D0876099

Cognitive Dynamics

Conceptual and Representational Change in Humans and Machines

Cognitive Dynamics

Conceptual and Representational Change
in Humans and Machines

Edited by

Eric Dietrich
Binghamton University

Arthur B. Markman
University of Texas, Austin

LEA LAWRENCE ERLBAUM ASSOCIATES, PUBLISHERS
2000   Mahwah, New Jersey   London

Copyright © 2000 by Lawrence Erlbaum Associates, Inc.
All rights reserved. No part of this book may be reproduced in any
form, by photostat, microfilm, retrieval system, or any other means,
without prior written permission of the publisher.

Lawrence Erlbaum Associates, Inc., Publishers
10 Industrial Avenue
Mahwah, NJ 07430

Cover design by Kathryn Houghtaling Lacey

Library of Congress Cataloging-in-Publication Data

Cognitive dynamics : conceptual and representational change in
humans and machines / edited by Eric Dietrich, Arthur B.
Markman.
    p. cm.
    Includes bibliographical references and index.
ISBN 0-8058-3408-7 (alk. paper)
1. Mental representation. 2. Thought and thinking. 3. Cognitive
science. I. Dietrich, Eric. II. Markman, Arthur B.
BF316.6.C64 1999
153—dc21   99-30505
                                 CIP

Books published by Lawrence Erlbaum Associates are printed
on acid-free paper, and their bindings are chosen for strength and
durability.

Printed in the United States of America
10   9   8   7   6   5   4   3   2   1

To my friends and fellow sojourners:
Rodney, Chris, and Maggi
—ESD

To my grandparents:
Emanuel and Libby Gold
—ABM

Contents

Preface

It has become unfashionable to be a cognitive scientist and to believe in representation. A number of books and articles have suggested that ideas about representation, many of which are derived from a computational view of the mind, are not sufficient to explain the details of cognitive processing. These attacks on representation have focused on the importance of context sensitivity in cognitive processing, on the range of individual differences in performance, and on the relationship between minds and the bodies and environments in which they exist. In each case, models based on traditional assumptions about representation are assumed to be too rigid to account for these aspects of cognitive processing.

These aspects of cognitive processing are all concerned with the *dynamics* of mind. Context sensitivity involves cases in which the same concept has a different meaning in different situations (though sometimes the differences may be subtle). Individual differences highlight the way a given process can manifest itself in a unique way across individuals, or even in the same individual at different times. The relationships among mind, body, and environment are dynamic, because the body and environment are constantly changing, and cognitive processing must adapt to these changes. Beyond this, the mind itself is in a constant state of activity, even when the environment is relatively stable (during sleep, for example).

In place of a representational view of mind, researchers have proposed other formalisms and methodologies, such as nonlinear differential equations (or dynamical systems) and situated robotics. These new approaches are touted as better explanatory tools for understanding cognition. We must say at the outset that we are fully in favor of exploring a range of approaches to cognitive processing. It seems unlikely that any single explanatory approach is going to suffice.

However, we suggest that the flexibility that is inherent in cognitive processing does not require a radically new approach to cognitive science.

Instead, traditional representational approaches to mind can be adapted and used in new explanations for the dynamics of cognition. We refer to this course of research as *cognitive dynamics*.

To illustrate the power of cognitive dynamics, we have collected original essays by prominent researchers in cognitive science. Each of the chapters in this volume explores some aspect of the dynamics of cognitive processing while still retaining representations as the centerpiece of the explanations of these phenomena. We see this work as the antidote to arguments that representation is incompatible with the dynamics of cognitive processing.

The book is divided into three sections. Each section is introduced by a brief overview of the chapters that appear in it. In the first section, the chapters focus on foundational issues about the use of representation in cognitive science. These chapters explore what it means for something to be a representation, and how representations come to have their content. The second section examines the dynamics of low level cognitive processes such as visual and auditory perception and simple lexical priming. The third section examines the dynamics of higher cognitive processes including categorization, analogy, and decision making.

We are very excited about the cognitive dynamics approach. There are important insights in the approaches to cognition that stress the variability and context sensitivity of cognitive processing. These insights have often been overlooked by cognitive scientists working with traditional explanatory constructs. Understanding these insights will be critical for the future success of cognitive science. There is much exciting work yet to be done. We hope that this volume helps to point the way

—*Eric Dietrich*
—*Arthur B. Markman*

Acknowledgments

Putting together an edited volume is a difficult task, and we could not have done it without the help of a number of important people. First, we must thank the contributors, who wrote stellar chapters. We must also thank Julia Kalmanson, Page Moreau, Tomislav Pavlicic, Adalis Sanchez, Takashi Yamauchi and the rest of the Similarity and Cognition lab, as well as the students of a seminar on computational theories of mind for their tireless efforts reading all of the chapters and making first-rate comments.

Over the years, we have discussed issues relating to representation and its importance to cognitive processing with many of our colleagues. Many of these ideas managed to find their way into this book and its organization. In addition to the contributors to this volume, we would like to thank Bob Davidson, David Krantz, Robert Krauss, Lewis Loren, and Clay Morrison.

We would also like to thank Judi Amsel for being so supportive of this project. The production staff at LEA, led by Linda Eisenberg did a wonderful job of putting this book together. The results speak for themselves.

List of Contributors

Lawrence W. Barsalou
Emory University

Mark H. Bickhard
Lehigh University

Curt Burgess
University of California, Riverside

Eric Dietrich
Binghamton University

Dedre Gentner
Northwestern University

Robert L. Goldstone
Indiana University, Bloomington

Keith J. Holyoak
University of California, Los Angeles

John E. Hummel
University of California, Los Angeles

Alan Kersten
Indiana University, Bloomington

Kevin Lund
University of California, Riverside

Gary F. Marcus
New York University

Arthur B. Markman
University of Texas, Austin

C. Page Moreau
Southern Methodist University

Jesse J. Prinz
Washington University, St. Louis

Robert E. Remez
Barnard College

Jesse Spencer-Smith
Indiana University, Bloomington

Mark Steyvers
Indiana University, Bloomington

Phillip Wolff
Northwestern University

Shi Zhang
University of California, Los Angeles

I

FOUNDATIONS

The chapters in the first part of this book are devoted to foundational issues: the nature of representation and computation, the nature of representational dynamics, and the role these theoretical concepts play in explanations in cognitive science. Although very friendly to the notion of representation, in general, none of these chapters defends a classical notion of representation, which views representations as static data structures. Instead, each chapter takes seriously both the representational dynamics necessary to explain cognitive processing and the need for explicit systems of representation.

This section begins with our introductory chapter: "Cognitive Dynamics: Computation and Representation Regained." In this chapter, the stage is set for discussions of representation to follow. To this end, we begin by defining the term *cognitive dynamics*, which forms the basis of this book. Then, we define and explain in detail the computational and representational hypotheses in cognitive science. Along the way, we also discuss the notion of virtual machines, as well as the relation between philosophical and psychological problems of representation.

Mark H. Bickhard's chapter "Dynamic Representing and Representational Dynamics" argues that there are at least two kinds of representational dynamics whose existence is empirically established but that cannot be accommodated in classical accounts. The first is dynamic change that happens to representations. This change occurs to representations as a result of external operations on them. Classical computer models of

1

cognitive capacities, with their operations on data structures, capture external operations on representations quite well. Because they assume static and inert representational elements, however, they fail to capture the fact that changes might thereby occur internal to the representations operated on. The second kind of dynamics is internal to, and inherent in, the construction of representations themselves. On Bickhard's view, representation is dynamic at a number of levels. First, his theory of *interactivism* posits that representation emerges through interactions between an organism and its environment. Furthermore, the substrate of the representations is itself dynamic. Thus, through a process Bickhard calls microgenesis, the dynamics of the brain influence dynamics at the level of representation. Both interactive representational dynamics and the dynamics of microgenetic construction contribute to explaining the changes induced by "external" operations. None of these phenomena of dynamic representation can be accounted for by classical models using inert representations or by dynamical views that eschew representation altogether.

Jesse J. Prinz and Lawrence N. Barsalou, in "Steering a Course for Embodied Representation," argue that we can enjoy the main benefits of the dynamical systems approach—namely, its ability to explain cognition's context sensitivity, embodiment, and inherent temporality—while preserving the unique and powerful role of representation in cognition. First, they defend the notion of representation in cognitive science and discuss among other things, van Gelder's antirepresentational arguments and the role of representation in the evolution of cognition. Then they discuss context sensitivity, embodiment, and temporality and show that each complements representation and, in general, that representations can be context sensitive, embodied, and temporally based. Finally, Prinz and Barsalou discuss their *perceptual symbol systems theory* of mental representation. Perceptual symbol systems ground cognition in perception to form a context-sensitive representational system that is also embodied and temporally based. Perceptual symbols have several interesting properties. They are schematic rather than holistic; they are multimodal, including motor modalities; and they get integrated into conceptual simulations that are run when that concept is activated (for more detail about perceptual symbols and perceptual symbol systems, see Barsalou, 1999).

Part I closes with Gary F. Marcus' chapter "Two Kinds of Representation." Marcus argues that two kinds of representations must be included in anyone's taxonomy of representational capacities: categories and rules. A category is some sort of internal state that allows treating all members of some group equally. A rule is a relation between abstract variables. This definition of a rule is perhaps slightly nonstandard, but it captures something that Marcus, and many others, regard as crucial to representation and cognition: the ability to generalize and reason with free and bound variables. As an example of rule, consider a young grade schooler who has learned the concept of an even number: "An even number is any number n that can be divided by two with no remainder." It is clear that rules require both learning and the ability to abstract. Hence, rules are crucial to cognition. Marcus argues that any new approach to studying cognition, for instance, connectionism, must be able to incorporate rules and categories if it is to be useful. Versions of connectionism or dynamics systems that try to eliminate representations, especially rules and categories, are doomed to failure on Marcus' view.

All these chapters provide a groundwork for thinking about representation in cognitive processing. Furthermore, all of them reject the classical view of representations as inert data structures waiting to be operated on or influenced by a set of processes. Despite these commonalities, these authors' views differ significantly in their underlying assumptions. They reveal that accepting the dynamics of cognitive processing still leaves plenty of room for exploration.

REFERENCE

Barsalou, L. (in press). Perceptual symbol systems *Behavioral and Brain Sciences*.

Cognitive Dynamics: Computation and Representation Regained

Eric Dietrich
Binghamton University, State University of New York

Arthur B. Markman
University of Texas, Austin

INTRODUCTION

A young infant named Lucas flails about in his environment. In a few weeks, he can detect that his hand has brushed against his face and can then move his face until his hand is in his mouth. A month after that, he can expertly pop a finger into his mouth.

A psychology professor stands in front of a class and gives a lecture. When she introduces the topic of representation, she gives a definition, and heads in the class nod in agreement. Each of the students has learned something about representation, but not all of them have learned the same thing.

How do humans, both young and old, develop the ability to coordinate their movements and to plan their actions? How do humans process language, communicate, learn new concepts and use them later? How do humans reason about their social and physical world? The goal of cognitive science is to answer questions like these. Doing this crucially involves understanding how behavior changes and develops over time, and that in turn requires understanding how the mind changes and develops over time. That is, an understanding of the *dynamics* of the mind is ultimately needed.

The dynamics of cognitive systems has been at the center of an important debate in cognitive science. Since the late 1950s, cognitive science's dominant working assumption has been that cognitive systems are *computational systems*. Just as computer programs can be described as sequences of steps carried out over data structures, it has been hypothesized that cognition can be described as computational processes operating over mental representations. This assumption has proved enormously fruitful.

Recently, however, a growing number of cognitive scientists have suggested that the dynamics of cognitive processing is incompatible with the hypothesis that the mind is a computational device. They have suggested that it is no accident that psychological processing is dynamic, because the brain is a dynamic system, and it is well known that the brain's dynamism gives rise to mind. The mind, then, is an *emergent entity* or *emergent property* of the brain. To some cognitive scientists, the dynamics of cognitive processes cry out for explanations couched in the language of the brain's dynamics. To these researchers, explanations at any other level are mere approximations that do not provide a good basis for the study of the mind.

The contrast between the computational view and the view that the dynamics of cognition require explanations in terms of the dynamics of the brain is the core of the current debates. The question is whether understanding the complexity of cognitive processes requires focusing only on the dynamics of brain states, thereby eliminating the computational hypothesis of the mind and by extension eliminating all discussion of processes operating over representations. Perhaps no worthwhile generalizations that involve representations and processes can be made about cognitive processing. Perhaps the proper language of psychology is one of dynamical systems—differential equations and the like.

In this book, our colleagues and we argue that the computational level of explanation in cognitive science is real and that this level of explanation is crucial for understanding the dynamics of cognitive processing. No doubt the mind's dynamics supervene on underlying brain dynamics, but cognitive dynamics are not the same as brain dynamics. Consider an analogy with computers. The underlying electronics of computers are dynamic and continuous and best explained by using differential equations. No one suggests, however, that this level of description is useful or adequate for explaining how word processors or web software works. Imagine trying to debug an application by dropping down to the level of electrons, watts, amps, and differential equations.

To introduce this discussion in greater detail, we first define the notion of cognitive dynamics and illustrate it with some examples. Then, we discuss theoretical approaches to psychology advocating abandoning computation and representation. Finally, we provide key definitions for *computation, virtual machine, representation,* and related notions, and we fully and carefully explain the need for these theoretical ideas in cognitive science. The rest of the book takes up the task of using these theoretical notions to explain various aspects of the dynamics of cognitive processing.

WHAT IS COGNITIVE DYNAMICS?

What do we mean by the phrase *cognitive dynamics?* Cognitive dynamics are any changes in an organism directly affecting that organism's cognitive processing or cognitive capacities. These changes in behavior include motor and sensory development, all types of learning, and conceptual change of all kinds. Such changes occur in a variety of forms, at different levels of cognition, and with numerous degrees of complexity. We include all these kinds and levels in our definition of cognitive dynamics.

Cognitive dynamics also occur at a variety of time frames. At the shortest time frames, the dynamics of visual object recognition require rapid representation and processing of visual images and comparisons of those images to stored representations of objects seen in the past. At a somewhat longer time frame, the dynamics of preference may involve short-term shifts in the value ascribed to particular objects as a function of goals active in a given situation. These changes may take place over minutes or hours. Finally, conceptual change may occur over a lifetime of experience: Information is added to concepts, and properties are forgotten. These changes may be mediated by a variety of factors including analogical retrieval and comparison.

Cognitive dynamics are dynamics that are intrinsic to cognition, and they are to be studied at the levels where cognitive processing exists. Cognitive dynamics are not ancillary to neural dynamics or the brain's dynamics. Because on our view, cognition requires representation, cognitive dynamics are first and foremost the dynamics of representational change. This subject is what this book is about. There are two broad classes of representational change: processes acting *on* representations and processes *intrinsic to* the existence or production of the representations themselves. Both classes are discussed in this book.

It is well known that cognitive processes are dynamic. What is in dispute is the best way to deal with these dynamics. As we discuss in the next section, the observed dynamics has led some researchers to recommend that we abandon the computational hypothesis about the mind and move toward other formalisms for understanding cognitive processing. They have suggested that insufficient progress has been made in understanding cognitive processing by using traditional computational approaches and that this absence of progress is a symptom of a foundational ailment in the field.

To argue against this attack, we must defend the computational foundation of cognitive science (see also Markman & Dietrich, in press). Despite the best efforts of theorists interested in other formalisms like dynamic systems, they have yet to come up with a viable, alternative way to conceptualize cognitive processes that does not involve representations.

Furthermore, once representations are adopted into a cognitive model, *algorithms* must be included as well. Representation and computation go hand in hand; we cannot have one without the other. In this book, we want to reinforce the methodological point that cognitive science cannot proceed without representations and computational processes defined over them. That is, cognitive science requires a computational view of the mind. This point is easily misunderstood, so we will devote a fair amount of time to clarifying it. But first, we discuss why the computational view of mind is not as popular as it once was.

SOME PROBLEMS WITH REPRESENTATION AND COMPUTATION

The notions of mental representation and computation have fallen on hard times lately and are utterly in disfavor in some quarters in cognitive science—an odd fate for two notions that are responsible for *all* the success cognitive science has enjoyed to date. It is in part the word *success* that causes the problem. Many cognitive scientists think that what success we have had is minimal and that unless we change tactics, we are unlikely to progress much further.

What are the reasons for this unease? There are many. But we think that five failures are primarily to blame.

First, we have failed to explain the plasticity of human intelligence. We have only vague ideas about how the mind works on novel problems and in novel situations and how it works so well with degraded input. We cannot say where new representations come from or how new concepts are acquired. We have done a better job of explaining generative processes like syntax than of explaining content-bound processes like semantics.

Second, we have failed to tell an integrative story about cognitive and sensorimotor behavior. For most of the history of cognitive science, cognition got the lion's share of research attention. Sensorimotor behavior and robotics were considered afterthoughts. Many researchers, however, have come to the conclusion that this list of priorities is exactly backward. These researchers have suggested that cognitive science must concentrate first on the sensorimotor aspects of organisms and the development of systems that interact with their environment. Only when these processes are fully understood can cognitive science graduate to the study of higher level processes.

Third, we have failed to tell an integrative story about brains and cognition. Again, throughout the history of cognitive science, the *mind* got all the attention. Understanding how the brain carried out cognitive processes was assumed to be an implementational detail. Again, researchers have suggested that the priorities of the field should be reversed. The behavior and structure of brains seem crucial to the flow and structure of cognition. The slogan is that mind emerges from the brain. Cognitive science, it is argued, should be the science of this emergence.

Fourth, our explanations of human development and maturation typically do not characterize the trajectory of development. Instead, developmental theories often capture snapshots at different stages of development and then posit mechanisms to jump from one stage the next.

Fifth, we have failed to make an intelligent machine. If cognition is computation over representations, then why is it so proving so hard to make an intelligent computer? Note the way the first and fifth failures work together. Computers do not seem like the right things for grounding research into the nature of plasticity and representational content. To the extent that these latter are crucial aspects of cognition, then computation must be the wrong way to think about cognition. Here is an analogy: if the Wright brothers had failed at building a flying machine, then it would have been reasonable to question their theory of flight (namely, that it requires lift).

In sum: many cognitive scientists are dismayed at the robustness and complexity of human cognition, and they do not think that mental representations and computation are up to the task of explaining them.

How should we respond to these indictments of representation and computation? The approach taken by a number of antirepresentationalist theorists—like those working on dynamic systems, situated action, and some connectionists—is to abandon computation in favor of another formalism. This approach is a good idea. There is no knockdown argument that the brain is a computational system (but neither is there an argument that it is not). Hence, we need to have researchers exploring alternative possibilities for conceptualizing the mind–brain system.

A second approach is to insist (or assume) that we are generally on the right road and that all we need is more time. This approach is typical of research in classical artificial intelligence. There is a burgeoning industry examining a variety of logical formalisms for representing knowledge, making inferences, and constructing causal explanations. There is also substantial work on formalisms to permit defeasible reasoning and other forms of belief maintenance (Pollock, 1994, 1995). Finally, some studies of machine learning focus on selecting the appropriate set of features to permit new objects to be classified (e.g., DeJong & Mooney, 1986; Michalski, 1994). This approach should also continue being pursued for the reasons that it has been successful to some degree and no other approach has been vastly more successful.

The second approach, however, has left many important questions unanswered, and the first approach has yet to realize its advertised promise. We advocate a third approach: We should change the way we think about representation and cognitive computation. On this view, the foundational assumptions of cognitive science are solid, but more attention needs to be paid to the details of these assumptions and to their roles in our cognitive theories. In this book, we focus on this approach. We are not the only ones who advocate taking it. This approach is most often taken by experimental psychologists and mental modelers, those of a certain pragmatic bent who are nevertheless sensitive to the fact cognitive science must make its current computational and representational foundations more robust if it is to progress much further.

COMPUTATION AND REPRESENTATION
FOR THE PRACTICING COGNITIVE SCIENTIST

In this section, we explain the nature of computation and representation required for cognitive science. We show how computation and representation work in cognitive science, and we defend the notions against several objections.

Computation is an Explanatory Tool

Because the computational hypothesis about the mind is the core assumption that binds together modern cognitive science, one might think that its tenets should be firmly grasped by cognitive scientists. In this light, it is striking how often this hypothesis is misunderstood. We begin by stating the hypothesis and then working through some of the typical misunderstandings.

> The Computational Hypothesis about the Mind:
> Cognition is best *explained* as algorithmic execution of Turing-computable functions. Such computational explanations have three properties (explained next): They explain cognitive *capacities*; they are *systematic*; and they are *interpretive*.

That is all the hypothesis says. Before we discuss its properties, we note two things. First, the computational hypothesis is only a *foundational* hypothesis. All the hypothesis gives us is a framework in which to work. It does not specify which particular functions constitute cognition. Therefore, the hypothesis does *not* tell us what models to build, nor which experiments to run. The computational hypothesis is *not* a theory of mind.

Second, the hypothesis is *not* committed to mental representations of any particular variety. Rather, it is compatible with a myriad of different kinds of representations, from mental spaces to vectors to nodes in a semantic network. Together, these two points mean that the hypothesis leaves all the hard work to do. We still need to roll up our sleeves and get down to the difficult business of developing a theory of mind. The computational hypothesis does tell us what this theory will look like—but only broadly. Now for the three properties.

Computational explanations explain capacities or abilities of a system to exhibit certain behavior. Hence, computational explanations differ from better known causal explanations that subsume behavior under a causal law. This property guarantees that cognitive capacities (or capacities for exhibiting certain behaviors) are understood (by the explainers) as capacities for computing certain functions and that exhibiting the behavior is seen as actually computing the function.

Second, computational explanations are systematic. For any system of reasonable complexity (say, anything from a paramecium up), computational explanations posit interdependent functions that interact to produce the output from the input. Given a system, a computational explanation analyzes the system-sized function, which explains the system's gross behavior, into subfunctions and then shows how those subfunctions interact to produce the system's behavior.

Third, computational explanations are interpretive. To explain some bit of behavior as computing function F, say, we must be able to interpret the initial state of the system as being the requisite input for F, the final state of the system ("final" in a teleological sense) as being the requisite output of F, and all the system's intermediate states as being the subfunctions of F.

This last property has been misunderstood by some, even by computationalists (e.g., Chalmers, 1994). It's important to get the order of events right. We do not want to show how a computation is implemented in some system, contra Chalmers. Precisely the opposite: We want to show how some system implements some computation. This change of order is quite important. As cognitive scientists, we do not pick a computation and then look for a system that implements it. Rather, we want to explain how some system does what it does by *interpreting* it as executing some computation. That is, we begin with a physical system's behavior and look for what explains it, where the explanans are computations performed over representations.[1] Computational explanations are grounded in a system's behavior; such behaviors are the explanations' raison d'être. With the computationalist, as with any scientist, a system's behavior is

---

[1]This is not to say that cognitive science does not care about the brain or how the brain implements cognitive processes. At a pragmatic level, data about how the brain functions help to constrain explanations of how representations and processes interact. At a theoretical level, we care about how brains implement cognition, because brains are the substrate from which our cognitive abilities are constructed. The functional architecture of the brain places limits on the kinds of functions that we can compute.

central; the computation that explains this behavior is important, but it is second on the list.[2] Interestingly, this is true even in artificial intelligence (AI). In AI, we do implement computer programs, but the point of the program is that it explains the behavior of the virtual machine, which in turn is used to model some aspect of intelligent behavior. This point can be readily observed when one considers scientific AI rather than engineering AI (for two examples, see MAC/FAC, Forbus, Gentner, & Law, 1995; LISA, Hummel & Holyoak, 1997; and chap. 9, this volume).

For those with a formal bent, we provide a formal description of the explanatory strategy that the computational hypothesis posits. Given a physical system S, exhibiting behavior through time, its behavior is successfully explained by a computable function F when the researcher explains the execution of F in terms of a sequence of functions $< g_1, \ldots, g_n > (n > 1)$ such that:

$$(1) \quad F = g_n \circ g_{n-1} \circ \ldots \circ g_1;$$

(2) S passes through a sequence of states corresponding via an interpretation function I to either the domain or range of all the g_is, and each state of S between the first and final states is both the range of some g_i and the domain of some g_{i+1}; and (3) we antecedently understand the g_is (i.e., they are very simple, primitive recursive functions, for example). When all of this occurs, we say that the sequence $< g_1, \ldots, g_n >$ *analyzes* the computation of F by S and *explains* the capacity of S to exhibit the relevant behavior. (See Fig. 1.1; for more detail on the computational hypothesis, see Dietrich, 1990, 1994; Fields, 1994).

It is crucial to bear in mind that the computational hypothesis is a hypothesis that can be proven false. Not all functions are Turing computable (i.e., computable by a Turing machine). For example, the computational hypothesis would be false if researchers showed that some aspect of cognition was in fact a non-Turing-computable function. This would not be hard to do, in principle. For example, one could show that true continuity—i.e., the cardinality of the real numbers—is crucial to cognition. In practice, however, this seems unlikely. Any physical device is finite, or at least it has only finitely many measurable states (see Fields, 1989), and any finite, descriptive function is computable. Moreover, the classical theory of computation (Turing machines, NP-completeness, un-

---

[2]Chalmers would probably at least partly agree that explanation grounds the use of computations, but in his writings, this point gets lost. He seems more interested in the abstract computation and its implementation, rather than in the physical system and its explanation, which goes in precisely the opposite direction. We darkly suspect that Chalmers is more interested in metaphysics than is your typical cognitive scientist working in the field.

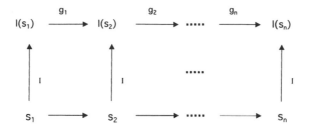

FIG. 1.1. The explanatory strategy of the computational hypothesis. A cognitive process goes through states S_1 to S_n. An interpretation function, I, is then used to interpret the states as input and output for a Turing computable function F, where $F = g_n \cup g_{n-1} \cup \ldots \cup g_1$. F, explains the capacity of the cognitive system to exhibit the relevant cognitive process.

decidability, partial recursive functions, automata, etc.) has been extended to certain "well-behaved," continuous rings of real numbers (Blum, Shub, & Smale, 1989). Hence, one can no longer argue that cognizers are non-computational because they are best described by the mathematics of continuous systems because that description can be compatible with cognizers still being computational. Rather, what must be done is to show that the system's continuity is of a particularly complex type that is *not* "well behaved" (suppose it crucially involves the set of transcendental numbers, numbers like π), and it must then be shown that this type of continuity is crucial to the system's being cognitive. Put another way, it must be shown that any computation on some physical device (which can approximate the continuity of the set of real numbers to an arbitrary degree of precision) always falls short of true cognition. No one has come close to showing this; indeed, it is completely implausible. Often, arguments that attempt to do this simply insist that natural systems are continuous and then argue that because computation is (allegedly) not continuous, it cannot be the right way to theorize about cognition (Port & van Gelder, 1995, p. 22). This approach obviously will not work.

Systems designed to carry information are unlikely to require internal states that are complexly continuous (or even continuous at all). In other work, we pointed out that another information-carrying system, the genetic code, must be constructed from discrete units (Dietrich & Markman, 1998). The ability to mix the genomes of two different organisms requires an information-bearing system with discrete units. Otherwise, sexual reproduction would yield a blend of the genetic codes of a pair of organisms and would gradually lead to organisms that have a common set of smeared properties. Likewise, combining concepts and other higher cognitive processes is likely to require discrete units in cognitive representations.

The plausibility (but not necessarily the truth) of the computational hypothesis would be undermined if it were shown that the human brain routinely solves, in an exact manner, arbitrarily large versions of problems that are computationally intractable. A classic problem of this type is the traveling salesman problem, in which one must find the path between a set of cities, which minimizes the distance traveled. This problem is one for which all known solutions take an amount of time that is exponential to the size of the set of cities. Problems like this belong to the set of NP-complete computational problems, which means that in all likelihood, they are intractable. If the brain is routinely and quickly solving problems that are NP complete (or intractable), then computation, *as it is currently understood*, is obviously not a good foundation for cognitive science. In this case, we should look elsewhere for a foundation, possibly to a new theory of computation.

So far, however, no one has shown that the brain or any part of the nervous system routinely *and exactly* solves NP-complete problems. It is well known that the brain *heuristically* solves NP-complete problems all the time, but these solutions are heuristic, not exact. They leave open the possibility of error, although they do manage to run in real time.

Finally, some researchers have rejected the computational hypothesis because computers cannot do what the brain allegedly can do: solve an unbounded set of problems (Horgan & Tienson, 1996). According to these researchers, the brain's processes are continuous, and our solutions go beyond what a computer can do; in short, they think brains can do what computers cannot. The first problem with this argument is that what computers can and cannot do is irrelevant here. What matters is what the notion of computation can *explain*. This point cannot be overstressed. The second problem with this argument is that we are only now beginning to understand what computation is and what computers can and cannot be. Studies with DNA computers challenge our notions of what can be tractably computed. The third problem with arguments about human unboundedness is that it is implausible that the brain can really solve an unbounded set of robust problems. Rather, at best, it heuristically copes with a large but bounded set of problems.

Throughout this discussion, we have not said that the mind is a computer. We have avoided this term, because there is a computer metaphor of the mind that is a specification of the computational hypothesis, but we do not endorse this metaphor here. The computer metaphor is just one of many metaphors that have been used in the history of the study of the mind to explain cognitive processes. The computer metaphor assumes that the core components of the cognitive system are analogous to the core components of a modern digital computer. The top of Fig. 1.2 shows an oversimplified schematic of the components of a digital computer. This diagram has a central processor (fittingly illustrated in the middle of the diagram). The central processor carries out the instructions

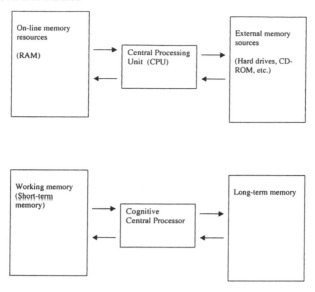

FIG. 1.2. *Top:* a simplified schematic of a standard computer. *Bottom:* the analogous architecture used (often implicitly) in many cognitive models. The computational hypothesis of the mind does not entail that cognitive architectures have to resemble standard computers.

of the program. It has access to both an active memory system (random-access memory, or RAM) that stores the program and current active data structures. It also has access to a long-term memory store (like a hard drive) that can be used to access new parts of a program or additional data structure information.

This simplified model of a digital computer has parallels in the architecture of many cognitive models that have a mechanism for carrying out processes. The processes themselves are conceptualized as steps in a program. Online processing is done using working memory, which is a short-term store that holds onto information that is relevant to the process being carried out. Online processing also influences and is influenced by long-term memory, which stores autobiographical memories, semantic information, and known processes. This architecture is implicit in many cognitive models. In addition, a number of assumptions that come with this architecture are ingrained in cognitive science. For example, research in cognitive psychology often focuses on average behavior rather than on individual behavior under the assumptions that all cognitive processing uses the same central processor and that differences in performance reflect factors that can be treated as "noise." This architecture also underlies divisions between areas of research, so that researchers can study short-term memory capacity independently from long-term memory, and each of these can be studied independently from reasoning processes and problem-solving abilities. Of course, there is some evidence that the distinction between working memory and long-term memory is a reasonable one, and thus this research is not based solely on a metaphor.

Of importance for the present discussion is that the computer metaphor for the mind is not a requirement of the computational hypothesis. A variety of architectures can carry out functions that are Turing computable. The particular architecture of the modern personal computer need not bear any relation to the architecture of the brain or even to the natural description of the mind at an algorithmic level. Thus, the computer metaphor of the mind may be right or wrong. Demonstrating that it is wrong does not undermine the foundational assumption that the mind is a computational system. We explore this issue in more detail in the next section.

Computation and Virtual Machines

At the end of the previous section, we touched on a crucial point: Computation does not carry with it specific requirements for the processor that carries it out. Instead, a computation can be described by specifying a certain representation (or data structure) and its attendant processes. These processes are defined to directly operate on the representations as specified. A computation thus specified defines a *virtual machine*.

More formally, a set of representations of a certain kind and its attendant set of processes that transform the representations form an ordered pair $< R, P >$. The pair $< R, P >$ specifies a machine that directly computes a function. For any Turing-computable function, F, there is, in principle, such a machine (usually *not* a classic Turing machine) that computes F directly. This machine is called a *virtual machine*. Given F, a virtual machine is therefore a machine, $< R_F, F >$, which computes F and whose base machine language consists of the representations in R_F and their transformations. (Here we view the function F as an algorithm and hence as a process or sequence of processes. If readers tend to think of functions extrinsically, as sequences of ordered pairs, then redefine the notion of a virtual machine as $< R_F, A_F >$, where A is the algorithm or process that produces the ordered pairs.) This virtual machine can be implemented on *any* standard computer (this point is just the physical version of Turing's famous theorem that there exists a universal Turing machine that can compute any recursive [i.e., Turing-computable] function).

As a simple example of a virtual machine, day-of-week (calendar date) returns the name of the day of the week for any calendar date given: Day-of-week (6/5/98) = Friday. This function works on calendar dates and names of days of the week and can execute in one step. That is not how it is ultimately implemented, but that is what the function does at the level the user is interested in. The function is implemented in terms of other, lower level functions that operate on character strings, then bit strings; finally, the function is implemented in terms of the physics of the relevant microprocessor.

There are plenty of more robust yet familiar examples of virtual machines. A word processor is a computer program that helps us write papers and books. A word processor runs on the hardware of a computer. As long as you are running your word processor, the machine you are interacting with is, for all intents and purposes, a hardware version of your word processor. Another virtual machine on standard, multitasking computers makes everything happen at the right time: the operating system. In the case of the word processor, the operating system typically loads it into RAM and then runs it (i.e, passes control to it).

Virtual machines give us the capacity to implement our programs in *hierarchical layers*. This layering of programs can reach several levels when, for example, an AI researcher runs experiments written in an interpreted language (like LISP), which in turn runs on a more basic virtual machine (using a more basic language, like C), which in turn is compiled by a compiler and loaded by an operating system and then run, finally, on actual physical hardware.

Here computational cognitive science makes its critical bet. The field assumes that the brain is just a specific implementation of a process carrying out the program that is cognition. Just as a modern digital computer has a number of layers that intervene between the electric circuits and your word processor, so too does the brain have a (large) number of layers (one of the interesting similarities between brains and computers). These layers or levels range from the electrochemistry of the brain (or maybe even lower) up to such processes as reasoning, understanding, and recognizing. Explaining all these layers is required if we are to explain how minds supervene on brains. The bet is that the important generalizations about *cognitive* processing are to be found at the levels of the higher virtual machines, that is, at the levels of processes running over mental representations of roughly the sort we use today. (The classical view of this bet is that cognitive processes run over representations with some sort of *propositional content*. We think this view is probably too strong, but do not argue this point here; see Markman & Dietrich, in press). Of course, not all explanations relevant to cognitive science will occur at the level of cognitive processing. As with computers, not every capacity or process in the brain is best explained in terms of computation. Even in a computer, the lowest level is best explained by the physics of electricity and the electrochemistry of materials such as silicon. It is reasonable to suppose that in the brain, the lowest levels will be explained by neurochemistry, electrochemistry, and the like.

So, the feature of the virtual machine property of computation crucial to understanding the brain and the mind is that it allows researchers working at different levels to use different technical vocabularies and different notions of representation. No level, no vocabulary, and no particular kind of representation is privileged. By adopting the computational hypothesis and the notion of virtual machines, researchers are free to use whatever fits their purposes. No one, for example, is forced to use static, enduring, proposition-sized representations such as production system rules defined over propositions like "The cat is on the mat." If such representations suit the level where one is working, however, they can and should be used. In this light, the debate between dynamic systems researchers and more classical cognitive scientists is pointless. Both groups need to do their work at their respective levels and then marry them for us to one day have a robust theory of the mind and brain.

Representation by Triangulation

It is impossible to do cognitive science without the notion of representation. The essential nature of all cognitive systems is that they must have internal states that mediate their behavior. Some of these states act as representations of situations external to the cognitive system; others may act as representations of other internal states of the system. That is, modern cognitive science rests on a *representational hypothesis* about the mind.

The Representational Hypothesis about the Mind:
Thinking or cognizing crucially involves manipulating internal structures that stand for other structures in the organism's or system's environment (internal structures may also stand for other internal structures). Such structures *mediate* between the organism (or system) and its environment.

Broadly speaking, the dynamic systems approach contrasts with the computational hypothesis discussed earlier (van Gelder, 1998), and the *situated action* approach (defined next) contrasts with (or is intended to modify) the representational hypothesis. In this section, we concentrate on situated action, comparing and contrasting it with the representational hypothesis.

Like the computational hypothesis, the representational hypothesis is merely a framework that gets us started. It is *not* a theory of mind, nor does it entail a theory of mind. It leaves completely unspecified how representations actually work, what kinds of representations need to be studied, and how representation is even possible. Again, all the hard work remains to be done.

A significant question about cognitive systems is how much of the external world needs to be represented. An important insight by Gibson

(1950, 1986) is that we may not need to represent that much of the world. He pointed out that the standard assumption in models of perception is that the perceptual system must find a way to represent the information in the image reaching the retina, such as the lines, edges, objects, and depths of objects in the visual field. He suggested that it may unnecessary to represent all this information explicitly, because the organism is constantly a part of its environment. Instead, he suggested that the goal of perception is to determine the aspects of the world that can be used to satisfy the organism's goals. Thus, he argued that what we perceive and represent about the visual world are the *affordances* of objects rather than their perceptual characteristics.

This insight has been broadened by recent research in *situated action* (also called *situated cognition* and *embodied cognition*). This research takes as its starting point that cognizers are embedded in their environment. Thus, they need not represent all aspects of problems they are solving or all situations in which they are engaged, because they can use the world itself as a form of external representation. Some researchers who take a situated action perspective have suggested that the fact that cognitive systems are embedded in an environment means that we can dispense with the notion of representation altogether (e.g., Brooks, 1991; Clancey, 1993). Nonetheless, much of the situated action camp takes representation seriously. For example, Agre (1995) argued that a system cannot maintain goal-directed behavior without being able to represent the goals and the desirable and undesirable states of the world that are objects of the goals. Also, Bickhard (1998) argued that representations emerge from a system's nonrepresentational interaction with its environment (see also Bickhard & Terveen, 1995).

The work in situated action is welcome, because it is an area of cognitive science that begins to point out how we may be able to move beyond models that have *hand-coded* representations with strictly derivative semantic contents. Hand-coded representations are those that are designed by the modeler for the purposes of developing the particular system. But in naturally occurring cognitive systems, the representations are *not* hand coded.[3] An important question for cognitive science to answer is where the representations in naturally occurring cognitive systems (like humans and other animals) come from. For too long, most cognitive scientists have relied on philosophers to answer this question. Philosophers have done a good job; in fact, most of what we know about representations and representational content is due to philosophers. But developing a

---

[3]Some cognitive scientists try to solve this hand-coding problem by saying that the representations are innate. This does not work for the simple reason that we have all kinds of representations in our heads whose contents cannot possibly be innate, such as "worldwide web." For more on this and other alleged solutions to the hand-coding problem, see Bickhard and Terveen (1995).

theory of content is proving to be enormously difficult, and the philoso-phers need help. Theorists working in situated action can perhaps help develop a theory that tells us how representations emerge from a system's interactions with things in its environment. However, contrary to the way some situated action researchers talk, situated action does *not* mean that we can move beyond methodological solipsism. No organism checks the contents of its representations with an *unmediated* external world; that is physically impossible. All information in the cognizing organism or sys-tem is mediated by the organism's sense organs. In short, there exist only surface tickles and the representational structures built up from them.

A robust theory of representational content, therefore, must begin with the idea that all information in the organism or system is *mediated*. This simple truth entails something profound about representational content, namely, the idea that semantic content emerges from a process of hy-pothesizing and comparing. We call this process *interactive triangulation*. Because the mind triangulates, its content is *coherentist*. A central aspect of a representation is whether it is veridical; after all, it is generally in an organism's best interests to represent its environment correctly. Saying that the mind is coherentist is saying that the process of establishing correct representations (establishing truth) is a comparison process *among the representations themselves*. Minds do not compare their representations to the world. Rather, they compare their representations to other repre-sentations derived at other times and via other modalities. To put it another way, representational content crucially depends on the repre-sentations internal to a system maintaining some *self-consistency* (coher-ence). Any future theory of representation and representational content, situated action included, must be formulated to accord with this fact.

The coherentist property of representational content is only one prop-erty of representations. Formulating a theory in accord with this property is just one condition of a good theory of representation. There are two others we briefly discuss. We do not know whether the three properties form a complete set; they may, but we take no position on that here.

The first remaining property is that representations are *causally connected* to the system's environment. It is well known that a theory of repre-sentational content cannot be based on this fact alone because the notion of causation is itself not sufficiently constrained to fix individual contents. Nevertheless, that representations are part of a causal chain reaching from the environment into the system (and back out again) is important and somehow must be folded into a future theory of representation.

The second property is closely related to the coherentist property. According to the coherentist property, content emerges from hypothesiz-ing and comparing. A given representation's semantic role in the overall behavior of the system (both internal and external) is also part of what fixes its content. This is called the representation's *conceptual role*. However, it is well known that conceptual role theories founder on the fact that conceptual roles are so fine grained that representational content becomes completely idiosyncratic to the system possessing the representations. This problem is often called *holism* (Fodor & Lepore, 1992). Consider the representations of *car* in the heads of two people. The conceptual roles of these two representations are different for each person because each person's entire knowledge base is different. Because the conceptual role of the car representation is just its connection to the rest of a person's entire knowledge base, it follows that the two representations have different conceptual roles. So, since conceptual roles are part of what establishes a representation's content, the representational content of the car representations differs. However, this conclusion seems intuitively wrong, because we do manage to communicate about and refer to cars (as we are doing now). We discuss a possible solution to this problem in the next section.

In sum, we think that the three notions of coherence, causation, and conceptual role should be merged or blended in developing a good, strong theory of representation and representational content. We are not saying that these three are all that there is to explaining representational content, but they must be part of the final picture.

Causation and Conceptual Role:
Toward a Psychological Theory of Representation

As discussed in the previous section, the use of both causation and conceptual roles in developing a theory of representation is problematic. In this section, we briefly discuss our proposed solutions to the main problems besetting causation and conceptual roles.

Causal models specifying representation in terms of causation or causally mediated information exchange are very common and over the years have become quite sophisticated. The sophistications center around two problems: accounting for representational error and accounting for the distinction between proximal and distal cause.[4]

---

[4]There are several technical versions of each of these two problems in the philosophical literature, and each version has its own complications and subtleties. An interesting complication relevant here involves what are called twin cases and Frege cases (Fodor, 1994). Twin cases have the consequence that identical computational states of systems can have different content, and Frege cases show that different computational states can have the same contents. The question then becomes: How is psychology to proceed? If computation and representational content can easily be pulled apart, then which should we use for our theorizing: the computational description of the mental state or the semantic description? Are models of cognition supposed to be couched in computational or semantic

The problem of representational error is that we can be mistaken about what we perceive. We can mistake a skunk in the dark for a dog. In this case, the skunk in the world should cause our mental representation, but we think "dog" instead, so something has gone awry. Thus, pure causation cannot be all there is to representing.

If, on the other hand, we see the skunk clearly, on a bright sunny day, we have a second problem: The causal chain connecting our representation of the skunk to the skunk itself is part of a vastly long causal chain of events that extends back to the Big Bang. Our representations are not of these events. So, causation alone is not sufficiently constrained to be a good model of representation.

This second problem can be solved by changing what the causal component of a theory of representation is about. It is *not* about causation abstractly conceived. Of course, we are causally connected to events clear back to the Big Bang. But our perceptual organs are not designed to register the vast majority of these events. Our eyes, for example, register sunlight bouncing off the skunk, not the three-degree Kelvin background radiation left over from the Big Bang. A theory of representation needs not causation per se but very specific kinds of information exchange such as light waves of such and such a wavelength.

Increased specificity about the kinds of causal connections between a cognizing organism and its environment will not solve the first problem about representational error. To solve this problem, we need a theory of concepts, especially concept acquisition (learning) and concept activation (how and under what conditions are concepts activated?). In fact, we need these theories to adequately theorize about representations even in supposedly easy cases. For example, when we see a dog, light bouncing off the dog causes us to see it. Therefore, it may seem that all we need for a theory of at least visual representation is a theory that explains how light and the visual system work. Such a theory is not enough, however. Imagine standing on a green lawn in someone's backyard on a bright summer's day looking at a dog. The image on the back of your retina contains information about the dog, as well as other elements like the grass, trees, and sky. You do not know which of these is actually the dog until after some high-level object recognition systems have done significant work. The question is, how does this system know which information of all the information coming in is the information representing the dog? The only answer seems to be that you have learned what dogs look like

---

terms? This split allows some researchers to claim to be anticomputationalist because they are prosemantics. It allows others to completely jettison semantics and representations, because they are procomputation. The literature on these questions is extensive. For an introduction, see Fodor (1994), Fodor and Lepore (1992), Putnam (1975).

(you have some sort of "dog" concept) and your high-level object recognition system uses that knowledge to pick the right information thereby enabling you to see the dog as a dog. At this point, the problem of developing a theory of representation has been replaced with the problem of developing a theory of learning or concept acquisition, which is no easier than developing a theory of representation. So we have made no progress; we have merely replaced one hard job with another (for more on this, see Bickhard & Terveen, 1995).

This situation is not a cause for despair. It merely means that the problem of representational error runs as deep as the problem of representation itself, which we already knew was hard. We can solve them both by more or less at once developing several different theories that play off one another. Not an easy task, but for all that, not a task that is philosophically mysterious (not in the way that developing a theory of consciousness is, for example). To solve the problem of representational error, what is needed is (at least) theories of conceptual development and change, learning, and perceptual information processing. Coming up with these theories is not going to be easy, but we have every reason to be optimistic. We just have to roll up our sleeves and get to it.

We are not saying that merely having all these theories will be sufficient to solve the problem of representational error: The theories will have to be brought together to tell a unified story. In our opinion, the key to this story lies in specifying how the causal chains between organisms and their environments flow *both* ways—from the environment to the organism as well as from the organism to its environment. Information that flows from the organism to the environment amounts to testing hypotheses that the organism has about what it is perceiving (see Bickhard, 1998; Bickhard & Terveen, 1995; Loren & Dietrich, 1997). Organisms test these hypotheses by using multiple sensory modalities as well as multiple versions of a single sensory modality collected at different times. This is a restatement of our thesis that representational content is fixed by triangulation. Again, we are not saying that working out the details of this proposal is easy. But we are saying it is possible to do it.

Now for conceptual roles. As we said, the problem with using conceptual roles in representations is that, in theory, the meaning of any given concept or representation depends on the way that concept is connected to every other concept in the web of knowledge possessed by the cognizing organism. Because every individual has different experiences, everyone has differences in the overall structure of conceptual knowledge; and because meaning depends on this overall structure, concepts differ in meaning. This observation contrasts with the empirical fact that people do communicate with one another effectively. (Recall that this is called the problem of holism.) We think that the problem of holism is more apparent than real and that the part that is real is solved heuristically. We will take these in order.

The part of holism that is only apparently problematic stems from confusing the level of individual, very detailed, particular meanings and the level of social, communicative, more global meanings. Individual humans do have different meanings for their representations at a very detailed level. The total meaning of Dietrich's concept of *cat* (i.e., its total inferential capacity) is not identical to Markman's for the simple reason that we have had different cat experiences. But Dietrich and Markman do manage to communicate rather successfully about cats. This fact looks like a problem only if one assumes that when they communicate they have to somehow convey all and only their cat information, or that somehow they each must activate all and only the same cat and cat-related representations. But neither of these is needed. Dietrich and Markman need only share enough information for the conversation to proceed and for them to accomplish their goals. This they can easily do in the case of cats in part because the intersection of their knowledge is high. Now we come to the heuristic part. In cases where the intersection of information is not high (for example, if Dietrich and Markman were to talk about some rare and strange animal that lives only at the Bronx Zoo, which Markman frequents), various learning procedures and procedures for making guesses about which information is relevant in the current context kick in, and then that information is used to communicate. This solution leads to some errors in communication, but the errors are almost always correctable, so this solution works in practice. (Actually, the guessing procedures are always used, even when talking about cats, but in these cases, the guessing procedures are enormously reliable and almost never fail.)

To be more specific, it is well known that presenting a word to someone makes it easier for him or her to recognize some other words. This phenomenon is called *lexical priming* (e.g., Meyer & Schvaneveldt, 1971). For example, presenting someone with the word *doctor* makes him or her recognize more quickly that the string of letters NURSE is a word than does presenting someone with the word *hockey* or with a string of asterisks. What this facilitation suggests is that only a limited amount of semantic knowledge is activated by the presentation of a given concept. The information that is activated is the basis of the meaning of the concept in that discourse setting.

Activating only a subset of the information in a knowledge base is only part of the solution to the problem, because there is no guarantee that different people activate the same knowledge or that the structure of the knowledge that is activated is compatible across individuals. However, people develop their concepts in a social setting where they communicate with other members of a common cultural group. This membership in a communicative group has the effect of synchronizing the meanings of words across individuals, because they must be able to communicate with other members of the group (Garrod & Doherty, 1994; Markman & Makin, 1998).

This solution to the problem of holism is similar in structure to the proposed solution of the problem of common ground or mutual knowledge (Stalnaker, 1978). The general problem here involves understanding how people come to represent the knowledge that they share with another person. For example, John and Mary might be sitting across from each other at a table in a restaurant, and there might a sugar bowl between them. If Mary wants John to pass the sugar bowl to her, she may say to John, "Pass me the sugar bowl." To make this request, she must know that there is a sugar bowl on the table. Furthermore, she must believe that John knows that there is a sugar bowl on the table. Unfortunately, there seems to be an infinite regress of these beliefs: John must believe that Mary believes that John believes that there is a sugar bowl on the table, etc. While it might be possible to argue that a particular utterance requires only a very limited subset of these recursive, mutual beliefs, a canny philosopher can always construct a scenario that requires one additional recursive belief beyond that point (one such canny philosopher is Schiffer, 1972).

Just as with the alleged problem of holism, the common ground problem does not seem to be a serious problem on psychological grounds. Clark (1996) suggested that the common ground problem is solved heuristically. In particular, he suggested that people are sensitive to a few indicators of common ground, which they use to judge whether a given utterance is acceptable. For example, people make judgments about possible communities that they may share with other people. If you are at a party, and discover that someone else there is a cognitive scientist, you may ask them what they think about connectionist models. This question is not one you would ask of a person randomly, but you deem it to be acceptable in the context where you share a group membership with the person you are talking to. A second indicator of mutual knowledge involves personal situations. For example, you generally assume that salient perceptual events in your environment will be perceived by all people in the vicinity. If John and Mary are sitting at the restaurant, and they hear the crash of a tray of dishes being dropped, and John then comments, "Ah, the sound of a job opening up," he can be reasonably confident that Mary will attach this comment to the salient noise.

Hence, the suggested solutions to both holism and the determination of common ground assume that the cognitive system is designed to make guesses about what information is relevant in a given situation. These guesses are needed to make tractable potentially unbounded situations.

In essence, the problems philosophers have pointed to are really problems about how humans and other cognitive agents communicate. The problems therefore are to be solved by psychological theories of communication and concept activation. These problems have no philosophical solution, no in-principle, complete solution derivable from basic truths. Instead, they have a pragmatic solution that relies on heuristics to do the best job possible in the face of processing limitations.

In this section, we have suggested that some logical problems with the concepts of representation used by psychologists may have psychological solutions rather than logical or philosophical solutions. There is, obviously, much more that we could say to elaborate on these suggestions, but we have said enough to achieve our goal which was to show that representations and the computational hypothesis are capable of providing a scientific foundation for cognitive science.

A ROAD MAP OF THE BOOK

This book is organized into three sections. At the beginning of each section, we present some introductory material that binds together the chapters in that section, but we want to briefly preview the content of the chapters here.

The first section, "Foundations," includes four chapters (of which this chapter is one) that examine foundational issues in the study of representation and representational dynamics in cognitive systems. The second chapter by Bickhard takes a situated action perspective and argues that the dynamics of representation run deep: Not only are representations subject to dynamics that happen to them and transform them, but representation itself is a dynamical phenomenon. On Bickhard's view, representations emerge from dynamical interactions between an organism and its environment; representations themselves are not static objects. Prinz and Barsalou distinguish between perceptual and amodal representational systems. They suggest that most research in cognitive science has assumed representations that are not tied to any particular perceptual modality and hence are amodal. They argue that this approach is wrongheaded and that many problems with amodal symbol systems can be solved with representations derived from perceptual symbol systems. Finally, Marcus defends the role of variables in cognitive processing and demonstrates that models that fail to implement variables and binding (like many connectionist models) cannot account for a number of complex linguistic phenomena.

The second section, entitled "Words and Objects," focuses on representation and dynamics in aspects of language and object recognition.

This section begins with a chapter by Remez, who argues that speech perception is first a matter of analyzing speech signals for phonemic contrasts, rather than fixed, Platonistic phonemes, and as such requires flexible, dynamic representations on both the talker's and listener's parts. In the second chapter, Burgess and Lund describe HAL, a model of the representation of word meaning derived from a corpus of 300 million words of text taken from the Internet. This spatial representation captures a number of interesting low-level aspects of word meaning such as priming and similarity. Next, Hummel examines a debate in research on object recognition between those who adopt view-based models and those who adopt structural description models. Only the latter, he claims, use what can truly be called representations, and only the latter, therefore, can truly explain object perception and recognition.

Finally, the third section, "Concepts, Concept Use, and Conceptual Change," examines dynamics in higher cognitive processing. Goldstone, Steyvers, Spencer-Smith, and Kersten begin by discussing the role of conceptual information and concept learning in perceptual representation. They provide important data demonstrating that construction of perceptual representations is guided by the concepts a cognitive system learns. This view makes constructing perceptual representations quite a dynamic process, because such representations are influenced both by transduced, external information and by higher level conceptual information.

The next three chapters deal with types of concept-comparison processes and their role in the dynamics of representation. Holyoak and Hummel use this topic to make their case that connectionist architectures must be married with physical symbol systems. Their project, "symbolic connectionism," is an explicit attempt to get a connectionist system to use symbolic representations. Next, Dietrich examines the nature of analogical reminding. He argues that the best explanation for what happens during an episode of analogical reminding is that the concepts involved in the reminding change in the very process of retrieval, prior to the completion of the analogy. He then argues that this view requires concepts to be malleable, so malleable, in fact, that it is probably best to think of concepts in terms of constructive, representational processes rather than static representations. Finally, Gentner and Wolff discuss four ways that metaphor comprehension results in conceptual change. Their proposals are rich in detail and supported by both empirical data and robust computer models.

In the last chapter of the book, Markman, Zhang, and Moreau examine the dynamics of decision making. They suggest that preferences are often constructed in the process of making decisions and that what is learned about choice options is affected by how those options are compared in the process of making a choice. They present data about the dynamics of preferences, which are best explained by representations—indeed dynamic representations.

All the contributions to this book take seriously both dynamics and representation. There is a serious temptation to use demonstrations of the flexibility and fluidity of cognitive processing as evidence that there are no representations, or at least no complex structured representations (e.g., Hofstadter, 1995; Thelen & Smith, 1994). What the chapters in this book demonstrate is that the flexibility and fluidity of cognitive processing are actually good arguments for taking representation and processing seriously. At times, the dynamics of cognition is well modeled by simple unstructured representations that change flexibly with context (see chaps. 5 and 6). At other times, dynamics is well modeled by processes operating over complex structured representations (as in the chapters in Part III). What is crucial is that cognitive dynamics do not obviate the need for representation. Instead, different aspects of dynamics call for different representational assumptions. The hard work involves deciding which types of representations are necessary and how different representational approaches can be combined into models that explain the fine details of dynamics in cognitive processing.

REFERENCES

Barsalou, L. (in press). Perceptual symbol systems. *Behavioral and Brain Sciences*.

Bickhard, M. (1998). Levels of representationality. *Journal of Experimental and Theoretical Artificial Intelligence, 10*(2), 179–215.

Bickhard, M., & Terveen, L. (1995). *Foundational Issues in artificial intelligence and cognitive science: Impasse and solution*. Amsterdam: Elsevier.

Blum, L., Shub, M., & Smale, S. (1989). On a theory of computation and complexity over the real numbers: NP-completeness, recursive functions, and universal machines. *Bulletin of the American Mathematical Society, 21*(1), 1–46.

Brooks, R. (1991). Intelligence without representation. *Artificial Intelligence, 47*(1–3), 139–159.

Chalmers, D. (1994). A computational foundation for cognition. *Minds and Machines, 5*(4), 391–402.

Clancey, W. J. (1993). Situated action: A neuropsychological interpretation. *Cognitive Science, 17*, 87–116.

Clark, H. H. (1996). *Using language*. New York: Cambridge University Press.

DeJong, G., & Mooney, R. (1986). Explanation-based learning. *Machine Learning, 1*, 145–176.

Dietrich, E. (1990). Computationalism. *Social Epistemology, 4*(2), 135–154.

Dietrich, E. (1994). Thinking computers and the problem of intentionality. In E. Dietrich (Ed.), *Thinking computers and virtual persons* (pp. 3–34). San Diego: Academic Press.

Dietrich, E., & Markman, A. (1998). All information processing entails computation, or If R. A. Fisher had been a cognitive scientist. (Commentary on van Gelder's "The Dynamical Hypothesis in Cognitive Science"). *Behavioral and Brain Sciences, 21*(5), 637–638.

Fields, C. A. (1989). Consequences of nonclassical measurement for the algorithmic description of continuous dynamical systems. *Journal of Experimental and Theoretical Artificial Intelligence, 1*, 171–189.

Fields, C. A. (1994). Real machines and virtual intentionality. In E. Dietrich (Ed.), *Thinking computers and virtual persons* (pp. 71–90). San Diego: Academic Press.

Fodor, J. A. (1994). *The elm and the expert.* Cambridge, MA: MIT Press.

Fodor, J. A., & Lepore, E. (1992). *Holism: A shoppers guide.* Cambridge, MA: Blackwell.

Forbus, K., Gentner, D., & Law, K. (1995). MAC/FAC: A model of similarity-based retrieval. *Cognitive Science, 19,* 141–205.

Garrod, S., & Doherty, G. (1994). Conversation, co-ordination and convention: An empirical investigation of how groups establish linguistic conventions. *Cognition, 53,* 181–215.

Gibson, J. J. (1950). *The perception of the visual world.* Westport, CT: Greenwood Press.

Gibson, J. J. (1986). *The ecological approach to visual perception.* Hillsdale, NJ: Lawrence Erlbaum Associates.

Hofstadter, D. R. (1995). *Fluid concepts and creative analogies.* New York: Basic Books.

Horgan, T., & Tienson, J. (1996). *Connectionism and the philosophy of psychology.* Cambridge, MA: MIT Press.

Hummel, J., & Holyoak, K. J. (1997). Distributed representations of structure: A theory of analogical mapping. *Psychological Review, 104*(3), 427–466.

Loren, L., & Dietrich, E. (1997). Merleau-Ponty, embodied cognition, and the problem of intentionality. *Cybernetics and Systems, 28*(5), 345–358.

Markman, A. B., & Dietrich, E. (in press). In defense of representations. *Cognitive Psychology.*

Markman, A. B., & Makin, V. S. (1998). Referential communication and category acquisition. *Journal of Experimental Psychology: General, 127,* 331–354.

Meyer, D. E., & Schvaneveldt, R. W. (1971). Facilitation in recognizing pairs of words: Evidence of a dependence between retrieval operations. *Journal of Experimental Psychology, 90*(2), 227–234.

Michalski, R. S. (1994). Inferential theory of learning: Developing foundations for multi-strategy learning. In R. S. Michalski & G. Tecuci (Eds.), *Machine Learning* (Vol. 4, pp. 3–61). San Francisco: Morgan Kaufmann.

Pollock, J. L. (1994). Justification and defeat. *Artificial Intelligence, 67,* 377–407.

Pollock, J. L. (1995). *Cognitive carpentry.* Cambridge, MA: MIT Press.

Port, R., & van Gelder, T. (1995). *Mind and motion.* Cambridge, MA: MIT Press.

Putnam, H. (1975). *Mind, language, and reality.* New York: Cambridge University Press.

Schiffer, S. (1972). *Meaning.* Oxford: Oxford University Press.

Stalnaker, R. C. (1978). Assertion. In P. Cole (Ed.), *Syntax and semantics 9: Pragmatics* (pp. 315–322). New York: Academic Press.

Thelen, E., & Smith, L. B. (1994). *A dynamic systems approach to the development of cognition and action.* Cambridge, MA: MIT Press.

van Gelder, V. (1998). The dynamics hypothesis in cognitive science. *Behavior and Brain Sciences, 21*(5).

2

Dynamic Representing and Representational Dynamics

Mark H. Bickhard
Lehigh University

Contemporary cognitive science is caught between two poles regarding representation and cognition: Representations are considered to be important, even fundamental, but they are conceived of as inherently static entities or states; or the dynamics of systems and agents is considered to be everything, with representation relegated to a nugatory position or denied any existence at all. At the first pole, in either classical symbol manipulation approaches or connectionist approaches, representations undergo dynamics—of differing kinds in the two cases—but the representations themselves are static and even atemporal in the correspondences with things in the world that are taken to constitute them as representations. In contrast, at the second pole, there are strong movements in situated cognition and autonomous agents to deny representations any relevant existence at all. Workers have claimed that dynamics is everything, and the very notion of representation is at best unimportant and at worst misleading or even incoherent (Port & van Gelder, 1995).[1]

Neither of these camps can naturally account for some obvious phenomena in cognition. In particular, neither can account for the dynamics

---

[1]Discussion of such movements and their rationales can be found in Bickhard and Terveen (1995). Not everyone involved in situated cognition or autonomous agent research advocates abandoning representation. Bickhard (1998) and Bickhard and Terveen (1995) show how the apparently opposed sides of this issue may both be accommodated.

inherent in multiple forms of representational change. There are at least two forms of such dynamics—dynamics that *operate on* representations and result in changes internal to those representations and dynamics that are inherent and internal to representations per se (Bickhard, 1993, 1998; Bickhard & Campbell, 1996; Freyd, 1987; Shanon, 1993). Both versions pose serious challenges to the standard stances toward representational phenomena. Representations as static symbols or states can model the construction of new representations as compositions of atomic representations, perhaps as the result of some program operating on symbol strings, but cannot easily accommodate changes wrought on (or in) particular representations per se.[2] Positions that deny any role to representations obviously cannot account for any kind of dynamics of representations. Yet such dynamics clearly occur. This is likely the case even for simple representations in relatively simple animals, but it is most easily demonstrated with respect to higher level human cognitions (see next).

The dynamics of cognition and representation, then, serve as strong counterexamples, if not refutations, of standard theoretical approaches to cognition and representation. Taken seriously, they would induce a genuine crisis. They *should* be taken seriously—there should be a serious crisis in the field.

The cognitive dynamics that has such rational force (which is not to claim that it has had or will have the impact that it logically deserves) is well established empirically, especially in recent work. The basic point that there is in fact a rich dynamics of cognition is obvious to casual observation—its neglect in recent theoretical literature is likely fostered by typical blinders imposed by too much immersion in some misguiding theory. If our favorite theory, as well as our favorite professors' theories and all our textbooks, all preclude cognitive dynamics of this rich sort, then we simply overlook and ignore such phenomena—until still richer data force us to notice that there may be some blinders around our thinking.

I argue that the rich dynamics of cognition that is beginning to be noticed is not only a set of empirical phenomena that is embarrassing to

---

[2]Particular instances of such phenomena can be addressed by postulating and modeling internal representational structure to particular representations, such as internal string or network structure, and modeling changes created in such internal structure, perhaps by a computer program. Such approaches are ad hoc, however, and seriously limited with respect to the general phenomena of cognitive change because each instance requires its own ad hoc model. There are also difficult conceptual issues involved in specifying what internal changes leave the identity of the structured representation unchanged and what internal changes yield a resultant change in the identity of the structured representation—not to mention the issues involved in accounting for the representational atoms out of which such structures are constructed. If the presupposed representational atoms themselves undergo any dynamics, then we encounter either a contradiction of assumption or an infinite regress seeking the true atoms that do not change, that have no dynamics.

contemporary cognitive science, but that it is an expected consequence of an alternative conception of the nature of representation and, therefore, of cognition. Just as standard views tend to hide the dynamics of cognition, a more valid view of representation makes such dynamics highly perspicuous. Standard models of representation arguably have deep, even fatal, problems, which, if corrected, yield an alternative in which representational dynamics are inherent in the nature of representational phenomena. Representation, properly understood, is a dynamic phenomenon itself, not merely something that may undergo, or be subject to, dynamics.

REPRESENTATION: ENCODINGS AND ACTIONS

Since the ancient Greeks, conceptions of representation have been dominated by one underlying assumption: Representation is some kind of correspondence between representing elements in the mind and things or properties being represented in the world. These correspondences are usually assumed to be created by causal influences in perception, such as light causing various transductions into representations in the visual system. The analogy here is that mental representations are like external representations, such as pictures, statues, and maps. Representational correspondences are variously presumed to be causal, covariational, structural, isomorphic, or informational.

Such correspondence representations are presumed to encode what they represent. Just as a map encodes its territory, a mental representation encodes the desk before us. Because the assumption is that all representations have some version of this form, I have come to call these approaches to representation *encodingism*. Note that encodings are inherently static. They can undergo transformation—they can be used as atoms for construction—but the representational elements themselves are inert (qua representations), and the representational relationships, the correspondences, are not only static, they are generally assumed to be atemporal, logical, in nature (Shanon, 1993). A map exists in time and can be created, destroyed, and altered in time, but the relationship between the map and the territory is not itself temporal. The representational relationship has no inherent dynamics.

Clearly encodings do exist—that is not at issue—but the assumption that *all* representation is of the nature of encodings is at issue. In particular, encodingism—the assumption that all representation *is* of that form—encounters fatal difficulties when addressing mental representation.

Before turning to any of these arguments, however, I first point out that this general encodingist approach is no longer the only available approach to representation. Contrary to occasional announcements, it is not the only game in town. In the last century, Darwin, Peirce, and others introduced *action* as a focus for analysis of things mental as a replacement for the classical assumption that consciousness was the locus of mind (Joas, 1993). Clearly, both action and consciousness must ultimately be accounted for, but the assumed framework within which the analysis might best begin had not changed in millennia.

Furthermore, the classical assumptions about consciousness were passive, with no necessary output or action. Consciousness was a matter of contemplating the world in Plato's cave. Action was distinctly secondary or absent, but the pragmatism that Peirce introduced suggests that action and interaction may be essential for understanding consciousness as much as for understanding any other aspects of mind.

In any case, action and interaction—pragmatism—constitutes an alternative to encodingism in considering representation and cognition (Bickhard, 1993; Murray, 1990; Rosenthal, 1983, 1987; Thayer, 1973). The possibility that representation and cognition are somehow emergent in action and interaction is a distinct alternative to encodingism. With respect to current issues, if representation—and, therefore, cognition—is emergent in interaction, then representation and cognition are inherently dynamic.

In this chapter, I argue that encodingism is a failed and even incoherent approach, whereas pragmatic approaches to representation and cognition hold promise. Observed dynamics of cognition already strongly support pragmatic approaches. Within the pragmatic, or interactive, approach, I illustrate some of the dynamics that should be naturally found and, therefore, naturally explained if found. I call the assumption that representation is fundamentally emergent in interaction *interactivism*. Interactivism is inherently richly dynamic.

WHAT'S WRONG WITH ENCODINGISM?

The general encodingist approach has innumerable flaws. Some have been noted from earliest times; some are still being discovered. The only reason this approach is still around is that there has been no alternative; the assumption has always been that any problems found were specific to the models being considered and that some other version of encodingism would prove to be the correct model. That assumption is still dominant.

Encodingism is no longer without alternative, but pragmatism is only a century old, and its explication is still underway. Throughout much of this century, pragmatism was buried by the encodingism of positivism and even by encodingist interpretations of pragmatist positions. Peirce, for example, has often been misinterpreted as a verificationist. Suffice it to say, then, that there has been no alternative to encodingism for most of its history, and now that there is an alternative, it is only slowly being recognized as a real and viable alternative.

I argue that the pragmatic and interactive alternative deserves strong consideration. The flaws in encodingism are deeply serious—fatal, in fact—and the interactive model of representation avoids them. But, most important for current purposes, interactivism is inherently dynamic.

I cannot rehearse all the problems with encodingism here, but illustrate with a few. (For more complete discussions, see Bickhard, 1993, 1999; Bickhard & Terveen, 1995; Shanon, 1993.) One approach to the problems of encodingism is to look at genuine encodings, such as maps or Morse code. Such codes require that the person interpreting them already know the encoding relationships in order to engage in that interpretation. Furthermore, they need such an interpreter in order to function as representations at all. If knowledge of the encoding relationship were required for *mental* representations to be representational, then they could never provide new knowledge. New encodings would be impossible, and old encodings mysterious: How did the organism come to understand those old encoding relationships? The need for an interpreter singlehandedly eliminates this notion: If mental representations required an interpreter, then who is to interpret the results of that interpretation? Who interprets the results of the next? A vicious regress is initiated. Mental representations cannot require interpreters.

The inability to account for new encodings relates to another difficulty. The only extant models of how to create new encoding representations are models of how to combine already existing encodings into new structures of encodings. There is no model of the emergence of new basic or atomic encodings. There cannot be, because they require an interpreter to provide them with representational content and to interpret that content once provided (Bickhard & Richie, 1983). So the only new encodings that can emerge are those created by human beings, but, again, like Morse code, those cannot be our basic epistemological contact with the world— because we would have to already know, have encodings for, everything that we could represent about that world. In this situation, any genuine learning would be impossible. All representation would have to be innate (Bickhard, 1991; Fodor, 1981). But if it is logically impossible to create new atomic encodings, then it is also impossible for evolution to create them, so they cannot be innate. On the other hand, because no representation existed at the moment of the big bang, and representation exists now, representation *must* be capable of emergence.[3] The implication of encodingism—that representation cannot be emergent—provides still an-

---

[3]Emergence is itself a metaphysically problematic notion. For a discussion of how to make sense of emergence, see Bickhard with D. Campbell (in press).

other perspective on its logical failure. Representation must be capable of emergence (Bickhard, 1993; Bickhard with D. Campbell, in press).

The impossibility of encoding representation to emerge turns on the impossibility of providing new representational content, new specification of, knowledge of, what a new encoding would represent. That is, the impossibility of emergent encodings reflects the impossibility of emergent representational content. Content can be provided to encodings if that content already exists. "X" can be defined in terms of "Y", and thereby pick up the same content as "Y", so long as "Y" is already an encoding—so long as "Y" already has content. Or "X" can be defined in terms of some structure of "Y" and "Z" and perhaps others, again so long as they already have content to be provided via the definition. But, although "X" can be defined in terms of "Y", and "Y" perhaps in terms of "Z", such a chain must halt in finitely many steps. There must be some bottom level of encodings in terms of which all others are defined. Where do they come from?

Again, it does not suffice to simply posit that this level is innate—if such emergence is impossible, then evolution cannot accomplish it either. On the other hand, if such emergence *is* possible, then how? And why not for single organisms—why not in learning? Bottom-level encodings cannot emerge, and they cannot be defined in terms of any other representations without violating the assumption that they are at the bottom level. Thus they cannot be given any representational content at all, which means that they cannot be encodings at all. This is in contradiction to the original assumption. So, the assumptions of encodingism have yielded a contradiction. It cannot be correct. This perspective on the inadequacies of encodingism I call the *incoherence argument* (Bickhard, 1993).

Piaget (1970) had a variant of these general arguments against encoding representations: If our representations of the world are copies of that world, then how do we know what the world is in order to construct our copies? Again, representational content, the knowledge that representation is supposed to provide, must be already present in order to account for that very representational content. This is the same circle with a slightly different aspect.

Still another member of this family of arguments is that of radical skepticism. We cannot check whether our representations are correct or in error, because to do so is simply to use those same representations again. Any such check is circular. We cannot get any independent access to the other end of the presumed encoding relationship. Therefore, there is no way to determine the truth or falsity of our representations. System- or organism-detectable error of representation is impossible, and it becomes superfluous to even posit an independent world that we can never have access to. Solipsism or some other idealism is a classical—and contemporary—reaction to such realizations (Bickhard, 1987, 1995).

These problems arise from the basic conception or definition of representation as encoding correspondence. There are also many problems that arise as what appear to be technical difficulties within the project of providing an encoding account of representation. An example of one of these is the "too many correspondences" problem. Suppose that representation is constituted by some causal relationship between the representation and what it represents in the world: perhaps a mental representation of a desk and the desk itself via the causal connection of light. But, if representation is constituted as causal correspondence, which correspondence is the right one, and how can the organism tell the difference? The point is that if there is any such correspondence in existence, then there are an unbounded number of such correspondences: not only with the desk per se, but also with the chemical activity in the retina, the light activity in the air, the molecular activity in the surface of the desk, the quantum activity in the surface electrons of the desk, the desk a minute ago, last week, a year ago, and when it was built, the trees that provided the wood (or the oil for the plastic), the evolution of such trees, and so on, all the way back to the origin of the universe. Where in this unbounded regress of correspondences in time is the one correspondence that is supposed to be representational? How is that single correspondence specified? What is the nature and source of the representational content that selects what that correspondence is with for the organism or system?

There are many more such problems, but I stop here. Typically, insofar as there is any awareness of these problems, it is assumed that someday they will be solved. I assume, on the contrary, that there is good reason to conclude that these problems are impossible to solve within the encodingist framework. If encodingism is not viable, however, what is this interactive alternative?

INTERACTIVISM

The underlying intuition of the interactive model is that interactions sometimes succeed and sometimes fail. If the interactions are performed well, whether they succeed depends on whether particular enabling conditions in the environment are true. If they are, the interaction succeeds; if not, the interaction fails. Engaging in an interaction, then, presupposes about the environment that the interaction's enabling conditions do in fact hold. That is, engaging in an interaction predicates of the environment: "This environment is appropriate for this interaction—the enabling conditions hold." That presupposition, that predication, of course, can be false.

In this manner, two related aspects of representation—aboutness and truth value—emerge. The predication is about the environment, and it is true or false. This is a minimal, primitive sense of representation. It holds in a pure version only in very simple organisms—perhaps bacteria and worms. I argue, however, that this is the basic form of representation, from which all others are constructed and derived.

There are three issues I briefly address about the interactive model: a comparison with encodingism, an indication of how these intuitions can be realized, and an outline of how more standard kinds of representations, and associated challenges to the adequacy of interactivism, can be accounted for. (For more complete discussions, see Bickhard, 1993, 1996b; Bickhard & Terveen, 1995; Christensen, Collier, & Hooker, 1999.) For this chapter, developing the deficiencies of encodingism and outlining interactivism are preliminaries to the main topic: the senses in which interactive representation and cognition are intrinsically dynamic.

Interactivism and Encodingism: A Comparison

Encodingist models are oriented toward the past. They "look backwards" down the causal input stream toward whatever the light (say) last reflected from. Pragmatists called this the spectator model (Smith, 1987). Encodings are (most simply) of what is factual; they are non-modal. Encodings are explicit about what they represent.

Interactivism, in contrast on all these points, looks toward the future. It is concerned with what sorts of interactions would be possible in given situations—what classes of presupposed enabling conditions exist. In this sense, it is anticipatory: anticipations of courses and outcomes of successful interactions. It is inherently modal: concerned not just with what actually existed in the past causal chain, but with the realm of possibility in the future. It is implicit: The enabling conditions, the properties predicated of the environment, are not represented explicitly, only implicitly.[4] Explicit representations can be constructed, however: If *this* interaction succeeds (these enabling conditions hold), then *that* interaction will succeed (those enabling conditions also hold).

Realization

Notions such as anticipation, in terms of which the interactive intuitions have been presented, can have a worrying flavor of already being mental terms and therefore committing a circularity in attempting to account for mental representation in a manner that makes use of mentality. As a first point about the realization of interactive representation, therefore, I out-

---

[4]This implicitness is a source of great power: It allows, for example, for the solution of the frame problems (Bickhard & Terveen, 1995). Simply put, implicit representations are inherently unbounded in scope.

line a minimally adequate form of realization that eliminates such worrisome terms by making fairly simple use of standard notions from abstract machine theory and programming theory.

The truth value of an interactive representation presents itself when the anticipations involved turn out to be correct or incorrect, when the interaction succeeds or fails. Such anticipations are relevant because they are the basis for the selection of interactions: Select those with anticipated outcomes that satisfy current goals.[5] In fact, I argue that it is the function of action selection that yielded the initial evolution of primitive representation and similarly that is introducing interactive representation into contemporary robotics (Bickhard, 1996a; Bickhard & Terveen, 1995).[6] Anticipation-for-the-purpose-of-action-selection is almost trivially realizable with simple pointers, however. Pointers to subsystems can indicate that the interactions that would be executed by those subsystems are appropriate or would be appropriate, and pointers to potential internal states can indicate the anticipated internal outcomes of those interactions. Selection of subsystems can then be made on the basis of the indicated anticipated outcomes. Anticipation, then, can be successfully naturalized and does not introduce a circularity into the model.[7]

A deeper consideration, however, drives realizations of interactive representation to a different kind of architecture. That consideration is intrinsic timing, and it initiates the investigation of the intrinsic dynamic aspects of interactivism. Interactive representation is emergent in systems for interaction with the environment. Successful interaction requires successful timing. Therefore, interactive representation cannot be realized without the ability to engage in proper timing.

In computers, timing is introduced by a common clock that drives the steps of the processing, but such a clock has at least two problems for

---

[5]If goals were necessarily representational, this would be still another point of potential circularity. But goals in the sense needed here are no more than conditional switches that shift control out of the subsystem under some (the goal) conditions and return control to the subsystem under others. Those conditions, in turn, can be strictly internal and functionally accessible to the system—functionally detectable by the system—without requiring any representation of them. Once representation *has* emerged, of course, goal systems can make use of them.

[6]For a discussion of the relationship of this model to the beliefs and desires of folk psychology, see Bickhard (1998).

[7]There is another requirement here, however, that I have not discussed. It is not sufficient to make a distinction that we can label as successful and unsuccessful. The normativity of success and failure must itself be naturalized. An automobile does not care whether it is working "correctly" or not—that designation is completely dependent on human users. If the same point could be made about the notions of success and failure involved in the interactive model of representation, then there would be a hidden reliance on human mind in modeling representation—a hidden circularity. The normativity of success and failure, therefore, must also be naturalized. I develop such a model in Bickhard (1993).

my current purposes. (a) It is an introduction at the level of the engineering design of the computer, not an intrinsic aspect of either the encodings that are presumably being manipulated or of the mathematics upon which such machines are based. Turing machines have no intrinsic timing. (b) A common clock running the complexities of the computer can succeed as a design, but it is an impossible solution within the framework of evolution. It would require exquisite coordination between the processing circuitry and the timing circuitry, and, worse, it would require that the exquisite coordination be maintained over eons of evolution of the circuitry of the nervous system. Such simultaneous coordinated change is of vanishing probability to occur even once; it is beyond any serious consideration over evolutionary time spans.

There is, however, an "easy" solution to the timing problem. Instead of a single clock that somehow controls all processes, put clocks every-where and realize all control processes as relationships among clocks. This solution sounds odd, but when we realize that clocks are "just" oscillators, this solution becomes: Realize an interactive system as a system of oscillators or even as a dynamic oscillatory field, with all functional relationships being realized as modulatory relationships among oscilla-tions. Such an architecture is capable of at least Turing–machine–equiva-lent computational power because a limit form of modulation is switching on and off and switches are sufficient for constructing a Turing machine. It is, in fact, of greater than Turing-machine power because Turing ma-chines cannot have any intrinsic timing (Bickhard & Richie, 1983; Bickhard & Terveen, 1995). If this model is correct, it is not an accident of evolution that the central nervous system seems to function on precisely these principles of oscillation and modulation (for an extensive discussion, see Bickhard & Terveen, 1995).

Representations of Objects

According to the interactive model, representation emerges from interac-tion and, in particular, in response to the problem of the selection of interaction. Most primitively, it captures the emergence of truth values in implicit predications about the appropriateness of particular interac-tions to particular environments. At this level, we have truth-value norm-ativity, certainly the classically most vexing problem about the nature of representation, but we do not have representations of the familiar sort, such as of physical objects.

The issue here is not one of detecting or differentiating objects—that is almost trivial. Any interaction that does succeed in reaching particular outcomes does so only if its presupposed enabling conditions hold. If those enabling conditions involve particular properties, then success in that interaction detects, differentiates, those properties. If those enabling conditions involve the interaction with particular kinds of objects, then success in that interaction detects, or differentiates, an object of one of those kinds.

But, unlike in the encoding account, here there is no claim or assumption that detection or differentiation suffices for the organism to know anything about, to have representational content about, what has been detected or differentiated. A photocell can detect a break in its light beam, but it does not thereby have representations of what has interrupted that light. In the standard encodingist story, in contrast, a visual interaction that differentiates particular patterns of light thereby "transduces" repre sentations of the properties of that light (Fodor & Pylyshyn, 1981) or even of the objects and surfaces and edges that produced those light patterns. Differentiation, however, is not representation. Only the blindness of a false encodingist framework ever yields the conclusion that they are the same (Bickhard & Richie, 1983).

If interactive differentiation of objects does not constitute representation of those objects, however, then the task remains of accounting for such representations—for such representational content. The key to the model is to recognize that interactive differentiations and interactive anticipations (thus implicit predications) can link up with each other in conditional and potentially quite complex ways. A simple instance has already been introduced earlier: If this interaction, then that interaction.

Such indicative linkages, indications of interactive potentiality conditional on prior interactions, can form complex webs and patterns. Some of these patterns, in turn, manifest a *closed reachability* among all of the participating kinds of interactions. A visual scan of a manipulable object, for example, indicates the possibility of multiple manipulations. Each such manipulation, in turn, yields the possibility of its own visual aspect of the object to scan. Each such scan indicates all the other manipulations and consequent scans, including the original. All points in such a web of potentialities indicate the potentiality, possibly conditional on intermediate interactions, of all the others.

Such closure of reachability is one of the critical properties of the representation of objects. A second critical property is that such a closed pattern remain invariant under particular classes of interactions. The potentialities of an object remain invariant under multiple kinds of manipulations, locomotions of the organism, transportings of the object, hidings of the object, and so on—but not under others, such as crushing or burning. Manipulable physical objects, from a simple representational perspective such as characterizes an infant or toddler, are represented by closed patterns of interactive potentiality, which remain invariant under strong classes of physical transformations. This is a basically Piagetian model of the construction of object representations out of organizations of potential interaction (Piaget, 1954). Clearly, many details remain to be specified, but I take it that this suffices to demonstrate that accounting for object representations from within an interactive framework is not an *aporia*.

Many additional challenges can be made to the interactive model, but I do not address them here. The key point is that the interactive model of representation is not limited to primitive representation and provides resources for developing models of more complex representations. It remains, therefore, a candidate for the fundamental nature of representation—of all kinds.[8]

At this point, we have the emergence of primitive representation in the dynamics of action selection on the basis of processes of anticipation, which are realizable in systems of oscillatory dynamic systems, and a sense of how more complex representations can be constructed on this primitive basis. In this view, the very foundations of representation and cognition are dynamic (Bickhard, 1993, 1996b; Bickhard & Terveen, 1995; Christensen, Collier, & Hooker, 1999; Hooker, 1996). Yet there is more to the story of cognitive dynamics.

MICROGENESIS

The notion of microgenesis—in a local region of the brain, for example—is relatively simple, yet it involves a subtlety. It depends on a distinction between the processes that a (sub)system engages in and the manner or mode of that engagement. A local brain region may engage in differing modes of processing from one occasion to another, even if the external sources of influence are identical. This phenomenon is akin to a single processor in a computer functioning in different modes depending on the program it is running (a more precise example of computer architecture is discussed next). If the arguments about brain functioning given here are correct, however, microgenesis involves altered baseline oscillatory properties and altered modulatory relations—not changes in "program."

---

[8]One interesting challenge to the interactive model is to question how it can account for the classic paradigmatic encoding phenomena of perception. How can visual perception, for example, be *other* than the generation of encodings about the environment based on the processing of visual inputs? Perception, however, is fundamentally a matter of interaction, both in its process and in the nature of the representations generated (Bickhard & Richie, 1983; Rizzolatti, Fadiga, Fogassi, & Gallese, 1997).

Another interesting challenge concerns abstract representations, such as of electrons or numbers. What can the system interact with to constitute such representations? The answer to the challenge of abstract representation is interesting and important in its own right, but requires significant development and discussion (Campbell & Bickhard, 1986).

If the mode of functioning of a system changes from time to time, then some process must yield that change. Some process must set up or construct whatever local states and properties manifest the altered mode—the altered oscillatory and modulatory properties. Such a construction or genesis of local modes of process is different from (although related to) the more macroconstructive processes involved in development and learning: A local construction of appropriate mode of functioning must be engaged in even for processes that have been well learned. I call construction at this local or microlevel *microgenesis*.

Notions of microgenesis have a moderately long history, but are nevertheless not common (Catán, 1986; Deacon, 1989; Hanlon, 1991a, 1991b). As with timing, I argue that microgenesis is of critical importance to representation and cognition, even though largely ignored in contemporary cognitive science. Like timing, something akin to microgenesis occurs even in von Neumann computers, but is considered to be an implementation issue—not of theoretical importance. The analogue in a computer is the sense in which a single register in the central processing unit at one time adds two numbers and at the next instant performs a logical *or*. The processes (and circuitry) that set up the different modes of functioning of such registers are the core of a computer design, but not part of the computer metaphor of brain functioning (however bad that metaphor may be, this is just one additional defect).[9] Such setup processes are register-level microgenesis processes.

Consider the following two aspects of microgenesis: It occurs continuously and throughout the central nervous system simultaneously, and it realizes an implicit topology on the space of what might be microgenetically constructed. Briefly, the importance of these two points is that first, the ongoing processes of microgenesis proceeding concurrently throughout multiple parts of the nervous system will manifest mutual influences on one another—a context-sensitive synergistic process internal, or foundational, to processes of representation and cognition; and second, such a topology in a space of potential representations and modes of thought underlies similarity, metaphor, analogy, and creative problem solving. All these depend on a functionally real sense in which representations and cognitive processes can be "near to" or "far from" one another, and such relationships are constitutive of a topology.

---

[9]I am referring to the *computer metaphor of the brain* here, not to the *computational theory of mind*. The computer metaphor imports various aspects of computer design and function into hypotheses about the structure and functioning of the brain, quite often yielding false hypotheses (Bickhard, 1997). Such importation yields, for example, notions of neurons as threshold switches or the strong differentiation between information transmission and information processing that we find in von Neumann computer models. With regard to microgenesis, however, a process that does occur in standard computers ironically has *not* been imported into brain studies, but should have been.

Topologies are essential to any kind of heuristic problem solving—to any judgments about or formations of senses of similarity. Correspondingly, they are present in all models of such processes, but are usually not recognized in their full topological generality. Models of analogy, for example, must introduce some sort of similarity comparisons and usually do so via the introduction of some set of features together with a function that calculates nearness in terms of the respective sets of features. Features generate a distance measure, or metric, which is a very rich form of topological structure.

There are many objections to feature structures as the basis for similarity and analogy models. One is simply that features are instances of encodings and, as such, cannot ultimately be correct. A second problem, one that interacts with the first, is that there is no way in such a feature-based model to create new spaces of possible representations with their own new topologies or to learn a new topology on an old space. The impossibility of creating novel new encodings precludes the creation of novel new features just as much as any other kind of representation. Feature-based models, then, require the hand coding of all relevant topological information and block the modeling of the natural learning of such information and related processes (Bickhard & Campbell, 1996; Morrison, 1998).

Microgenesis introduces a topology into the spaces of its possible constructions in terms of overlaps in the microgenesis constructive processes. *Nearness* in such a space is constituted as overlap in the processes of microgenesis.[10] If we assume that current microgenesis sets the initial conditions from which microgenesis proceeds into the future, then we can expect that microgenesis will, other things being equal, tend to honor a nearness relationship in subsequent constructions (such as is manifested in word associations)—"nearby" constructions will be already partially constructed. Similarly, new constructions will tend, other things being equal, to make use of similar constructive heuristics or patterns—they are already activated and available. Microgenetic search in such a space will honor the topologies induced by the microgenetic processes.

Microgenesis, then, induces topologies into processes of representation and cognition, topologies that inherently tend to be honored in those processes. These are manifested in similarity-based processes such as analogy.

---

[10]There are, in general, different kinds of overlap, or overlap of different components or aspects of microgenetic process, not just degree of overlap. In this sense, there is more structure than a topology, although still not generally all the structure of a metric space. A mathematical structure that captures this kind of structure intermediate between a topology and a metric space is a uniformity (Geroch, 1985; Hocking & Young, 1961; James, 1987). Uniformities are of importance in physics and appear to be potentially so in cognitive science as well.

This point is far from the limit of the cognitive importance of micro-genesis. I argue that the locus of learning processes must be in these processes of microgenesis. I do not relate the full arguments (Bickhard & Campbell, 1996), but the general point is as follows. Learning generates the ability to engage in new interactive processes, which, in turn, must be engaged in by nervous system modes of functioning—modes that must be microgenetically constructed. Learning, therefore, must alter micro-genesis. Conversely, any alteration in microgenesis processes alters modes of functioning, which alter interactive processes. If such changes are at all sensitive to selection effects, they constitute learning.

Recognizing that learning takes place at the level of microgenesis has interesting implications when considered together with the parallelism of microgenesis throughout the central nervous system. In particular, we can expect concurrent microgenesis processes to influence one another. We can expect context sensitivities in microgenesis, thus in learning and other topology-based processes. Furthermore, there is in general a base construc-tion involved, which is privileged with respect to the similarity processes, so that there is an a priori possibility of asymmetry. The microgenesis model, then, suggests the possibility of mutual influence, context sensitivi-ties, asymmetries, and even context-sensitive asymmetries.

All these in fact occur.[11] It is clear, for example, that the creation of analogies is a process, not an automatic recognition (Medin, Goldstone, & Genter, 1993). Such processes, in turn, exhibit context sensitivity and can undergo reorganization with experience, whether on the scale of individual development or of the historical development of ideas (Gent-ner, 1988, 1989; Gentner & Jeziorski, 1993; Gentner & Markman, 1995; Gentner & Rattermann, 1991; Medin et al., 1993). Even in a single task, a target domain may be representationally reorganized—microgenetically reorganized—so as to improve the comparisons that can be made with a source. The resources for creating analogies, and the criteria for good analogies, change over time—again, on both historical timescales and individual development timescales (Gentner & Grudin, 1985; Gentner & Jeziorski, 1993). The creation of analogies, therefore, must be a constructive process, and, unless we posit prescience, it must be a variation and selection construction process (Medin et al., 1993). That is, it must be a variation and selection microgenesis process.

---

[11]These do not constitute confirmations of novel predictions because the phenomena were noted empirically before the model was published, but, nevertheless, no available alternative model is consistent with these phenomena in a non-ad hoc manner. All combinations of context sensitivity and asymmetry can be built into any standard computer model, but the point is that they must be specifically built in. They are ad hoc; nothing about the architecture or process of encoding models suggests either property.

We find similar *context sensitivities* in similarity judgments. For example, the context of the list *Austria, Sweden, Poland, Hungary* leads to the similarity grouping of Austria and Sweden, whereas *Austria, Sweden, Norway, Hungary* yields the grouping of Austria and Hungary (Medin et al., 1993; Tversky, 1977; Tversky & Gati, 1978). For another, Italy and Switzerland have lower similarity in the context of other European countries than in the context of European and American countries (Tversky, 1977). We find *asymmetry* in such examples as North Korea being more similar to China than China is to North Korea, and a different kind of context sensitivity in the fact that judgments of political similarity can be different from judgments of geographical similarity (Tversky, 1977; Tversky & Gati, 1978).

To accommodate these and related results, some models propose that analogy processes may work by comparing the steps by which the items to be compared are constructed (Hofstadter, 1995; O'Hara, 1994; O'Hara & Indurkhya, 1995). This is microgenesis in everything but name—Procrusteanly squeezed, however, into narrow domains and constructions with inert encoding atoms.

In general, language and cognition exhibit massive context sensitivities. Even a simple question such as "Is there any water in the refrigerator?" can elicit very different answers if the context indicates that the questioner has drinking some water in mind rather than if the context indicates that the questioner wants to store some raw sodium (which reacts violently with water; Malt, 1994). Shanon has documented so many kinds of cognitive context sensitivity and such fundamental cognitive context sensitivity that he argued against encodingist atomism on the grounds that the unboundedness of context sensitivity requires a corresponding unboundedness in the number of basic encoding atoms to be able to capture that variation (Shanon, 1993; see also Bickhard & Terveen, 1995). The necessity for unbounded numbers of atomic encodings, among many other reasons, renders encodingism vacuous. It is clear from such considerations that representing and cognitive meaning are not restricted to an atomistic encodingism.

Empirical phenomena of the creation of analogies and similarity judgments have forced recognition of the inherent dynamics involved and of some of the resultant manifestations of context sensitivity, asymmetry, and so on. Relevant models, in turn, have become more sophisticated in attempts to keep up with these empirical recognitions. Models constructed within an encodingist framework, however, can approach such phenomena only in a limited and ad hoc manner: limited because the models are limited to whatever primitives they use as the atoms from which everything else is constructed, and ad hoc because there is *no* intrinsic representational dynamics in an encoding-based model. All representation-level dynamics must be built in to accommodate the data, that is, must be built in ad hoc. In contrast, all of these dynamics are precisely what should be expected from the inherent characteristics of the interactive microgenesis model (Bickhard & Campbell, 1996).

CONCLUSIONS

Encoding representations are inherently inert. Dynamical processes can manipulate them, but there is nothing dynamic in their nature. The evidence about human cognition, on the other hand, demonstrates unquestionable dynamic properties, of multifarious form (Freyd, 1987; Shanon, 1993). Such dynamics can be modeled in narrow domains with ad hoc encoding models that have the proper dynamical treatment of the encodings built into the models. The restriction to narrow domains derives from the necessity for unbounded numbers of encoding atoms to account for any realistic realm of cognition and representation. The frame problems, the unbounded context sensitivity, the impossibility of the emergence of content, and the myriads of additional problems demonstrate that encodingist approaches simply fail (Bickhard, 1993; Bickhard & Terveen, 1995; Shanon, 1993). These are the contemporary phlogiston theories of cognitive science. They work in restricted domains for restricted phenomena and can even sustain ongoing research programs, but they are ultimately false and inadequate. In the case of encodingism, the inadequacy is both empirical and conceptual (Bickhard, 1993; Bickhard & Terveen, 1995; Shanon, 1993).

The interactive model, in contrast, exhibits pervasive dynamics—intrinsically. Representing *is* the dynamics of anticipating, and the microgenesis of representational dynamics is itself a dynamics with ubiquitous consequences. Phenomena such as context sensitivity, mutual influence, and asymmetry of sensitivity are precisely what the interactive model predicts. No data can confirm a theory or theoretical perspective, but the extremely broad realm of approaches of encodingism is strongly *in*firmed by the evident dynamics of representation and cognition.

More broadly, encodingist approaches do not handle well the sorts of dynamics noted here. The various phenomena can be built into encoding models in narrow and ad hoc manners, but such accommodations to the data with no inherent motivation in the model itself signal a moribund metatheory. Researchers interested in the mind and cognition need to find alternatives. Cognition is dynamic, and it ultimately requires a model in which those dynamics are explained, not just accommodated. The only historical candidate for accounting for such dynamics is the general pragmatist approach, in which representation and cognition are understood to emerge out of systems of action and interaction. Cognitive science (not to mention philosophy, cognitive psychology, and so on) would be well advised to recognize and explore such inherently dynamic approaches.

ACKNOWLEDGMENTS

Thanks are due to Clay Morrison for comments on an earlier draft of this chapter and to the Henry R. Luce Foundation for support during its preparation.

REFERENCES

Bickhard, M. H. (1987). The social nature of the functional nature of language. In M. Hickmann (Ed.), *Social and functional approaches to language and thought* (pp. 39–65). New York: Academic Press.

Bickhard, M. H. (1991). The import of Fodor's anticonstructivist arguments. In L. Steffe (Ed.), *Epistemological foundations of mathematical experience* (pp. 14–25). New York: Springer-Verlag.

Bickhard, M. H. (1993). Representational content in humans and machines. *Journal of Experimental and Theoretical Artificial Intelligence, 5,* 285–333.

Bickhard, M. H. (1995). World mirroring versus world making: There's gotta be a better way. In L. Steffe & J. Gale (Eds.), *Constructivism in education* (pp. 229–267). Hillsdale, NJ: Lawrence Erlbaum Associates.

Bickhard, M. H. (1996a). *The emergence of representation in autonomous embodied agents.* [Papers from the 1996 AAAI Fall Symposium on Embodied Cognition and Action, November, Cambridge, MA]. (Tech. Rep. FS-96-02). Menlo Park, CA: AAAI Press.

Bickhard, M. H. (1996b). Troubles with computationalism. In W. O'Donohue & R. F. Kitchener (Eds.), *The philosophy of psychology* (pp. 173–183). London: Sage.

Bickhard, M. H. (1997). Cognitive representation in the brain. In R. Dulbecco (Ed.), *Encyclopedia of human biology* (2nd ed., pp. 865–876). San Diego: Academic Press.

Bickhard, M. H. (1999). Interaction and representation. *Theory and Psychology, 9*(4), 435–458.

Bickhard, M. H. (1998). Levels of representationality. *Journal of Experimental and Theoretical Artificial Intelligence, 10*(2), 179–215.

Bickhard, M. H., with Campbell, Donald T. (in press). Emergence. In P. B. Andersen, N. O. Finnemann, C. Emmeche, & P. V. Christiansen (Eds.), *Emergence and downward causation.* Aarhus, Denmark: University of Aarhus Press.

Bickhard, M. H., & Campbell, R. L. (1996). Topologies of learning and development. *New Ideas in Psychology, 14*(2), 111–156.

Bickhard, M. H., & Richie, D. M. (1983). *On the nature of representation: A case study of James J. Gibson's theory of perception.* New York: Praeger.

Bickhard, M. H., & Terveen, L. (1995). *Foundational issues in artificial intelligence and cognitive science—Impasse and solution.* Amsterdam: Elsevier Scientific.

Campbell, R. L., & Bickhard, M. H. (1986). *Knowing levels and developmental stages.* Basel, Switzerland: Karger.

Catán, L. (1986). The dynamic display of process: Historical development and contemporary uses of the microgenetic method. *Human Development, 29,* 252–263.

Christensen, W. D., Collier, J. D., & Hooker, C. A. (1999). *Autonomy, adaptiveness and anticipation: Towards foundations for life and intelligence in complex, adaptive, self-organizing systems.* Manuscript in preparation.

Deacon, T. W. (1989). Holism and associationism in neuropsychology: An anatomical synthesis. In E. Perecman (Ed.), *Integrating theory and practice in clinical neuropsychology* (pp. 1–47). Hillsdale, NJ: Lawrence Erlbaum Associates.

Fodor, J. A. (1981). The present status of the innateness controversy. *RePresentations* (pp. 257–316). Cambridge, MA: MIT Press.

Fodor, J. A., & Pylyshyn, Z. (1981). How direct is visual perception?: Some reflections on Gibson's ecological approach. *Cognition, 9,* 139–196.

Freyd, J. J. (1987). Dynamic mental representations. *Psychological Review, 94*(4), 427–438.

Gentner, D. (1988). Metaphor as structure mapping: The relational shift. *Child Development, 59,* 47–59.

Gentner, D. (1989). The mechanisms of analogical learning. In S. Vosniadou & A. Ortony (Eds.), *Similarity and analogical reasoning* (pp. 199–241). Cambridge: Cambridge University Press.

Gentner, D., & Grudin, J. (1985). The evolution of mental metaphors in psychology. *American Psychologist, 40*(2), 181–192.

Gentner, D., & Jeziorski, M. (1993). The shift from metaphor to analogy in Western science. In A. Ortony (Ed.), *Metaphor and thought* (2nd ed., pp. 447–480). New York: Cambridge University Press.

Gentner, D., & Markman, A. B. (1995). Similarity is like analogy: Structural alignment in comparison. In C. Cacciari (Ed.), *Similarity in language, thought and perception* (pp. 111–147). Milan, Italy: Brepols.

Gentner, D., & Rattermann, M. J. (1991). Language and the career of similarity. In S. A. Gelman & J. P. Byrnes (Eds.), *Perspectives on language and thought: Interrelations in development* (pp. 225–277). London: Cambridge University Press.

Geroch, R. (1985). *Mathematical physics.* Chicago: University of Chicago Press.

Hanlon, R. E. (1991a). Introduction. In R. E. Hanlon (Ed.), *Cognitive microgenesis: A neuropsychological perspective* (pp. xi–xx). New York: Springer-Verlag.

Hanlon, R. E. (Ed.). (1991b). *Cognitive microgenesis: A neuropsychological perspective.* New York: Springer-Verlag.

Hocking, J. G., & Young, G. S. (1961). *Topology.* Reading, MA: Addison-Wesley.

Hofstadter, D. R. (1995). *Fluid concepts and creative analogies: Computer models of the fundamental mechanisms of thought.* New York: Basic Books.

Hooker, C. A. (1996). Toward a naturalised cognitive science. In R. Kitchener & W. O'Donohue (Eds.), *Psychology and philosophy* (pp. 184–206). London: Sage.

James, I. M. (1987). *Topological and uniform spaces.* New York: Springer-Verlag.

Joas, H. (1993). American pragmatism and German thought: A history of misunderstandings. In *Pragmatism and social theory* (pp. 94–121). Chicago: University of Chicago Press.

Malt, B. C. (1994). Water is not H_2O. *Cognitive Psychology, 27,* 41–70.

Medin, D. L., Goldstone, R. L., & Gentner, D. (1993). Respects for similarity. *Psychological Review, 100,* 254–278.

Morrison, C. (1998). *Situated representations: Reconciling situated cognition and structured representation.* Doctoral dissertation, State University of New York, Binghamton.

Murphy, J. P. (1990). *Pragmatism.* Chicago: Westview Press.

O'Hara, S. (1994, May). *Towards a blackboard architecture for the solution of interpretive proportional analogy problems.* Paper presented at the Florida Artificial Intelligence Research Symposium, Pensacola Beach, FL.

O'Hara, S., & Indurkhya, B. (1995). Adaptation and redescription in the context of geometric proportional analogies. In *Adaptation of knowledge for reuse: Papers from the 1995 Fall Symposium* (pp. 80–86). (Tech. Rep. FS-95-04). Menlo Park, CA: American Association for Artificial Intelligence.

Piaget, J. (1954). *The Construction of reality in the child.* New York: Basic Books.

Piaget, J. (1970). *Genetic epistemology.* New York: Columbia University Press.

Port, R., & van Gelder, T. J. (1995). *Mind as motion: Dynamics, behavior, and cognition.* Cambridge, MA: MIT Press.

Rosenthal, S. B. (1983). Meaning as habit: Some systematic implications of Peirce's pragmatism. In E. Freeman (Ed.), *The relevance of Charles Peirce* (pp. 312–327). La Salle, IL: Open Court.

Rosenthal, S. B. (1987). Classical American pragmatism: Key themes and phenomenological dimensions. In R. S. Corrington, C. Hausman, & T. M. Seebohm (Eds.), *Pragmatism considers phenomenology* (pp. 37–57). Washington, DC: University Press of America.

Rizzolatti, G., Fadiga, L., Fogassi, L., & Gallese, V. (1997). The space around us. *Science, 277,* 190–191.

Shanon, B. (1993). *The representational and the presentational.* Hertfordshire, England: Harvester Wheatsheaf.

Smith, J. E. (1987). The reconception of experience in Peirce, James, and Dewey. In R. S. Corrington, C. Hausman, & T. M. Seebohm (Eds.), *Pragmatism considers phenomenology* (pp. 73–91). Washington, DC: University Press of America.

Thayer, H. S. (1973). *Meaning and action.* Indianapolis, IN: Bobbs-Merrill.

Tversky, A. (1977). Features of similarity. *Psychological Review, 84,* 327–352.

Tversky, A., & Gati, I. (1978). Studies of similarity. In E. Rosch & B. Lloyd (Eds.), *Cognition and categorization* (pp. 79–98). Hillsdale, NJ: Lawrence Erlbaum Associates.

Steering a Course
for Embodied Representation

Jesse J. Prinz
Washington University, St. Louis

Lawrence W. Barsalou
Emory University

Cognition is a dynamic process, continually changing over time. This truism has contributed to a growing interest in using dynamic systems theory to study and model cognitive phenomena. This development is by no means unwelcome. Already, dynamic approaches have inspired important new insights into cognition, and they are likely to inspire more. There is, however, need for caution. Some proponents of the dynamic approach have been too quick to dismiss convictions that have been widely held since the advent of cognitive science. Sometimes there is an unfortunate tendency to view a new approach as so revolutionary that important lessons of previous paradigms are prematurely discarded. The rapidly growing literature on dynamic approaches to cognition is rife with such revolutionary rhetoric. One of the most provocative claims is that the talk of internal representations should be seriously delimited or even eliminated from explanations of cognition (Freeman & Skarda, 1990; Thelen & Smith, 1994; van Gelder, 1995; see also Edelman, 1989).

In our opinion, representation has been a red herring in the dynamic systems revolution. In making strong eliminativist claims, dynamicists have probably obscured important ramifications of their position, as they appear increasingly to realize. For example, van Gelder (1997) de-emphasized the critique of representation in his most recent presentation of the dynamic approach and suggested that dynamic systems can accommodate representations in various ways. The critique of representations can be more instructively viewed as part of a larger campaign that dynamicists wage against the prevailing view in cognitive science. The central issue is no longer whether internal representations exist, but whether traditional representational approaches can account for the contextually sensitive, embodied, and inherently temporal character of cognition. Traditionally conceived, representations are context invariant, disembodied, and static. If representations are inextricably tied to these properties, dynamicists believe that representational theories of cognition are inadequate. If, on the other hand, representations are to be reconstrued as contextually sensitive, embodied, and temporal, then they should be identified with state-space trajectories, attractors, bifurcations, or some other construct of dynamic systems theory. In other words, the applicability of dynamic tools in studying cognition is alleged to either undermine or appropriate talk of internal representations. These two possibilities constitute two distinct challenges: an elimination challenge and an appropriation challenge.

We agree that cognition is contextually sensitive, embodied, and inherently temporal. We also agree that dynamic systems theory provides useful tools for describing cognitive systems. In that sense, we uphold the spirit of current dynamical systems approaches. At the same time, we think that internal representations should be neither eliminated nor appropriated by dynamic systems theory. First, we offer some general considerations in favor of representational approaches to cognition. In particular, we show that many dynamic systems lend themselves to representational interpretations, and we argue that representations contribute to the adaptive success of evolved cognitive systems. Then we take up context sensitivity, embodiment, and temporality in turn. While conceding the importance of these properties, we argue that none of them calls for the elimination of representations or for identification of representations with constructs posited by dynamic systems theory. After that, we introduce a perceptual symbols theory of mental representation, which can account for context sensitivity, embodiment, and temporality without being stated in terms of dynamic systems theory. None of these arguments is intended to show that dynamic tools should not be used in studying cognition. To the contrary, we conclude by proposing that dynamic systems theory and perceptual symbols theory are complementary. They can work in concert to describe different aspects of cognitive systems.

REPRESENTATION

A dynamic system is simply a physical system (or a physically realizable system) that changes over time. A mathematical description of a dynamic system contains a set of numbers that describe the system's states and a set of functions that specify how the system's current state evolves into its next state. Given this generic characterization, it should be obvious that representational systems can be dynamic. Implemented programs in classical computer languages, for instance, are representational systems that change over time (see Giunti, 1995). At every moment, an implemented program is in some state, and the changes it undergoes can be plotted as a trajectory through a space of possible states. Likewise, many connectionist networks lend themselves to representational interpretations. Individual nodes, in the case of localist networks, or activation patterns across nodes, as in distributed networks, can often be described as representations. The changing patterns of activity in such networks are, nevertheless, dynamic and can be usefully characterized by using standard tools of dynamic systems theory.

The challenge posed by dynamic approaches to cognition comes in recognizing that, although implemented representational systems are all dynamic, many dynamic systems are nonrepresentational. Perhaps, dynamicists have argued, natural cognitive systems fall into that category. They think we should study cognition by using the tools of dynamic systems theory (e.g., low-dimensional differential equations) instead of by appealing to internal representations.

Nonrepresentational Dynamics Systems

Van Gelder (1995) provided one of the most perspicuous arguments against internal representations based on the dynamic character of natural cognitive systems. It rests on an analogy to another quintessential dynamic system: Watt's centrifugal governor. Van Gelder first proposed that the Watt governor achieves a complex engineering feat without representations. He then urged us to consider the possibility that cognition is more like a Watt governor than a Turing machine, a classic representational system. We focus on problems with the first stage of van Gelder's argument, namely, that the Watt governor is not representational. In this discussion, we do not defend the claim that cognition is computational. Further doubts about both stages of his argument can be found elsewhere (Bechtel, 1996; Clark, 1997b; Clark & Toribio, 1994).

As Fig. 3.1 illustrates, the Watt governor is designed to translate the fluctuating pressure from a steam piston into the uniform rotations of a flywheel by adjusting a throttle valve. It achieves this remarkable feat with a simple arrangement of parts. First, a spindle is attached to the flywheel, then two arms with balls at their ends are attached by hinges to the spindle, and finally the arms are linked to the throttle valve. As steam pressure increases, the flywheel's rotation causes the spindle to rotate faster; the spindle's rotation causes the arms to move outward by centrifugal force; and the arms' outward motion closes the throttle valve, decreasing pres-

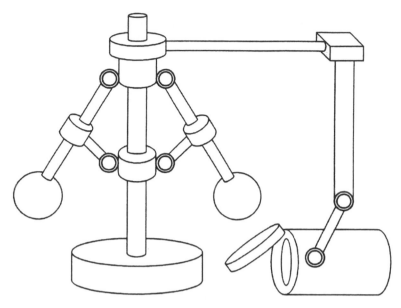

FIG. 3.1. A centrifugal governor.

sure. When steam is decreased, the flywheel slows, the arms fall, and the valve opens again, increasing pressure. By modulating pressure in this manner, the flywheel maintains a relatively constant speed.

On our definition and van Gelder's, the Watt governor is a dynamic system, a physical device that changes continuously in time. Like other dynamic systems, its behavior can be described by using differential equations, which van Gelder provided. These equations do not include variables or parameters that correspond in any obvious way to representations. However, these equations neither demonstrate nor corroborate van Gelder's claim that the Watt governor is not a representational device.

Van Gelder anticipated an obvious objection to this claim by acknowledging the "initially quite attractive intuition" (1995, p. 351) that arm angle of a centrifugal governor represents flywheel speed. Despite this intuition, van Gelder insisted that the relation between arm angle and engine speed is not representational. To support this claim, he provided four arguments that "are not based on an unduly restrictive notion of representation." Bechtel (1996) criticized these arguments effectively, so we do not review them all here. Instead, we focus on positive reasons for believing that the Watt governor harbors representation.

To make this case, we first need to determine what it means to represent. On many current accounts, representation is defined with synonyms. Something is a representation if it denotes, designates, stands for, refers to, or is about something else. Debate rages over what conditions must be met to stand in this kind of relation (Stich & Warfield, 1994). Entering into this debate would take us too far afield. Instead, we simply describe one theory of representation that epitomizes the prevailing family of views. If the Watt governor counts as representational on this account, we have reason to doubt van Gelder's diagnosis.

Many philosophers believe that representation involves information. A state represents a property only if it carries information about it (Dretske, 1981; Fodor, 1990). Carrying information is, in turn, analyzed in terms of nomic, or law-like, covariation. To a first approximation, a state s carries information about a property F just in case instantiations of F reliably cause tokens of s. Although arguably necessary, information is not sufficient for representation. Fire reliably causes smoke, but smoke does not represent fire. An information-bearing state must satisfy one further condition to count as a representation. For Dretske (1995), this extra ingredient is teleological: Something can represent something else only if it has the *function* of carrying information about it. Representations can acquire such functions through a variety of different histories, including natural selection, learning, and design. For example, the word *fire* has the function of carrying information about fires, because it was created to linguistically indicate their presence. In contrast, smoke, even though it covaries with fires, does not have the function of carrying information about them and therefore does not represent them.

In sum, Dretske said that two conditions must be met for something to represent something else. First, the former must carry information about it through covariance. The Watt governor certainly satisfies this condition. To say that arm angles carry information about engine speed just means that arm angles causally covary with engine speed in a law-like way. Van Gelder revealed the satisfaction of this condition when he provided a law correlating changes in arm angle with engine speed (1995, p. 356). Second, to count as a representation on Dretske's account, an information-bearing state must have the function of bearing that information. Once again, the Watt governor complies. Watt *designed* the governor to regulate the relation between steam pressure and engine speed. Most important, he designed the arm angles to covary with engine speed, to release the right amount of steam. Because design confers function, arm angle *represents* engine speed. In Dretske's framework, it is the function of arm angles to carry information about engine speed.

We do not necessarily claim that Dretske's theory is correct in all its details. What is crucial is that it is exemplifies a class of accounts that currently dominate philosophical approaches to representation. Because the general form of this account is readily applicable to the states of many dynamic systems, we have good reason to believe that these systems are representational.

Van Gelder might complain that this analysis fails to address one of his arguments against representational interpretations of the Watt governor. On this particular argument, representation is the wrong conceptual tool for explaining the relation between arm angle and engine speed. Instead, this relation is better understood as an instance of *coupling*, a central construct in dynamics "more subtle and complex" than representation (1995, p. 353). Van Gelder considered this his most important argument, and it is the only one included in his most recent treatment of representation (van Gelder, 1997).

We find this argument puzzling. Why must coupling be incompatible with representation? To simply assume that it is begs the question. On examining the construct of coupling more closely, no incompatibility is apparent. To see this, consider Dretske's characterization of thermostats as paradigmatic representational systems, in particular, thermostats that use bimetal strips to control temperature (Dretske, 1988, p. 49). Each side of a bimetal strip contains a different temperature-sensitive metal. When the strip cools, the different expansion rates of the two metals cause it to bend in one direction; when the strip warms up, they cause it to bend in the opposite direction. As Fig. 3.2 illustrates, bending in these two directions turns a furnace on or off. As the temperature of the room falls, the metal strip bends toward an electrical contact, eventually touching it and closing a circuit to activate the furnace. As the furnace warms the room, the metal strip bends in the other direction, thereby opening the circuit and deactivating the furnace.

As this example illustrates, the thermostat and room temperature constitute coupled dynamic systems. The dynamic behavior of the thermostat is coupled with dynamic changes in room temperature. Most important, however, this relation is also representational. On the generic account of representation just provided, the thermostat carries information about room temperature by functional design. Thus, the relation between the thermostat and room temperature simultaneously constitutes examples of coupled systems *and* representation.

The compatibility of coupling and representation can be illustrated by another example. In cognitive neuroscience, it is widely supposed that the brain can be functionally decomposed into different systems (Mundale & Bechtel, 1996; Van Essen, Felleman, DeYoe, Olavarria, & Knierim, 1990; Zeki, 1992). These systems are often presumed to carry out representational functions. For example, different portions of the visual system are said to represent different aspects of a visual signal. Cells in brain area V3 respond to dynamic form, area V4 responds to color and color form, and area MT responds to motion. Following Dretske, these cells can be said to represent those properties in virtue of the fact that they are reliably caused by them. Such reliable causal relations are exactly

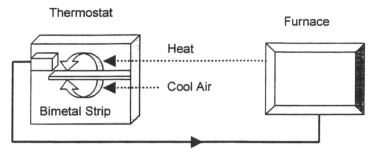

FIG. 3.2. A bimetal thermostat.

what neuroscientists appeal to in mapping the cortex. At the same time, different regions of the visual system are thought to interact. Direct and indirect pathways between these regions give rise to a complex coupled system. Activity in one area can both affect and by affected by its neighbors. Such coupling can play various roles. For example, dynamic coupling can allow for temporal synchronization, which, in turn, may be necessary for generating a unified conscious percept (Crick & Koch, 1990). As in the thermostat, representation and coupling are compatible and complementary in the nervous system. Omitting either of these components from one's analysis significantly diminishes understanding. Each underwrites distinct, but equally important and often interrelated, explanatory projects.

The upshot of this discussion is that many systems that readily lend themselves to dynamic analysis also lend themselves to representational analysis. It is sometimes thought that the mere applicability of dynamic tools, such as differential equations, tells against representational analyses of a system. This is not the case. Many interesting dynamic systems, such as Watt governors and thermostats, *are* representational. Furthermore, it appears that construing these dynamic systems as representational offers an important and essential level of analysis in characterizing them. If governor arms did not carry information about flywheel speed and thermostat strips did not carry information about temperature, they would not be able to carry out the functions for which they were designed. To the extent that dynamicists believe that cognition is anything like Watt governors and thermostats, it follows that cognition, too, is inherently representational.

The Evolutionary Fitness of Representation

We have argued that the dynamic systems sometimes used to characterize cognition are inherently representational. However, our final remarks alluded to a much stronger point: Representation is extremely useful. In the case of natural cognitive systems, we believe that evolution has selected representation as a central design function of cognition, because representation confers substantial advantages in fitness on organisms that implement it powerfully. In the spirit of our earlier discussion, we believe that representational ability is analogous to other high-level functions that organisms exhibit, such as reproduction and digestion. Because these functions increase fitness, evolution attempts to implement them in organisms.

In his evolutionary theory of cognition, Donald (1991, 1993) elegantly postulated an important relation between representational ability and fitness. Donald argued that all nonhuman species are relatively limited in their representational abilities. To a large extent, nonhuman organisms represent only their current environment and internal state. Although these organisms may anticipate short-term events that are not present (e.g., the future acquisition of prey on initially perceiving it), they do not typically represent nonpresent situations that have nothing to do with current circumstances.

The major transition leading to human intelligence, Donald continued, occurred when humans acquired powerful new abilities for representing nonpresent situations. By being able to review past events and preview future events, humans became better able to learn from the past and to control the future. Furthermore, as humans developed new communicative abilities for inducing representational states in others, their cooperative activities gained even further leverage on environmental resources. Together, multiple individuals could review past events, control current events, and plan future events. In addition, humans developed extensive cultural systems capable of accomplishing much more than a single individual could accomplish alone.

In our opinion, dynamic accounts of cognition that eschew representation essentially create organisms at Donald's first level of intelligence. Because these organisms have minimal representational ability, they are relatively limited in their ability to represent nonpresent situations. Instead, they simply have the reactive ability to encode the current situation and to generate appropriate actions. Certainly, these abilities are important and sophisticated. Nevertheless, an organism with only these abilities is much less powerful than organisms that can represent and manipulate nonpresent situations. Like Donald, we believe that evolution selected increasingly powerful representational abilities to create an unusually fit species, namely, humans.

Roles of Representation in Human Cognition

As just discussed, we believe that representation plays one essential role of "standing in" for situations that are not present in the physical world. For example, by jointly representing a herd of buffalo traversing a valley, a group of hunters can review past hunting episodes and plan future ones. Rather than simply reacting to an actual herd, the hunters can imagine various scenarios that may be factual or counterfactual. By considering these scenarios systematically and evaluating their properties, the hunters can converge on optimal hunting practices. Most important, because these representations correspond systematically to actual situations, they support offline simulations that are truly effective in guiding future action.

A second essential role of representation is to support productivity. In cognitive science, it is widely agreed that humans have the ability to construct infinite representations from a finite set of building blocks. Not only does productivity manifest itself in the infinite production of sentences from finite words (Chomsky, 1957), it also manifests itself in the infinite production of conceptualizations from finite concepts (Fodor & Pylyshyn, 1988). Having such an unbounded capacity is invaluable, because it allows us to cope with an environment that is constantly changing. Anticipating and understanding new situations require us to recombine previous knowledge in novel ways.

We agree with Fodor and Pylyshyn when they criticize dynamic models (qua connectionism) that fail to account for this basic property of human cognition. We agree that any viable theory of cognition must exhibit productivity. However, we strongly disagree with other aspects of Fodor and Pylyshyn's proposal. We reject their underlying commitments to classical representations that are static, context invariant, and disembodied. In other words, we embrace only Fodor and Pylyshyn's emphasis on the importance of combinatorial representations as a means of achieving productivity. Dynamic approaches that repudiate productive representations give up valuable resources for explaining our ability to cope with a changing environment. Many connectionists agree and have tried to meet Fodor and Pylyshyn's challenge by generating networks that use combinatorial representations. For reasons to be discussed below, we have reservations about many connectionist accounts. We support these connectionists, however, for conceding the importance of representations and for seeking alternatives to traditional, static accounts.

CONTEXT SENSITIVITY

Cognitive science has traditionally conceived of representations as enduring, context-insensitive entities. On this view, the representation of a category may be a single node, a stable pattern of activation, a fixed set of features, a constant set of predicates, a static network, an immutable mental word, and so forth. This approach assumes that an invariant structure represents a category in all contexts. Different contexts do not require that context-sensitive representations be tailored to fit them. This picture seems deeply problematic. Natural cognitive systems exhibit remarkable variability. Our behaviors and inner states adapt differently to different contexts. This suggests that the traditional concept of representations is inadequate. Dynamic systems theorists claim that our extreme sensitivity to context is best captured by using the tools of dynamic systems theory. Some have even taken context sensitivity as support for the mandate to banish representational talk from our explanatory repertoire (Thelen & Smith, 1994). Although we are sympathetic to the underlying spirit of these arguments, we think this case is overstated. Context sensitivity coexists with a degree of stability that is best captured by appeals to representations.

Context Sensitivity in Dynamic Systems

Complexly coupled dynamic systems often process inputs of the same type in different ways. Because such systems' behaviors are a product of activities in numerous interconnected components, they are typically incapable of identically reproducing an earlier state. Even when a focal point in the environment contains the same input as it did on a previous occasion, active inner states and peripheral environmental features make up a distinct context. These influence the way the focal input is processed. Thus, when confronted with exactly the same focal input, the system responds to it somewhat differently. In these ways, dynamic systems produce context-sensitive responses to inputs, making these systems significantly different from more traditionally conceived systems that process identical inputs in exactly the same way.

One crusader for context specificity is Walter Freeman. Using the tools of dynamic systems theory, Freeman has explored the neural processing of categories and has found that the neural states underlying categories are far more context specific than previously suspected (Freeman, 1991). On the basis of these findings, Freeman has concluded that cognition does not traffic in representations, which he assumed are inherently stable.

As an example of Freeman's important findings, consider his work on rabbit olfaction. Freeman demonstrated that rabbit olfactory states change dramatically as rabbits learn to distinguish new odorants. Using electroencephalogram recordings, Freeman showed that different odorants are associated with different spatial patterns in the amplitudes of waves across a rabbit's olfactory bulb. Repeated exposure to a given training stimulus, such as sawdust, invokes the same pattern under the same conditions. This continuity is ephemeral, however. When a rabbit is conditioned to another stimulus, such as bananas, the patterns associated with previously learned odorants change. Freeman explained this by appeal to the distributed and interconnected nature of neural states. The neural state for an odorant on a given occasion does not reflect only the stimulus; it also reflects the rabbit's learning history. If the neural state corresponding to an odor changes across learning contexts, the traditional faith in enduring, invariant representations cannot be maintained.

Freeman's results provide a fascinating look into how the brain works. A population of neurons mediating one odor engages in complex inter- actions with populations of neurons mediating other odors, producing dynamic changes in each. However, dynamic variability at the neural level does not froth upward into functional properties of the system. Indeed, Freeman's behavioral results clearly indicate that dynamic vari- ability is confined to the neural level. At the behavioral level, a rabbit's response to a particular odor remains constant while the underlying neural states vary. Different patterns in a rabbit's olfactory bulb mediate the same functional relation between an odor input and a behavioral output. In other words, these different neural states serve the same in- put–output (I/O) function.

This observation suggests that one must be cautious when arguing for context specificity. Observing radical variability at the neuronal level can give the appearance that cognitive systems are contextually sensitive all the way up. From this perspective, it looks as if there is no level at which one can postulate stable representations, and, as a result, the very notion of a representation seems to get no foothold. If this were correct, it would be appropriate to treat the brain as a purely nonrepresentational dynamic system. The fact that neurally distinct states serve common I/O func- tions points to another interpretation: Although there is extreme context sensitivity at the lowest level of analysis, there is also a somewhat higher level of analysis at which stability emerges through function. For certain explanatory purposes, it is appropriate to treat neurally distinct states as the same precisely because of their functional equivalence. If we did not co-classify such states, it would be extraordinarily difficult to explain how we manage to recognize the same inputs again and again. Thus, the applicability of dynamic tools at the lowest level does not vitiate a rep- resentational account at a somewhat higher level. Indeed, it seems to demand high-level analysis if we want an explanatory psychology.

The longstanding importance of emergent properties in science consti- tutes a good reason for bestowing a stable representational interpretation on the neural states that implement a common I/O function. Consider emergent properties such as reproduction, digestion, flying, and life. Just because multiple physical states instantiate reproduction, for example, does not mean that we eschew it as a useful scientific construct. It is indeed interesting and significant that reproduction can be achieved in many ways, yet it remains critical that the same state is achieved in all cases. Indeed, one can argue that evolution selects for these higher level properties and cares more about achieving and preserving them than about the particular mechanisms that implement them. As a result, different life forms achieve the same ability but in ways that vary widely. Eschewing representations because they supervene on disparate lower level activities makes as much sense as eschewing reproduction and digestion on the same grounds.

Context Sensitivity in Representational Models

To this point, we have argued that low-level context sensitivity is compatible with higher level stability. This suggests that complex neural dynamics cannot refute representational accounts of the brain. At the same time, it is important to show that representational accounts are compatible with context sensitivity. If stable representations precluded this, representational theories of cognition would be intolerably inflexible. We believe that representational accounts can readily exhibit context sensitivity. We also believe that the context sensitivity of representational accounts can be neatly interfaced with context sensitivity in dynamic systems models to provide unified multilevel accounts of this important property.

Barsalou (1987, 1989, 1993) demonstrated that concepts exhibit considerable context sensitivity. When representing the same category, different subjects represent it with different information. In the feature-listing task, for example, the features active for one subject overlap only about 40% with the features active for another subject. Similarly, when the same individual represents a category on different occasions, he or she represents it differently. In the feature-listing task, the features that a subject produces for a category on one occasion overlap only about 65% with the features produced 2 weeks later. Finally, context substantially biases the features active for a subject on a given occasion (Barsalou, 1982; Medin, Goldstone, & Gentner, 1993). For example, subjects do not usually activate the property *pet* for snake but do so in the context of other pets. All these results clearly document the context sensitivity that dynamicists champion.

All these discoveries were made and explained in a representational framework (e.g., Barsalou, 1989, in press). For example, one can view an individual's knowledge of a category as containing many representations of features and relations that have accrued over a lifetime of experience with category members. On a given occasion, only a very small subset of this representational base becomes active to represent the category. In particular, the features that become active are those that have been processed most frequently, those that have been processed most recently, and those that are most associated to the current context. Note that frequency, recency, and context are exactly the sorts of statistical factors central to dynamic theories. However, they have been conceptualized and implemented in the representational framework. Indeed, such flexibility has become a hallmark of many representational models. For example, the prototypes of prototype models and the exemplars of exemplar models are readily viewed as context-sensitive representations whose specific form varies widely across contexts (e.g., Barsalou, 1990). On this approach, context sensitivity is achieved not by eradicating stability, but by creating novel and adaptive combinations of relatively stable feature representations.

The fundamental error of more traditional representational theories is not stability as such, but too much stability. On such theories, categories are represented by the very same collection of features on each occasion. On the present view, categories are represented by different collections of features as context demands. On both accounts, features are construed as representations, and they can be relatively stable entities stored in memory. The latter account improves on the former, however, by insisting that features be retrieved, combined, and deployed in ways that vary. From this perspective, one can capture the dynamists' intuition that our cognitive systems are never in the same state twice without giving up the notion of representation.

Prinz (1997) developed one further argument reinforcing the message that context sensitivity does not vitiate representation. As we defined the term, something counts as a representation when it has the function of being reliably caused by something external to it. Representations, on this view, are something like tracking devices. Tracking, it turns out, is no trivial matter. The things we track tend to vary from one context to the next. Therefore, a tracking device is successful only if it can adapt to these changes. Tracking is necessary for representation, and sensitivity to context is necessary for tracking. It follows that context sensitivity is necessary for representation, not incompatible with it.

EMBODIMENT

Traditional theories in cognitive science adopt representations that are inherently disembodied. A disembodied representation is one harbored by a system that lacks a sensory-motor system capable of interacting with the environment. As a result, disembodied representations do not rely on sensory-motor systems to do their work—instead they rely solely on their intrinsic representational resources. By focusing on disembodied representations as paradigms for exploring cognition, cognitive scientists have failed to develop theories that are well suited for actual performance in the real world. Because disembodied representations typically take the form of arbitrary language-like codes, nothing inherent in their structure supports grounding them in bodies and environments.

We agree with dynamicists that disembodiment is a fatal flaw for any representational theory and that embodied forms of these theories cry out for development. We further agree with dynamicists that brain–body–environment interactions are central to many, if not all, intelligent functions. However, we do not believe that embracing embodiment implies that dynamic systems must be the correct account of cognition and that representational approaches must be incorrect. On the one hand, representational theories can be made inherently embodied, as we demonstrate later in presenting perceptual symbol systems. On the other hand, dynamic theories are not necessarily embodied. Indeed, disembodied dynamic theories are widespread in cognitive science.

Embodiment in Connectionist Systems

As we have already observed, some dynamicists do not repudiate representations. Instead, they try to appropriate them in a dynamic framework. Connectionists typically fall into this camp. Many of them have even tried to meet Fodor and Pylyshyn's (1988) demand for representations that can be productively combined (van Gelder, 1990). For example, Pollack (1990) and Smolensky (1990) have developed distributed connectionist systems that superimpose vectors for finite elements to productively create complex representations. Because such systems can apparently construct infinite numbers of complex representations from finite elements, they are productive. Furthermore, they seem to improve on classic computational accounts of productivity by implementing elemental concepts in dynamic and context-sensitive manners. As the same concept is superimposed in different complex representations, it adopts context-sensitive forms that have dynamic properties. These approaches openly admit that cognitive systems are representational, but they identify representations with activation patterns in artificial neural networks. So construed, representations can be analyzed by using the tools of dynamic systems theory.

Although these connectionist representations implement productivity in a context-sensitive manner, they are inherently disembodied. The vectors that represent elemental concepts are essentially arbitrary strings that bear no systematic relation to their perceptual and motor referents. To see this, consider a standard feed-forward connectionist net that implements completely distributed representations in a single layer of hidden units. As Barsalou (in press) discussed, the layer of input units is often interpreted as a perceptual system that detects the presence or absence of sensory features. In contrast, the layer of hidden units is often viewed as providing conceptual interpretations of inputs. Most critically, the mapping from input units to hidden units is arbitrary and reflects the small random weights assigned to the connections between them before learning. Depending on different random assignments, the mappings from input to hidden units vary arbitrarily. As a result, conceptual interpretations in a feed-forward net are disembodied, just like those in standard computational representations. In both cases, conceptual interpretations have nothing in common with perceptual states, with the two having an arbitrary relation.

As this example illustrates, dynamic approaches to cognition are not necessarily embodied, although they can be. In this regard, dynamic approaches do not differ from their more traditional counterparts. As we show shortly in our discussion of perceptual symbol systems, it is feasible to develop accounts of productive representation that are context sensitive *and* embodied.

Embodiment in Situated Robotics

Researchers in situated robotics have been more fervently committed to embodiment than have other researchers. Exciting developments in this area have exposed serious problems with classical theories. To be effective, the cognitive system that guides a robot's behavior must interface well with perception and action. A system that simply computes abstract functions does not suffice. Instead, a system must be able to use sensory information effectively and to implement action effectively. Whereas cognitive systems inspired by traditional computational theories have fared poorly in these regards, cognitive systems inspired by dynamic systems have fared much better (Brooks, 1991).

Perhaps the most important lesson learned from these recent developments is that using the resources of a cognitive system solely to accomplish perception and action is misguided. It may well be the case that no formulation of a cognitive system in isolation can ever accomplish these tasks on its own. Instead, a much more successful tack is to use resources inherent in the body and the environment. Rather than relying solely on cognitive mechanisms, intelligence evolves from dynamic interactions between brains, bodies, and environments (Clark, 1997a, 1997b; Thelen & Smith, 1994). All three components are essential, and no one alone suffices.

To accomplish these dynamic interactions, dynamicists often call for the elimination of representations altogether. However, the representations that inspire these calls are the classical representations of traditional cognitive science, namely, representations that are static, context independent, and disembodied. We have already argued that advanced intelligent systems simply cannot do without representations. In our discussion of context sensitivity, we began to argue that important alternatives exist to classical representations, alternatives that are compatible with dynamicists' aims. A similar moral applies with regard to embodiment. Rather than dispensing with representation, we should look for forms of representation that are more intimately connected to sensory-motor systems, which mediate our interaction with the world. We will pursue this possibility more fully when we discuss perceptual symbol systems below. The interim moral is that, on the one hand, connectionist nets do not guarantee embodiment, and, on the other hand, situated robots try to do without representation. We want to steer a course between these options by adopting embodied representations.

TEMPORALITY

Of all the features emphasized by proponents of dynamic systems theory, temporaility is claimed to be the most important (van Gelder, 1997). Traditional approaches in cognitive science are atemporal. We define a cognitive model as atemporal if it does not explicitly define states or state transitions with reference to real time. In contrast, the differential equations used by dynamic systems theorists typically include variables for time. In so doing, they can capture temporal distances between events, rates of change, and duration of processes. Traditional approaches often use classical computational models, which can explain such phenomena only in terms of computational steps. Such steps are defined without reference to real time, so that they fail to capture truly temporal properties of a system. Dynamic models are to be applauded for their ability to capture such properties. Their introduction into cognitive science promises to shed light on phenomena that cannot be readily modeled with more traditional tools. Some dynamicists seem to endorse a stronger claim, however. They think we can do away with models that fail to explicitly capture temporal properties. These include most standard representational models. We are uncomfortable with this move.

Abstracting Over Real Time

In sharp contrast to the dynamicists, we think the ability of traditional representational theories to abstract over real time is one of their strongest virtues. By ignoring the spatiotemporal details of neural activity, traditional representational models identify the stable, functional properties of cognition. On these approaches, cognitive activity can be characterized in terms of the representations that are used and the processes that govern them without reference to how long such processes take. In this manner, representational models establish the high-level, functional properties of cognition, while ignoring the low-level details of implementation. Indeed, one can infer from the absence of real time in many traditional models that timing belongs to a noncognitive level of analysis.

To bolster the intuition behind this approach, consider the following thought experiment. Imagine Slow World, a place exactly like Earth except that everything takes twice as long. Each of us has a doppelgänger on Slow World. Of course, the snail-paced speeds of people on Slow World do not impair them, because everything else in their world occurs at the same slow pace. In fact, if we were to view a sped-up video recording of Slow World, it would be indistinguishable from our own. Our doppelgängers would do just what we do in comparable situations (compare Block, 1978).

This comparability suggests that our Slow twins should be classified with us from the perspective of psychology. They have minds just like ours and can be subsumed under a common psychological theory. However, if psychological laws defined cognition only in terms of real time, this commonality would not be apparent. Laws that solely specify the real-time properties of Earth cognition would be inapplicable to Slow World cognition. Laws focusing only on real time would be inadequate to capture the important similarities between these two forms of cognition. Instead, establishing an account of cognition that captures these similarities requires an atemporal analysis—exactly the type of analysis that traditional representational models provide. Traditional models that abstract over real time can exactly establish those *relative* temporal properties we share with our Slow World doppelgängers.

Dynamicists might respond in several ways to this core assumption of the traditional representational approach. First, they might argue that the obvious similarities between individuals in the two worlds can be captured by saying that they share similar dynamic systems, with one running at twice the rate of the other. To specify how these dynamic systems are similar, however, one must abstract from their temporal properties, which concedes that there is a useful level of explanation that ignores real time. Taking a more offensive tack, dynamicists might respond by arguing that ignoring the dimension of real time leads to the omission of critical mechanisms. In particular, a traditional account of people in the two worlds we are considering fails to capture the very temporal properties that distinguish them. This response raises a valid point, but it only points to the compatibility of dynamic and atemporal approaches. We need the former to explain the differences between Slow World and the real world, and we need the latter to explain the similarities.

Implementing Real-Time Constraints

One can underscore the importance of real-time constraints by considering the 100-step rule of Feldman and Ballard (1982). Using physiological facts about the rate of neural firing, Feldman and Ballard arrived at a conservative estimate of how long a neural-processing step takes in real time. By establishing the time to perform some task and dividing it by this estimate, one arrives at the maximum number of steps an account of that task can include. Of course, this analysis makes assumptions about the seriality of steps, which might not hold in a cascade model (McClelland, 1979). Nevertheless, the point remains that real time must play a critical role in evaluating cognitive theory. Theories of cognition that do not address real time not only fail to account for important phenomena, but may also be implausible once the implications of real-time processing are considered.

At first blush, this seems to be an argument against cognitive models that do not define operations in terms of real time. On closer analysis, however, the lesson of Feldman and Ballard is that we should construct models that can be implemented in a way that respects real time regardless of whether they are temporal models. Numerous atemporal models appear capable of implementing real-time performance. For decades, traditional computational models in mainstream psychology have been developed to explain all sorts of real-time processing, including activation, matching, search, retrieval, transformation, and response generation. So many models exist that trying to cite them all here takes more space than allowed for this chapter (for a few examples, see Just & Carpenter, 1992; Logan, 1988, 1996; McClelland, 1979; Nosofsky & Palmeri, 1997; Ratcliff, 1978; Townsend, 1990; Van Zandt & Ratcliff, 1995). Our present point is not to argue that classical computational models are adequate, but to argue that adequate models can abstract away from real time. It is simply not true that atemporal models cannot naturally and elegantly implement real-time processing. Put differently, a model that is atemporal in the sense of lacking explicit real-time variables can be temporal in the sense of satisfying real-time constraints. So conceived, atemporality and temporality are perfectly compatible.

Dynamicists might be inclined to reformulate their temporal challenge in another way. Cognitive models that abstract from real time are typically discrete. Discrete models, it is argued, cannot explain the continuous properties of cognitive systems (van Gelder, 1995). Most obviously, discrete models fail to capture the fact that natural cognitive systems reside in some state at every moment of continuous time. As a result, such models cannot provide adequate accounts of cognition.

There are a number of replies to this objection. The first we owe to Eric Dietrich, who pointed out (personal communication) that the continuity assumption may concede too much to proponents of dynamic systems theory. Nature may ultimately bottom out into discrete interactions between discrete particles. In that case, apparent continuity rests on a discontinuous foundation. We are also grateful to Dietrich for suggesting a delightful thought experiment. Imagine Strobe World, a place that appears much like our own world, but where people and objects flicker very quietly in and out of existence. Strobe World is certainly discrete, but we would not deny that its inhabitants think.

The continuity challenge can be met even if we concede that real cognitive systems are continuous. Fifty years ago, Alan Turing (1950) anticipated this challenge and responded as follows:

> Strictly speaking, there are no [discrete state] machines. Everything moves continuously. But there are many kinds of machines that can be profitably *thought of* as being discrete machines. For instance in considering the switches for a lighting system it is a convenient fiction that each switch must be definitely on or off. (p. 441)

As this passage illustrates, when discrete models are *implemented*, they are discrete only in a fictitious sense, because their physical states change continuously over time. It is simply false that such models are inherently noncontinuous. An implemented model can occupy different states at every point in time. In some cases, these differences do not make a difference. State individuation can abstract from minute changes if these play no explanatory role from the point of view of psychology. On this approach, the fiction of discreteness is profitable, because continuity plays no theoretically interesting role.

Adopting another strategy, proponents of computational approaches can admit that continuous properties in real time are theoretically significant, while insisting that atemporal theories constitute useful approximations. In general, it is always possible to provide a continuous interpretation of a discrete model. For example, when computers compute integrals, they sometimes approximate them in discrete steps at the programming level. Nevertheless, the users of these computations often interpret them as reflecting continuous mathematical processes. Similarly, when cognitive scientists implement activation functions in computational models (e.g., Anderson, 1976), they implement them discretely at the programming level but interpret them continuously at the theoretical level. As these examples illustrate, it is readily possible to conceive of computational mechanisms as having continuous properties, even though they are discrete at the programming level. At the physical level, they once again become continuous, but typically in ways that differ considerably from their conceptions at the theoretical level (e.g., the continuous transition of states in a silicon chip does not correspond to the continuous transitions in a theoretical activation function). Again, our aim is not to defend computational approaches, but to demonstrate that atemporal models can be defended against the charge that they fail to capture continuity. In some cases continuity does not make a theoretical difference, and, in others, discrete models provide useful approximations of theoretically interesting continuities.

It must be reiterated that we are not arguing against models that make reference to real time. Cognitive systems have real-temporal properties that are interesting and important. We only suggest that admitting the value of such models poses no threat to models that abstract from real time. If they are capable of satisfying real-time constraints, such models may be adequate and useful for certain explanatory purposes. There is no reason to think that cognitive models must explicitly use real-time variables.

There is a further argument that concedes this point, but continues to insist that the accommodation of temporal properties poses a threat to traditional representational models. According to this line, traditional representations are too cumbersome or inefficient to satisfy real-time constraints. Natural cognitive systems negotiate complex environments with remarkable speed and do so under considerable temporal pressure. For example, if one encounters a hungry tiger in the wild, one had better be able to quickly come up with an escape strategy. Too much cogitation is deadly. Those interested in situated cognition have taken such examples to heart. A growing number of researches believe that we do not achieve behavioral success by internally representing the situations that confront us. Brooks (1991), for example, has repudiated representation on the grounds that it takes too much time. Meeting real-world demands does not give us the luxury of representation.

We think this line of argument is partially correct. Time constraints have implications for what kinds of representations situated agents can deploy. They do not, however, show that no representations are deployed. This point is taken up again in the next section after we introduce perceptual symbol systems. Perceptual symbol systems show that a representational account of cognition can explain context sensitivity and embodiment while satisfying real-time constraints.

PERCEPTUAL SYMBOL SYSTEMS

We began our discussion by arguing that theories of cognitive systems should not dispense with internal representations. We then argued that representational accounts could be context sensitive, embodied, and accordant with real-time constraints. Along the way, we have suggested that such accounts can be formulated without identifying representations with constructs introduced by the tools of dynamic systems theory. At the same time, we have been happy to admit that such tools may be fruitfully employed to describe cognitive systems at nonrepresentational levels of analysis. To illustrate that representational systems can be context sensitive, embodied, and temporal, we present *perceptual symbol systems* as a theory of cognition. Because we develop detailed accounts of this approach elsewhere (Barsalou, in press; Prinz, 1997), we do not do so here. Instead, we simply provide a brief summary emphasizing the features most relevant to this discussion.

The first premise of perceptual symbol systems is that cognition and perception share common representational mechanisms, namely, the sensory-motor areas of the brain. This is analogous to the argument that imagery and perception share common neural bases on at least the visual, motor, and auditory modalities (e.g., Crammond, 1997; Farah, 1995; Jeannerod, 1995; Kosslyn, 1994; Zatorre, Halpern, Perry, Meyer, & Evans, 1996). Neuroscientists who study category-specific losses have reached a similar conclusion about category knowledge, namely, that it is grounded in the sensory-motor areas of the brain that process its referents (e.g., Damasio, 1989; Damasio & Damasio, 1994; Gainotti, Silveri, Danieli, & Giustolisi, 1995; Rösler, Heil, & Hennighausen, 1995). Intuitively, the idea is that conceptually representing a category involves running perceptual systems as if one were actually perceiving a member of that category. Thus, conceptually representing chairs involves running visual, haptic, motor, and somatosensory systems as if they were actually interacting with a physical chair. Of course, such simulations are not necessarily identical to the neural states that underlie perception, but they are cut from the same cloth, running the same systems in a similar manner.

Most important, this view of representation departs considerably from the disembodied views that permeate traditional computational theory. Rather than using amodal symbols that lie outside perceptual areas to represent knowledge, perceptual symbol systems use representations in these areas. As a result, they are inherently embodied.

Perceptual symbol systems are also inherently representational, because their primary purpose is to create representations that both detect physical objects, when used in recognition, and "stand in" for physical situations, when run offline (Clark, 1997a, 1997b; Donald, 1991, 1993). Furthermore, perceptual symbols, like classical representations, are capable of combing productively and representing propositions. Productivity results from the ability to compose perceptual simulations hierarchically and recursively. Propositions result from binding simulations to perceived individuals. We do not develop the details of these accounts here (see

Barsalou, in press; Prinz, 1997, 1998). Instead, we simply note these abilities to make the point that perceptual symbol systems are inherently representational, exhibiting classic representational functions.

Perceptual symbol systems must be context sensitive to achieve simulation competence (Barsalou, in press). Essentially, a simulation competence is a set of mechanisms that allow an individual to competently simulate the members of a category in their absence. The simulation competence for a particular category has two levels of structure. First, it contains a tremendous amount of perceptual category knowledge that has accumulated over a lifetime of experience with category members. For example, the simulation competence for *car* contains all the multimodal, sensory-motor knowledge that someone has acquired about cars. Second, a simulation competence produces specific simulations (mental models) of the category on specific occasions. For example, the simulation competence for *car* can produce an infinite number of specific simulations, thereby representing many different kinds of cars in many different situations. Besides being able to represent actual cars previously seen, a simulation competence can represent novel cars and schematic cars, using productive abilities to construct simulations.

Context sensitivity arises naturally from simulation competence. Rather than constructing a single simulation of *car* to represent the category in all contexts, a specific simulation is tailored to each one. Thus, representing cars on the French Riviera may produce simulations of expensive European cars, whereas representing cars on a hippie commune may produce simulations of painted Volkswagen buses. Similarly, representing cars being driven may produce simulations from the driver's perspective, whereas representing cars being repaired may produce simulations of a car's mechanical systems. In this manner, a simulation competence implements a wide variety of context-sensitive phenomena, including framing effects, context-dependent features, and representational flexibility between and in subjects (Barsalou, in press).

Perceptual symbols systems also satisfy real-time constraints. This is best demonstrated by considering the Brooks (1991) objection that we glossed at the end of the last section. According to Brooks, cognitive systems ought to dispense with internal representations, because forming such representations precludes real-time success. When acting under time pressure, it is more efficient to bypass a representational stage and let sensory inputs issue directly into motor outputs. We think there is a very important kernel of truth to this argument, but it also makes an instructive mistake. A system that goes directly from sensory inputs to motor outputs is not, thereby, nonrepresentational. The sensory inputs and the motor commands can themselves qualify as representations. Such a system lacks only *amodal* representations. The perceptual symbol systems view repudiates amodal representations. It agrees with Brooks that postulating an amodal level of representation is dangerously inefficient. The remaining sensory-motor states, however, qualify as representational. Like traditional representations, they carry information about the world, and they can be run offline in planning. Unlike traditional representations, they bypass a costly transduction into an amodal code and are thereby more capable of satisfying real-time constraints.

Perceptual symbol systems exhibit another interesting temporal property. Because conceptual knowledge involves running perceptual and motor systems in roughly the same manner as in perception and action, conceptual knowledge re-enacts, at least somewhat, the temporal properties of these original experiences. Representing a category conceptually plays out temporally in at least somewhat the same manner as experiencing category members. As a consequence of this view, certain representations arc conceived as temporally extended sequences. A representation of an event is not a static description represented as a single processing step, but a temporally sequenced series of representations corresponding to the activities that make up that event. The theory itself does not need to introduce a real-time variable to describe such sequences, but the sequences would have a real-temporal profile when implemented. In this way, perceptual symbol systems make predictions about real-time performance.

As this brief summary illustrates, perceptual symbol systems attempt to reinvent the strengths of traditional approaches and dynamic systems approaches in a single theory. On the one hand, perceptual systems are inherently representational; on the other, they are inherently embodied, context sensitive, and temporal.

COMPLEMENTARY APPROACHES TO MODELING COGNITION

Perceptual symbol systems are not formulated by using the tools of dynamic systems theory. A perceptual symbol is characterized as a facsimile of a perceptual state that can stand in for external entities in offline simulations. We have not identified perceptual symbols with state-space trajectories, attractors, or other dynamic constructs. At the same time, we are open to the possibility that such identifications may be appropriate at another level of analysis. More generally, we believe that dynamic tools can be used in conjunction with perceptual symbols theory in providing a complete account of cognition. The two approaches have distinct, but complementary explanatory virtues. Dynamic systems provide a natural account of continuously varying processes and real-time profiles. Perceptual symbols theory provides a natural account of more stable properties such as internal representations. The best account of cognition would come from merging these resources.

Such a merger can be achieved in different ways. Obviously, the two approaches can be used to model different levels. Dynamic systems are well suited for capturing low-level neural events (as in Freeman's work). They may also be well suited for capturing a very high level of analysis, such as the movement of an organism toward a food source (Busemeyer & Townsend, 1995). In contrast, perceptual symbols can capture the stabilities that supervene on low-level states or the representational mechanisms that guide an organism's dynamic actions.

Perceptual symbols and dynamic systems can also be compatibly used to explain different phenomena. Dynamic systems can be fruitfully used in explaining environmentally responsive motor movement (Thelen & Smith, 1994). They can also be used to model developmental changes over time. For example, the notion of a bifurcation has been used to explain qualitative transitions without appeal to preordained developmental stages (Elman et al., 1996). Perceptual symbols, in contrast, may be better suited for explaining more cognitive phenomena such as categorization, analogical reasoning, and planning.

Perhaps the most intriguing possibility for demonstrating compatibility is to integrate perceptual symbols and dynamic systems into a unified model of a single phenomenon. For example, both may together explain context sensitivity. Earlier, we argued that a representational account can accommodate context sensitivity by forming novel combinations from a relatively stable feature set. The category of dogs, for example, may be represented by different perceptual symbols on different occasions. The feature selection process, however, may be usefully explained by postulating dynamic mechanisms that capture the rising and falling of features and the constraint satisfaction that converges on a final set. An integration of this kind may provide a more complete account of this process than an account stated in terms of either approach alone.

In our opinion, it is overly simplistic and limiting to argue that either dynamic or representational systems provide the best approach to modeling cognition. Although each approach captures important insights, neither captures everything that must be explained. The two can be integrated by modeling different levels of analysis, modeling different phenomena, or forming hybrid models of the same phenomena. The perceptual symbols approach invites integration with dynamic approaches, because it departs from the context-insensitive, disembodied, and static representations favored by more traditional theories. These shared objectives suggest that the two approaches may be complementary.

Clearly, the construction of unified theories constitutes an open frontier. We offer perceptual symbol systems as one preliminary attempt in this spirit, yet we are under no illusions about its current status. This approach obviously requires significant development before it satisfies the challenges we raise here. Much must be accomplished before its implementations of embodiment, context sensitivity, and temporal processing are adequately formulated and defended. Nevertheless, we believe that this sort of theory exemplifies the theory of the future. We should be attempting to develop theories that reinvent previous approaches, salvaging their strengths, and discarding their weaknesses. Rather than disavowing internal representations, we should reconstrue them in a way that accords with the demands of embodied, real-world cognition. In this endeavor, perceptual symbol systems and dynamic systems approaches can form a natural alliance.

ACKNOWLEDGMENTS

We thank our editors, Eric Dietrich and Arthur Markman, for their helpful comments on an earlier draft.

REFERENCES

Anderson, J. R. (1976). *Language, memory, and thought.* Hillsdale, NJ: Lawrence Erlbaum Associates.

Barsalou, L. W. (1982). Context-independent and context-dependent information in concepts. *Memory and Cognition, 10,* 82–93.

Barsalou, L. W. (1987). The instability of graded structure in concepts. In U. Neisser (Ed.), *Concepts and conceptual development: Ecological and intellectual factors in categorization* (pp. 101–140). New York: Cambridge University Press.

Barsalou, L. W. (1989). Intra-concept similarity and its implications for inter-concept similarity. In S. Vosniadou & A. Ortony (Eds.), *Similarity and analogical reasoning* (pp. 76–121). New York: Cambridge University Press.

Barsalou, L. W. (1990). On the indistinguisability of exemplar memory and abstraction in category representation. In T. K. Srull & R. S. Wyer (Eds.), *Advances in social cognition* (Vol. 3, pp. 61–88). Hillsdale, NJ: Lawrence Erlbaum Associates.

Barsalou, L. W. (1993). Flexibility, structure, and linguistic vagary in concepts: Manifestations of a compositional system of perceptual symbols. In A. C. Collins, S. E. Gathercole, & M. A. Conway (Eds.), *Theories of memories* (pp. 29–101). London: Lawrence Erlbaum Associates.

Barsalou, L. W. (in press). Perceptual symbol systems. *Behavioral and Brain Sciences.*

Bechtel, W. (1996, July). Yet another revolution? Defusing the dynamic systems theorists' attack on mental representations. Presidential address to the Society for Philosophy and Psychology, San Francisco.

Block, N. (1978). Troubles with functionalism. In C. W. Savage (Ed.), *Minnesota studies in the philosophy of science, vol. ix: Perception and cognition: Issues in the foundations of psychology* (pp. 261–362). Minneapolis: University of Minnesota Press.

Brooks, R. (1991). Intelligence without representation. *Artificial Intelligence, 47,* 139–160.

Busemeyer, J., & Townsend, J. (1995). Dynamic representation of decision making. In R. F. Port & T. van Gelder (Eds.), *Mind as motion: Explorations in the dynamics of cognition* (pp. 101–120). Cambridge, MA: MIT Press.

Chomsky, N. (1957). *Syntactic structures*. The Hague, Netherlands: Mouton.

Clark, A. (1997a). *Being there: Putting brain, body, and world together again*. Cambridge, MA: MIT Press.

Clark, A. (1997b). The dynamic challenge. *Cognitive Science, 21*, 461–481.

Clark, A., & Toribio, J. (1994). Doing without representing? *Synthese, 101*, 401–431.

Crammond, D. J. (1997). Motor imagery: Never in your wildest dreams. *Trends in Neuroscience, 20*, 54–57.

Crick, F., & Koch, C. (1990). Towards a neurobiological theory of consciousness. *Seminars in the neurosciences, 2*, 263–275.

Damasio, A. R. (1989). Time-locked multiregional retroactivation: A systems-level proposal for the neural substrates of recall and recognition. *Cognition, 33*, 25–62.

Damasio, A. R., & Damasio, H. (1994). Cortical systems for retrieval of concrete knowledge: The convergence zone framework. In C. Koch & J. L. Davis (Eds.), *Large-scale neuronal theories of the brain* (pp. 61–74). Cambridge, MA: MIT Press.

Donald, M. (1991). *Origins of the modern mind: Three stages in the evolution of culture and cognition*. Cambridge, MA: Harvard University Press.

Donald, M. (1993). Precis of "Origins of the modern mind: Three stages in the evolution of culture and cognition." *Behavioral and Brain Sciences, 16*, 739–791.

Dretske, F. I. (1981). *Knowledge and the flow of information*. Cambridge, MA: MIT Press.

Dretske, F. I. (1988). *Explaining behavior: Reasons in a world of causes*. Cambridge, MA: MIT Press.

Dretske, F. I. (1995). *Naturalizing the mind*. Cambridge, MA: MIT Press.

Edelman, G. M. (1989). *The remembered present: A biological theory of consciousness*. New York: Basic Books.

Elman, J. L., Bates, E. A., Johnson, M. H., Karmiloff-Smith, A., Parisi, D., & Plunkett, K. (1996). *Rethinking innateness: A connectionist perspective on development*. Cambridge, MA: MIT Press.

Farah, M. (1995). The neural bases of mental imagery. In M. S. Gazzaniga (Ed.), *The cognitive neurosciences* (pp. 963–975). Cambridge, MA: MIT Press.

Feldman, J. A., & Ballard, D. H. (1982). Connectionist models and their properties. *Cognitive Science, 6*, 205–254.

Fodor, J. A. (1990). *A theory of content and other essays*. Cambridge, MA: MIT Press.

Fodor, J. A., & Pylyshyn, Z. W. (1988). Connectionism and cognitive architecture: A critical analysis. *Cognition, 28*, 3–71.

Freeman, W. J. (1991, February). The physiology of perception. *Scientific American, 264*, 78–85.

Freeman, W. J., & Skarda, C. A. (1990). Representations: Who needs them? In J. L. McGaugh, N. M. Weinberger, & G. Lynch (Eds.), *Third conference, brain organization and memory: Cells, systems and circuits* (pp. 375–380). New York: Guilford Press.

Gainotti, G., Silveri, M. C., Daniele, A., & Giustolisi, L. (1995). Neuroanatomical correlates of category-specific semantic disorders: A critical survey. *Memory, 3*, 247–264.

Giunti, M. (1995). Dynamic models of cognition. In R. F. Port & T. van Gelder (Eds.), *Mind as motion: Explorations in the dynamics of cognition* (pp. 549–571). Cambridge, MA: MIT Press.

Jeannerod, M. (1995). Mental imagery in the motor context. *Neuropsychologia, 33*, 1419–1432.

Just, M. A., & Carpenter, P. A. (1992). A capacity theory of comprehension: Individual differences in working memory. *Psychological Review, 99*, 122–149.

Kosslyn, S. M. (1994). *Image and brain*. Cambridge, MA: MIT Press.

Logan, G. (1988). Toward an instance theory of automatization. *Psychological Review, 95*, 492–527.

Logan, G. (1996). The CODE theory of visual attention: An integration of space-based and object-based attention. *Psychological Review, 103*, 603–649.

McClelland, J. L. (1979). On the time-relations of mental processes: An examination of systems of processes in cascade. *Psychological Review, 86*, 287–330.

Medin, D. L., Goldstone, R. L., & Gentner, D. (1993). Respects for similarity. *Psychological Review, 100*, 254–278.

Mundale, J., & Bechtel, W. (1996). Integrating neuroscience, psychology, and evolutionary biology through a teleological conception of function. *Minds and Machines, 6*, 481–505.

Nosofsky, R. M., & Palmeri, T. J. (1997). An exemplar-based random walk model of speeded classification. *Psychological Review, 104*, 266–300.

Ratcliff, R. (1978). A theory of memory retrieval. *Psychological Review, 85*, 59–108.

Pollack, J. (1990). Recursive distributed representations. *Artificial Intelligence, 46*, 77–105.

Prinz, J. J. (1997). *Perceptual cognition: An essay on the semantics of thought.* Unpublished doctoral dissertation, University of Chicago.

Prinz, J. J. (1998). *Regaining composure: A defense of prototype compositionality.* Manuscript submitted for publication.

Rösler, F., Heil, M., & Hennighausen, E. (1995). Distinct cortical activation patterns during long-term memory retrieval of verbal, spatial, and color information. *Journal of Cognitive Neuroscience, 7*, 51–65.

Smolensky, P. (1990). Tensor product variable binding and the representation of symbolic structures in connectionist systems. *Artificial Intelligence, 46*, 159–216.

Stich, S., & Warfield, T. A. (Eds.). (1994). *Mental representation: A reader.* Oxford: Blackwell.

Thelen, E., & Smith, L. B. (1994). *A dynamic systems approach to the development of cognition and action.* Cambridge, MA: MIT Press.

Townsend, J. T. (1990). Serial vs. parallel processing: Sometimes they look like Tweedledum and Tweedledee but they can (and should) be distinguished. *Psychological Science, 1*, 46–54.

Turing, A. M. (1950). Computing machinery and intelligence. *Mind, 59*, 433–466.

Van Essen, D. C., Felleman, D. J., DeYoe, E. A., Olavarria, J., & Knierim, J. (1990). Modular and hierarchical organization of extrastriate visual cortex in the macaque monkey. *Cold Spring Harbor Symposia on Quantitative Biology, 55*, 679–696.

van Gelder, T. (1990). Compositionality: A connectionist variation on a classical theme. *Cognitive Science, 14*, 355–384.

van Gelder, T. (1995). What might cognition be, if not computation? *Journal of Philosophy, 92*, 345–381.

van Gelder, T. (1997). Dynamics and cognition. In J. Haugeland (Ed.), *Mind design II* (pp. 421–450). Cambridge, MA: MIT Press.

Van Zandt, T., & Ratcliff, R. (1995). Statistical mimicking of reaction time: Single-process models, parameter variability, and mixtures. *Psychological Bulletin and Review, 2*, 20–54.

Zatorre, R. J., Halpern, A. R., Perry, D. W., Meyer, E., & Evans, A. C. (1996). Hearing in the mind's ear: A PET investigation of musical imagery and perception. *Journal of Cognitive Neuroscience, 8*, 29–46.

Zeki, S. (1992, September). The visual image in mind and brain. *Scientific American, 267*, 68–76.

4

Two Kinds of Representation

Gary F. Marcus
New York University

The key advance of cognitive science over behaviorism is often taken to be the fact that cognitive science comes clean with its commitment to representations (e.g., Gardner, 1985); still, the idea that the mind might do its work without representations is making a comeback. Advocates of dynamic systems theories (e.g. Thelen & Smith, 1994), for instance, claim that representations are unnecessary baggage, that "cognition may be something other than represented hypotheses and beliefs." Likewise, computer scientists such as Brooks (1991) aim to build robots that lack representations. (Radical connectionists do not deny that there are representations but do sometimes deny that the representations could be innate: e.g., Elman et al., 1996; more about this later.)

Part of the reason that researchers periodically deny the existence of representations is that there is no strong consensus about what counts as a representation. In this chapter, I argue for two kinds of representation, which I call *categories* and *rules*. My aim here is not to provide a complete inventory of all the kinds of representations that are exploited by the mind (a job that requires the full resources of cognitive science) but only to show that there is good reason for cognitive science to remain committed to representations.

POSITIVE PROPOSAL

Categories

One kind of a representation that is central to all models of the mind is the internally-represented category. An internally-represented category is

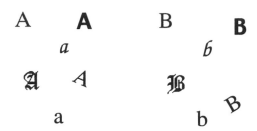

FIG. 4.1. Items on the left tend to be encoded by an internal representation of the letter A; items on the right by an internal representation of the letter B.

an encoding that treats all members of some group equally.[1] To the extent that categories encode all instances of a class with a common code, categories serve as filters, ignoring or suppressing some range of variation. For example, in many computational models of cognition, each of the percepts in the left half of Fig. 4.1 belongs to the category *Letter A*, while each of the percepts in the right half of Fig. 4.1 belongs to the category *Letter B*. The internally represented category Letter A, for instance, suppresses (or ignores) variations between instances of the letter A that may appear in different fonts, sizes, colors, orientations, and so forth.

In a similar way, the phonetic segment /ba/ abstracts over a variety of physical instantiations of the sound /ba/, rendered in different pitches, at different amplitudes, and even, within limits, different voice-onset timings: each member of this equivalence class is (with respect to certain computations) treated equally. Likewise, an internal representation of the category *bird* encompasses not only a prototypical bird like a robin but also atypical exemplars like penguins, and an internally represented category *male* allows us to abstract across all males, regardless of how typical they are.

Plainly, not all organisms represent the same categories; asking what categories a given organism can represent amounts to asking what equivalence classes are encoded by the organism. For instance, people represent some categories (e.g., dictators and standup comics) that presumably no other organisms represent. Even within a species, there can be variation as to what categories are internally represented. A person who treated the minerals jadeite and nephrite as a single undifferentiated equivalence class *jade* would, by hypothesis, represent (encode) them identically, whereas a person who distinguished between jadeite and nephrite would represent (encode) them differently. Thus individuals can vary as to what classes they represent.

To be sure, researchers vary on the range of internally generated categories that they assume are represented, but even foes of representations like Brooks build some low-level perceptual categories into their models. Hence even they build in some (perhaps small) set of representations. As

---

[1]I use the term *feature* only to refer to encodings in the head, not to refer to properties in the world.

Markman and Dietrich (in press) put it, the proper debate is not *whether* representations exist, but rather what *kinds* of representations exist; internally-represented categories appear to be at least one kind of representation that all cognitive systems share.

How we manage to compute what category (or categories) a given exemplar belongs to remains unknown, and deciding exactly what categories we represent internally is very much an open question. So long as we argue only about *which* categories are internally represented, we are firmly within a framework that incorporates some set of categories, hence some set of representations.

Rules

The idea that categories might be the *only* kind of representational devices needed for an adequate account of cognition appears to serve as an unspoken background assumption in a significant strand of thinking in cognitive science, one that has its origin in the notion of a *feature detector*. Feature detectors in visual systems are devices that detect whether some percept belongs to some (internally represented) category, say *vertical line* or the *Letter A*. Classic work such as Hubel and Wiesel's pioneering research on receptive fields and Fukishima and Miyake's (1982) Neocognitron model of character recognition shows how such feature detectors might be arranged hierarchically. Figure 4.2 provides one illustration of this idea of a hierarchy of interacting features.

There is reasonably strong evidence from neurophysiology that such hierarchies of feature detectors play some role in our visual system (Hubel, 1988; Hubel & Wiesel, 1962), thus raising the question of whether such hierarchies might extend all the way to the highest reaches of cognition, obviating the need for any other kind of representation. (One modern rendition of this view is a kind of neural network model known as the multilayer perceptron, discussed in the next section.)

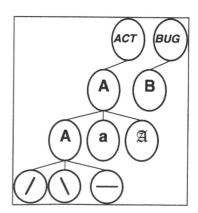

FIG. 4.2. A partial hierarchy of categories. Not all nodes drawn, not all connections drawn.

What I argue in this section is that models of hierarchies of features—essentially devices that represent relations between features (i.e., categories)—are not by themselves sufficient to account for an important part of cognitive life. In particular, my suggestion is that our knowledge of relations between specific features must be supplemented by a second kind of representation, which I call a *rule*.

By a rule I mean a relationship between abstract variables rather than between specific entities. For example, consider the notion of a *pair*, as it is used in a card game. In principle, we could learn this notion of pair by brute force, by memorizing a comprehensive list of all possible pairs (two aces form a pair, two twos form a pair, and so forth). Alternatively, we could learn the notion of the word *pair* by learning a relation between variables; for instance, we could represent the notion of a pair by a rule such as "For all cards x and y, if the rank of Card x equals the rank of Card y, x and y form a pair."

The key virtue of a system that can represent relations between variables is that it can generalize those relationships to arbitrary instances. Just as the equation $y = x + 2$ tells us that whatever value of x that we are presented with, we can compute the corresponding value of y by adding two to the value of x, the above-given definition of a pair allows us to generalize the notion of a pair to any new instance. Indeed, if we introduce a new card, say a *Duke*, we immediately can infer that two Dukes form a pair—we need not see the relationship *pair* instantiated with every possible instance of pair to be able to generalize it.

This sort of free generalization is pervasive throughout cognition. Many of the most obvious examples come from language. For instance, we can easily extend the rules of syntax to unfamiliar instances of grammatical categories. Even if the name *Dweezil* is unfamiliar to us, we can use it in any syntactic context that permits names, such as "That idea would appall my dear friend Dweezil." Likewise, we freely generalize the -ed past tense inflection to novel words, even those with unfamiliar sounds (Prasada & Pinker, 1993); we say, for instance, "Yeltsin outgorbacheved Gorbachev."

The ability to generalize freely is not, however, restricted to language. We can freely generalize syllogisms to novel instances: If all gronks are bleems, and all bleems are freebles, then we can infer that all gronks are freebles (Smith, Langston, & Nisbett, 1992). We can freely generalize the notion of sibling to any two people: If we know that Dweezil is a sibling of Moon, we can infer that Moon is a sibling of Dweezil. Our ability to make this generalization does not depend on how familiar we are with the people to whom we apply the generalization. We can freely generalize the cultural principle that (all things being equal) a son inherits the last name of his father even to unusual-sounding names (Joe Bfltspk's son Theo bears the name Bfltspk), and so forth.

This ability to freely generalize abstract relations to new instances appears to be present even in very young children; my colleagues and I have recently found evidence that 7-month-old infants are capable of generalizing abstract relations to new items (Marcus, Vijayan, Bandi Rao, & Vishton, 1999). After familiarizing infants with sentences in an artificial grammar such as "la ta la," "ga na ga," and "ta gi ta," we found, using a habituation paradigm, that infants listen longer to sentences composed of novel words that followed sequences with an unfamiliar patterns (like "wo fe fe") than to sentences composed of novel words that followed the same abstract pattern as the familiarization stream (such as "wo fe wo").

The many cases of free generalization suggest that rather than merely remembering relations between specific instances, we also have an "algebraic" system that allows us to represent (and generalize) relations between variables.

AN ALTERNATIVE

Connectionism

The rules-and-categories view that I am arguing for is standardly assumed in linguistics and "classical" artificial intelligence, and to some readers, the rules-and-categories view that I am defending seems obviously true. Recently, however, this view has been challenged, chiefly by some of the most radical[2] advocates of an approach to computational models of cognition known as "connectionist" or "parallel distributed processing" models (McClelland, Rumelhart, & the PDP Research Group, 1986; Rumelhart, McClelland, & the PDP Research Group, 1986) that seek to understand how massively interconnected units working largely in parallel can support cognition.

The challenge to the rules-and-categories view has come primarily from a class of "neural network" models known as multilayer perceptrons. These networks consist of a large set of interconnected nodes that process information in parallel. Nodes are connected to one another by weighted connections, and the output of a given node is a function of the sum of the activations of the units that feed the node multiplied by the weights of the connections from those units to the node. These networks learn on

---

[2]Connectionism in principle is orthogonal to the question of whether the mind represents rules, and it is important to note that not all connectionist researchers advocate multilayer perceptrons. Some connectionist researchers (e.g., chap. 9, this volume; Shastri & Ajjanagadde, 1993) have argued for more structured connectionist models that implement rather than eliminate representations of rules and categories. The criticisms in this section apply only to those models that eliminate rules.

the basis of exposure to input–output pairs, by adjusting the weights of the connections between nodes on the basis of an error-correction algorithm such as "back-propagation" (Rumelhart, Hinton, & Williams, 1986).

Such models have been applied to a wide array of problems, ranging from linguistics tasks such as learning the past tense of English verbs and the syntax of English sentences to aspects of cognitive development such as object permanence (for a review, see Elman et al., 1996; for recent critiques, see Marcus, 1998a, 1998b, 2000).

For our purposes here, the crucial question is whether these models can obviate the need for representations of rules and categories. Some (but, again not all) connectionist researchers take them to eliminate both rules and innately given categories.

The first claim—that connectionist models can dispense with innately given categories—seems to me to be mistaken. Elman et al. (1996), for instance, argued that representations (which presumably include categories) are not innate to their models[3]—but each of the models that they discussed actually presupposes some set of categories. What these authors overlooked is the fact that input and output encoding schemes that are assumed by the models that they advocated are in fact (innately given) representations: In each network, each input node (and each output node) encodes—hence, represents—a different category. (In practice, the choice of what a given node stands for is made before learning, by a programmer external to the model.) In one model, one particular node would be activated if and only if the input contains the speech segment /ba/, and another node would be activated if and only if the input contains /pa/; in another model, this node turns on if and only if the speech stream contains the word *cat*, that node only if the input contains the word *dog*.[4] Each input node is thus a category that, from the perspective of the model,

---

[3]Elman et al. followed in the Piagetian tradition of supposing that our higher level representations are constructed during the life span, but take an even stronger line than Piaget himself in denying that there are any innate representations. Thus whereas Piaget's program was to try to specify how higher level representations could be formed out of lower level representations, Elman et al. argued for a theoretical position in which even the lower level representations "emerge." As I have argued elsewhere (Marcus, 1998a), the models that Elman et al. advocated are not consistent with their theoretical position, because the models that they advocated do not actually construct any new representations. Instead, these models perform transformations between innately given classes of representations.

[4]Among the things that are represented by input or output nodes in models advocated in Elman et al.'s *Rethinking Innateness* are the following: sequences of phonetic features, the presence or absence of a consonant or vowel in a word's slot, the presence or absence of particular phonetic features in particular positions, the presence or absence of morphological feature in a given position, the presence or absence of a grammatical feature, sequences of letters, sequences of phonemes, graphemes in specified slots, phonemes in specified slots, the visibility or lack thereof of abstract objects, properties of objects, the distance of some weight on a balance beam from a fulcrum, the number of weights on a particular side of a balance beam, words,

is innately given, innately responding to that which it represents. (For a similar point, see Bloom & Wynn, 1994.)

The second claim—that some multilayer perceptrons perform computations without making use of explicit rules—is more interesting. For example, Rumelhart and McClelland (1986) aimed to provide "a distinct alternative to the view that children learn the rule of English past-tense formation in any explicit sense . . . [by showing] that a reasonable account of the acquisition of past tense can be provided without recourse to the notion of a 'rule' as anything more than a *description* of the language." Models like Rumelhart and McClelland's dispense with rules by using connectionist networks to learn correlations between specific input and output nodes. Rumelhart and McClelland's model of the acquisition of the past tense learned relations between the sounds contained in the stem of a verb (the model's input) and the sounds contained in the past tense of a verb (the model's output); later models learn relations between words, relations between parts of words, relations between objects in particular locations, and so forth.

As a simplified illustration of how these models work, let us return to the example of the relation *pair*. One way of setting this up in a connectionist architecture (that is I think true to the spirit of many connectionist models) is illustrated in Fig. 4.3.

In this model, the input is a description of two playing cards, the output is a code, zero if the two cards differ, one if the two cards form a pair. The model initially starts with random weights and is unable to distinguish pairs from nonpairs. As the model is trained on the various possible input–output sets, the back propagation tends to adjust the weights on the connections between nodes in a such way that performance gradually improves, eventually converging on essentially perfect performance. The model achieves this perfect performance without having anything corresponding to a rule of the sort that I argued was necessary.

Given that the model (apparently) succeeds in learning the pair concept, the question then arises as to whether the multilayer network alternative provides an adequate account of human performance, and if so whether it suffices to eliminate representations of rules from our theories of cognition. If the two models made identical predictions, answering this question would be difficult indeed (that is, if two different approaches made indistinguishable empirical predictions, how would we choose which one is correct?). Happily, the models do make differing predictions: in their predictions about generalization. Although (as described in the last sec-

---

coordinates of cube vertices, coordinates of joint locations, the relative location of an object, the distance of one object from another object, the identity of an object identity, or the description of which of two tasks a model is participating in at any given moment.

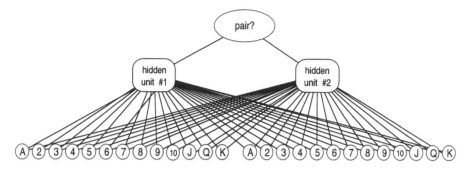

FIG. 4.3. One possible connectionist implementation of the *pair* concept. Input units are on the bottom; the output unit is on the top. The left bank of input units represents one card; the right bank of input units represents the other card. An activation value of 0 indicates the presence of some card, while an activation value of 1 indicates the absence of some card. The output unit is set to 1.0 if both cards are identical, to 0.0 otherwise. Weights are initially set at random values and then adjusted through training with the back-propagation algorithm.

tion) the rules-and-categories approach predicts that we should generalize to all instances of some category equally, the kind of network that I have just illustrated predicts that our generalizations would be far more constrained. That network predicts (incorrectly in this case, but see below) that we would be unable to generalize the *pair* relation to a new card (such as a Duke).

The network's prediction is a straightforward consequence of the mathematics of back propagation: On any trial in which the activation of some input i is set to zero, none of the weights leading from i changes; hence the model learns nothing about input i. If the network happens not to be trained on some unit, say the one representing the king, the network learns nothing about the relation between the node representing king and the output node.[5] (The example of pair provided here is of course a simplified example, but the same point holds for a variety of networks provided in the literature; it does not depend on factors such as the learning rate, the number of hidden units or hidden layers.)

When we train a network on the full range of possible inputs, the network appears at first blush to have "learned the rule" describing the relations between inputs and output. This is an illusion, however: The network appears to have learned the rule for the whole class of items

---

[5]In a multilayer network, training on other inputs affects the relation between the hidden layer(s) and the output layer, which can in some cases facilitate later learning on the untrained input node. Even in this case, the network still has to learn the relation between the input node and the hidden layer(s), and none of the training on other input units helps the network to do this. Thus the network's initial generalizations for the untrained unit will be incorrect.

only because it has done so for each item individually. The illusion is pierced if the network is trained only on a systematic subset of inputs that leave some input nodes untrained. For example, if the model is not trained on the node(s) encoding the king, the model does not accurately generalize the pair relation to the king.[6]

Thus, in a given domain in which we want to decide between a multilayer network account and the rule-and-categories account, a crucial empirical question arises: Can we freely generalize the relevant relation to arbitrary examples? In some domains (such as mappings between visual and motor space), our generalizations are quite restricted, and in those domains the rule-and-categories appears to be incorrect. Conversely, there appear to be at least some domains (e.g., those described at the end of the second section, such as generalization of the notion *pair*, a variety of syntactic principles, cultural principles, and so forth) in which our generalizations are free. In these cases, the multilayer network account seems inadequate, and the rule-and-memory account appears to provide the most plausible explanation.

Cases where we can freely generalize abstract relations to new instances cannot be accounted for by multilayer networks like the one in Figure 4.3 but provide support for the claim that the mind can represent (and generalize) rules. This is not to say that rules are necessarily used in all domains of cognition. In any given domain, it is a matter for empirical research whether rules or multilayer networks provide the best account, but there appears to be ample evidence that in at least some domains, rules play a crucial role in cognition.

SUMMARY

I have argued that at least two distinct kinds of representations are fundamental to cognition, categories and rules. Categories—internal representations of equivalence classes—appear to play a central role in all theories of cognitive architecture—even in connectionism. Moreover, although relatively unstructured connectionist models might be feasible in

---

[6]A thorny question that I avoid here concerns the nature of the input representation. If one constructed an input representation in which Duke *entirely overlapped* in its input representation with earlier examples (that is, if the input for Duke was made up of some set of low-level features, and if the network has specific experience with each of those low-level features), the network would generalize as a human would. If the overlap was not complete, however, the model would not generalize properly. In general, in domains in which we can generalize freely, regardless of the input representation that is chosen, it is possible to construct some input that does not entirely overlap with the earlier examples, and on that input, the network generalizes in a way that differs from the way in which humans generalize. See Marcus, 2000 for further discussion.

some domains, they cannot provide an alternative to a system that represents rules in those domains in which we can freely generalize to arbitrary examples. How the brain manages to represent rules and categories is still an open question—but a question well worth answering.

REFERENCES

Bloom, P., & Wynn, K. (1994). The real problem with constructivism. *Behavioral and Brain Sciences, 17*, 707–708.

Brooks, R. A. (1991). Intelligence without representation. *Artificial Intelligence, 47*, 139–159.

Elman, J. L., Bates, E., Johnson, M. H., Karmiloff-Smith, A., Parisi, D., & Plunkett, K. (1996). *Rethinking innateness: A connectionist perspective on development.* Cambridge, MA: MIT Press.

Fukishima, K., & Miyake, S. (1982). Neocognitron: A new algorithm for pattern recognition tolerant of deformations and shifts in position. *Pattern Recognition, 15*, 455–469.

Gardner, H. (1985). *The mind's new science: A history of the cognitive revolution.* New York: Basic Books.

Hubel, D. H. (1988). *Eye, brain, and vision.* New York: Scientific American Library.

Hubel, D. H., & Wiesel, T. N. (1962). Receptive fields, binocular interaction and functional architecture in the cat's visual cortex. *Journal of Physiology, 160*, 106–154.

Marcus, G. F. (1998a). Can connectionism save constructivism? *Cognition, 66*, 153–182.

Marcus, G. F. (1998b). Rethinking eliminative connectionism. *Cognitive Psychology, 37*(3), 243–282.

Marcus, G. F. (2000). *The algebraic mind: Reflections on connectionism and cognitive science.* Cambridge, MA: MIT Press.

Marcus, G. F., Vijayan, S., Bandi Rao, S., & Vishton, P. M. (1999). Rule learning in 7-month-old infants. *Science, 283*, 77–80.

Markman, A. B., & Dietrich, E. (in press). In defense of representation. *Cognitive Psychology.*

McClelland, J. L., Rumelhart, D. E., & the PDP Research Group. (1986). *Parallel distributed processing: Explorations in the microstructure of cognition, Vol. 1: Foundations.* Cambridge, MA: MIT Press.

Prasada, S., & Pinker, S. (1993). Similarity-based and rule-based generalizations in inflectional morphology. *Language and Cognitive Processes, 8*, 1–56.

Rumelhart, D. E., Hinton, G. E., & Williams, R. J. (1986). Learning representations by back-propagating errors. *Nature, 323*, 533–536.

Rumelhart, D. E., & McClelland, J. L. (1986). On learning the past tenses of English verbs. In J. L. McClelland, D. E. Rumelhart, & the PDP Research Group (Eds.), *Parallel distributed processing: Explorations in the microstructure of cognition, Vol. 2: Psychological and biological models* (pp. 216–271). Cambridge, MA: MIT Press.

Rumelhart, D. E., McClelland, J. L., & the PDP Research Group. (1986). *Parallel distributed processing: Explorations in the microstructure of cognition, Vol. 2: Psychological and biological models.* Cambridge, MA: MIT Press.

Shastri, L., & Ajjanagadde, V. (1993). From simple associations to systematic reasoning: A connectionist representation of rules, variables, and dynamic bindings using temporal synchrony. *Behavioral and Brain Sciences, 16*, 417–494.

Smith, E. E., Langston, C., & Nisbett, R. E. (1992). The case for rules in reasoning. *Cognitive Science, 16*, 1–40.

Thelen, E., & Smith, L. (1994). *A dynamic systems approach to the development of cognition and action.* Cambridge, MA: MIT Press.

II

WORDS AND OBJECTS

Part II considers the dynamics of representing speech perception, object perception, and meaning in memory. Robert E. Remez's chapter, "Speech Spoken and Represented," critically examines several different models of speech perception. All these models treat linguistic items as things—they reify linguistic entities. Remez is skeptical about this common methodological assumption because he is skeptical that speech perception is a statistical, lookup procedure. Speech perception is too fluid and dynamic for that approach, because speech itself is a messy, noisy affair. For example, different listeners hearing the same acoustic signal can, under different conditions, naturally interpret the signal as speech or as a series of changing tones. The fact that listeners can understand as speech sine wave replicas of speech that lack almost all the properties of naturally produced speech signals suggests that explanations that treat phonemes as independent, fixed elements with essential characteristics are not viable. Likewise, it is not viable to treat listeners as mere detectors who generate statistics to describe the samples of speech presented and to uncover the prototypical building blocks of the speech signal. Remez argues instead for a view that treats lexical identification as the exercise of a small set of phonemic contrasts and listeners as active participants in acts of speech perception whose first job is differentiation, rather than prototype identification and then lookup. The kinds of representations listeners must use on Remez's view are much more pliable and dynamic than the ones hypothesized in the views he criticizes.

Curt Burgess and Kevin Lund, in "The Dynamics of Meaning in Memory," first present their model of representation for word meaning in human memory. The model is called the hyperspace analogue to language (HAL). HAL learns its representations (in an unsupervised manner) from a large corpus of text fed to it gradually, via a window 10 words wide. From this text input, HAL constructs word vectors that encode co-occurrence information: how close one word is to another. The vector space these word vectors inhabit is huge: It is a 140,000-dimensional vector space. Word vectors are sparse and distributed, and words representing similar concepts have similar vectors. Another interesting property of such co-occurrence vectors is that all words (all word vectors) basically have as their features other words. The result of this is that representing abstract concepts is as easy as representing more basic ones. The central theory Burgess and Lund are exploring is that simple associations in context can, if enough information is considered, be aggregated into conceptual representations. Burgess and Lund then spend the rest of their chapter using HAL to investigate several well-known memory and cognitive phenomena such as the nature of association, the nature of several kinds of priming, and the nature of certain kinds of problem solving, which depend on similarity. Importantly, the HAL memory model is dynamic and sensitive to context.

In the final chapter in this part, "Where View-Based Theories Break Down: The Role of Structure in Human Shape Recognition," John E. Hummel takes on the hypothesis that object recognition depends on using template-like entities called views, which are stored in memory and used for matching against visual input. View-based theories claim that we recognize objects holistically, matching whole images of objects from one point of view with stored memory items of the observed objects. The problem with view-based theories lies in this very holism: View-based theories are elegant and simple. Hummel suggests, however, that they are too elegant and simple to explain human object perception. Hummel instead argues for a class of theories known as *structural description theories*. These theories complicate matters by saying that humans perceive objects by decomposing them into their volumetric parts and then representing those parts in terms of their relations to one another. Hummel's position is that structural description theories fare better both empirically and logically. (There seems to be one exception to this generalization, which Hummel notes: Face recognition is probably view based and not explained by a structural description theory. The view-based approach is likely to have been implemented in the case of faces, however, because of the importance of faces in the evolution of the perceptual system.) In his conclusion, Hummel extends his arguments to object to the general tendency in some quarters of cognitive science to try to get by without structured representations. The mind does not merely encode information about its environment in some flat, vector-like manner. Rather, the mind constructs compositional representations with all kinds of structure. Hummel points out that without such structured representations such important processes as general inferencing, creativity, and abstraction are impossible to explain.

The chapters in this section deal with aspects of perception and low-level language. As such, they take on an area that is also the province of many researchers in dynamic systems and situated action. Nonetheless, they provide a compelling case that representations and representational dynamics are crucial for understanding the fine details of these processes

5

Speech Spoken and Represented

Robert E. Remez
Barnard College

> *The nervous system appears to be using a radically different system of notation from the ones we are familiar with in ordinary arithmetics and mathematics: Instead of the precise system of markers where the position— and presence or absence—of every marker counts decisively in determining the meaning of the message, we have here a system of notations in which the meaning is conveyed by the* statistical *properties of the message. [T]his leads to a lower level of arithmetical precision but to a higher level of logical reliability: a deterioration in arithmetics has been traded for an improvement in logics.*
>
> —von Neumann, 1958

> *Form ever follows function.*
>
> —Sullivan, 1896

Language is a representational medium. Utterances stand for other things: the cat, the mat, the way you wear your hat, the way you sing off-key. It is not surprising that cognitive psychology, aiming to supplant the probabilistic functionalism of the behaviorists, extended its early roots in research on language. This arguably occurred in Lashley's (1951) break-through, a speculation about the form of communicative plans and the internal representations implicated in their expression. In critical ways, the issues that move the field today were determined by an intellectual and scientific trajectory set long ago, and the paths of some of the deter-minants are marked here. Of course, research on speech and language has also provided a hearty nonalgoristic welcome to ideas and techniques taken from a dynamical systems approach, and several contemporary research programs amalgamate dynamical and representational components in describing and explaining production and perception. The varied premises of some contemporary approaches are illustrated here to contrast the representational notations of our theoretical accounts from assertions of cognitive representation in the acts of production and perception.

ROOTS

The psychological accounts of language available for Lashley to consider were plain in comparison to our elaborate contemporary models and held a principle of serial association in common. Specifically, the progression of an utterance in production and its perceptual reciprocation were described as a chain of events. The motor gestures of articulation composed the links in the chain at the finest grain, and the succession of mental images that ultimately caused the speech or that together amounted to the perception of its meaning were conceptualized as the links at the grossest grain. Human capability for action was cast as a strict procession, and conditional probability as the only function expressed in action. Lashley's gambit in overturning this approach was to drive a wedge between the specific linguistic form of an utterance and its semantic function, that is, to deny that form follows function in a symbolic process.

Why does an utterance take its specific form? The prevailing account of peripheral associative chaining was psychologically implausible as an account of linguistic utterances, in Lashley's presentation, because the elements of language, whether designated as phonetic segments, phonemes, or words, do not occur in an inevitable order, the way links in a response chain must. By the principles of associative chaining, the first item triggers the entire sequence. Indeed, Lashley considered any reliance on peripheral chaining to be physiologically implausible, because motor gestures succeed one another faster than a sensorimotor loop can return the sensory consequences of one link in the chain to spur the next.

To entertain alternatives to this reflex-arc conceptualization, Lashley sought evidence that sequential acts can be driven endogenously and centrifugally and found an example in the orderly swimming of deafferented fish. In this instance, the ongoing cyclic locomotor pattern is preserved despite surgical interruption of the sensorimotor control loop and is sustained without reafference by a central motor pattern generator. On this model rather remote from language, Lashley defended an account of the production of utterances under open loop control at the periphery.

This left him the prospect of central associative chaining to consider in turn as a cause of the form of the expression.

Classic introspective accounts had claimed that an associative chain of mental images was responsible for the form of a sentence. Referring to Titchener, Lashley considered whether a sequence of meaningful linguistic constituents could properly be attributed to a series of mental images and ingeniously used pig latin to deliver the fatal coup. The talker's representation of the semantic content of a sentence would necessarily also be responsible for its pig latin translation, because the denotation is equivalent. However, the transformation of the form of an utterance that does not alter its sense proved the autonomy of spoken forms and communicative functions however talker and listener represent the meaning. This prosaic evidence freed Lashley to speculate about the psychology and physiology underlying sentence production among serially ordered acts. Despite an arguably probabilistic nature of representation in neural tissue, the psychological manifestations of language indeed had the quality of logical expressions; sentences, clauses, phrases, and phonemes—the logical constituents—were conceived as formal objects. Ultimately, the theorist's problem is to explain this particular relation between form and function. Although the neural embodiment of language operates in a probabilistic manner, as von Neumann (1958) noted, the functions that this engine supports express logical relations.

Much of Lashley's psychology is dressed in physiological camouflage, and cognitive representations of words or of syntactic principles are only implied. For instance, lexical priming during speech production was conceptualized as a specific neural event employing the recently discovered self-stimulating neuron. Once activated by the neural process underlying communicative intentions, this cell continued to drive itself, in Lashley's view, leading to suprathreshold activation of lexical elements when the second influence of a serial-ordering neural array was imposed. Of course, the orderly production of primed expressive elements in language is the syntax, in a word; the derivation of syntactic constituent structure in the descriptions of Lashley's successors has attempted to unpack the logic of these imageless determining tendencies of serial order. This psycholinguistic project has often postulated a covert cognitive economy in which representations of one or another formal attribute compose a set of arguments for the action of grammatical functions (e.g., Frazier, 1995). Functions operate on syntactic forms, returning new syntactic forms during a multiple-stage derivation expressed as an algorithm. The syntactic relations among constituents are described in well-known bracketings and tree diagrams; syntactic functions and the arguments that they take during the derivation of a sentence are asserted to be psychologically real albeit abstract.

In his tentative model, Lashley actually furnished a durable sketch of the architecture of speech production while proposing that the form of utterances must derive from plans rather than associative chains. The formulation Lashley proposed is retained in contemporary models (Dell, 1995; Levelt, 1989). The production of utterances employs two great functions, one that readies the elements of expression for action by priming them semantically, and the other that scans the primed elements according to a syntactic map and issues motor commands to articulators by using a metrical driver to impose a regular temporal pattern. In contrast to Lashley's physiological predilection, the conceptual complexity of the syntactic derivation of serial order has often precluded claims of a specific probabilistic mechanism couched in the minutiae of excitatory and inhibitory synaptic activity. Models that admit physiological limits are rare (Klatt, 1989). The great increase in precision of the account has occurred in a proliferation of functional descriptions and explanations, among which are those concerned specifically with the production and perception of phonetic form.

THE PERCEPTION OF SPEECH

A complete account of speech perception eludes us, although we can readily describe and model the form of expression in some contexts. Much effort has aimed to gauge the variability that confounds our models, but other research clearly opposes the actuarial approach of a normative enterprise and instead seeks an account in underlying principles of the perception of contrast among linguistic constituents. This view represents the reappearance of an old, familiar idea in language study, perhaps original to Saussure, although it departs from accounts based on psychophysics and probabilistic functionalism. This section offers some of the evidence that encourages each approach to understanding the perception of speech, reviewing the motives and assumptions of some exemplary projects. Overall, the presentation is skeptical of the reification of linguistic entities—the treatment of linguistic properties as things—and is partial to the axiom of distinctiveness.

Thinginess or Distinctiveness in Speech Perception

Consonants and vowels are sometimes described as elementary, meaningless constituents of the grammar, the individual building blocks from which the meaningful elements of language are constructed (Hockett, 1955). This perspective is mistaken and ubiquitous. It is mistaken because the phonemic elements in actuality compose a system of contrasts intrinsic to the medium of linguistic representation (Jakobson & Halle, 1956). They are not really an aggregation of specific sounds or an assortment of specific movements of the articulators or much like building blocks at all, but rather are manifestations of linguistically governed contrasts in the production and perception of utterances. Perhaps the thinginess of consonants and vowels has been easy for reductionists to assert, and the linguistic standing of consonants and vowels has been easy for reductionists to overlook, for two reasons. First, the experience of literacy teaches an implicit albeit false equation between phonemes and letters of the alphabet, as if speaking itself were a form of spelling, as if the sounds of language were as separably and freely commutable as printed characters. Second, consonants and vowels are meaningless; they seem rather like the sounds that meaningful exchange requires but do not seem symbolic themselves. Alternatively, the meaningfulness of words makes them self-evidently symbolic and differentiates them from meaningless consonants and vowels, phonesthesia notwithstanding (Jakobson & Waugh, 1979). *Meaningless* and *nonlinguistic* are not synonymous, of course, although it is easy to recognize that these aspects of experience can be taken as kin. Moreover, talkers are able to produce nonlinguistic sounds, symbolic or not, in the same upper airway that is excited to produce speech. Consonants and vowels are readily likened to the acoustic effects of breathing (or wheezing) or swallowing (gulp!), indexical nonlinguistic sounds formed in the anatomy of respiration and deglutition. Such sounds stand on their own as deterministic consequences of states of the physiology. If consonants and vowels are similarly designated, as if their linguistic function was an artifact of their physiological function, it is easy to extrapolate that each phoneme is an independently realizable physiological state or transition, rather then emphasizing the contrastive nature of each phoneme relative to the set that composes the sound system of a language. (See Table 5.1.)

The building-block metaphor also allows an assertion that consonants and vowels are ordinary things without further proof, from which it is commonly supposed that the phonemic and phonetic grain of language admits the same kind of probabilistic description that we apply in explaining the role of likelihood in the perception of chairs, tables, and other items that populate a world of things. If consonants and vowels are produced by movements like any other, then the standards of goal-directed action are sufficient to understand the articulation of each segment in the sound inventory; if the auditory effects of speech by which a listener apprehends the words are sound qualities like any other, then an account of speech perception should be sought in the resolution of auditory form, via psychoacoustic investigations. Overall, if a phoneme is a thing in itself, then the proper study of its incidence requires an assessment of its likely manifestations as a pattern of motor activation, as a distribution of acous-

TABLE 5.1
The Phoneme Set of English, Arguably

English phonemes in IPA notation	A word exhibiting the segment
b	bee
p	pea
m	me
w	woe
d	day
t	tea
n	no
ɹ	ray
l	lie
g	goo
k	key
ŋ	ring
j	yeah
v	view
f	fee
ð	they
θ	thigh
z	zoo
s	see
ʒ	luge
ʃ	shoe
dʒ	jam
tʃ	chew
h	he
i	beet
ɪ	bit
ɛ	bet
æ	bat
ɑ	cot
ʌ	pup
ʊ	would
ɔ	caught
u	boot
ə	about
ɑi	bike
ɛi	late
ɑu	lout
o^w	moat
oi	toy

The left column shows the notation of the segment in the notation of the International Phonetics Association, while the right column gives a word containing the element. (See text.)

tic patterns, or as typical auditory effects, thereby to describe the characteristic attributes of each and the human ability to resolve them in action and in perception. Indeed, a similar rationale was applied in recent investigations by Diehl, Kluender, Walsh, and Parker (1991), Greenberg (1988), and Kingston (1992).

Perceptual Organization

Our examination of the theoretical cost of this perspective has focused on the speech mode of perception and the sensory conditions that evoke it. This is a problem of perceptual organization, in which a listener finds and follows a nonstationary speech signal through its modulations, often despite brief moments of masking by noise or by concurrent sound streams, some of them other voices. Most theoretical accounts of speech perception are silent on this issue and presume that auditory mechanisms are adequate to isolate a speech signal for phonemic analysis or that it is sufficient to begin a perceptual account by presupposing perceptual organization. These latter models implicitly assert that the perception of speech includes two components, one preliminary to phonetic analysis, which unerringly finds acoustic correlates of speech production in the buzz of sensory inflow. Once the domain of analysis has been established, a second component to perception extracts the phonetic attributes from the auditory elements.

Historically, the idea of a speech mode of perception was engendered by comparisons of synthetic acoustic patterns that elicited phonetic impressions of syllables to those that specifically evaded such effects. Much imagination was applied to developing nonspeech control test items to use for benchmarks in judging the identification and discrimination of speech sounds. The impetus for such study was straightforward, for the discriminability of syllables differing to small extent in *voicing* appeared to be far poorer than the simple temporal discrimination on which it was presumably based; likewise, a discrimination of small differences in consonantal *place of articulation* appeared to be far more difficult than a formant frequency discrimination on which it was presumably based. The finding that phonetic identification predicted discrimination more successfully than a familiar psychophysical power law was described as categorical perception, and a huge literature stands in the wake of these initial findings from the experimental phonetics laboratory (Harnad, 1987). In essence, the same sensory property was apparently analyzed in differing fashion to produce auditory form impressions or phonemes in each mode.

At least this was the conclusion, although in truth the nonspeech control conditions typically used an element isolated from an acoustic signal, a speech cue, which varied in rough approximation to phonetic impressions when it was embedded in a complete pattern of formants. When such an acoustic element was presented to listeners in isolation, it lost its phonetic effect and was perceived as an auditory form; in consequence, it was discriminable without the concurrent perception of phonetic attributes (Mattingly, Liberman, Syrdal, & Halwes, 1971). Whether this difference in sensory resolution occurred as a consequence of the perceptual mode it evoked or whether it was due to the presentation of an acoustic element in two completely different spectrotemporal contexts, two conclusions were apparent. First, an acoustic cue, an element of a speech signal, is not particularly speechlike extracted from its context; second, the non-speech control conditions were only approximate to speech in physical structure, not exact. Therefore, the proposed existence of a speech mode was never quite free of the suspicion that the complexity, redundancy, or familiarity of speech signals was responsible for performance differences, which therefore ought not be taken to indicate fundamental perceptual differences between speech and other sounds.

We reported the relevant evidence in a study testing the necessity of natural acoustic vocal products in the perception of speech (Remez, Rubin, Pisoni, & Carrell, 1981). We took a natural sentence, analyzed the frequency and amplitude variation of the vocal resonances, and imposed this pattern on time-varying sinusoids by using a digital oscillator to create the acoustic wave form. Physically, the sinusoidal signal was unlike natural speech, which exhibits a harmonic spectrum, broadband resonances, momentary aperiodicities, and sustained narrow aperiodic bands. Sine wave replicas speech lacked all these, and it was barely surprising that most of the naive listeners in our test failed to notice that the concurrently varying tones were derived from an utterance. Instead, they reported a variety of impressions of the auditory form of several simultaneous tones changing in pitch and loudness in an apparently incoherent manner, as if listening in a perceptual mode that produced auditory form impressions only. We instructed other groups of listeners instead to transcribe the synthetic sentence or to evaluate the success of the synthesis of a specific sentence, and neither of these groups had much difficulty in treating the sine wave signal as a reliable source of phonetic impressions.

Subsequent study resulted in several conclusions: The timbre of such sine wave items is anomalous; the apparent intonation of sine wave sentences is too high in pitch and strangely contoured; but listeners treat a sine wave sentence as if it issued from a talker whose production is scaled to the normal range of vocal variation; frequency variation preserves phonetic information in the absence of veridical amplitude variation; and, crucially for the issue of the speech mode, the oddity of a speechlike pattern imposed on arbitrary and nonvocal carriers produces a bistable perceptual experience of nonspeech auditory forms concurrent with phonetic attributes. In fact, perceivers are extremely successful in concurrently reporting aspects of each perceptual mode, although they are seldom clear about the correlation of auditory form impressions and the phonetic attributes with which they are paired.

This line of investigation (see Remez, Rubin, Berns, Pardo, & Lang, 1994) showed that a single acoustic pattern could be perceptually elaborated in completely distinct ways, one of them phonetic, leading to lexical access and perception of a spoken sentence, the other nonphonetic, leading to an impression of contrapuntally changing tones of distinct pitch, loudness, and reedy or whistling timbre. Because auditory bistabilities are apparently concurrently sustainable, in contrast to visual bistabilities that alternate perspective—for example in the case of Woodworth's equivocal staircase—the parallel nature of the phonetic and auditory modes is proved by this evidence. However, return for a moment to a listener hearing a sine wave replica of an utterance and consider the challenge implicit in understanding that the sensory flux at the ear is something to analyze phonetically. Does it consist of a single talker's speech stream? Of two? Of none? Familiarity with the kinds of acoustic elements that compose speech signals ought to guide a listener, and in fact this is a common presumption of many normative approaches to speech perception. Massaro (1994), for instance, proposed a probabilistic perceptual function by which an incident acoustic stream is assembled for analysis element by element, based on piecemeal assessment of likelihood. The acoustic ingredients that are taken to initiate the perceptual analysis are implausibly enumerated in advance as the ones likeliest to issue from a talker's mouth.

This view simply does not describe the flexibility of perceivers in organizing sine wave replicas of speech, for two reasons. First, an organizing filter apparently accepts the time-varying tones as phonetic in nature, which we can determine from the fact that listeners are able to transcribe them with little exposure or training. However, this acceptance of sine wave replicas of speech occurs despite their acoustic structure, which is unlike speech in detail; it is doubtful that a listener groups sine wave components into a single organized whole because their acoustic constituents or timbre are familiarly speechlike. Second, an organizing filter apparently also rejects sine wave signals or rejects them enough to let the analysis of their nonphonetic auditory form occur. This differs from the case of natural and synthetic speech in which the coherence of the signal elements is so strong that the formant frequency variation producing consonant and vowel impressions is not experienced as a collection of concurrent changes in spectral pitch. The bistability that proves the existence of the phonetic mode of perception is trouble for a familiarity-based account of perceptual organization. (See Fig. 5.1.)

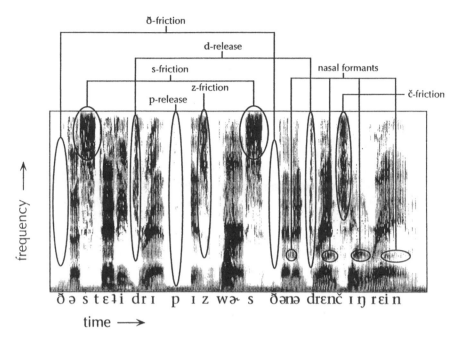

FIG. 5.1. A spectrographic representation of a sentence, "The steady drip is worse than a drenching rain," making up a varied set of acoustic signal elements. Similar elements are marked together: friction, broadband pops, rapidly and slowly changing formant configurations. From R. E. Remez, P. E. Rubin, S. M. Berns, J. S. Pardo, & J. M. Lang (1994). On the perceptual organization of speech. *Psychological Review, 101*, p. 132. Copyright © 1994 by American Psychological Association. Reprinted by permission.

Our research on this topic led to an inventory of the signal components of speech, as a method of appraising the suitability of the preeminent auditory approach to perceptual organization, Auditory Scene Analysis (Bregman, 1992; Cooke, 1991; Ellis, 1996). Perceptual organization is explained in general auditory terms as a process of sorting an incident complex spectrum by the mutual likeness of its momentary components. It presumes that sounds issuing simultaneously and successively from a single acoustic source are similar, a conjecture that is perhaps true of oboe melodies, although is unlikely to be true of clarinets across different registers (cf. Rossing, 1990), and is false in the case of speech. Figure 5.1 spotlights the acoustic constituents of the sentence "The steady drip is worse than a drenching rain," by grouping similar components. We argued that reliance on Auditory Scene Analysis to find a speech signal in a quiet room fractured it rather than promoted its coherence, because of the simple heterogeneity of the physical acoustic constituents emitted from a natural vocal source. To hold the components of a natural speech signal together requires the perceptual organizational finesse to disregard dissimilarities in excitation, discontinuities in the spectrum, differential rates of frequency variation, and, as the sine wave studies show, gross departures from typicality.

The property of a sine wave speech replica that allows the perceiver to organize it phonetically is its spectrotemporal form. This dynamic property of the acoustic signal is evidently effective even when familiarity of the signal elements is lacking. Overall, the intelligibility of sine wave sentences, words, and nonsense syllables offers counterevidence to perceptual explanations of speech based simply on remembering familiar cues or their likely variation, and shows that completely unlikely sensory effects are satisfactory when the pattern they compose preserves the dynamic properties of a phonologically organized act. The phenomena are difficult to explain in the framework that each phoneme is an independent element of language exhibiting essential acoustic correlates for perceivers to detect.

A System of Contrasts

Although a complete causal account of the perception of speech by listening surely requires an understanding of the detailed auditory effects of utterances, speech perception has rarely seemed to proceed through acts of categorization or fine discrimination of the details of auditory experience. Often, this has been readily and prominently acknowledged (Hirsh, 1988; Liberman, Harris, Hoffman, & Griffith, 1957). Very little that we do well and so casually can require optimal resolution for success, either in the control of action or in the resolution of sensory forms, and, indeed, speech is reasonably articulated with motoric constraint (under mandibular block, with teeth clenched, with food in the mouth, etc.) and reasonably well comprehended from signals that depart from ideal circumstances (shouted across a reverberant enclosure, spoken over a noisy channel, croaked in a voice wracked by influenza, etc.). Spoken communication does not require performance to approach the physiological limits. Language governs performance well within the limits of physiology.

In simpler terms, the perception of an instance of /t/ requires distinguishing it only from other phonemes (1 in 39), from other consonants (1 in 24), from other voiceless consonants (1 in 9), from other stop consonants (1 in 7), or from other voiceless stop consonants (1 in 4), surely not from other brief aperiodic sources of sound (1 in ?: a snapping twig, the striking of a match, the crackle of a log in the fire, etc.) or from other brief sounds (1 in ?: a timer on the oven, a squeaking door hinge, cable clatter in the dashboard, etc.), which never satisfy the boundary conditions for perceptual analysis in a speech mode (Remez et al., 1994). To distinguish the relevant dimensions of control, the production and perception of speech require facility in wielding a finite and small set of phonemic contrasts. Perception of objects and other events does not enjoy such powerful restriction, and the inventory of such entities is neither finite nor small in any case.

In explaining the perception of objects and events, the theoretical emphasis falls on the perceiver's facility in registering and remembering the characteristic attributes of each, the properties that together compose a relevant description of each. In an adequate explanation of the perception of speech, a description of the creation, and susceptibility to the distinctive attributes, of the phonemic constituents is critical. A survey of distinctive attributes and characteristic attributes of speech segments shows that they differ enormously (Halle, 1983; Ladefoged, 1980). Indeed, perceptual research aiming to catalog the characteristic attributes of consonants and vowels differs from research aiming to understand the robustness of speech communication in conditions that depart widely from the allegedly typical or essential manifestations of the building blocks.

Prototypes

Our theories ought not to treat the elements of a phoneme inventory as if they were ordinary conceptual types, but this has been a dominant point of departure for a statistically well-armed cognitive psychology. In this familiar conceptualization, a stock of consonants and vowels exists in the perceptual and motor repertoire of each individual in a language community, and the syntactically ordered words are spoken or identified by means of the subordinate phonemes. Each phoneme is articulated by performing a particular set of motor gestures, and each is identified in perception by noting and evaluating the specific sensory consequences of the segmental constituents of a talker's utterance.

This formal approach to the production and perception of speech segments is familiar from classical studies of categorization (Osgood, May, & Miron, 1975). The goal is to identify the manifestations of each item considered as an instance of a specific type and to treat variation among the instances in a normal way. Accordingly, each phoneme is conceptualized as a characteristic pattern of coordinated gestures. These gestures in turn produce a typical acoustic manifestation of each segment. Once the acoustic spectrum reaches the perceiver, a typical auditory experience ensues. Variation across different individuals, across different rates of production, or across different contexts of occurrence is to be treated as error, that is, departure from the statistically typical manifestation. If this manner of explaining perception appears congenial to the notion of the prototype, then it is not surprising to note an explicit prototype-based classification system envisioned in recent research on vowel perception. Studies by Kuhl (1991) and colleagues have clearly shown that perceivers readily choose the best instance from a range of variants of vowels. In explaining this finding, the researchers likened the variation in goodness to differing degrees of departure of each token from a prototype. Differing likeness to a prototype translates into experiences of relative goodness.

When a good and a less good instance of /i/ are compared perceptually, they seem less different from each other than do two poor instances of this type, as if the sensory discrimination was nonuniform, deformed by an attractor at the prototype. This general coincidence of discrimination findings and goodness findings is described as a perceptual magnet effect, and it is claimed to underlie the disposition of infants to learn the phoneme inventory of their language (Kuhl et al., 1997). An extraordinary observation in this regard is an absence of evidence of perceptual magnets in the performance of macaques judging vowels (although they may have native preferences of their own; see Rauschecker, Tian, & Hauser, 1995). Despite sensitivity in the same frequency range over which the vowel tokens occurred, monkeys lacked the nonuniformities of discrimination and goodness distributions that might promote the crystallization of likely human phonemes during language acquisition. If perceptual magnets are driven by an infant's experience of the adult language, then this comparative finding explains why the acoustic properties of phonemes exhibit specific distributional properties: The centers of perceptual and productive categories are the likely acoustic spectra of the magnets. An infant who exhibits this sensitivity expresses a propensity to use phonemes that adults use, and these perceptual magnets provide spectral targets for the juvenile vocal apparatus while a child learns to produce speech.

Is a set of perceptual prototypes matched to the phoneme elements in the adult inventory? The appeal of this conceptualization is its potential to explain whatever congruence happens to be observed among goodness judgments, categorization and discrimination performance in psychophysical tests, and the acoustic dispersion of vowels. In this respect, the natural language magnet combines psychoacoustic building blocks and cognitive finesse (cf. Posner & Keele, 1970) to define the precocious ability of human infants (Kuhl et al., 1997).

Alone, an appeal to a notion of prototype in explaining vowel perception is insufficient to elicit skepticism, unless one is automatically suspicious of an approach presuming that the variation in correspondence of token to type is due to chance and unanalyzable. Truly, the reason to reserve endorsement comes first from tests of its empirical adequacy and then from the evaluation of the claim in light of what we already think we know and understand about vowels.

Some of the research that has aimed to correct the claims of the proposal of vowel perception by perceptual magnets has focused on method. For instance, Lively and Pisoni (1997) endeavored to determine the cause of goodness judgments and found, for example, that it is possible in this testing paradigm to discover that an instance of /ɛ/ is reported as a bad instance of /i/ without affecting the outcome of the tests. Indeed, it is likely that this occurred in some of the original tests establishing the phenomenon. Is an /ɛ/ a poor instance of /i/? Is the whistle of a kettle a poor instance of the vowel /i/? Lively argued that a test to assess goodness is valid only if the items under consideration all belong to the same category. It is hardly fair to prove the differential distribution of goodness impressions for a particular vowel if the test includes items from other vowel categories. On such grounds, Lively suggested that the role of perceptual magnets is not proved.

Similar evidence is offered by Frieda, Walley, Flege, and Sloane (1999) against the simple claim of magnetism by noting that the best example of a vowel among the acoustic items in their test set differed from the test item that appeared to be the attractor in the discrimination tests. Remember, the appealingly simple claim of perceptual magnetism was that an internal auditory prototype acted as a standard for judging varying impressions of quality and also as a center of the discriminable variants of the category. Discrimination and goodness must coincide for the explanation to enjoy a single underlying principle. Both Lively and Frieda et al. were critical of the prototype account offered in the perceptual magnet studies because it failed well-justified empirical tests.

Would we have expected an empirical failure? It is difficult to reconcile two prominent observations about sound production in language with the notion that individual consonants and vowels are identifiable by likeness to a motor, acoustic, or auditory prototype. For one, each individual exhibits unique motoric and acoustic manifestations of the shared phoneme set, because of anatomical differences that affect articulation and resonant frequencies. (Whether subtle individual differences in the audiogram are likewise sufficient to bring about differences in vowel quality, all other things being equal, is not known.) These differences are supplemented by other drivers of variation in dialect and idiolect. The upshot is that even monozygotic twins raised together and therefore speaking the same regional dialect of English differ nonetheless in idiolect, owing to idiosyncratic but consistent differences in articulating phoneme contrasts (Laver, 1980). If such twins exhibit a common prototype set, these must be abstract, indeed.

Second and no less important in assessing the validity of a prototype account is the effect of the local phonetic environment on the expression of a segment, consonant or vowel. The concurrent articulation of consonant and vowel in production guarantees that their acoustic effects mingle, and although it is difficult at the lab bench to analyze the acoustic contributions of each segment, the listener has little difficulty in telling which aspect of the production is caused by which segmental influence (Fowler & Brown, in press; Fowler & Smith, 1986). Historically, the nonlinearity and lack of invariance in the correspondence of consonants and vowels to their acoustic effects have been discussed according to such considerations (Liberman, Cooper, Shankweiler, & Studdert-Kennedy, 1967). To accommodate variation in the acoustic manifestations of a single segment because of coarticulation in a prototype conception, the number of prototypes required just to handle the perception of syllables spoken by a single individual multiplies greatly: There must be one for every possible coarticulatory combination permitted by the language (Wickelgren, 1969). In the instance of Japanese, the consonant–vowel (CV) structure of each syllabic constituent yields a potential allophone set far less numerous than found in English, in which the kinds of syllable types are more varied—for example, CCCVCCC ([skɹætʃt]) is a potential phonetic form of the word *scratched*, to cite a prosaic instance.

To an extent, the counterevidence already exists for a perceptual account that appeals to prototypes of consonants and vowels, although not in the same sense as the specific tests of the psychophysical paradigms that we have mentioned. The premise of prototype accounts is that there is a core of consistency in the sensory manifestations in types and that perception of an unknown instance is accomplished by reference to this statistical fiction of the likely auditory pattern.

The scope of the problem can be gauged in the database of fluent speech collected and analyzed by Crystal and House (1988). Their enterprise included a labeling project that permitted a comparison of segmental duration across different contexts of occurrence. One may suppose that such data are useful primarily to prepare a catalog of the acoustics of spoken metrical variation, but these proved far more useful. To take the provocative instance of stop consonants, careful psychophysical studies show that a /b/ that lacks a hold portion is perceived as /w/ or /v/ or as the vowel with which it is produced; a /d/ that has no hold is perceived as /l/ or possibly as /ɹ/, and so on. In collecting the measures, these authors were somewhat surprised to note that fully one half of the stop consonants produced in fluent reading lacked the hold portions that are definitive of their type (Halle, Hughes, & Radley, 1957). Because the speech was obtained from readers who implicitly understood that they were to provide a fluent normative reading, we can safely guess that this proportion of nonstopping stops underestimates the incidence in spontaneous speech. None would deny that a nonstopping stop is a poor example of a stop consonant, but evidently we hardly notice that we hear so many.

The phenomenon that House and Crystal witnessed is perhaps a variant of Lieberman's (1963) classic observation that the perception of a word extracted from the fluent context in which it was produced is predictable from its role in the original utterance. If the target word was relatively difficult to infer from context, then it was far easier to identify when extracted and presented in isolation than if the target word had been relatively easy to infer from its original context. Lieberman concluded that talkers modulated articulatory precision according to the communicative load borne by the word. Here, the relevant conceptualization of information is akin to the uncertainty notion of Shannon and Weaver (1949). Each word is 1 among 100,000 that a talker speaking English might say. When context reduces the search set to nouns, count nouns, numbers, or the number that completes the proverb "A stitch in time saves . . . ," this reduces uncertainty to the extent that the word "nine" can be precisely indicated merely by articulating its coarsest phonetic features. Lieberman also noted that individual talkers differed in realizing the phoneme contrasts of English, which directly implies that the listener's facility in understanding fluent speech depends on a specific accommodation to the style of neutralization of contrasts that a particular talker uses. This rapid tuning of perceptual sensitivity does not seem compatible with fixed prototypes based on statistically likely acoustic manifestations of the items of the phoneme set, but more likely reflects a talker's expressive range and a perceiver's ability to detect instances of the phoneme contrasts of the language under a wide variety of acoustic guises.

Contrasts in Lexical Identification

The idea of the *lexical neighborhood* (Luce, Pisoni, & Goldinger, 1990) expresses this sense of contrast plainly. A talker who says a word and a listener who aims to understand it each face a problem of differentiation, although this is not quite the psychophysical understanding of discrimination tied to an anatomical channel. The grain of discriminative resolution required by lexical identification is nowhere near as fine as auditory frequency discrimination, for instance, and is in fact prescribed by the number of words in the lexicon rather than by the biophysics of the organ of Corti, or by the number of units in the cochlear nucleus. Of all lexical candidates—English speakers of college age have been benchmarked at recognition vocabularies approximating 100,000 items (Miller, 1951)—the talker must indicate the one that suits the immediate occasion with sufficiently precise articulation.

For the listener, the perceptual problem is reciprocal, that of determining which of the possible words the talker has uttered. In this circumstance, the domains in which the talker and listener find a word are delineated by the language and are often roughly matched. The talker's act and the listener's perceptual reciprocation converge on a method contrasting the intended word from its lexical neighbors, those words of the language that are slightly different in form. The dimensions of difference are not semantic, however. If the semantically similar words for *sheep* are *ewe, ram, lamb, bighorn, merino, romney,* and so on, the lexical neighbors of *sheep* are *sheet, ship, sheaf, seep, she, sea,* and so forth. In this respect, the differentiation of words occurs by virtue of contrasts in phonemic form, contrasts that the language allows; the phonemes constitute a matrix of potential contrasts for distinguishing among lexical items.

The picture of the lexicon considered in this light is complex; neighborhood density appears to be nonuniform and subject to various influences. Initially, the organizing principles of this aspect of language were thought to be simplicity and distinctiveness. Simplicity here means that the sound system tends to use an efficient inventory and to sustain unique and spare correspondence between meaning and form, all other things being equal. Distinctiveness is a crossing principle warranting that, simplicity aside, the relation of sound and meaning maximizes the potential for differentiation in the system. Clearly, simplicity and distinctiveness are opposing principles, and were they equal in strength, or were they the only principles active, we might expect to see a lexicon of uniform contrast and complexity in English, for instance. In such a lexicon, each word would be simple to make and would be optimally distinct from its neighbors.

In fact, the English lexicon is lumpy, with many common words falling into dense neighborhoods of similar words and rarer words inhabiting far sparser regions of the contrast space. Evidently, the lexicon is ordered according to more, or more subtle, principles than simplicity and distinctiveness.

A burst of attention to the perception of spoken words in the past decade has undermined the claim that simplicity is a dominant principle in the organization of the lexicon (see Cutler, 1995, for a review). In a traditional view, each word is composed of a mix of formal attributes, some of which are regular to its lexical class and others of which are irregular or unique. These include the way to make a singular noun plural, the way to form a cluster of consonants at the beginning of a word, and the way vowels differentially occur in open or closed syllables. Applying the principle of simplicity motivates a representation of regular properties by rule rather than by explicit specification and a list of the exceptions to the rule in every other case (Halle, 1985). At the very least, a description of lexical memory derived from these first principles requires the service of a specific perceptual function, and tests of this definition of perception have driven recent studies of word recognition and the organization of lexical memory.

When a talker speaks a familiar word and the listener identifies it, what has the listener done? In a traditional view, the waveform that strikes the ear is subject to an analytical transformation that has as its goal the abstraction of the utterance to a phonemic form. Once suitably pared of the sensory effects of the situation in which it was uttered—the idiosyncratic personal and circumstantial characteristics of the talker who said it, including the vocal tract scale, affective state, rate of speech, distance, and direction from which the talker's waveform propagated—the representation that results is general to all instances of the word and specific to none. At that point, a phoneme string derived perceptually is useful for probing the lexicon for a match, inasmuch as the access code for spoken words requires this abstract phonemic form. In this description, the lexicon is sensitive to linguistic form but deaf to specific utterances.

The counterevidence to this characterization of the lexicon and its perceptual premises is still emerging, but we can at least gauge the adequacy of a traditional conceptualization by considering two crucial phenomena. In one, listeners appeared to be sensitive to the exact acoustic form of a spoken word presented on repeated occurrences, as if the lexical process itself were retaining an impression of an unanalyzed auditory form (cf. Klatt, 1979). For lexical priming to be susceptible to the specific auditory form of test items, instance-specific properties of a spoken word must paradoxically survive the very abstracting functions of perception aimed to eliminate them; moreover, the contact between an unidentified sensory form and the lexical item it expresses must be transacted at a grain of analysis far less abstract than phonemic form.

Perhaps even more troubling for a traditional account than this notion is the proposal that contact between an unidentified sensory trace of a spoken word and an item inscribed in lexical memory is mediated by a representation of spoken words that is completely instance specific and through which lexical access can occur. This has seemed to undermine the notion of simplicity through abstraction, in the instance of Goldinger (1997), who considered the functional characteristics of an exemplar-based model of the lexicon; and in the instance of Church and Schacter (1994), whose description of concurrent activation of declarative and nondeclarative memory offers a unitary system of unrestricted capability.

However, until we see a radical reinterpretation of several decades of psychophysics and information-processing studies of speech, exemplar-based models that are utterly free of abstraction appear untenable. This appraisal does not stem from theoretical inertia, but is justified by long-standing findings that the perception of phonetic attributes occurs concurrently with the perceiver's ignorance of the auditory forms that promote perception. Some of this research is now classic (Pisoni, 1973), and shows that the ephemeral auditory form of a consonant is represented phonetically with an urgency and automaticity that denies the perceiver an opportunity to preserve the raw auditory form of an instance. The limits to the representation of the sensory form of speech sounds are well understood, and the means to evade them are unknown.

In this regard, a related finding (Nygaard, Sommers, & Pisoni, 1995) offers a clue about the fit of perceptual analysis and lexical access codes. This study used words spoken in isolation by a large number of different talkers. After learning to identify some of the talkers by name from speech samples of a single word, listeners took a test of intelligibility in which single words were presented in a noise load. Words in the intelligibility test had been spoken either by talkers whom subjects had learned to identify by listening or by unfamiliar talkers. A differential effect of familiarity on intelligibility was observed, although in this case none of the speech samples that benefited from a listener's familiarity with its speaker was at all familiar. Here, the familiarity of the talker mattered, not the instance-specific characteristics of the sample. Can these processes have a common mechanism?

A study of ours hinted at the potential solution, by determining that a perceptual analysis of a single level of linguistic attribute has the potential to promote the identification of words and talkers alike. In this project, we asked whether linguistic attributes can contribute to the identification and recognition of a familiar talker (Fellowes, Remez, & Rubin, 1997; Remez, Fellowes, & Rubin, 1997). We were confident that our acoustic manipulation, in which the natural acoustic products of vocalization were replaced by time-varying sinusoids, had eliminated the typical acoustic attributes on which individual qualitative identification is said to depend. The timbre of our test items was anomalous, and none of the acoustic correlates of voice pitch was present. Despite the strange nonvocal quality, listeners identified their acquaintances from the transformed test items without training and surely without an opportunity to rely on instance-specific encoding: Listeners were not familiar with the sound of their acquaintances in sine wave form. Although the tradition holds that rather different sensory attributes participate in lexical identification and personal identification, clearly the ability to identify a talker without access to acoustic correlates of voice pitch and quality depended on the phonetic attributes that listeners were able to extract from the sine wave analogs of speech. This encourages a conclusion that the ability to identify unfamiliar instances of words spoken by familiar talkers noted by Nygaard et al. (1995) can be explained if familiarization with a talker incorporates knowledge of a talker's allophonic habits. To know the talker is to expect a specific set of allophonic realizations, and if the contact between unidentified spoken words and the lexicon allows phonetic strings as well as phoneme sequences, then this phonetic level of abstraction, sufficient to represent the fine phonetic attributes of a speech sample, may suffice.

In reviewing this literature, Remez et al. (1997) noted the cases in which instance-specific properties included phonetic variants and those that did not and found that conservation of phonetic properties was required to show the benefits of form-based sensitivity in lexical processing. Of course, this line of investigation is still gathering momentum across the field, and we expect to see additional effort applied to determine whether perception serves lexical identification by delivering an unanalyzed auditory form to memory or by adjusting the level of analysis to the degree of abstraction required by the task.

Conclusion

This chapter has aimed to survey several contemporary views of speech perception, in the motivation and justification that each presumes and not simply in the methods and technical models that each proposes. We know a great deal about the physics and physiology of speech production and perception, although a unified account incorporating the creation and detection of linguistic contrast remains to be formed. By noting the limitations of a distributional analysis of reified phonetic and lexical entities— and of the manifestations of the speech mode of perception itself—we sought to elaborate the problem facing the theorist of language. Because the elements of language are articulated, radiated, and transduced, our crucial debates have tended to settle into predictable discussions of the relations among these phases of phonemes. However, utterances are also intended as representations, and the approach recommended here is to view the perceiver in complementary fashion, as a listener rather than simply as a sensory system feeding auditory states to a powerful actuarial faculty for encoding and tallying. In this view, the listener attempts to determine which of the potential linguistically governed contrasts is represented by the talker at any instant. Research on this question will determine whether this notion of representation contributes to the explanatory adequacy of new models.

ACKNOWLEDGMENTS

The author gratefully acknowledges the generosity of Carol Fowler and Philip Rubin, who corrected mistakes of fact and argument in an earlier version of this chapter. Errors of fact and argument evident in the present version have been introduced since their scrutiny occurred, and their consent should not be inferred.

The patience, support, and goodness of the editors, for which the author is thankful, was essential in the execution of this chapter.

This research was supported by a grant from the National Institute on Deafness and Other Communication Disorders (DC00308).

REFERENCES

Bregman, A. S. (1992). *Auditory scene analysis.* Cambridge, MA: MIT Press.

Church, B. A., & Schacter, D. L. (1994). Perceptual specificity of auditory priming: Implicit memory for voice intonation and fundamental frequency. *Journal of Experimental Psychology: Learning, Memory, and Cognition, 20,* 521–533.

Cooke, M. P. (1991). *Modeling auditory processing and organization.* Unpublished doctoral dissertation, University of Sheffield, England.

Crystal, T. H., & House, A. S. (1988). Segmental durations in connected speech signals: Current results. *Journal of the Acoustical Society of America, 83,* 1553–1573.

Cutler, A. (1995). Spoken word recognition and production. In J. L. Miller & P. D. Eimas (Eds.), *Speech, language, and communication* (pp. 97–136). San Diego, CA: Academic Press.

Dell, G. S. (1995). Speaking and misspeaking. In L. R. Gleitman & M. Liberman (Eds.), *Language: An invitation to cognitive science* (Vol. 1, 2nd ed., pp. 183–208). Cambridge, MA: MIT Press.

Diehl, R. L., Kluender, K. R., Walsh, M. A., & Parker, E. M. (1991). Auditory enhancement in speech perception and phonology. In R. R. Hoffman & D. S. Palermo (Eds.), *Cognition and the symbolic processes: Applied and ecological perspectives* (pp. 59–76). Hillsdale, NJ: Lawrence Erlbaum Associates.

Ellis, D. P. W. (1996). *Prediction-driven computational auditory scene analysis.* Unpublished doctoral dissertation, Massachusetts Institute of Technology, Cambridge. (Self-published via http://sound.media.mit.edu/~dpwe/pdcasa/)

Fellowes, J. M., Remez, R. E., & Rubin, P. E. (1997). Perceiving the sex and identity of a talker without natural vocal timbre. *Perception & Psychophysics, 59,* 839–849.

Fowler, C. A., & Brown, J. (in press). Perceptual parsing of acoustic consequences of velum lowering. *Perception & Psychophysics.*

Fowler, C. A., & Smith, M. R. (1986). Speech perception as "vector analysis": An approach to the problems of invariance and segmentation. In J. S. Perkell & D. H. Klatt (Eds.), *Invariance and variability in speech processes* (pp. 123–139). Hillsdale, NJ: Lawrence Erlbaum Associates.

Frazier, L. (1995). Issues of representation in psycholinguistics. In J. L. Miller & P. D. Eimas (Eds.), *Speech, language and communication* (pp. 1–27). San Diego, CA: Academic Press.

Frieda, E., Walley, A., Flege, J. E., & Sloane, C. (1999). Adults' perception of native and nonnative vowels: Implications for the perceptual magnet effect. *Perception & Psychophysics, 61,* 561–577.

Goldinger, S. D. (1997). Words and voices: Episodic traces in spoken word identification and recognition memory. *Journal of Experimental Psychology: Learning, Memory, and Cognition, 22,* 1166–1183.

Greenberg, S. (1988). The ear as a speech analyzer. *Journal of Phonetics, 16,* 139–149.

Halle, M. (1983). On distinctive features and their articulatory implementation. *Natural Language and Linguistic Theory, 1,* 91–105.

Halle, M. (1985). Speculations about the representation of words in memory. In V. A. Fromkin (Ed.), *Phonetic linguistics: Essays in honor of Peter Ladefoged* (pp. 101–114). New York: Academic Press.

Halle, M., Hughes, G. W., & Radley, J.-P. A. (1957). Acoustic properties of stop consonants. *Journal of the Acoustical Society of America, 29,* 107–116.

Harnad, S. (1987). *Categorical perception.* Cambridge: Cambridge University Press.

Hirsh, I. J. (1988). Auditory perception and speech. In R. C. Atkinson, R. J. Herrnstein, G. Lindzey, & R. D. Luce (Eds.), *Stevens' handbook of experimental psychology* (Vol. 1, pp. 377–408). New York: Wiley-Interscience.

Hockett, C. (1955). *A manual of phonology.* Bloomington: Indiana University Publications in Anthropology and Linguistics, 11.

Jakobson, R., & Halle, M. (1956). *Fundamentals of language.* The Hague, Netherlands: Mouton.

Jakobson, R., & Waugh, L. (1979). *The sound shape of language.* Bloomington: Indiana University Press.

Kingston, J. (1992). The phonetics and phonology of perceptually motivated articulatory covariation. *Language and Speech, 35,* 99–113.

Klatt, D. H. (1979). Speech perception: A model of acoustic-phonetic analysis and lexical access. *Journal of Phonetics, 7,* 279–312.

Klatt, D. H. (1989). Review of selected models of speech perception. In W. D. Marslen-Wilson (Ed.), *Lexical representation and process* (pp. 169–226). Cambridge, MA: MIT Press.

Kuhl, P. K. (1991). Human adults and human infants show a "perceptual magnet effect" for the prototypes of speech categories, monkeys do not. *Perception & Psychophysics, 50,* 93–107.

Kuhl, P. K., Andruski, J. E., Chistovich, I. A., Chistovich, L. A., Kozhevnikova, E. V., Ryskina, V. L., Stolyarova, E. I., Sundberg, U., & Lacerda, F. (1997). Cross-language analysis of phonetic units in language addressed to infants. *Science, 277,* 684–686.

Ladefoged, P. (1980). What are linguistic sounds made of? *Language, 56,* 485–502.

Lashley, K. S. (1951). The problem of serial order in behavior. In L. A. Jeffress (Ed.), *Cerebral mechanisms in behavior* (pp. 112–136). New York: Wiley.

Laver, J. (1980). *The phonetic description of voice quality.* Cambridge: Cambridge University Press.

Levelt, W. J. M. (1989). *Speaking.* Cambridge, MA: MIT Press.

Liberman, A. M., Cooper, F. S., Shankweiler, D. H., & Studdert-Kennedy, M. (1967). Perception of the speech code. *Psychological Review, 74,* 431–461.

Liberman, A. M., Harris, K. S., Hoffman, H. S., & Griffith, B. C. (1957). The discrimination of speech sounds within and across phoneme boundaries. *Journal of Experimental Psychology, 54,* 358–368.

Lieberman, P. (1963). Some effects of semantic and grammatical context on the production and perception of speech. *Language and Speech, 6,* 172–187.

Lively, S. E., & Pisoni, D. B. (1997). On prototypes and phonetic categories: A critical assessment of the perceptual magnet effect in speech perception. *Journal of Experimental Psychology: Human Perception and Performance, 23,* 1665–1679.

Luce, P. A., Pisoni, D. B., & Goldinger, S. D. (1990). Similarity neighborhoods of spoken words. In G. T. M. Altmann (Ed.), *Cognitive models of speech processing* (pp. 122–147). Cambridge, MA: MIT Press.

Massaro, D. W. (1994). Psychological aspects of speech perception: Implications of research and theory. In M. A. Gernsbacher (Ed.), *Handbook of psycholinguistics* (pp. 219–263). New York: Academic Press.

Mattingly, I. G., Liberman, A. M., Syrdal, A. K., & Halwes, T. G. (1971). Discrimination in speech and nonspeech modes. *Cognitive Psychology, 2,* 131–157.

Miller, G. A. (1951). *Language and communication.* New York: McGraw-Hill.

Nygaard, L. C., Sommers, M. S., & Pisoni, D. B. (1995). Speech perception as a talker-contingent process. *Psychological Science, 5,* 42–46.

Osgood, C. E., May, M. H., & Miron, M. S. (1975). *Cross-cultural universals of affective meaning.* Urbana: University of Illinois Press.

Pisoni, D. B. (1973). Auditory and phonetic memory codes in the discrimination of consonants and vowels. *Perception & Psychophysics, 13*, 253–260.

Posner, M. I., & Keele, S. W. (1970). Retention of abstract ideas. *Journal of Experimental Psychology, 83*, 304–308.

Rauschecker, J. P., Tian, B., & Hauser, M. (1995). Processing of complex sounds in the macaque nonprimary auditory cortex. *Science, 268*, 111–114.

Remez, R. E., Fellowes, J. M., & Rubin, P. E. (1997). Talker identification based on phonetic information. *Journal of Experimental Psychology: Human Perception and Performance, 23*, 651–666.

Remez, R. E., Rubin, P. E., Berns, S. M., Pardo, J. S., & Lang, J. M. (1994). On the perceptual organization of speech. *Psychological Review, 101*, 129–156.

Remez, R. E., Rubin, P. E., Pisoni, D. B., & Carrell T. D. (1981). Speech perception without traditional speech cues. *Science, 212*, 947–950.

Rossing, T. D. (1990). *The science of sound, 2nd edition.* Reading, MA: Addison-Wesley.

Shannon, C. E., & Weaver, W. (1949). *The mathematical theory of communication.* Urbana: University of Illinois Press.

Sullivan, L. H. (1896). The tall office building artistically considered. *Lippincott's Monthly Magazine, 57*(26), 403–409.

von Neumann, J. (1958). *The computer and the brain.* New Haven: Yale University Press.

Wickelgren, W. A. (1969). Context-sensitive coding, associative memory and serial order in (speech) behavior. *Psychological Review, 76*, 1–15.

6

The Dynamics of
Meaning in Memory

Curt Burgess
Kevin Lund
University of California, Riverside

Semantics. The curse of man.

—Maxwell, 1976

[H]ow a word "stands for" a thing or "means" what the speaker intends to say or "communicates" some condition of a thing to a listener has never been satisfactorily established.

—Skinner, 1957

[S]emantic structure of natural languages evidently offers many mysteries.
—Chomsky, 1965

Meaning provides the fundamental bridge between the various language, cognitive, and perceptual components of the language comprehension system. As such, it is important to attempt to model how meaning can be acquired from experience and what is the specific nature of its representational form. In this chapter, we attempt to deal with the particularly difficult problem of how meaning can be specified. In particular, we are interested in the way that meaning can be represented in a computational model of meaning and the process by which these representations are formed. Although a review of previous models of word meaning is outside the scope of this chapter (but see Komatsu, 1992), three psychological models deserve mention because they have in many ways inspired current computational approaches. Collins and Quillian (1969, 1972; see also Collins & Loftus, 1975) developed a hierarchical network model of semantic memory. It is a node and link model where knowledge is represented by both concepts (the nodes) and the relations among concepts (the links). Superordinate and subordinate relations (hence, the hierarchical nature of the model) are represented via the links. The later version of the model, the spreading activation model (Collins & Loftus, 1975), de-emphasized the hierarchical nature of the mental representations in favor of a more general notion of semantic relatedness. The information-retrieval process occurs as a function of spreading activation in the structured network. There has been considerable support for the model; the spreading activation approach to meaning retrieval and representation has been extensively used (see Neely, 1991, for a review). The notions of semantic connectedness, spreading activation, and perceptual thresholds for conceptual retrieval are present in many more contemporary localist connectionist models (Burgess & Lund, 1994; Cottrell, 1988).

Smith, Shoben, and Rips (1974), in their feature comparison model, hypothesized that there were two types of semantic features: defining features that were essential to the meaning of the concept and characteristic features that were usually true of the concept. Processing in this model hinged on whether an overall feature comparison or only a comparison using defining features was required for a semantic decision. The processing characteristics of both the spreading activation model and the feature comparison model have been better described than have their representational characteristics.

A different approach to developing a semantic system was taken by Osgood and his colleagues (Osgood, 1941, 1952, 1971; Osgood, Suci, & Tannenbaum, 1957). Their work is likely the most ambitious attempt to empirically derive a set of semantic features. Osgood pioneered the use of the semantic differential in developing a set of semantic indexes for words. With this procedure, a person rates a word by using a likert scale against a set of bipolar adjective pairs (e.g., *wet-dry, rough-smooth, angular-rounded, active-passive*). For example, the concept *eager* may be rated high on *active* and intermediate on *wet-dry*. The meaning of a word, then, is represented by this semantic profile of ratings on a set of adjectives. The aspect of meaning represented by each adjective pair is a dimension in a high-dimensional semantic space. Distances between words in such a space essentially constitute a similarity metric that can be used to make comparisons among words or sets of words. An advantage of the semantic differential procedure is that all words have coordinates on the same semantic dimensions, and thus comparisons are straightforward. A drawback of the procedure is that it requires considerable overhead on the part of human judges. In one study reported by Osgood et al. (1957), 100 likert-scale judgments were collected for each of the 50 adjective scales for 20 words. Thus, 100,000 human judgments were required for a set of semantic features for these 20 words. Human semantic judgments were used by Rips, Shoben, and Smith (1973), who had people make typicality judgments on a small set of words to generate a two-dimensional semantic representation. Although meaning-based models can be developed by using judgments about word meaning, the effort is extensive for even a small set of words. Both the semantic differential and word association norms (Deese, 1965) share the problem that there is considerable human overhead in acquiring the information. There is, perhaps, a more serious problem at a theoretical level. As Berwick (1989) argued, selecting semantic primitives is a "hazardous game" (p. 95). These different procedures do not begin to deal with issues such as the way that word meaning acquisition occurs, the role of simple associations in learning more general knowledge, a mechanism for linking environmental input to the form of a mental representation, the relation between episodic and semantic representations, and the creation of abstract representations.

REPRESENTING MEANING IN COMPUTATIONAL MODELS

The use of semantic representations in computational models very much corresponds to that in the psychological models just discussed. In this section, three means of representing semantic features that encompass most computational approaches are described.

The spreading activation model of Collins and Loftus (1975) and the feature comparison model of Smith et al. (1974) provide the inspiration for many aspects of contemporary connectionist models. Feature vectors representing meaning can be found in distributed connectionist models (Hinton & Shallice, 1991; McClelland & Kawamoto, 1986; Plaut & Shallice, 1994). In these models, the semantic features are specifically delineated (humanness, shape, volume, etc). The limitation of these connectionist models, however, is that there is usually only an intuitive rationale for the semantic features. For example, McClelland and Kawamoto used a set of distributed representations in their model of thematic role assignment and sentence processing. Words were represented by a set of semantic microfeatures. Nouns had features such as *human, softness, gender,* and *form*. Verbs had more complex features such as *cause* (whether the verb is causal) or *touch* (whether the agent or instrument touches the patient). This model was important in that it demonstrated that distributed semantic representations can account for case–role assignment and can handle lexical ambiguity. Similar approaches to feature designation have been frequently used in the connectionist literature for more basic models of word recognition (Dyer, 1990; Hinton & Shallice, 1991; Plaut & Shallice, 1994).

A more empirically derived set of semantic features was developed by McRae, de Sa, and Seidenberg (1997). McRae et al. had 300 subjects list what they thought were features to 190 words. This procedure resulted in a total of 54,685 responses. In their experiments, they found that these feature representations and the pattern of intercorrelations among them predicted the pattern of behavioral priming results for natural kind and artifact categories. These feature lists were also used as the source for word vectors in a connectionist model of word representation.

Masson (1995) used a different approach in his model of semantic priming. Rather than have vector elements correspond to any actual aspect of meaning, he simply used 80-element word vectors such that related words had more elements that matched than did unrelated words. Thus, his semantic vectors indicated only a degree of similarity between two items, not any particular relation because the vectors are inherently "non-meaningful." The vector representations make no commitment to a particular set of features or theory of meaning, although the vector representations imply a certain degree of relatedness to model cognitive effects.

All three approaches use binary vectors. In some cases, the vector elements correspond to specific featural aspects of word meaning; in other cases, the proportion of similar elements simply dictates the general relatedness of word meaning. All these approaches have certain advantages in developing models of meaning in that they are straightforward to set up and they work well in complex learning models. What is not clear, however, is what features one would select for a more general model of semantic representation (beyond some small set of items) or for concepts that are abstract in nature. A drawback to developing a set of features from human feature list norms is that many human responses are required for each word of interest. This situation is not unlike the semantic differential technique in which the experimenter must choose the semantic dimensions on which words are rated and then gather a large number of human judgments. These approaches do seem to facilitate the development of processing models.

Gallant (1991) attempted to extract semantic information directly from text by using large-scale corpora. He developed a methodology that extracts a distributed set of semantic microfeatures by using the context in which a word is found. However, a drawback to his approach is that the features for the core meanings must be determined by a human judge.

The limitation of all these approaches (although less so with the feature list procedure) is that the nature of the representations does not foster much evolution of representational theory. Given the theoretical and computational importance of developing some principled set of meaning features, it is surprising that so little has been attempted in deriving such a set. The hyperspace analog to memory (HAL) model to be discussed next relies on no explicit human judgments in determining the dimensions that are used to represent a word (other than deciding that the word is the unit) and acquires the representations in an unsupervised fashion. The model learns its representations of meaning from a large corpus of text. The concept acquisition process, referred to as global co-occurrence, is a theory of how simple associations in context are aggregated into conceptual representations. Memory is not a static collection of information—it is a dynamic system sensitive to context. This dynamic relation between environment and representation provides the basis for a system that can essentially organize itself without recourse to some internal agent or "self." The HAL model is a model of representation. As presented in this chapter, HAL models the development of meaning representations, and, as implemented here, it is not a process model.[1] The primary goal of this chapter is to address the critical issues that a dynamic model of memory must confront when providing a representational theory. We argue that the HAL model provides a vehicle that has caused us to rethink many assumptions underlying the nature of meaning representation.

THE HAL MODEL

Words are slippery customers.
                    —Labov, 1972

Developing a plausible methodology for representing the meaning of a word is central to any serious model of memory or language comprehension. We use a large text corpus of approximately 320 million words to initially track lexical co-occurrence in a 10-word moving window. From the co-occurrences, we develop a 140,000-dimensional context space (see Lund & Burgess, 1996, for full implementational details). This high-dimensional context or memory space is the word cooccurrence matrix. We refer to this high-dimensional space as a "context" space because each vector element represents a symbol (usually a word) in the input stream of the text. Each symbol is part of the textual context in the moving window.

---

[1]We discuss later some exceptions to the statement that HAL is not a processing model. We have implemented HAL as a processing model of cerebral asymmetries (Burgess & Lund, 1998) and as a model of concept acquisition (Burgess, Lund, & Kromsky, 1997). Chad Audet is working on one of our newest initiatives: developing a connectionist model that includes HAL context vectors for a meaning component along with phonology and orthography.

Constructing the Memory Matrix

The basic methodology for the simulations reported here is to develop a matrix of word co-occurrence values for the lexical items in the corpus. This matrix is then divided into co-occurrence vectors for each word, which can be subjected to analysis for meaningful content. For any analysis of co-occurrence, one must define a window size. The smallest useable window is a width of one, corresponding to only immediately adjacent words. At the other end of the spectrum, one may count all words in a logical division of the input text as co-occurring equally (see Landauer & Dumais, 1994, 1997; Schvaneveldt, 1990).

In this 10-word window, co-occurrence values are inversely proportional to the number of words separating a specific pair. A word pair separated by a 9-word gap, for instance, gains a co-occurrence strength of 1; the same pair appearing adjacently receives an increment of 10. Cognitive plausibility was a constraint, and a 10-word window with decreasing co-occurrence strength seemed a reasonable way to mimic the span of what might be captured in working memory (Gernsbacher, 1990). The product of this procedure is an N by N matrix, where N is the number of words in the vocabulary being considered. This matrix, as we demonstrate, contains significant amounts of information that can be used to simulate a variety of cognitive phenomena. A sample matrix is shown in Table 6.1. This sample matrix models the status of a matrix using only a 5-word moving window for just one sentence, "The horse raced past the barn fell." An example may facilitate understanding this process. Consider the word *barn*. The word *barn* is the next-to-last word of the sentence and is twice preceded by the word *the*. The row for *barn* encodes preceding information that co-occurs with *barn*. The occurrence of the word *the* just before the word *barn* gets a co-occurrence weight of 5 because there are

TABLE 6.1
Sample Global Co-occurrence Matrix for the Sentence
The horse raced past the barn fell

	Barn	Horse	Past	Raced	The
Barn		2	4	3	6
Fell	5	1	3	2	4
Horse					5
Past		4		5	3
Raced		5			4
The		3	5	4	2

The values in the matrix rows represent co-occurrence values for words preceding the word (row label). Columns represent co-occurrence values for words following the word (column label). Cells containing zeroes were left empty in this table. This example uses a 5-word co-occurrence window.

no intervening items. The first occurrence of *the* in the sentence gets a co-occurrence weight of 1 because there are four intervening words. Adding the 5 and the 1 results in a value of 6 recorded in that cell. This example uses a 5-word moving window; it is important to remember that the actual model uses a 10-word window that moves through the 320 million-word corpus.

Characteristics of the Corpus

The corpus that serves as input for the HAL model is approximately 320 million words of English text gathered from Usenet. All newsgroups (about 3,000) containing English text were included. This source has a number of appealing properties. It was clear that to obtain reliable data across a large vocabulary, a large amount of text was required. Usenet was attractive in that it could indefinitely supply about 20 million words of text per day. In addition, Usenet is conversationally diverse; virtually no subject goes undiscussed, which allows the construction of a broadly based co-occurrence data set. Such a data set is useful when attempting to apply the data to various stimulus sets because there is little chance of encountering a word not in the model's vocabulary. One goal for HAL was to develop its representations from conversational text that was minimally preprocessed, not unlike human concept acquisition. Unlike formal business reports or specialized dictionaries that are frequently used as corpora, Usenet text resembles everyday speech. That the model works with such noisy, conversational input suggests that it can deal robustly with some of the same problems that the human-language comprehender encounters.

Vocabulary

The vocabulary of the HAL model consisted of the 70,000 most frequently occurring symbols in the corpus. About one half of these had entries in the standard Unix dictionary; the remaining items included proper names, slang words, nonword symbols, and misspellings. These items also presumably carry useful information for concept acquisition.

Data Extraction

The co-occurrence tabulation produces a 70,000 by 70,000 matrix. Each row of this vector represents the degree to which each word in the vocabulary preceded the word corresponding to the row; each column represents the co-occurrence values for words following the word corresponding to the column. A full co-occurrence vector for a word consists of both the row and the column for that word. The following experiments use groups of these co-occurrence vectors. These vectors (length 140,000) can be viewed as the coordinates of points in a high-dimensional space, with each word occupying one point. With this representation, differences between two words' co-occurrence vectors can be measured as the distance between the high-dimensional points defined by their vectors (distance is measured in Riverside context units, or RCUs; see Lund & Burgess, 1996).

Vector Properties

As described previously, each element of a vector represents a coordinate for a word or concept in high-dimensional space, and a distance metric applied to these vectors presumably corresponds to context similarity (not just item similarity; this is discussed later). The vectors can also be viewed graphically as can be seen in Fig. 6.1. Sample words (e.g., *dog*, *cat*) are shown with their accompanying 20-element vectors (only 20 of the 140,000 elements are shown for viewing ease). Each vector element has a continuous numeric value (the frequency-normalized value from its matrix cell). A gray scale is used to represent the normalized value, with black corresponding to a zero or minimal value. The word vectors are very sparse; a large proportion of a word's vector elements is zero or close to zero. A word's vector can be seen as a distributed representation (Hinton, McClelland, & Rumelhart, 1986). Each word is represented by a pattern of values distributed over many elements, and any particular vector element can participate in the representation of any word. The representations gracefully degrade as elements are removed; for example, there is only a small difference in performance between a vector with 140,000 elements and one with 1,000 elements. Finally, words representing similar concepts have similar vectors, although this similarity can be subtle at times (see Fig. 6.1). (See Lund & Burgess, 1996, for a full description of the HAL methodology.)

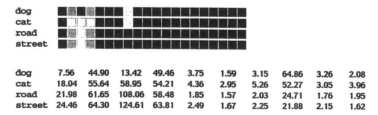

dog	7.56	44.90	13.42	49.46	3.75	1.59	3.15	64.86	3.26	2.08
cat	18.04	55.64	58.95	54.21	4.36	2.95	5.26	52.27	3.05	3.96
road	21.98	61.65	108.06	58.48	1.85	1.57	2.03	24.71	1.76	1.95
street	24.46	64.30	124.61	63.81	2.49	1.67	2.25	21.88	2.15	1.62

FIG. 6.1. Sample 20-element word vectors for four words. Each vector element has a continuous value (the normalized value from its matrix cell) and is gray scaled to represent the normalized value with black corresponding to zero. Below the gray-scaled vectors are the normalized numeric representations for the first 10 vector elements.

The HAL model has been used to investigate a wide range of cognitive phenomena. The goal of this chapter is to address a series of issues that are central to any theory of memory representation, rather than to discuss any particular cognitive phenomenon in detail. As a precursor to that, Fig. 6.2 was prepared to illustrate a variety of categorization effects that the HAL model has been used to investigate. In later sections, the primary literature where more extensive results can be found is referred to, but for now, Fig. 6.2 can serve as a conceptual starting point. The results in Fig. 6.2 are analyses of stimuli from earlier papers using a multidimensional scaling algorithm (MDS), which projects points from a high-dimensional space into a lower dimensional space in a nonlinear fashion. The MDS attempts to preserve the distances between points as much as possible. The lower dimensional projection allows for the visualization of the spatial relations between the global co-occurrence vectors for the items. Fig. 6.2a is an example of how the vector representations carry basic semantic information that provides for the categorization of animals, foods, and geographic locations.[2] In-category semantics can be seen as well. Alcoholic liquids cluster together in the food group; young domestic animals cluster separately from the more common labels (*dog*, *cat*). Distances between items have been used to model a variety of semantic priming experiments (discussed in the next section). The stimuli in Fig. 6.2b illustrate a particular feature of HAL's meaning vectors, namely, that they can be used to model abstract concepts that have been notably problematic for representational theory. Abstract concepts such as weather terms, proper names, and emotional terms all segregate into their own meaning spaces. One advantage of representing meaning with vectors such as these is that, because each vector element is a symbol in the input stream (typically, another word), all words have as their "features" other words. This result translates into the ability to have a vector representation for abstract concepts as easily as one can have a representation for more basic concepts (Burgess & Lund, 1997b). This is important, if not absolutely crucial, when developing a memory model that purports to be general in nature. The other major aspect of categorization that the HAL model can address is the grammatical nature of word meaning. A clear categorization of nouns, prepositions, and verbs can be seen in Fig.

---

[2]Visual inspection of the MDS presentations in this chapter all appear to show a robust separation of the various word groups. However, it is important to determine whether these categorizations are clearly distinguished in the high-dimensional space. Our approach is to use an analysis of variance that compares the intragroup distances to the intergroup distances. This is accomplished by calculating all combinations of item–pair distances in a group and comparing them with all combinations of item–pair distances in the other groups. In all MDS presentations shown in this chapter, these analyses were computed, and all differences discussed were reliable.

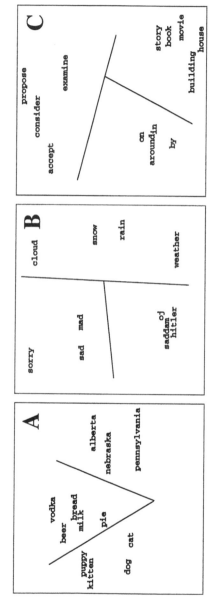

FIG. 6.2. Two-dimensional multidimensional scaling solutions for: (A) common nouns, (B) abstract words, and (C) grammatical categories.

6.2c. The generalizability of the HAL model to capture grammatical meaning as well as more traditional semantic characteristics of words is an important feature of the model (Burgess, 1998; Burgess & Lund, 1997a) and was part of our motivation to refer to the high-dimensional space as a context space rather than a semantic space.

These and other characteristics of word meaning that the model encodes have led us to rethink a number of assumptions about the dynamics of memory and concept acquisition that we address in the following sections. The HAL model offers a clearly defined way to think about what an association is in the learning process and what the relation of basic associations is to higher order word meaning. The grammatical characteristics encoded in the word vectors provoke a reconsideration of syntactic constraints and representational modularity. The global co-occurrence mechanism at the heart of the model provides the vehicle for rethinking what is meant by similarity. We think that HAL offers a more general statement about similarity than do other models. One result of how the global co-occurrence mechanism works has allowed a proposal of the way high-dimensional memory models can address the failure of previous computational models to deal with the symbol-grounding problem. The role of context is central to all these issues that we address. In one section, a comparison is made of the HAL implementation of a context-based model and a recurrent neural network implementation. The similarity of the results of these two very different implementations makes a strong case for the strength of the contextual constraint in language input in forming conceptual representations. We now turn to the evidence for these arguments.

RETHINKING THE NATURE OF ASSOCIATIONS

In the HAL model, an association and semantic or categorical knowledge are clearly defined. These operational definitions can be used to shed light on an ongoing controversy in the priming literature as to what is meant by "semantic" priming and under what conditions it is obtained. Critical to this discussion is a distinction between semantic and associative relations. In most experiments, word association norms are used to derive stimuli. However, word norms confound semantic and associative relations. *Cat* and *dog* are related both categorically (they are similar animals) and associatively (one tends to produce the other in production norms). The typical assumption behind associative relations is that associations are caused by temporal co-occurrence in language (or elsewhere in the environment). Stimuli can be constructed such that these semantic-categorical and associative relations can, for the most part, be orthogonally manipulated. To illustrate, *cat* and *dog* are semantically and associatively

TABLE 6.2
Example Prime–Target Word Pairs from the Semantic, Associated,
and Semantic + Associated Relatedness Conditions

Semantic		Associated		Semantic + Associated	
table	bed	cradle	baby	ale	beer
music	art	mug	beer	uncle	aunt
flea	ant	mold	bread	ball	bat

The full set of these stimuli was taken from Chiarello, Burgess, Richards, & Pollock (1990).

related. However, *music* and *art* are semantically related, but *art* does not show up as an associate to *music* in word norms. Conversely, *bread* tends to be one of the first words produced in norms to the word *mold*, but *bread* and *mold* are not similar. This is not to say there is no relation between *bread* and *mold*; they are just very different items. As the story goes, *mold* and *bread* are likely to co-occur. Examples of these types of word pairs can be seen in Table 6.2.

Semantic and Associative Priming

Our claim is that HAL encodes experience such that it learns concepts more categorically. Associative—more episodic—relations have been aggregated into the conceptual representation. This can be seen by re-examining Table 6.1. The vector representation for *barn* includes the row and column of weighted co-occurrence values for the words that co-occurred with *barn* in the moving window. The representation for *barn*, as it stands in Table 6.1, is episodic. *Barn* has occurred in only this one context. As more language is experienced by HAL, the vector representation for *barn* accrues more contextual experience; as a result, the weighted co-occurrences sum this experience, resulting in a more generalized representation for *barn*. This aspect of HAL is important for attempting to model priming. It follows that the distances in the hyperspace should be sensitive to more generalized, categorical relations. Furthermore, the more associative relations should not have a strong correlation to HAL's distance metric. We tested these hypotheses in two experiments (Lund, Burgess, & Atchley, 1995) using the three different types of word relations illustrated in Table 6.2. These word relations have various combinations of semantic and associative properties—semantic only, associative only, and combined semantic and associative properties. Considerable research shows that human subjects are sensitive to all three of these types of word relations (Lund et al., 1995; Lund, Burgess, & Audet, 1996; see Neely, 1991). We replicated that finding: Subjects made faster lexical decisions to related word trials (in all three conditions) than to the targets in the unrelated pairs (Lund et al., 1995). In a second experiment, we computed the context distance between the related and unrelated trials in all three conditions using HAL. Priming was computed in this experiment by using the distances; there should be shorter distances for the related pairs than for the unrelated pairs in the representational model. In this experiment, we found robust priming for the semantic-only and the semantic-plus-associative conditions. There was no distance priming in the model for the associated-only pairs. This result raises some intriguing questions about the representational nature of words and the ongoing controversy in the priming literature as to what is meant by "semantic" priming and under what conditions it is obtained.

The controversy exists, in part, because of a mixed set of results in the literature, some investigators obtaining semantic priming without association, others not finding semantic-only priming in conditions that seem to limit strategic processing. Fischler's (1977) finding was one of the earliest showing that strength of association did not correlate with priming. Similarly, Chiarello, Burgess, Richards, and Pollock (1990) found semantic-only priming by using a low proportion of related trials and a naming task. However, Lupker (1984) did not find priming for semantically related word pairs that were not also associatively related. Shelton and Martin (1992) found similiar results. They used a single presentation lexical decision task where words were presented one after another with lexical decisions made to each word. Such a procedure masks the obviousness of prime–target relations to a subject. Shelton and Martin did not find semantic priming under these conditions. A comparison of experiments such as these usually entails a comparison of the methodologies. Experiments that do not obtain semantic-only priming typically avoid the lexical decision task, unless it is part of the individual presentation procedure (i.e., Shelton & Martin). The naming task is thought to be less sensitive to strategic effects (which may also limit its sensitivity to semantic relations). Clearly, experimental procedures and task differences play a part in these results. Focusing on task differences, however, may divert attention from important representational issues that are likely just as important. In developing representational theory, it is important not to make representational conclusions based solely on procedural issues.

We have argued that an experiment's sensitivity in reflecting the semantic-only priming effect is guided by the strength of the semantic (contextual) relation (Lund et al., 1995, 1996). One set of stimuli that we have evaluated in detail with the HAL model is the items used by Shelton and Martin (1992). We found that many of their semantic pairs (e.g., *maid-wife, peas-grapes*) were not closely related by using HAL's semantic distance metric. Furthermore, a number of their semantic and associated pairs were very strongly related categorically (e.g., *road-street, girl-boy*; see

Lund et al., 1995). Using HAL, we argued that the semantic-only condition did not produce priming simply because the prime–target pairs in that condition were not sufficiently similar.

Two experiments offer compelling evidence that increased similarity results in priming under task constraints usually associated with a lack of semantic-only priming. Cushman, Burgess, and Maxfield (1993) found priming with the semantic-only word pairs used originally by Chiarello et al. (1990) with patients who had visual neglect as a result of brain damage. What is compelling about this result is that the priming occurred when primes were presented to the impaired visual field. These patients were not unaware that a prime had even been presented, which made it difficult to argue for any strategic effect. A more recent result by McRae and Boisvert (1998) confirmed our earlier hypothesis, generated by our HAL simulation, that Shelton and Martin's (1992) failure to find priming was due to insufficient relatedness in their semantic-only condition. Recall that they used an individual-presentation lexical decision methodology. McRae and Boisvert replicated this methodology but used a set of nonassociatively related word pairs that subjects rated as more similar than Shelton and Martin's items. McRae and Boisvert replicated Shelton and Martin's results with their items, but, using the more similar items, found a robust semantic-only priming effect. Thus, increased attention to the representational nature of the stimuli seems to afford a more complete understanding of the semantic constraints as well as the methodological issues involved in priming.

HAL's distance metric offers a way to evaluate stimuli in a clearly operationalized manner. The roughly 70,000-item lexicon provides the basis for which the stimuli from various experiments can be directly evaluated. In most experiments, word association norms are used to derive stimuli, and it is important to realize that word norms confound semantic and associative relations.

We argue that HAL offers a good account of the initial bottom-up activation of categorical information in memory. It provides a good index of what information can be automatically activated. Although others have argued that associative, not semantic, information facilitates the automatic, bottom-up activation of information (Lupker, 1984; Shelton & Martin, 1992), some of the confusion is a result of not having a clear operational definition of what an association is and how "an association" participates in learning. On one hand, an association is operationally defined as the types of word relations produced when a person free-associates. Yet at a theoretical level this definition is unsatisfying because it divorces the acquisition process from the nature of the representation. It also confounds many types of word relations that can be found by using a word-association procedure.

Word Association Norms

One intuitive concept of word association is that it is related to the degree to which words tend to co-occur in language (Miller, 1969). Spence and Owens (1990) empirically confirmed this long-held belief. To see whether this relation between word association ranking and lexical co-occurrence held for the language corpus that we use for HAL, we used 389 highly associated pairs from the Palermo and Jenkins (1964) norms as the basis for this experiment (Lund et al., 1996). We replicated Spence and Owens' effect; word association ranking was correlated (+ .25) with frequency of co-occurrence (in the moving window). Our correlation was not as strong as theirs probably owing to the fact that we used only the five strongest associates to the cue word. However, using all strongly associated word pairs allowed us to test a further question. To what extent is similarity, at least as operationalized in the HAL model, related to this co-occurrence in language for these highly associated words? We divided these strongly associated pairs into those that were semantic neighbors (associates that occurred in a radius of 50 words in the hyperspace) and those that were non-neighbors (pairs that were farther than 50 words apart). Because all these items are strong associates, one might expect word association ranking to correlate with co-occurrence frequency for both HAL's neighbors and non-neighbors (recall that these two groups of words collectively show a + .25 correlation between ranking and co-occurrence). The results were striking. The correlation using the close neighbors is + .48; the correlation for the non-neighbors is + .05. These results suggest that the popular view that association is reflected by word co-occurrence seems to be true *only* for those items that are similar in the first place.

Word association does not seem to be best represented by any simple notion of temporal contiguity (local co-occurrence). From the perspective of the HAL model, word meaning is best characterized by a concatenation of these local co-occurrences, that is, global co-occurrence—the range of co-occurrences (or the word's history of co-occurrence) found in the word vector. A simple co-occurrence is probably a better indicator of an episodic relation, but a poor indicator for more categorical or semantic knowledge. One way to think about global co-occurrence is that it is the contextual history of the word. The weighted co-occurrences are summed indexes of the contexts in which a word occurred.

Lesioning Word Meaning Vectors

Another way to consider what little effect the local co-occurrence information has on vector similarity is to remove it from the vector and to recompute similarity. Consider, for example, the *cat–dog* example. Somewhere in the vector for *cat* there is the vector element that is the weighted local co-occurrence of *cat* when preceded by *dog* (matrix row) and the weighted co-occurrence of *cat* when followed by *dog* (matrix column). For any word pair, one can remove the vector elements that correspond to the local co-occurrences for those two words. We did this for the prime–target pairs for the stimuli that were used in the semantic priming studies described previously (e.g., Lund et al., 1995, 1996; originally from Chiarello et al., 1990). There were several items that were not in the HAL lexicon, but this left 286 related prime–target pairs. The procedure resulted in two sets of vectors for these related pairs: an original set with all vector elements and another set in which the elements corresponding to the words themselves had been removed. This lesioning of the vector elements that correspond to the words themselves removes the effect of their local co-occurrence. The correlation was then computed for the prime–target distances for these two sets of items. There was virtually no impact of the removal of these vector elements (the correlation was 0.99964). This may not seem so counterintuitive when one considers that removing the local co-occurrence amounts to the removal of only $1/70,000$ of the word's vector elements. What is important is the overall pattern of vector similarity (global co-occurrence), particularly for the rows and columns for which the variance is largest (thus indicating greater contextual exposure).

RETHINKING SYNTACTIC CONSTRAINTS

That a common word representation can carry information that is both semantic and grammatical raises questions about the potential interaction of these kinds of information and subsequent sentence-level comprehension. Burgess and Lund (1997a) addressed this issue by using the semantic constraint offered by a simple noun phrase on the syntactic processing of reduced-relative sentences. English is a language with an SVO (subject-verb-object) bias (Bever, 1970) where the sentential agent is typically in the subject position (e.g., 1a, 1b, 1c). Sentence 1a follows this construction and is simple past tense. Sentence 1b has the same initial three words, *The man paid*, which might lead the parser to construct a past-tense construction. However, when the preposition *by* is encountered, it becomes clear to the comprehension system that the sentence structure is past participle. These reduced-relative past-participle constructions are usually difficult to understand. When the semantics of the initial noun phrase constrain the interpretation, such that the initial noun is not a plausible agent for the verb (as in 1c), reading difficulty can be reduced. Although it makes intuitive sense that semantic plausibility facilitates interpretation, an important question in psycholinguistics has been the speed at which this can take place and the implication of processing on architectural modularity. Various investigators have shown that semantic plausibility plays an immediate role in the interpretation of these constructions so that syntactic reinterpretation is not necessarily required (Burgess & Hollbach, 1988; Burgess & Lund, 1994; Burgess, Tanenhaus, & Hoffman, 1994; MacDonald, 1994; MacDonald, Pearlmutter, & Seidenberg, 1994; Tanenhaus & Carlson, 1989; Trueswell, Tanenhaus, & Garnsey, 1994; Trueswell, Tanenhaus, & Kello, 1993; see MacDonald et al., 1994, for a review). Other investigators, however, have found that this type of semantic constraint does not immediately affect this sentential interpretation and that the reader always initially misinterprets a construction like 1c even with the strong semantic constraint (Ferreira & Clifton, 1986; Frazier, 1978; Rayner, Carlson, & Frazier, 1983).

1a. The man paid the parents.
1b. The man paid by the parents was unreasonable.
1c. The ransom paid by the parents was unreasonable.

Several studies directly compared stimulus sets used by various investigators. Some sets produced results that reflected this initial semantic effect, and other sets did not (Burgess & Lund, 1994; Burgess et al., 1994; Taraban & McClelland, 1988). These studies have found that the strength of the semantic constraint differed in important ways between some of these experiments and that this difference predicts whether the reading difficulty is eliminated.

Burgess and Lund (1997a) pursued this issue of the strength of semantic constraint on syntactic processing by evaluating how well distance in a high-dimensional context space model (HAL) corresponded to the constraint offered by a sentence's initial noun and past-participle verb (e.g., *man-paid* versus *ransom-paid*). They theorized that the context distance between noun–verb pairs would be inversely correlated with reading ease. Burgess and Lund used context distances for stimuli from three different studies that all used these reduced relative past-participle sentence constructions to simulate the results from these three experiments. One study did not find an effect of this noun context on the reading time in the disambiguating region. The other two studies, which they simulated, did find this context effect, suggesting a more constraining relation between the biasing noun and the verb. Burgess and Lund's results showed that HAL's context distances were shorter for the stimuli used in the two studies that did find a context effect than for the study that did not find the context effect. Thus, it appears that HAL's representations can be sensitive to this interaction of semantic and grammatical information and that context distance provides a measure of the memory processing that must accompany sentence comprehension, because HAL's similarity measure is essentially a measure of contextuality, a notion on which we expand later. These results suggest that a high-dimensional memory model such as HAL can encode information that can be relevant beyond the word level. Based on these results, we certainly cannot make any general claims about modeling syntax with high-dimensional meaning spaces. At the same time, however, the distance metric clearly corresponds to constraints between different grammatical classes of words that have specific contextual relations in sentences. Furthermore, Elman (1990) has shown that sentential meaning can be tracked in an attractor network (a 70-dimensional space). His results demonstrated that a network can learn grammatical facts about complex sentences (relative clauses, long-distance dependencies). The relation between what these high-dimensional spaces can represent and their correspondence to higher level syntactic forms remains an exciting and controversial domain.

RETHINKING REPRESENTATIONAL MODULARITY

Whether the syntactic processor can use contextual information to guide its parsing decision has been a controversial issue; the question itself presupposes a parsing mechanism. Recent theories of parsing have been driven by lexical-semantic models of word recognition. The notion of a two-stage parser, where a syntactic structure is built without initial recourse to the available semantics, continues to be a dominant theory in psycholinguistics (Clifton & Ferreira, 1989; Frazier & Clifton, 1996). More recent models of syntactic processing have increasingly relied on the richness of the lexical-semantic system to provide the varied semantic, thematic, and local co-occurrence information required to correctly assign meaning to word order (Burgess & Lund, 1994; MacDonald et al., 1994; Tanenhaus & Carlson, 1989). Basic constraint satisfaction models are free to use a broad range of information and further demonstrate that these different sources of information vary in their relative contribution to the sentence comprehension process. The evidence that supports a constraint-satisfaction approach calls into question any strict notion of modularity of processing. Recent results suggest that the language processor is not modular and that whether modular performance is observed is a function of a variety of constraints that may or may not be available.

A parallel issue exists with respect to modularity of representations. Most theories of language comprehension assume that different forms of representations (e.g., syntactic, grammatical, lexical, and semantic) are linguistically distinct, regardless of their position on processing modularity (Burgess, 1998; Burgess & Hollbach, 1988; Burgess & Lund, 1994;

Frazier, 1978; Frazier & Fodor, 1978; MacDonald et al., 1994; Tanenhaus & Carlson, 1989). Connectionist word recognition models have tended to blur this distinction by consolidating the learning from different representational sources into a single layer of hidden units (Elman, 1990; Seidenberg & McClelland, 1989). HAL's vector acquisition process simply accumulates a word's representation from the word's surrounding context. Each vector element for a particular word corresponds to a symbol (usually another word) in the input stream that was part of the contextual history for that particular word. The word's representation, then, corresponds to the complete contextual learning history that is a function of the word's context, the frequency of co-occurring symbols, and the relative weight in the moving window. Our previous work with semantic priming, word association norms (Lund et al., 1995, 1996), and other grammatical effects (Burgess, Livesay, & Lund, 1998; Burgess & Lund, 1997a; see also Finch & Chater, 1992) suggests that HAL's representations carry a broad range of information that accounts for a variety of cognitive phenomena. This generality of HAL's representations suggests that it is possible to encode many "types" of semantic, grammatical, and possibly syntactic information into a single representation and that all this information is contextually driven.

With the increased reliance on contextual factors and their influence in syntactic processing, the need for a representational theory is vital. We propose that the vector representations that are acquired by the HAL model can provide at least a partial resource. These vector representations are a product of considerable language experience (approximately 320 million words of text in these simulations) that reflects the use of words in a highly diverse set of conversational contexts. The model does not presuppose any primitive or defining semantic features and does not require an experimenter to commit to a particular type or set of features. Rather, the model uses as "features" (i.e., the vector elements) the other words (and symbols) that are used in language. That is, a word is defined by its use in a wide range of contexts.

RETHINKING SIMILARITY

The notion that word meaning and similarity are somehow constrained by the contexts in which they are found is uncontroversial. Many possible relations between context and word meanings were delineated by Miller and Charles (1991). Their strong contextual hypothesis that "two words are semantically similar to the extent that their contextual representations are similar" (p. 8) seems superficially consistent with much of what we have been presenting, and in many ways, it is. However, Miller and

Charles relied heavily on a (commonly held) assumption that we think becomes problematic for a general model of meaning acquisition. It is important for Miller and Charles that similarity is closely attached to grammatical substitutability. Much of HAL's generalizability would be quite limited if the acquisition process somehow hinged on grammatical substitutability. The context in which a word appears in HAL is the 10-word window that records weighted co-occurrences before and after the word in question. However, this local co-occurrence is immediately abstracted into the more global representation. The result is that a word's meaning ultimately has little to do with the words that occur in temporal proximity to it.

The role of context is transparent in the HAL model. Word meanings arise as a function of the contexts in which the words appear. For example, *cat* and *dog* are similar because they occur in similar sentential contexts. They are not similar because they frequently co-occur (locally). This is a departure from traditional views on similarity, which focus on item similarity. The vector-lesioning experiment produced an important insight by simply removing the vector elements that correspond to the locally co-occurring words in a pair of vectors and recomputing their distance in the hyperspace. This manipulation made virtually no difference. Another example that illustrates the lack of effect of local co-occurrence is the relation between *road* and *street* (see Fig. 6.1). These two words are almost synonymous but seldomly locally co-occur. They do, however, occur in the same contexts. This lack of effect from local co-occurrence is also found with Landauer and Dumais' (1997) high-dimensional memory model and seems to be a general feature of this class of model.

As a result of the role of contextual similarity, words may possess elements of items' similarity, but this is due to the role of the context. An advantage of this notion of contextual similarity (rather than the traditional item similarity) is that words that are related in more complex, thematic ways have meaningful distance relations. For example, *cop* and *arrested* are not traditionally "similar" items. However, they are contextually similar, and as a result, the distance between such items reflects the relation between the agent and action aspects of the lexical entities (see Burgess & Lund, 1997a). This interpretation greatly expands the potential role of similarity in memory and language models that incorporate meaning vectors such as these.

A COMPARISON OF DYNAMIC LEARNING MODELS

Although it is argued that HAL is a dynamic concept acquisition model (the matrix representing a momentary slice in time), the prototypical "dynamic learning model" is probably the more established connectionist model. In this section, we compare the output of the global co-occurrence learning algorithm with a simple recurrent network (SRN) when both are given the same input corpus. The motivation for this comparison is that both claim to be models that learn from context. HAL uses a weighted 10-word moving window to capture the context that surrounds a word. The example SRN used for this comparison is that of Elman (1990) in which the context for a target word in a sentence is the recurrent layer that provides an additional set of inputs from the previous word to the hidden units encoding the current word whose representation is being learned. HAL and this SRN also have in common that the words are represented in a distributed fashion and in a high-dimensional meaning space. The mean ing space in HAL is the 140,000 elements defined by the input symbols that are weighted by the global co-occurrence procedure. The meaning space in Elman's SRN is a function of the hidden unit activations.

Elman (1990) used an SRN that was trained to predict upcoming words in a corpus. When the network was trained, hidden unit activation values for each input word were used as word representations. The corpus Elman used was one constructed from a small grammar (16 sentence frames) and lexicon (29 words); the grammar was used to construct a set of two- and three-word sentences resulting in a corpus of around 29,000 words. The corpus was simply a sequence of words without sentence boundary markers or punctuation. This corpus was fed into a neural network consisting of input, hidden, and output layers plus a fourth context layer that echoed the hidden layer (see Fig. 6.3). The network was trained to predict the next word, given the current word and whatever historical information was contained in the context layer. At the end of training, the hidden layer activation values for each word were taken as word representations.

Our approach to replicating this SRN used the global co-occurrence learning algorithm in the HAL model. A co-occurrence matrix was con-

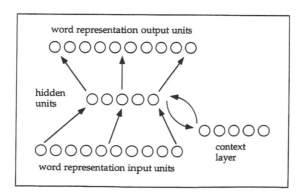

FIG. 6.3. Elman's (1990) simple recurrent neural network architecture.

structed for the Elman (1990) corpus by using a window size of one word. As the context represented in Elman's neural network consisted of only previous items, word vectors were extracted from the co-occurrence matrix by using only matrix rows (representing previous co-occurrence), yielding 29 vectors of 29 elements each. These vectors were normalized to constant length to account for varying word frequency in the corpus.

A gray-scaled representation of the co-occurrence matrix for the 29 lexical items is shown in Fig. 6.4. In this figure, darker cells represent larger co-occurrence values, with rows storing information on preceding co-occurrence and columns following co-occurrence. For example, the matrix shows that the word $glass_{row}$ was often preceded by the words *smash* and *break*; eat_{column} was often followed by all the animates except *lion*, *dragon*, and *monster* (which were presumably the agents involved). A casual examination of this matrix suggests that semantic information has been captured, as words with similar meanings can be seen to have similar vectors. To more closely examine the structure of these vectors, we constructed a hierarchical clustering of HAL's vectors, shown in Fig. 6.5b, alongside the clustering obtained by Elman (1990) in Fig. 6.5a. HAL

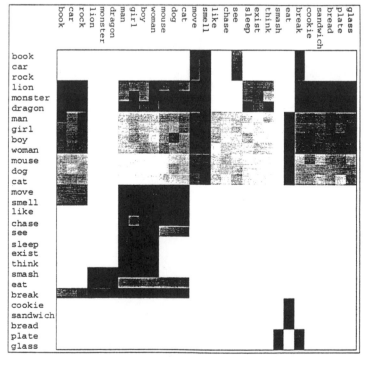

FIG. 6.4. Gray-scaled representation of the global co-occurrence matrix for the 29 lexical items used in Elman (1990).

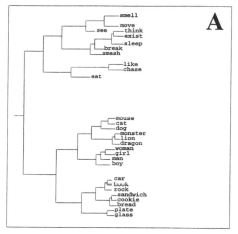
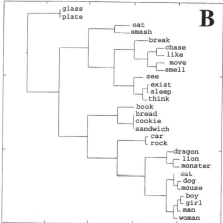

FIG. 6.5. Hierarchical cluster diagrams of (A) Elman's (1990) results with hidden unit activation vectors from a simple recurrent neural network, and (B) results using the global co-occurrence vectors from HAL model trained on Elman's corpus.

performed reasonably in separating animate objects (with subdivisions for people, dangerous animals, and safe animals), edible objects, verbs, and fragile objects. These categorizations are similar to those found by Elman. Although the clustering produced by HAL is not as clean as that of Elman's SRN, it should be noted again that the matrix was formed with a very conservative one-word window, whereas the test sentences were often three words long.

Similar results were produced by two approaches to the generation of semantic structure. Why should such apparently dissimilar approaches yield the same results? The answer is that both techniques capitalize on the similarity of context between semantically and/or grammatically similar words to construct representations of their meanings. Virtually the only thing that the two approaches have in common, in fact, is that both have context information available to them. That they both find the same basic underlying structure in the vocabulary argues strongly that context is a valid and fundamental carrier of information pertaining to word meaning. The SRN appears to be a little more sensitive to grammatical nuances. It also produces more compact representations, as the vectors are shorter than the vocabulary size (one element per hidden unit). However, it has a drawback in that it does not scale well to real-world vocabularies. If tens of thousands of words are to be tracked (not just 29), not only would the network be enormous, but training it would be difficult and time consuming (if not impossible) owing to the sparseness of the representations to be learned. It is important to know that global co-occurrence models yield virtually the same result as the SRN. The equivalence of these two approaches should facilitate the understanding of the general role of context as well as helping to develop hybrid models.

THE SYMBOL-GROUNDING PROBLEM

Glenberg (1997) raised two issues that he claimed are serious problems for most memory models. First is the symbol-grounding problem. The representations in a memory model do not have any extension to the real world. That is, lexical items cannot be understood only with respect to other lexical items. There must also be a grounding of the representation of the lexical item in its physical reality in the environment (cf. Cummins, 1996). A model that represents a concept by a vector of arbitrary binary features or by some set of intuitively reasonable, but contrived semantic features does not have a clear mapping onto the environment that it is supposed to represent. HAL takes a different approach to this problem. In HAL, each vector element is a coordinate for a word in high-dimensional space. What is important to realize about each vector element is that the element *is* a direct extension of the learning environment. A word's vector element represents the weighted (by frequency) value of the relation between the part of the environment represented by that element and the word's meaning. The word's meaning is made up of the complete vector. Symbol grounding is typically not considered a problem for abstract concepts. Abstract representations, if memory models have them, have no grounding in the environment. Again, however, HAL differs in this regard. An advantage to the representational methodology used in HAL is that abstract representations are encoded in the same way as more concrete words. The language environment, the incoming symbol stream that HAL uses as input, is special in this way. Abstract concepts are, in a sense, grounded.

The second problem faced by models that develop "meaningless" internal representations is that the variety of input that a human can experience does not get encoded, and, therefore, the memory representation is inevitably impoverished. With the current implementation of HAL, this problem is certainly a limitation: The learning experience is limited to a corpus of text, which raises an important but currently unanswerable question. Are the limitations in HAL's representations due to the impoverished input, or are higher level symbolic representations required to flesh out a complete memory system as argued by Dietrich and Markman (chap. 1, this volme)? We think that a HAL-like model sensitive to the same co-occurrences in the natural environment as a human-language learner (i.e., a model that is completely symbol grounded, using more than just the language stream) could capitalize on this additional information and could construct more meaningful representations. Any answer to these questions is premature and speculative. That said, however, these issues are important for a general model, and we present what we think are intriguing (although speculative) arguments that high-dimensional memory models can capture some aspects of schemata and decision making.

HIGHER LEVEL COGNITION

We have previously argued that HAL's word vectors generated by the global co-occurrence learning mechanism are best regarded as encoding the information that models the initial bottom-up activation of meaning in memory. Semantic and grammatical structure emerges from what we refer to as global co-occurrence, which is the (weighted) concatenation of thousands of simple, local co-occurrences or associations. However, others have maintained that statistical associations are unlikely to produce sophisticated knowledge structures because they do not encode the richness of the organism's interaction with the environment (Glenberg, 1997; Lakoff, 1987; Perfetti, 1998). Lakoff argued that schemata are a major organizing feature of the cognitive system and that the origin of primary schemata involves the embodiment of basic sensory-motor experience. Glenberg took a similar stance and concluded that complex problem solving is beyond the scope of simple associationist models. Although simple association can be part of some similarity judgments (Bassok & Medin, 1997), Gentner and Markman (1997) maintained that higher level structure is typically involved in making similarity judgments. It is easy to imagine that a model such as HAL is less than adequate for representing higher level cognition. Markman and Dietrich, in this volume, suggested that the adequacy of a cognitive model requires multiple grain sizes. Symbolic representations may not represent the fine grain necessary for context sensitivity. Conversely, distributed representations are limited in how they can manage contextual invariance. In this section, we address how high-dimensional memory models may offer a plausible representational account of schematic representations and some forms of decision making.

Rethinking Schemata

A schema is typically considered a symbolically structured knowledge representation that characterizes general knowledge about a situation (Schank & Abelson, 1977). Schemata can be instantiated in distributed representations as well (Rumelhart, Smolensky, McClelland, & Hinton, 1987). Rumelhart et al. modeled the notion of "rooms" by having a set of microfeatures that corresponded to aspects of various rooms (e.g., television, oven, dresser, etc). Each of these microfeatures can fill a slot in a schema. The primary difference between a symbolic account and a distributed account is that in the distributed account the schema is not a structured representation—a distributed schema is a function of connection strengths.

In HAL, the notion of a schema best corresponds to the context neighborhood. A word in HAL's lexicon can be isolated in the high-dimensional space. Surrounding this word are other words that vary in distance from it. Neighbors are words that are close. Table 6.3 shows the context neighborhoods for three words (*beatles, frightened,* and *prison*). An MDS solution can demonstrate that different sets of words can be plausibly categorized. It remains unclear exactly what the space in an MDS figure represents. The context neighborhood provides more of an insight into the nature of the meaningful information in the hyperspace. A schema is more specifically structured than is a context neighborhood. Both have in common that components of a schema or context neighbors of a word provide a set of constraints for retrieval. The context neighborhoods are sufficiently salient to allow humans to generate the word from which the neighbors were generated or a word closely related to it (Burgess et al., 1998). The neighborhoods provide a connotative definition or schema of sorts, not the denotative definition one finds in a dictionary.

One criticism of spatial models such as HAL is that the words in the meaning space have sense, but no reference (Glenberg, 1997). This is generally true; many models have features that are provided by intuition, hand coded, or are derived from word norms. As a result, there is no actual correspondence between real input in a learning environment and the ultimate representations. Several models, including HAL, differ in this regard (see also Landauer & Dumais' [1997], LSA model; Deerwester, Dumais, Furnas, Landauer, & Harshman, 1990; and Elman's [1990] connectionist approach to word meaning). In other words, they are symbol

TABLE 6.3
Nearest Neighbors for *Beatles, Frightened,* and *Prison*

Beatles	Frightened	Prison
original	scared	custody
band	upset	silence
song	shy	camp
movie	embarrassed	court
album	anxious	jail
songs	worried	public

grounded with respect to the environment that serves as input (a stream of language in these cases). Edelman (1995) has taken a similar approach to constructing representations of the visual environment.

Another criticism of high-dimensional space models is that they do not adequately distinguish between words that are synonyms and words that are antonyms (Markman & Dietrich, in press). This criticism can be illustrated by the neighbors of *good* and *bad*. *Bad's* closest neighbor is *good*. Such examples also highlight the difference between item similarity and context similarity, which is usually seen with adjectives. *Good* and *bad* occur in similar contexts (good and bad are in the eye of the beholder) and tend to be close in meaning space. Spatial models tend to have this problem. Although this is a limitation, it may not be as problematic as suggested by Markman and Dietrich. *Good's* immediate neighbors contain more items related to its core meaning (*nice, great, wonderful, better*) than items related to *bad*. Likewise, *bad's* neighbors share its meaning (*hard, dumb, stupid, cheap, horrible*) more so than *good's* meaning. Despite this limitation, we argue that the neighborhoods offer sufficient constraint to characterize meaning.

Problem Solving

Problem solving and decision making are complex cognitive events, both representationally and from the view of processing. It is premature indeed to suggest that high-dimensional memory models can purport to model the range of representations that must provide the scaffolding for complex problem solving. High-dimensional memory models may, however, be useful in modeling aspects of problem solving that hinge on similarity. For example, Tversky and Kahneman's (1974) approach to decision making about uncertain events relies on representativeness and availability. In HAL, representativeness can be captured by context similarity. Likewise, a frequency metric is likely to predict availability. Tversky's (1977) feature contrast model has been used to model many kinds of similarity judgments. Before Tversky, similarity relations were, for the most part, considered to be symmetric. Tversky has shown that asymmetry is more likely the rule. An example from Tversky illustrates this: North Korea is judged to be more similar to China than China is to North Korea. Featural asymmetry is now acknowledged to be an important component of many models of similarity (Gentner & Markman, 1997; Medin, Goldstone, & Gentner, 1993; Nosofsky, 1991) and of metaphor (Glucksberg & Keysar, 1990).

The metric typically used in the HAL model is the distance metric. For example, *tiger* and *leopard* are 401 RCUs apart in the high-dimensional space. This information is useful; we know that *tiger* and *leopard* are more

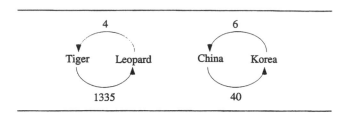

FIG. 6.6. Diagram illustrating the asymmetry in the number of context neighbors separating two word pairs.

contextually similar than *tiger* and *bunny* or *eagle*. However, context distance is symmetrical, and this seems to be an important limitation of HAL. Others have noted that the areas around items in a high-dimensional space can vary in density (Krumhansl, 1978; Nosofsky, 1991). HAL is no different. Tversky (1977) pointed out that *tiger* is a more probable response to *leopard* in a word association task than *leopard* is to *tiger*. Although *tiger* and *leopard* are 401 units apart; their context neighborhoods differ in the items they contain and in their density. In HAL's high-dimensional space, *tiger* is the 4th neighbor to *leopard*, whereas *leopard* is the 1,335th neighbor to *tiger*—an asymmetry in the direction one finds with word norms (see Fig. 6.6). Tversky's Korea–China example shows a similar asymmetry in the number of intervening neighbors (see Fig. 6.6). China is Korea's 6th neighbor in HAL's hyperspace; Korea is China's 40th neighbor. Density in the HAL model can also be an important metric in predicting semantic effects. Buchanan, Burgess, and Lund (1996) found that context density was a better predictor of semantic paralexias with brain-damaged patients than was either context distance or word association norm rankings.

The characteristics of context neighborhoods (density and neighbor asymmetries) seem to be important factors in modeling the representations important to the problem-solving process. This is not to say that distance is not. The ability to use similarity information in sorting is an important ability. Tversky and Gati (1978) had subjects select from a set of three one country that was most similar to a comparison target. They found that the choice frequently hinged on the similarity of the other two possible choices. Before simulating the similarity component among country choices and the implication of similarity in the sorting task, it was important to show that HAL's vector representations could reflect the semantic characteristics of geographic locations. To do this, names of cities, states, and countries were submitted to an MDS procedure (see Fig. 6.7). The figure reflects how the vectors can be used to categorize locations. It is important to note that English-speaking countries seem separated in this space from Asian countries because our analysis of the

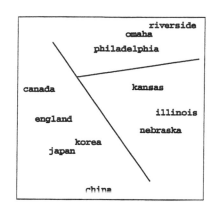

FIG. 6.7. Two-dimensional multi-dimensional scaling solutions for countries, cities, and states.

Tversky and Gati sorting experiment requires that the vector representations for countries reflect semantic distinctions of countries.[3]

In this demonstration, we attempted to show that low-level contextual information can support high-level decision making. In the Tversky and Gati (1978) experiment, subjects were asked to match a country to the most similar of three other countries. One of the three countries varied, with the assumption that changing the third-choice country could affect which of the other two countries was chosen as the closest match to the comparison target. Indeed, the manipulation of the third-choice country tended to cause a reversal in which of the other two choices was chosen as the closest match to the comparison target.

After Tversky and Gati (1978), the assumption was made that subjects were not actually finding the closest match to the target country (if they had been, there would have been no reversal), but that instead they were finding the most similar pair among the choices and then assigning the remaining item as the closest match to the comparison target. This is a rather simplistic model, disregarding the target item, but in theory it can account for the choice reversal found by Tversky and Gati.

To evaluate this theory, context distances were computed for each triplet of choices (Tversky & Gati, 1978, table 4.4). No distances were computed relating to the target item. The two countries that had the smallest context distance between them were considered to form their own match, with the third country then being considered to be matched to the target. For an example of this procedure, see Fig. 6.8. Here it was predicted that, in Set 1, Israel would be matched with England because

---

[3]Proper name semantics have a tradition of being notoriously difficult to model (see Burgess & Conley, in press-a, in press-b). The simulation of the Tversky and Gati (1978) experiment with HAL vector representations is notable in that it represents another successful application of the model to the implementation of proper name semantics.

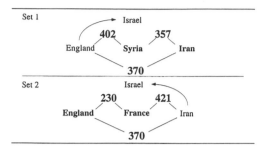

FIG. 6.8. An example of two sets of countries from Tversky and Gati (1978). Context distances (in RCUs) are indicated for all possible pairs of choice words. Word pairs with the shortest distance are in bold.

Syria and Iran tend to form their own grouping. When Syria is replaced by France, in Set 2, the prediction is that France now tends to pair with England, leaving Iran as the best match to Israel. In fact, this reversal was found by Tversky and Gati 61.2% of the time.

This result is well replicated by using HAL distances. In Set 1, Syria and Iran do indeed have the smallest interitem distance (357 RCUs), leading to England's being paired with Israel. In Set 2, England and France are very similar in HAL's hyperspace (230 RCUs), which brings about the same result found in humans: Israel is now paired with Iran. Across all of Tversky's stimuli, the analysis using context distances from the HAL model led to the expected country's being picked 62% of the time, a result similar to the human data.

The contrast model of Tversky and Gati (1978) computes similarity between items as a combination of their common and distinctive features. With humans, the sorting task requires that attention be directed to common features of the choices with the result that these features become more salient. A different choice option redirects attention to other common features and results in the different pairing. HAL is a representational model and, as implemented, does not have a mechanism that corresponds to attention. Consequently, these results suggest that the contextual information available in HAL's vector representations is sufficient for this type of decision making. It should be emphasized that we are not claiming that HAL is a decision-making model. Rather, we feel that a contextual model of meaning can provide sufficiently rich information about concepts such that this information can be useful in higher level decision making.

WHAT ARE HAL's VECTOR REPRESENTATIONS?

> Form and function are one.
> —Wright (1943, p. 146)

The inner workings of many models are rather opaque. Shepard (1988) illustrated this criticism well with connectionist models: "[E]ven if a connectionist system manifests intelligent behavior, it provides no understanding of the mind because its workings remain as inscrutable as those of the mind itself" (p. 52). It is difficult at times to understand the precise representational nature of hidden units or the psychological reality of "cleanup" nodes. Conversely, the HAL model is transparent, and it is also simple. One goal of the HAL project has been to "do much with little," to the extent possible. For some, these features are problematic because they cannot possibly capture the "range of human abilities that center on the representation of non-co-occurring units, especially in language" (Perfetti, 1998, p. 12). Addressing the question of what HAL's vector representations represent involves a number of subtle descriptive and theoretical issues.

What Are HAL's Vector Representations?
A Descriptive Answer

The meaning vector is a concatenation of local co-occurrences in the 10-word window. The first time two words co-occur, there is an episodic trace. An example in Table 6.1 would be a co-occurrence value of 5 for *raced* as preceded by *horse*. This 5 represents a strong episodic relation in the window between *horse* and *raced*; it is a strong relation because the words occur adjacently. As soon as *raced* co-occurs with some other word, this cell in the matrix starts to lose its episodic nature. As experience accrues, the vector elements acquire the contextual history of the words they correspond to. The more a word experiences other words, the richer its context vector. Although a complete vector has the 70,000 row elements and the 70,000 column elements, approximately 100 to 200 of the most variant vector elements provide the bulk of the meaning information. The vector (whether full or a smaller set of features) is referred to as a global co-occurrence vector; local co-occurrence is simply a co-occurrence of one item with another.

What Are HAL's Vector Representations?
A Theoretical Answer

There are probably three ways in which one can coherently consider what these vector representations are. The representations are of words; thus, in a sense they are symbolic. The vectors also have some characteristics of distributed representations. Finally, one can consider the vector representations simply as documentation of the learning history of a word in many contexts and not worry about mediationism and representation. Each of these possibilities is briefly addressed to answer the question "What are HAL's vector representations?"

Vectors as Symbolic Representations

Each element in a vector representation provides one coordinate in the high-dimensional space. The vector provides a set of coordinates or constraints that converge on a symbol (usually a word). In the hyperspace, one can retrieve a word's neighbors, which are usually other words. In addition, each vector element directly corresponds to a symbol in the input stream. Of course, this correspondence is a result of using text as input. Evidence, however, suggests that a process similar to global co-occurrence can deal with the speech segmentation problem at the phonetic level (Cairns, Shillcock, Chater, & Levy, 1997; Christiansen, Allen, & Seidenberg, 1998). One can imagine a global co-occurrence system that operates at two cascaded levels in which the speech segmentation processor can present the meaning processor with its output.

Vectors as Distributed Representations

The meaning of a word is a function of a pattern of values (of the different vector elements). A word is a point in the hyperspace, but this point is the convergence of thousands of flexible constraints. The memory matrix is a slice in time of the history of the system as it encounters language experience. HAL's vectors have several important characteristics of distributed representations. They degrade gracefully. This characteristic is clear in the extreme when one considers that several hundred of the 140,000 vector elements suffice for most purposes. Another characteristic of distributed representations is that they are made up of subconceptual elements. A typical connectionist example is that *dog* and *cat* may have subconceptual features such as <has-legs> and <does-run> (from Hinton & Shallice, 1991). Presumably, these features are some of the perceptual components from which the concept develops. HAL's representations are acquired from the language environment, and the representations take on a more abstract form than does a set of concrete objects. The "subconceptual" features in HAL are not just other symbols, but the weighted co-occurrence value with the other symbol. In a sense, calling word features subconceptual is misleading—it depends on how and where in the nervous system the perceptual apparatus parses the input. What is probably more important at this point in the development of the theory of meaning is the notion that concepts are made up of a large set of co-occurrence elements. These co-occurrence values form the contextual history of a word. Thus, *dog* and *cat* are similar in HAL because they occur in similar contexts, not because they both are furry, small, have four legs, and are pets (although these features constrain their appearance in particular contexts). As a result, the degree to which items locally co-occur is of little relevance in the development of the distributed meaning vector. Recall the experiment in which the locally co-occurring vector elements were lesioned. When similarity was recomputed, the effect was negligible. This result runs counter to many uses of co-occurrence in memory models (Perfetti, 1998). HAL's distributed vector representations are representations of contextual meaning (very much like LSA; Landauer & Dumais, 1997).

The representation of meaning in a high-dimensional space means that there are parallels to earlier high-dimensional models of similarity (Osgood et al., 1957; Shepard, 1988; Smith et al., 1974; Tversky, 1977). An important difference is that HAL is also an acquisition model that relies on context, not human similarity judgments or normative data, for its derivation of meaning.

Vectors as Representations of Learning History

Associationist theory holds at its core the notion of temporal contiguity. In the HAL model, temporal contiguity is closely related to local co-occurrence. Contextual similarity is a function of global co-occurrence, not local co-occurrence. Each vector element is one of many measures of a word's experience in the context of another word. As Deese (1965) pointed out over 30 years ago, the basic principles of association are best viewed in the context of distributions of associations to particular events or stimuli. These higher order associations (or global co-occurrence) reveal the structure in memory and language. Simply incorporating first-order association (temporal contiguity) into a memory model is an invitation to either underestimate the effect of association or to set up a straw-person model. Classical and sometimes instrumental learning principles have found a home in connectionist models and are certain to find a home in high-dimensional memory models that essentially instantiate very high-order association to build semantic and grammatical structure. Viewing meaning vectors as a learning history seems to obviate the need for representations per se. A disadvantage to this view is the discomfort it generates in legions of cognitive scientists. Giving up mediationism forces a theorist into the realm of functionalism. This approach focuses on the relation of the learning environment and the contextual history of the learner. The failure of associationist models to have a more influential role in the last 30 years may hinge more on their reliance on word association methodologies than on their theoretical limitations. Current high-dimensional memory models can simulate the acquisition process by using substantial amounts of experience to model the psychological plausibility of a range of cognitive phenomena. The closer relation among the actual learning environment, context, and vector behavior may reduce the need for a reliance on a host of memory metaphors currently employed in cognitive science. Such a view of HAL's representations is likely to be viewed as radical (Markman & Dietrich, in press) or terribly misguided (Glenberg, 1997). However, Watkins (1990) argued that it is a mistake to try to justify complex models because one is trying to model complex phenomena. Regardless, global co-occurrence offers a principled approach to developing structured representations from real environment.

It may be premature to decide on the ultimate veracity of these views of HAL's representations. These three views all have some relevance to high-dimensional memory models—at a minimum, we hope that these multiple perspectives facilitate further discussion about the nature of high-dimensional representations.

CONCLUSIONS

The notion of similarity can be found in many psychological models of memory and language. In high-dimensional memory models such as HAL (Burgess, 1998; Burgess & Lund, 1997a, 1997b; Lund & Burgess, 1996), LSA (Foltz, 1996; Landauer & Dumais, 1997), or other similar approaches (Bullinaria & Huckle, 1996; Finch & Chater, 1992; Schutze, 1992), the conceptual representations are a product of the contexts in which words are found. The HAL model is distinguished by a number of very simple assumptions about how concepts are acquired. Despite these limitations (or perhaps because of them), the cognitive phenomena that the model has been applied to range from basic word recognition and meaning retrieval (Lund et al., 1995, 1996), semantic dyslexia (Buchanan et al., 1996), grammatical effects (Burgess & Lund, 1997a), to abstract meaning and emotional connotation (Burgess & Lund, 1997b) and sentence and discourse comprehension (Burgess et al., 1998; see also Foltz, 1996; Landauer & Dumais, 1997). Most of the work with the HAL model has focused on the nature of representations rather than on processing issues. The memory matrix is a slice in time of the concept acquisition process. An advantage to this is that representational issues can be explored independently of processing constraints. The drawback, of course, is that one can not evaluate the interaction of the two. There are currently two exceptions to this in the research with the HAL model. The process of acquisition as presented in this chapter affords a look at important issues such as the role of associations in the learning process and the way categorical knowledge is formed from these simpler constructs (Burgess, Lund, & Klomsky, 1997). HAL's representations have been incorporated in a mathematical memory processing model of hemispheric asymmetries (Burgess & Lund, 1998). Furthermore, the results of the global co-occurrence mechanism compare favorably with neural net implementations as presented earlier.

The ability to separate the representational and the processing components in a computational model and to provide a set of real-valued meaning vectors to the process provides the initiative to begin rethinking a host of important issues such as the nature of similarity and representational modularity and the way a computational model can have its representations grounded in its environment. The HAL model is proposed as a model of the initial bottom-up component of meaning activation. Higher level meaning and problem solving may not be beyond the scope of the model as previously thought. Despite the range of problems that the HAL model has been applied to, there are many unanswered and exciting questions. One of the most important is the extent to which global co-occurrence and distributed representations can account for higher level cognition as the model is expanded to encounter a more plausible environment beyond only language input. Clearly, however, HAL's focus on context has been very beneficial and is likely to continue to provide insights into the contextually dynamic form of mental representations and their role in cognitive processing.

ACKNOWLEDGMENTS

This research was supported by a National Science Foundation Presidential Faculty Fellow award SBR-9453406 to Curt Burgess. Catherine Decker, Art Markman, Sonja Lyubomirsky, and two anonymous reviewers provided many helpful comments, and we thank Jeff Elman for providing his corpus. More information about research at the Computational Cognition Lab, a HAL demo, and reprint information can be found at http://HAL.ucr.edu.

REFERENCES

Bassok, M., & Medin, D. L. (1997). Birds of a feather flock together: Similarity judgments with semantically rich stimuli. *Journal of Memory and Language, 36*, 311–336.

Berwick, R. C. (1989). Learning word meanings from examples. In D. L. Waltz (Ed.), *Semantic structures: Advances in natural language processing* (pp. 89–124). Hillsdale, NJ: Lawrence Erlbaum Associates.

Bever, T. G. (1970). The cognitive basis for linguistic structures. In J. R. Hayes (Ed.), *Cognition and the development of language* (pp. 279–362). New York: Wiley.

Buchanan, L., Burgess, C., & Lund, K. (1996). Overcrowding in semantic neighborhoods: Modeling deep dyslexia. *Brain and Cognition, 32*, 111–114.

Bullinaria, J. A., & Huckle, C. C. (1996). *Modelling lexical decision using corpus derived semantic representations in a connectionist network.* Unpublished manuscript.

Burgess, C. (1998). From simple associations to the building blocks of language: Modeling meaning in memory with the HAL model. *Behavior Research Methods, Instruments, and Computers, 30,* 1–11.

Burgess, C., & Conley, P. (in press-a). Developing a semantics of proper names. In *Proceedings of the Cognitive Science Society.* Hillsdale, NJ: Lawrence Erlbaum Associates.

Burgess, C., & Conley, P. (in press-b). Representing proper names and objects in a common semantic space: A computational model. *Brain and Cognition.*

Burgess, C., & Hollbach, S. C. (1988). A computational model of syntactic ambiguity as a lexical process. In *Proceedings of the 10th annual Cognitive Science Society Meeting* (pp. 263–269). Hillsdale, NJ: Lawrence Erlbaum Associates.

Burgess, C., Livesay, K, & Lund, K. (1998). Explorations in context space: Words, sentences, discourse. *Discourse Processes, 25,* 211–257.

Burgess, C., & Lund, K. (1994). Multiple constraints in syntactic ambiguity resolution: A connectionist account of psycholinguistic data. In A. Ram & K. Eiselt (Eds.), *Proceedings of the Sixteenth Annual Conference of the Cognitive Science Society* (pp. 90–95). Hillsdale, NJ: Lawrence Erlbaum Associates.

Burgess, C., & Lund, K. (1997a). Modelling parsing constraints with high-dimensional context space. *Language and Cognitive Processes, 12,* 177–210.

Burgess, C., & Lund, K. (1997b). Representing abstract words and emotional connotation in high-dimensional memory space. In M. G. Shafto & P. Langley (Eds.), *Proceedings of the Nineteenth Annual Conference of the Cognitive Science Society* (pp. 61–66). Hillsdale, NJ: Lawrence Erlbaum Associates.

Burgess, C., & Lund, K. (1998). Modeling cerebral asymmetries of semantic memory using high-dimensional semantic space. In M. Beeman & C. Chiarello (Eds.), *Right hemisphere language comprehension: Perspectives from cognitive neuroscience* (pp. 215—244). Hillsdale, NJ: Lawrence Erlbaum Associates.

Burgess, C., Lund, K., & Kromsky, A. (1997, November). *Examining issues in developmental psycholinguistics with a high-dimensional memory model.* Paper presented at the Psychonomics Society Meeting, Philadelphia, PA.

Burgess, C., Tanenhaus, M. K., & Hoffman, M. (1994). Parafoveal and semantic effects on syntactic ambiguity resolution. In *Proceedings of the Cognitive Science Society* (pp. 96–99). Hillsdale, NJ: Lawrence Erlbaum Associates.

Cairns, P., Shillcock, R., Chater, N., & Levy, J. (1997). Bootstrapping word boundaries: A bottom-up corpus-based approach to speech segmentation. *Cognitive Psychology, 33,* 111–153.

Chiarello, C., Burgess, C., Richards, L., & Pollock, A. (1990). Semantic and associative priming in the cerebral hemispheres: Some words do, some words don't, . . . sometimes, some places. *Brain and Language, 38,* 75–104.

Chomsky, N. (1965). *Aspects of the theory of syntax.* Cambridge, MA: MIT Press.

Christiansen, M. H., Allen, J., & Seidenberg, M. S. (1998). Learning to segment speech using multiple cues: A connectionist model. *Language and Cognitive Processes, 13,* 221–268.

Clifton, C., & Ferreira, F. (1989). Ambiguity in context. *Language and Cognitive Processes, 4,* 77–103.

Collins, A. M., & Loftus, E. F. (1975). A spreading-activation theory of semantic processing. *Psychological Review, 82,* 407–428.

Collins, A. M., & Quillian, M. R. (1969). Retrieval time from semantic memory. *Journal of Verbal Learning and Verbal Behavior, 8,* 240–247.

Collins, A. M., & Quillian, M. R. (1972). How to make a language user. In E. Tulving & W. Donaldson (Eds.), *Organization of memory* (pp. 309–351). New York: Academic Press.

Cottrell, G. W. (1988). A model of lexical access of ambiguous words. In S. L. Small, G. W. Cottrell, & M. K. Tanenhaus (Eds.), *Lexical ambiguity resolution in the comprehension of human language* (pp. 179–194). Los Altos, CA: Morgan Kaufmann.

Cummins, R. (1996). *Representations, targets, and attitudes.* Cambridge, MA: MIT Press.

Cushman, L., Burgess, C., & Maxfield, L. (1993, February). *Semantic priming effects in patients with left neglect.* Paper presented at the International Neuropsychological Society, Galveston, TX.

Deerwester, S., Dumais, S. T., Furnas, G. W., Landauer, T. K., & Harshman, R. (1990). Indexing by latent semantic analysis. *Journal of the American Society for Information Science, 41,* 391–407.

Deese, J. (1965). *The structure of associations in language and thought).* Baltimore: Johns Hopkins University Press.

Dyer, M. G. (1990). Distributed symbol formation and processing in connectionist networks. *Journal of Experimental and Theoretical Artificial Intelligence, 2,* 215–239.

Edelman, S. (1995). Representation of similarity in 3D object discrimination. *Neural Computation, 7,* 407–422.

Elman, J. L. (1990). Finding structure in time. *Cognitive Science, 14,* 179–211.

Ferreira, F., & Clifton, C. (1986). The independence of syntactic processing. *Journal of Memory and Language, 25,* 348–368.

Finch, S., & Chater, N. (1992). Bootstraping syntactic categories by unsupervised learning. In *Proceedings of the Fourteenth annual meeting of the Cognitive Science Society* (pp. 820–825). Hillsdale, NJ: Lawrence Erlbaum Associates.

Fischler, I. (1977). Semantic facilitation without association in a lexical decision task. *Memory and Cognition, 5,* 335–339.

Foltz, P. W. (1996). Latent semantic analysis for text-based research. *Behavior Research Methods, Instruments, and Computers, 28,* 197–202.

Frazier, L. (1978). *On comprehending sentences: Syntactic parsing strategies.* Unpublished doctoral dissertation, University of Connecticut.

Frazier, L., & Clifton, C. (1996). *Construal.* Cambridge, MA: MIT Press.

Frazier, L., & Fodor, J. D. (1978). The sausage machine: A new two-stage parsing model. *Cognition, 6,* 291–325.

Gallant, S. I. (1991). A practical approach for representing context and for performing word sense disambiguation using neural networks. *Neural Computation, 3,* 293–309.

Gentner, D., & Markman, A. B. (1997). The effects of alignability on memory. *Psychological Science, 8,* 363–367.

Gernsbacher, M. A. (1990). *Language comprehension as structure building.* Hillsdale, NJ: Lawrence Erlbaum Associates.

Glenberg, A. M. (1997). What memory is for. *Behavioral and Brain Sciences, 20,* 1–55.

Glucksberg, S., & Keysar, B. (1990). Understanding metaphorical comparisons: Beyond similarity. *Psychological Review, 97,* 3–18.

Hinton, G. E., McClelland, J. L., & Rumelhart, D. E. (1986). Distributed representations. In D. E. Rumelhart, J. L. McClelland, & the PDP Research Group (Eds.), *Parallel distributed processing: Explorations in the microstructure of cognition, Vol. 1: Foundations* (pp. 77–109). Cambridge, MA: MIT Press.

Hinton, G. E., & Shallice, T. (1991). Lesioning an attractor network: Investigations of acquired dyslexia. *Psychological Review, 98,* 74–95.

Komatsu, L. K. (1992). Recent views of conceptual structure. *Psychological Bulletin, 112,* 500–526.

Krumhansl, C. L. (1978). Concerning the applicability of geometric models to similarity data: The interrelationship between similarity and spatial density. *Psychological Review, 85,* 445–463.

Labov, W. (1972). Some principles of linguistic methodology. *Language in Society, 1,* 97–120.

Lakoff, G. (1991). *Women, fire, and dangerous things: What categories reveal about the mind.* Chicago: University of Chicago Press.

Landauer, T. K., & Dumais, S. (1994, November). *Memory model reads encyclopedia, passes vocabulary test.* Paper presented at the Psychonomics Society, St. Louis, MO.

Landauer, T. K., & Dumais, S. T. (1997). A solution to Plato's problem: The latent semantic analysis theory of acquisition, induction and representation of knowledge. *Psychological Bulletin, 104,* 211–240.

Lund, K., & Burgess, C. (1996). Producing high-dimensional semantic spaces from lexical co-occurrence. *Behavior Research Methods, Instrumentation, and Computers, 28,* 203–208.

Lund, K., Burgess, C., & Atchley, R. A. (1995). Semantic and associative priming in high-dimensional semantic space. In J. D. Moore & J. F. Lehman (Eds.), *Proceedings of the Seventeenth Annual Conference of the Cognitive Science Society* (pp. 660–665). Hillsdale, NJ: Lawrence Erlbaum Associates.

Lund, K., Burgess, C., & Audet, C. (1996). Dissociating semantic and associative word relationships using high-dimensional semantic space. In G. W. Cottrell (Ed.), *Proceedings of the Eighteenth Annual Conference of the Cognitive Science Society* (pp. 603–608). Hillsdale, NJ: Lawrence Erlbaum Associates.

Lupker, S. J. (1984). Semantic priming without association: A second look. *Journal of Verbal Learning and Verbal Behavior, 23,* 709–733.

MacDonald, M. C. (1994). Probabilistic constraints and syntactic ambiguity resolution. *Language and Cognitive Processes, 9,* 157–201.

MacDonald, M. C., Pearlmutter, N. J., & Seidenberg, M. S. (1994). The lexical nature of syntactic ambiguity resolution. *Psychological Review, 101,* 676–703.

Masson, M. E. J. (1995). A distributed memory model of semantic priming. *Journal of Experimental Psychology: Learning, Memory, and Cognition, 21,* 3–23.

Maxwell, A. (1976). *The Singer enigma.* New York: Popular Library.

McClelland, J. L., & Kawamoto, A. H. (1986). Mechanisms of sentence processing: Assigning roles to constituents. In D. E. Rumelhart, J. L. McClelland, & the PDP Research Group (Eds.), *Parallel distributed processing: Explorations in the microstructure of cognition, Vol. 2: Psychological and biological models* (pp. 272–325). Cambridge, MA: MIT Press.

McRae, K., & Boisvert, S. (1998). Automatic semantic similarity priming. *Journal of Experimental Psychology: Learning, Memory, and Cognition, 24,* 558–572.

McRae, K., de Sa, V., & Seidenberg, M. S. (1996). The role of correlated properties in computing lexical concepts. *Journal of Experimental Psychology: General, 126,* 99–130.

Medin, D. L., Goldstone, R. L., & Gentner, D. (1993). Respects for similarity. *Psychological Review, 100,* 254–278.

Miller, G. (1969). The organization of lexical memory: Are word associations sufficient? In G. A. Talland & N. C. Waugh (Eds.), *The pathology of memory* (pp. 223–237). New York: Academic Press.

Miller, G. A., & Charles, W. G. (1991). Contextual correlates of semantic similarity. *Language and Cognitive Processes, 6,* 1–28.

Neely, J. H. (1991). Semantic priming effects in visual word recognition: A selective review of current findings and theories. In D. Besner & G. W. Humphreys (Eds.), *Basic processes in reading: Visual word recognition* (pp. 264–336). Hillsdale, NJ: Lawrence Erlbaum Associates.

Nosofsky, R. M. (1991). Stimulus bias, asymmetric similarity, and classification. *Cognitive Psychology, 23,* 94–140.

Osgood, C. E. (1941). Ease of individual judgment-processes in relation to polarization of attitudes in the culture. *Journal of Social Psychology, 14,* 403–418.

Osgood, C. E. (1952). The nature and measurement of meaning. *Psychological Bulletin, 49,* 197–237.

Osgood, C. E. (1971). Exploration in semantic space: A personal diary. *Journal of Social Issues, 27,* 5–64.

Osgood, C. E., Suci, G. J., & Tannenbaum, P. H. (1957). *The measurement of meaning*. Urbana: University of Illinois Press.

Palermo, D. S., & Jenkins, J. J. (1964). *Word association norms grade school through college*. Minneapolis: University of Minnesota Press.

Perfetti, C. A. (1998). The limits of co-occurrence: Tools and theories in language research. *Discourse Processes, 25*, 363–377.

Plaut, D. C., & Shallice, T. (1994). *Connectionist modelling in cognitive neuropsychology: A case study*. Hove, England: Lawrence Erlbaum Associates.

Rayner, K., Carlson, M., & Frazier, L. (1983). The interaction of syntax and semantics during sentence processing: Eye movements in the analysis of semantically biased sentences. *Journal of Verbal Learning and Verbal Behavior, 22*, 358–374.

Rips, L. J., Shoben, E. J., & Smith, E. E. (1973). Semantic distance and the verification of semantic relations. *Journal of Verbal Learning and Verbal Behavior, 12*, 1–20.

Rumelhart, D. E., Smolensky, P., McClelland, J. L., & Hinton, G. E. (1987). Schemata and sequential thought processes in PDP models. In D. E. Rumelhart, J. L. McClelland, & the PDP Research Group (Eds.), *Parallel distributed processing: Explorations in the microstructure of cognition, Vol. 2: Psychological and biological models* (pp. 7–57). Cambridge, MA: MIT Press.

Schank, R. C., & Abelson, R. P. (1977). *Scripts, plans, goals and understanding: An inquiry into human knowledge structures*. Hillsdale, NJ: Lawrence Erlbaum Associates.

Schutze, H. (1992). Dimensions of meaning. In *Proceedings of Supercomputing '92* (pp. 787–796). New York: Association for Computing Machinery.

Schvaneveldt, R. W. (Ed.). (1990). *Pathfinder associative networks: Studies in knowledge organizations*. Norwood, NJ: Ablex.

Seidenberg, M. S., & McClelland, J. L. (1989). A distributed, developmental model of word recognition and naming. *Psychological Review, 96*, 523–568.

Shelton, J. R., & Martin, R. C. (1992). How semantic is automatic semantic priming? *Journal of Experimental Psychology: Learning, Memory, and Cognition, 18*, 1191–1210.

Shepard, R. N. (1988). How fully should connectionism be activated? Two sources of excitation and one of inhibition. *Behavioral and Brain Sciences, 11*, 52.

Skinner, B. F. (1957). *Verbal behavior*. New York: Appleton-Century-Crofts.

Smith, E. E., Shoben, E. J., & Rips, L. J. (1974). Structure and process in semantic memory: A featural model for semantic decisions. *Psychological Review, 81*, 214–241.

Spence, D. P., & Owens, K. C. (1990). Lexical co-occurrence and association strength. *Journal of Psycholinguistic Research, 19*, 317–330.

Tanenhaus, M. K., & Carlson, G. N. (1989). Lexical structure and language comprehension. In W. Marslen-Wilson (Ed.), *Lexical representation and process* (pp. 529–561). Cambridge, MA: MIT Press.

Taraban, R., & McClelland, J. (1988). Constituent attachment and thematic role expectations. *Journal of Memory and Language, 27*, 597–632.

Trueswell, J. C., Tanenhaus, M. K., & Garnsey, S. M. (1994). Semantic influences on parsing: Use of thematic role information in syntactic ambiguity resolution. *Journal of Memory and Language, 33*, 285–318.

Trueswell, J. C., Tanenhaus, M. K., & Kello, C. (1993). Verb-specific constraints in sentence processing: Separating effects of lexical preference from garden-paths. *Journal of Experimental Psychology: Learning, Memory, and Cognition, 19*, 528–553.

Tversky, A. (1977). Features of similarity. *Psychological Review, 84*, 327–352.

Tversky, A., & Gati, (1978). Studies of similarity. In E. Rosch & B. B. Lloyd (Eds.), *Cognition and categorization* (pp. 79–98). Hillsdale, NJ: Lawrence Erlbaum Associates.

Tversky, A., & Kahneman, D. (1974). Judgment under uncertainty: Heuristics and biases. *Science, 185*, 1124–1131.

Watkins, M. J. (1990). Mediationism and the obfuscation of memory. *American Psychologist*, 45, 328–335.

Wright, F. L. (1943). *Frank Lloyd Wright: An autobiography*. New York: Duell, Sloan and Pearce.

7

Where View-Based Theories Break Down: The Role of Structure in Human Shape Perception

John E. Hummel
University of California, Los Angeles

In the object recognition community, recent years have seen the growth of a movement based on the idea that visual object recognition is mediated by the activation of template-like *views*. This chapter reviews the evidence and motivation for the view-based account of object representation, describes in detail the nature of this account, and discusses its logical and empirical limitations. I argue that view-based theory is fundamentally and irreparably flawed as an account of human shape perception and object recognition. I then present the most plausible and common objections to my arguments and respond to each. Finally, I relate view-based theories of object recognition to other models based on formally similar types of knowledge representation and conclude with a discussion of why such accounts must necessarily fail as an account of human perception and cognition.

STRUCTURAL DESCRIPTIONS, THE PROBLEM OF VIEWPOINT, AND THE MOTIVATION FOR THE VIEW-BASED ACCOUNT

It is almost traditional to begin writing about object recognition by noting that we can recognize objects in novel viewpoints, even though different views can project radically different images to the retina. One of the most important mysteries of human object recognition is the question of what makes this possible. One influential class of theories—*structural description* theories—holds that this capacity reflects the way our visual systems represent object shape (Biederman, 1987; Hummel & Biederman, 1992; Marr, 1980; Marr & Nishihara, 1978). The general idea is that we decompose an object's image into regions corresponding to volumetric parts (such as *geons*; Biederman, 1987), and then explicitly represent those parts in terms of their relations to one another. For example, a coffee mug might be represented as a curved cylinder (the handle) side-attached to a straight vertical cylinder (the body). The relations are critical: If the curved cylinder is attached to the top of the straight cylinder, then the object is a bucket rather than a mug (Biederman, 1987).

Structural descriptions based on categorical parts and relations—for example, specifying the handle as simply "curved" rather than specifying its exact degree of curvature, and specifying the relation as "side-attached" rather than specifying the metric details of the attachment—permit recognition of novel viewpoints as a natural consequence (Biederman, 1987). Our description of a mug remains the same as the mug is translated across the visual field, moved closer to or farther from the viewer, or rotated in depth (provided the handle does not disappear behind the body and provided the mug does not appear in a view—such as directly end on—that makes it impossible to perceive the shapes of the parts; see Biederman, 1987; Hummel & Biederman, 1992; Marr, 1982). Recognition based on this kind of description is likewise unaffected by these changes in the mug's image. Rotating the image 90 degrees about the line of sight, however, so that the body is horizontal and the handle is on top, changes the description and makes recognition slower, more error prone, or both. Like human object recognition, our categorical structural description is sensitive to rotations about the line of sight, but insensitive to translation, scale, left-right reflection, and some rotations in depth (see Hummel & Biederman, 1992). Categorical structural descriptions are also useful because they permit generalization across members of a class (Biederman, 1987; Marr, 1982): "Curved cylinder side-attached to straight vertical cylinder" describes many different mugs, so that representing mugs in this fashion makes it easy to recognize new ones.

Structural description theories have attracted a great deal of attention, both as accounts of human object recognition and as approaches to object recognition in the machine vision literature. On both scores, they have also been vigorously criticized. As researchers in computer vision have discovered, it is not easy to develop algorithms to generate structural descriptions from object images (but see Dickenson, Pentland, & Rosenfeld, 1992; Hummel & Biederman, 1992; Hummel & Stankiewicz, 1996a; Zerroug, 1994, for substantial progress in this direction). Deriving structural descriptions from images is difficult in part because the resulting descriptions can be exquisitely sensitive to the manner in which the image is segmented into parts: The same image, segmented in different ways, may give rise to very different descriptions (Ullman, 1989). This problem has led many researchers to doubt the plausibility of structural descriptions as an approach to shape representation and object recognition. (However, it is important to point out that, although we have yet to develop machine vision systems that can reliably segment gray-level images into objects and their parts, people have absolutely no difficulty doing so: It is not that segmentation is impossible; we just do not yet fully understand how it is done.)

Behavioral data from experiments with human subjects have also been cited as evidence against structural descriptions in human object recognition. It is common (and mistaken) to assume that structural descriptions are completely object centered and view invariant (see, e.g., Bülthoff, Edelman, & Tarr, 1995; Diwadkar & McNamara, 1997; Schacter, Cooper, & Delaney, 1990). A number of researchers have shown that, under a variety of conditions and with a variety of stimuli, human object recognition is sensitive to rotation in depth (for reviews, see Tarr, 1995; Tarr & Bülthoff, 1995): We are slower to recognize some objects in novel views than in familiar views. Such findings demonstrate that object recognition is not completely viewpoint invariant, at least not in any strong sense.

In response to considerations such as these, some researchers have rejected structural descriptions in favor of the idea that we recognize objects on the basis of stored *views*. The claims of such view-based theorists are often very strong. The claim is not simply that object recognition is sensitive to variations in viewpoint; it is that we recognize objects by matching images to literal templates ("views") stored in memory. A complete list of references is too long to include in this chapter, but some of the more influential and/or explicit versions of this argument appear in Edelman (1998), Edelman and Weinshall (1991), Lawson and Humphreys (1996), Olshausen, Anderson, and Van Essen (1993), Poggio and Edelman (1990), Tarr (1995), Tarr and Bülthoff (1995), Tarr, Bülthoff, Zabinski, and Blanz (1997), Ullman (1989, 1996), and Ullman and Basri (1991).

According to this view-based account, the human object recognition system does not decompose an object's image into parts and specify the parts' inter-relations. Instead, the idea is that we recognize objects *holistically*, matching whole images directly to image-like views stored in memory. (Images are not matched in their "raw" retinal form. Rather, some preprocessing is typically assumed to normalize for illumination, absolute location and size on the retina, etc.; see Edelman & Poggio, 1991.) In most view-based models, the stored views are two dimensional (2D) and highly viewpoint specific. Objects are recognized in novel viewpoints by means of operations (detailed shortly) that bring viewed images into register with stored views.

View-based models have recently gained wide popularity in the object recognition community. Indeed, the view-based approach is arguably the dominant current approach to theorizing about shape perception and object recognition. In addition to the list of influential view-based sources already mentioned, there is a much longer list that, citing these (and other) sources, simply takes view-based theory as a given and proceeds from there (see, e.g., Diwadkar & McNamara, 1997). Part of the appeal of view-based models is their apparent consistency with the effects of depth rotations on human object recognition (see Bülthoff & Edelman, 1992; Tarr & Bülthoff, 1995; but see Biederman & Gerhardstein, 1995). Another, perhaps more important part of their appeal is their simplicity. In contrast to structural description theories, which postulate complex parts-based representations of shape, view-based theories postulate only that we store and match individual views. There is substantial parsimony in this assumption and substantial elegance in the routines that some view-based models use to recognize three-dimensional (3D) objects. However, this same simplicity renders these models inadequate as a general account of human object recognition. Although view matching is remarkably simple, human object recognition is not.

As elaborated in the remainder of this chapter, there is more to object recognition than recognizing objects in novel viewpoints, and most of it demands explanation in terms of structured rather than holistic representations of shape. The properties of human object recognition that I cite as evidence against the view-based approach are not subtle: They are intuitive and completely obvious to anyone with a working visual system. The only thing subtle about them are the reasons that they are fundamentally incompatible with view-based theories. This is not to say that holistic "view-like" representations play no role in human shape perception. There is evidence that face recognition is based on holistic representations (e.g., Cooper & Wojan, in press; Tanaka & Farah, 1993), and my colleagues and I have found evidence for both structural descriptions and view-like representations in common object recognition (specifically, view-like representations seem to mediate the recognition of unattended objects; Stankiewicz, Hummel & Cooper, 1998; see also Hummel & Stankiewicz, 1996a). However, very little of the interesting action in shape perception and common (nonface) object recognition is attributable to such representations.

The arguments I present against the view-based approach are not particularly new (except that they are perhaps a bit more formal than most previous arguments): Similar arguments have been around since 1967 (see Clowes, 1967; see also Palmer, 1978), and probably even earlier; and the old arguments are still right. The view-based approach is thus not only wrong, it is regressive.

ALGORITHMS FOR OBJECT RECOGNITION

To understand the core difference between structural descriptions and views, it is important to step back and consider the problem of object recognition, broadly defined. Object recognition is the process of matching a representation of an object's image to a representation in long-term memory. The properties of any given object recognition algorithm (including the algorithm that the human visual system uses, whatever that turns out to be) are determined jointly by the representations on which it is based and the operations that match those representations to memory. (More broadly, *any* algorithm is defined jointly by its representations and the processes that act on them.) Nonetheless, structural description and view-based theories differ in their emphasis on the role of representation versus process in object recognition. In general, structural descriptions emphasize the role of representation, postulating complex representations and matching those representations to memory on the basis of relatively simple operations (see, e.g., Hummel & Biederman, 1992). According to these theories, object recognition is robust to variations in viewpoint to the extent that the parts and relations on which it is based are robust to variations in viewpoint. By contrast, view-based theories postulate very simple representations (image-like views), and match them to memory by means of relatively complex operations (such as alignment and view interpolation). According to these theories, object recognition is robust to viewpoint to the extent that differing views can be brought into register with one another.

The fact that structural description theories postulate simple operations on "smart" representations whereas view-based theories postulate "smart" operations on simple representations is important because, within limits, simplicity in one domain (representation or process) can be compensated by intelligence in the other. The algorithm as a whole depends on both. This state of affairs can make things difficult for the vision scientist trying to understand human object recognition on the basis of behavioral data: Does our ability to recognize objects in novel views reflect the way we represent shape or the processes we use to match those representations to memory? More to the point for our current discussion, do findings of view sensitivity imply that object recognition is view based? As evidenced by recent debates in the literature (see, e.g., Biederman & Gerhardstein, 1995; Tarr & Bülthoff, 1995), this question can prove very difficult to answer. In fact, the question is worse than difficult. It is impossible, in principle, to decide between view- and structure-based theories based only on patterns of view sensitivity or view invariance in human object recognition.

The reason is that view sensitivity versus view invariance is not the core difference between view- and structure-based algorithms for object recognition. Models based on either approach can be modified to accommodate findings of greater or less view dependence in human object recognition. For example, the view-based model of Ullman (1989) can in principle predict complete view invariance in object recognition (see also Lowe, 1987). This model uses alignment to match 2D images to 3D models in memory. Although matching to memory is view based in the sense of modern view-based models (as elaborated shortly), the object models themselves are 3D and object centered. Similarly, the structural description model of Hummel and Stankiewicz (1998; Stankiewicz & Hummel, 1996) is based on parts and relations that are not strictly categorical (a departure from the [almost strictly categorical] models of Biederman, 1987, and Hummel & Biederman, 1992). This model predicts systematic effects of viewpoint at brief presentations and for unattended objects (see also Hummel & Stankiewicz, 1996a; Stankiewicz, Hummel & Cooper, 1998).[1] Even Biederman's original (1987) theory—which is often misconstrued as predicting complete or nearly complete view invariance—predicts systematic effects of viewpoint in recognition (Biederman & Gerhardstein, 1993, 1995). Thus, the role of viewpoint in object recognition is not the deciding issue in the view- versus structure-based debate. To understand what the deciding issue is, it is necessary to consider the nature of views and structural descriptions in greater detail.

What Is a "View"?

The terms *view* and *view based* encompass a variety of specific theories and computational models. However, all view based models share a common, defining assumption: that objects are represented and matched to memory in terms of their features' *coordinates* in a spatial reference frame (Edelman, in press; Edelman & Weinshall, 1991; Poggio & Edelman, 1990; Ullman, 1989; Ullman & Basri, 1991). The central tenet of the view

---

[1]The Hummel and Stankiewicz (1996a) model is based on a hybrid representation of shape, in which view-like representations are integrated into (i.e., serve among the components of) structural descriptions for recognition. The view-like components of these representations are both more view sensitive than the other components and faster to generate from an object's image. As a result, this model predicts (correctly; see, e.g., Ellis & Allport, 1986; Ellis, Allport, Humphrey, & Collis, 1989) that recognition is more view sensitive early in processing (i.e., immediately after an image is presented for recognition) than it is later in processing. The Hummel and Stankiewicz (1998) model extends the models of Hummel and Biederman (1992) and Hummel and Stankiewicz (1996a) with a more detailed account of how categorical properties are visually represented. In brief, because of noise (in the stimulus and in the processing system), this model requires both attention and processing time to generate a reliable (i.e., low noise) representation of an object's shape. As a result, the model predicts systematic effects of processing time and attention on shape representation.

based approach is that we represent objects in long-term memory as views and that—by means of operations on the coordinates of the features in those views—we bring new views into register with stored views (or, in the case of Ullman, 1989, and Lowe, 1987, into register with stored 3D models). The nature of these operations is the primary focus of most view-based theories, and the coordinate-based nature of a view plays an essential role in these operations.

Formally, a view is a vector of spatial coordinates. For example, in a 2D coordinate space (x, y), a view containing five features is the 10-dimensional vector $[x_1, y_1, x_2, y_2, \ldots x_5, y_5]$. Views have four properties that form the foundation of the view-based account: (a) All feature coordinates are expressed relative to a single reference point (namely, the origin of a coordinate system). (Edelman & Poggio, 1991, described a view-based model that codes each feature in terms of its angle and distance from one other feature. This model uses multiple reference points, but the coordinates are linear [as defined shortly], so that the model is formally equivalent to a single reference point linear coordinate system. The reason for this equivalence is discussed in detail in the Appendix. See also Edelman & Poggio, 1991; Hummel & Stankiewicz, 1996b.) (b) The coordinate system is spatial in the sense that vector elements code coordinates in a spatial reference frame. (Although any vector can be described as a point in a high-dimensional space, a vector is spatial in the sense described here only if the vector elements represent spatial coordinates.) (c) The value of each coordinate (vector element) varies linearly with the location of the corresponding feature in the reference frame: If moving a feature Distance d has Effect c on a given coordinate, then moving it $2d$ has Effect $2c$. (d) Views are *holistic*, in the sense that the various features in a view are not represented independently of their locations (list positions) in the vector. In contrast to a symbolic representation, in which symbols are free to "move around" without changing their meaning, features in a view are defined by their locations in the vector (cf. chap. 9, this volume; Hummel & Holyoak, 1997; Hummel & Stankiewicz, 1996b). For example, consider an object with five features, and assume that Feature A is located at location 1, 1, B at 2, 2, and so forth, up to E at 5, 5. If features are placed into the vector in alphabetical order, then the resulting vector (i.e., view) is [1, 1, 2, 2, 3, 3, 4, 4, 5, 5]. However, if we reverse the placement of A and B in the vector, then the same object is represented by the new vector [2, 2, 1, 1, 3, 3, 4, 4, 5, 5]: In a vector representation, feature identity is inexorably bound to list position. A related point is that, because coordinates are dependent on their list positions in the vector, a given value in one part of the vector bears no relation to that same value in another part of the vector: A 1 in the first position is a different thing entirely from a 1 in the second.

To anyone familiar with the properties of coordinate spaces and vectors, these four properties are so intuitive that they hardly seem to deserve mention. However, these properties are worth considering in detail because they constitute the foundation of the view-based approach to representing shape. These properties are also important because they distinguish view-based models from structural description models: Structural descriptions differ from views on each of these properties (Hummel & Biederman, 1992; Hummel & Stankiewicz, 1996a).

What Is a "Structural Description"?

The alternative to a holistic representation, such as a view, is a structured representation, such as a structural description. In a structured representation, complex entities (such as objects) are represented as collections of simpler elements (such as parts or part attributes) in specific relations (cf. Fodor & Pylyshyn, 1988; chap. 9, this volume). In contrast to a holistic representation, a structured representation codes elements *independently* of one another and of their inter-relations, making it necessary to actively (i.e., dynamically) bind elements to their relations (chap. 9, this volume; Hummel & Biederman, 1992; Hummel & Holyoak, 1997; Hummel & Stankiewicz, 1996a). For example, the simple shapes in Fig. 7.1 might be described by the elements *circle* and *square* and the relations *above ()* and *larger ()*. A structured representation of the shape in Fig. 7.1a would bind *circle* to the agent role of *above ()* and the patient role of *larger ()* and would bind *square* to the patient role of *above ()* and the agent role of *larger ()*, to form the structure *above (circle, square)* and *larger (square, circle)*. The form in Fig. 7.1b would be represented by rebinding the *very same elements* to form *above (square, circle)* and *larger (circle, square)*. The key difference between a holistic representation and a structured one is that the binding of elements to roles is fixed in a holistic representation, whereas a structured representation dynamically binds elements to relational roles; as a result, the elements of a structured representation are independent of their relations, whereas the elements of a holistic representation are not (see chap. 9, this volume).

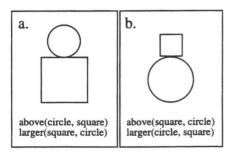

a.
above(circle, square)
larger(square, circle)

b.
above(square, circle)
larger(circle, square)

FIG. 7.1. Two simple shapes along with hypothetical structural descriptions.

Although the previous example used discrete symbols to denote elements and relations, a structural description can also be represented as a collection of vectors (chap. 9, this volume; Hummel & Biederman, 1992; Hummel & Holyoak, 1997; Hummel & Stankiewicz, 1996a, 1998; Shastri & Ajjanagadde, 1993). For example, each vector might code a separate set of bindings, with one vector binding *circle* to *above-agent* and *larger-patient* and another binding *square* to *above-patient* and *larger-agent*. (Note that although this is a vector, it is not a linear coordinate vector.) Augmented with a means for dynamically binding elements to relations (e.g., through synchrony of firing; Hummel & Biederman, 1992), a single vector can be part of a larger compositional structure (e.g., in the way that *circle* is part of *above (circle, square)*). But because relational structures are composed from collections of element–relation bindings (e.g., collections of vectors), no single vector can, by itself, be a complete relational structure (in the way that *circle* is not a complete relational structure). To represent relational structures—that is, explicit relations—a representational system must be able to dynamically bind relational roles to their fillers. "Flat" vector representations lack any means for dynamic binding and therefore cannot explicitly represent relations (cf. chap. 9, this volume). The capacity to bind simple elements into relational structures is the hallmark of a structured, *symbolic* representation (cf. Fodor & Pylyshyn, 1988; Gallistel, 1990; Halford, Bain, Maybery, & Andrews, 1998; chap. 9, this volume) and is the single most important difference between a structural description and a view.[2]

The Strengths of the View-Based Approach

View-based models are primarily concerned with understanding how the coordinates of an object's features (in an image) change as the object is rotated in depth and with exploiting these regularities to recognize objects in unfamiliar viewpoints. By this criterion, view-based models have been very successful. For example, Ullman and Basri (1991) noted that the coordinates of the features in any 2D view of an object can be expressed as a linear combination of their coordinates in a finite number of other views (provided the same features are visible in all views). Their view-based model exploits this fact to recognize objects in novel views. By discovering which linear combination characterizes a given new view,

---

[2]Most modern structural description models also happen to use complex parts as primitive elements of representation, whereas view-based models use simpler features. Although this difference is often cited as the major difference between the approaches, in fact it is incidental: It is just as easy to define a structural description on simple features as on complex parts, and it is perfectly possible to define a holistic view on parts rather than features (see Hummel & Stankiewicz, 1996a).

this model recognizes objects at novel orientations in depth, even though it stores only 2D views in memory. The models of Poggio, Edelman, and their colleagues (Edelman, 1998; Edelman, Cutzu, & Duvdevani-Bar, 1996; Edelman & Poggio, 1991; Edelman, & Weinshall, 1991; Poggio & Edelman, 1990; Poggio & Vetter, 1992) exploit similar relations between the coordinates of features in different views. Like Ullman and Basri's model, these models store only 2D views in memory, but can recognize 3D objects at novel orientations in depth. Because of the way they exploit the properties of linear coordinate vectors, view-based models have met with substantial success, both as accounts of how objects can in principle be recognized in novel viewpoints and as accounts of some effects of viewpoint in human object recognition (Bülthoff & Edelman, 1992; Edelman & Weinshall, 1991; see also Tarr, 1995; Tarr & Pinker, 1989, 1990).

The successes of these (and other) view-based models have made it clear that it is unnecessary to postulate complex structural descriptions to explain how we might recognize objects in unfamiliar viewpoints: Simple template-like representations can explain more than we have traditionally supposed. Some researchers have taken this idea even further and have suggested that it is unnecessary to postulate visual representations, per se, at all. For example, Edelman (1998) stated, "Indeed, the idea of second-order isomorphisms places the responsibility of representation where it belongs—in the world" (p. 18): Effectively, the claim is that visual systems need not bother to represent shape (see also Edelman et al., 1996). Not all view-based theories take such a hard antirepresentationalist line (see, e.g., Tarr, 1995; Tarr et al., 1997), but they all assume that we can explain all the interesting action in object recognition in terms of the way the coordinates of an object's features behave in a holistic linear spatial coordinate system. In making the leap from "view-based models can recognize objects at novel orientations in depth," to "we do not need structural descriptions to understand human object recognition," view-based theorists have thrown the baby out with the bathwater. They have gone from "object recognition is not completely view invariant" to "object representations are unstructured." As I argue in the remainder of this chapter, the representation of shape is decidedly structured, and this fact makes the view-based approach fundamentally and irreparably flawed as an account of human shape perception and object recognition.

LIMITATIONS OF THE VIEW-BASED APPROACH

Biederman and Gerhardstein (1995) discussed many limitations of the view-based approach, and I do not repeat that discussion here. Instead, I focus on the core limitation of the approach, which derives directly from its foundational assumption: that object shape is represented in a linear spatial coordinate system. The mathematics of view matching depend on the mathematics of linear spatial coordinates, so that there is a deep computational reason that views are—and must be—holistic vectors of linear spatial coordinates (see Edelman, 1998; Hummel & Stankiewicz, 1996b).

The independence of elements and relations in a structured representation makes two things possible that are impossible in a holistic representation. First, in a structured representation, it is possible to evaluate (i.e., respond to) entities and their relations independently (Halford et al., 1998). For example, our structured representation of Fig. 7.1 makes it possible to appreciate what Figs. 7.1a and 1b have in common and the ways in which they differ. By contrast, in a holistic representation, the shapes in Figs. 7.1a and 1b are simply different, and the specific ways in which they differ are not recoverable (see Edelman, 1998; Poggio & Edelman, 1990; Tanaka & Farah, 1993). The second property that derives from the independence of elements and relations in a structured representation is the capacity to recombine a finite number of elements and relations into a large (potentially infinite) number of specific structures. It is in this sense that structured representations are symbolic (see Fodor & Pylyshyn, 1988). In a holistic representation, a separate element (e.g., view) is required for each new entity, and recombination is not possible.

The holistic-structured distinction described here maps directly onto the more familiar integral-separable distinction discussed in the categorization literature (see Garner, 1974). Like the elements of a holistic representation, integral dimensions (such as the hue and brightness of a color), are not represented independently of one another and therefore cannot be responded to independently; like the elements of a structured representation, separable dimensions are represented independently and can be responded to independently. According to view-based theory, parts and relations should behave as integral dimensions, but in human shape perception, parts and their relations are decidedly separable. A brief glance at Fig. 7.1 reveals that we have no difficulty appreciating the similarity of the circle in (a) to the circle in (b) (even though the circles are not identical and would therefore activate different views). Similarly, Goldstone, Medin, and Gentner (1991) showed that people evaluate shapes and their relations independently in judging the similarity of different figures, and Saiki and Hummel (1998) showed that shapes and relations are perceptually separable in terms of the "classic" measures of perceptual integrality and separability. Although this point may seem minor, its importance is difficult to overemphasize: According to view-based theory, how we appreciate the similarity of the two circles in Fig. 7.1 is a *complete mystery*. (The question of how a view-based theorist would respond to this fact is addressed in detail later.)

A related point concerns the role of relational structures in similarity judgments. Not only *can* we explicitly evaluate relations for the purposes of computing similarity; in important respects we are *compelled* to. Markman and Gentner (1993) showed that subjects make similarity judgments by aligning structured representations of to-be-compared items. This phenomenon, too, is apparent in Fig. 7.1. Looking at the figure, we not only appreciate that both shapes contain a circle and a square; we also appreciate that the relations in (a) are reversed in (b). That is, on the basis of the parts' shapes, the circle in (a) corresponds to the circle in (b); on the basis of the relations, the circle corresponds to the square. The alternative correspondences are easy for us to appreciate, but they require us to represent the relations between the simple shapes both explicitly and independently of the shapes themselves. As such, they are impossible for a model based on holistic views to appreciate.

The role of relational structures in visual similarity is a fundamental issue with important implications for the question of how we generalize from familiar shapes to new ones. Our ability to generalize over variations in shape lies at the heart of our ability to recognize objects as members of a class and thus to generalize our knowledge about one object to others. The question of how we do this is at least as important as the question of how we recognize familiar objects from novel viewpoints. As a theoretical problem, it is even more difficult. The laws of projective geometry constrain the possible appearances of any single object in different views—a fact that lies at the heart of view-based theory. No such laws, however, constrain the possible shapes of the various members of a class. Consider, for example, the vast array of shapes in the class *chairs* and how the physical constraints on what makes an object a suitable chair differ from the constraints on, say, what makes an object a suitable knife. Although view-based models have met with some success in accounting for our ability to generalize from one object view to other views of that *same* object, they utterly fail to account for our ability to generalize from one shape to another (the claims of Edelman, 1998, notwithstanding).

Visual generalization is closely tied to visual similarity: We usually recognize a novel chair as a chair because it *looks like* a chair. (We can also categorize objects on the basis of more "theory-based" considerations [see, e.g., Rips, 1989], but the present discussion is concerned only with generalization based on visual similarity. As an aside, it is interesting to note that the kinds of knowledge that make theory-based categorization possible—e.g., the fact that an object has a horizontal surface of a size and height suitable for sitting—cannot be explained without appeal to explicit structural descriptions.) A model's predictions about visual similarity thus underlie its predictions about visual generalization. View-based models, as a class, make very general predictions about visual similarity: Two objects appear similar to the extent that they have the same features in the same coordinates (cf. Hummel & Stankiewicz, 1996b); the pairwise relations among their features (e.g., whether one feature is above or below another) do not matter *at all* except inasmuch as they are reflected in the features' coordinates.

Consider the Basis object and its variants (V1 and V2) in Fig. 7.2. Hummel and Stankiewicz (1996b) generated V1 from the Basis object by moving one line (the short vertical) six pixels; V2 was generated by moving that same line and the long horizontal to which it is attached the same direction and distance. In terms of their features' coordinates—that is, according to any view-based model—the Basis object is more similar to V1 (which differs in the location of one line) than to V2 (which differs in the location of two). Hummel and Stankiewicz (1996b) ran the Poggio and Edelman (1990) model on these and several similar figures, and the model does indeed rate the Basis-V1 match higher than the Basis-V2 match. To human observers, the Basis object looks much more like V2 than like V1. This demonstration holds for a wide variety of stimuli over a wide variety of tasks (Hummel & Stankiewicz, 1996b).

Virtually everyone is willing to agree that the Basis object looks more like V2 than V1, but few people are willing to believe that any modern model of object recognition can possibly predict otherwise. The prediction seems absurd. Indeed, it *is* completely absurd, but it is a general, fundamental prediction of all view-based models. The prediction derives directly from the view-based models' use of linear spatial coordinates, so that it holds for *any* view-based model, regardless of whether the model uses 2D or 3D coordinates, Cartesian or polar coordinates, viewer- or object-centered coordinates (Hummel & Stankiewicz, 1996b; see the Appendix for a formal discussion of why this is true). It is also independent of the feature set on which the coordinates are defined. A common objection to the example in Fig. 7.2 is that it is misleading because it is based on the wrong set of features: The difference between the Basis object

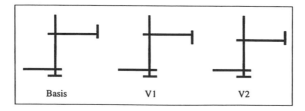

FIG. 7.2. Sample stimuli from the experiments of Hummel and Stankiewicz. V1 was made from the Basis object by moving the short vertical line six pixels down. V2 was made from the basis object by moving that same line and the long horizontal to which it is attached the same direction and distance.

and V2 is a small difference in the location of the T-shaped feature, whereas the difference between the basis object and V1 is that one feature (an upward-pointing T-shape) has been replaced with a qualitatively different feature (a downward-pointing T-shape); a view-based model based on the right set of features (more complex than simple lines) would predict the right similarity relations between the objects.

This objection does not work, however, because for any set of features—no matter how complex—it is always possible to create examples in which moving one feature results in a more detectable change than moving two: It is only necessary to change a categorical relation in the former case but not the latter. Figure 7.3 replicates the demonstration in Figure 7.2 with a series of increasingly complex "features." In each case, V2 looks more like the basis object than V1 does. It would be a simple matter to generalize this demonstration to 3D object-centered coordinates (e.g., by moving parts closer to or farther from the viewer), so it is not simply a function of the 2D viewer-centered coordinates on which the example is nominally based.

The reason the Basis object looks more like V2 than V1 is that we explicitly perceive the categorical spatial relations among the objects' parts. A categorical above-below relation differs in V1 and the Basis object;

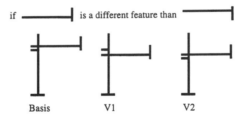

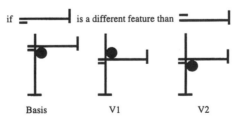

FIG. 7.3. Demonstration that, even with an increasingly complex definition of "features," it is possible to create a more detectable change in a stimulus by moving one feature and crossing a categorical boundary than is created by moving two features the same distance without crossing a categorical boundary.

in V2, twice as many coordinates differ, but no categorical relations differ. The Basis looks more like V2 than V1 because categorical relations—not coordinates—drive visual similarity, generalization, and object recognition (at least for attended objects; see Stankiewicz et al., 1998). As noted previously, explicit relations require non-holistic *structured* representations, that is, structural descriptions (Fodor & Pylyshyn, 1988; Halford et al., in press; Hummel & Biederman, 1992; Marr, 1982).

Because the view-based approach fails to capture the appropriate similarity relations among different objects, it fails to account for our ability to generalize from one object shape to another: To a view-based model, the wrong things look alike. A related limitation is that, although view matching can tell *which* things look alike (as long as we do not expect its intuitions to conform to our own), it cannot tell *why* they look alike. To a holistic representation, things are simply similar or not-so-similar (Edelman, 1998). This property of holistic view matching is evident in our own intuitions about the similarity of different faces (which we represent holistically). We can often say who looks like whom, but without obvious features such as scars or facial hair, it is typically difficult to say why (Tanaka & Farah, 1993). The output of holistic view matching is thus not very useful. To decide whether to sit on an object, it is necessary to know *why* it looks like a chair (i.e., does it have a surface suitable for sitting?), not simply *how much* it looks like a chair. A view-based model can tell you that some new object looks, say, 80% like a chair (i.e., by activating a "chair" view to 80% of its maximum activation); but this statement is as likely to apply to a trash compactor or a wheat thresher as to a footstool, and only one of these objects makes a suitable chair. (An electric chair also looks a lot like a chair, but most of us hope to avoid ever sitting in one.) This failing of the view-based approach is fundamental because it reflects the foundational assumptions of the approach. The same properties that allow view-based models to generalize from one object view to another—namely, the properties of linear spatial coordinate systems—preclude their generalizing in a human-like fashion from one object shape to another. There is no way to modify the view-based approach to overcome this limitation, short of discarding coordinates in favor of explicit relations—that is, discarding views in favor of structural descriptions.

ARGUMENTS IN SUPPORT
OF THE VIEW-BASED APPROACH

I am arguing that view-based theories are hopelessly flawed as a general account of human shape perception and object recognition, so no view-based theorist would take my arguments lying down. In the following, I try to anticipate the most likely objections to my arguments and respond to each.

Objection 1. You have missed the point. View-based theory is not about coordinates; it is about the role of information-rich, viewpoint-dependent features in object recognition. For example, Tarr et al. (1987) emphasized the role of features in views and stated: "View-based theories propose that recognition relies on features tied to the input image or images" (p. 282). This version of view-based theory makes no explicit reference to the role of coordinates in views.

Reply. The problems with this objection begin with the fact that the proposed features, and the operations that match them to memory, are undefined. (All *working* view-based models are of the coordinate-based type; see Hummel & Stankiewicz, 1996b.) As a result, this version of view-based theory, although it does not explicitly endorse the coordinate-based approach to coding an object's features, also does not escape it. Let us grant the view-based theorist any population of features he or she desires and allow him or her to add or delete features from the theory at will. The question still remains: How do these features combine to form representations of whole objects? Unless the features alone somehow uniquely specify object identity (i.e., in the way that a linear combination of global Fourier components uniquely specifies an image), it is necessary to know the features' configuration (i.e., where they are located, either in the image or relative to one another).[3] The view-based theorist must therefore choose some basis for representing the features' configuration. If he or she chooses coordinates, then the theory is subject to the limitations detailed earlier; if he or she chooses explicit relations (the right choice), then he or she has abandoned views in favor of structural descriptions.

Objection 2. The view-based claim is not about features or about coordinates versus relations, but about the nature of the reference frame. Whereas structural description models assume an object-centered reference frame, view-based theories assume "Interobject relations are mentally represented in a viewpoint-dependent manner" (Diwadkar & McNamara, 1997, p. 307).

Reply. This objection is simply factually incorrect. Not all structural descriptions are object centered. In fact, the question of structural descriptions versus views is *unrelated* to the question of object- versus viewer-centered reference frames (Hummel, 1994). The structural description

---

[3]Recognition by simple feature listing is inadequate as a theory of human object recognition (see Hummel & Biederman, 1992). Unless the features serving object recognition are like global Fourier components (which they are not [see, e.g., Tanaka, 1993]), then simply listing an object's features (e.g., "14 horizontal lines, 16 vertical lines") no more specifies its shape than listing colors specifies the appearance of the Mona Lisa.

models of Hummel and Biederman (1992) and Hummel and Stankiewicz (1996a, 1998) are all based on relations defined in a *viewer-centered* reference frame. Following Biederman's (1987) theory, the models' capacity to discount variations in viewpoint derives from their use of categorical part attributes (e.g., straight versus curved major axis) and categorical relations (e.g., above versus below). Based on these (and other) categorical attributes and relations, the models account for both the invariances of human object recognition (e.g., invariance with translation, scale, and left-right reflection) and the sensitivity of human object recognition to rotation in the picture plane (see Hummel & Biederman, 1992).

The models' ability to simulate the effects of picture-plane rotation is especially interesting. When human observers recognize pictures of common objects, response times and error rates increase monotonically as the image is rotated to about 135 degrees and then decrease between 135 and 180 degrees (see, e.g., Jolicoeur, 1985). Although this function is usually interpreted as evidence for "mental rotation" in object recognition, the Hummel and Biederman model simulates it without performing rotations of any kind. Rather, this function simply reflects the way an object's categorical attributes and relations change as its image is rotated in the picture plane. For example, if Part A is above Part B in an upright image, then A is beside B after a 90-degree rotation and below B after a 180-degree rotation. If the model's structural descriptions were based on an object-centered reference frame, as is often incorrectly assumed, then the model would be unable to simulate this aspect of the human data.

Objection 3. The Hummel and Stankiewicz (1996b) experiments falsified models based on the use of literal retinotopic (x, y) coordinates, but we already knew that one cannot explain object recognition by using those kinds of coordinates. Not all view-based models use literal x, y coordinates, so the Hummel and Stankiewicz experiments did not falsify all view-based models.

Reply. In fact, the Hummel and Stankiewicz experiments falsified models based on *any* set of linear coordinates, not just retinotopic (x, y) coordinates. If the coordinates are linear (as they are in all view-based models), then the prediction is the same regardless of the reference frame (as elaborated in the Appendix): Moving two features a given distance always affects similarity more than moving only one of those features that distance (Hummel & Stankiewicz, 1996b).

Objection 4. Your argument, most notably your claim that a view-based model could not appreciate the equivalence of the two circles in Fig. 7.1, attacks a straw man. It is perfectly plausible to postulate a hierarchy of views for any given object. For example, the object in Fig.

7.1a could activate three different views: one for the circle, one for the square, and a third for the entire circle-above-square configuration. Because a "circle" view would be activated by both Figs. 7.1a and 7.1b, the view-based model would appreciate the equivalence of the two circles.

Reply. If the view-based model could ignore the fact that the circles are different sizes, then said model would indeed make the equivalence of the two circles explicit. However, even this model would fail to make explicit either the part–whole relation between the circle and the circle–square configuration or the spatial relation between the circle and the square. To the hierarchy-of-views representation, the "circle" view is a completely different thing from the "circle-above-square" view. In terms of this representation, they have no more in common than the "circle" view has in common with a view of the Eiffel Tower. (This is a consequence of the views' being holistic: By definition, only a compositional representation makes explicit the relations between the parts and the whole; see, e.g., Tanaka & Farah, 1993.) By contrast, the human visual system appreciates not only that both Figs. 7.1a and 7.1b contain circles, but also that the circle in Fig. 7.1a is a subset of the figure as a whole. Making this relation explicit in the view-based model would allow the model to appreciate the same thing, but it would turn the view-based model into a structural description.

A related limitation of the hierarchy-of-views proposal is that it still assumes that each part is represented as an indivisible whole. This assumption also falls short of human perception, because there is good reason to believe that even individual parts (e.g., geons) are themselves composed of properties that can be shared by other parts. We can appreciate that a cylinder has one property in common with a cone (both have round cross sections) and another in common with a brick (both have parallel sides). If "cylinder," "cone," and "brick" were represented as separate holistic views, then we would be unable to appreciate their shared properties. The only thing a view makes explicit (i.e., the only thing it represents) is the coordinates of an object's features. That is, coordinates are the one and only currency for expressing similarity in a view-based representation, but the property *round cross section* cannot even be expressed in the language of feature coordinates. "Round cross section" is an *abstract invariant* that is both more and less than any finite set of feature coordinates (see Hummel & Kellman, 1998). It is more because a new set of coordinates might arise from a new instance of a volume with a round cross section, and it is less because many attributes of those new coordinates have nothing to do with their forming a round cross section. Views are thus inadequate—in principle—to capture the fact that cylinders and cones share the property *round cross section*.

By contrast, the structural description models of Hummel & Biederman (1992) and Hummel and Stankiewicz (1996a, 1998) can and do capture this shared property. These models represent geons, not as "geon views," but as collections of abstract invariants (such as *round cross section* and *nonparallel sides;* see Hummel & Biederman, 1992). Specifically, geons are represented as patterns of activity distributed over units representing geon attributes (abstract invariants) and relations. Geons that share attributes share the units representing those attributes, thereby making explicit what the geons have in common. Units are bound dynamically into geons (and geons are bound to their inter-relations) by synchrony of firing. For example, a cone is represented by firing *round cross section* in synchrony with *nonparallel sides;* a cylinder is represented by firing *round cross section* in synchrony with *parallel sides.* This capacity for dynamic binding makes these models structured and, effectively, symbolic (see chap. 9, this volume).

Objection 5. Your arguments about the similarity relations among the Basis objects and their variants (Figs. 7.2 and 7.3) fail to take into consideration that a view-based model might differentially weight an object's features (e.g., as proposed by Edelman & Poggio, 1991): The greater a feature's weight, the more important that feature's coordinates are for recognition. With the right feature weightings, a view-based model can account for the demonstration in Fig. 7.2 and the findings of Hummel and Stankiewicz (1996b).

Reply. No, it cannot. The only difference between V1 and V2 is the location of the long horizontal line, which is in its original (Basis object) location in V1 but not in V2. Therefore, the only way to make a view-based model rate the Basis-V1 match *lower* than the Basis-V2 match (in accord with the human data) is to assign a *negative* weight to the long horizontal. The negative weight would "penalize" the Basis–V1 match for having the long horizontal in the same location in both objects. As a result, the Basis–V2 match (which would not be penalized, because the long horizontal changes location from Basis to V2) is greater than the Basis–V1 match. (Giving the long horizontal a weight of zero does not do the trick, as it simply causes the Basis–V1 match to equal the Basis–V2 match. To make the Basis–V1 match lower than the Basis–V2 match, the weight on the horizontal *must* be negative.) Although this feature weighting makes the Basis object less similar to V1 than to V2, it also makes the Basis object less similar to *itself* than to a variant in which the long horizontal has moved.

Objection 6. Your arguments (and the experiments of Hummel & Stankiewicz, 1996b) are based on coordinates expressed relative to a single reference point (i.e., the origin of the coordinate system). However,

Edelman and Poggio (1991) showed that their model can also be implemented with multiple reference points, where each feature location is expressed, not relative to the origin of the coordinate system, but relative to the location of some other feature.

Reply. Even this version of the Edelman and Poggio model assumes coordinates that vary linearly with the location of the feature in the reference frame. As detailed in the Appendix, a linear coordinate system with $N > 1$ reference points is formally equivalent to a linear coordinate system based on a single reference point (Hummel & Stankiewicz, 1996b). As a result, the feature-to-feature version of the Edelman and Poggio model makes exactly the same predictions as the coordinate-based version (as noted by Edelman & Poggio).

Objection 7. Ullman (1989, 1996) explicitly acknowledged that a complete view-based theory requires "deformable templates" to recognize nonrigid objects. For example, recognizing an object as a person requires a model to tolerate variations in the location of the arms relative to the body. A view-based model augmented with routines to tolerate such deformations would likely also be able to account for the findings of Hummel and Stankiewicz (1996b) and related findings. The idea of a transformable template is an example of the point you made earlier about an algorithm's being defined by both its representations and the processes that act on them: With the right processes, even simple templates can account for the properties of human object recognition.

Reply. This objection is directly analogous to Objection four, and its limitations are likewise analogous. A model based on deformable templates must know which parts of the template are free to move and in what directions. That is, the model must have knowledge of the parts and their legal relations. For example, the deformable template must know which parts of the template correspond to arms, which parts correspond to the torso, and what kinds of relations between arms and torso are legal. Adding this knowledge to the view-based model turns it into a structural description model. Even if the model knows these legal relations, then as long as the parts are represented as individual subtemplates (rather than as collections of abstract invariants), the deformable template model is still unable to appreciate what different parts have in common (as detailed in the reply to Objection four).

Objection 8. In light of your own work on multiple representations of shape for object recognition—including the Hummel and Stankiewicz (1996a) model, which postulates both holistic (viewlike) and structural representations of shape, and the empirical findings of Stankiewicz et al. (1998), which reports evidence in support of that model—it seems more accurate (and more moderate) to say that views are simply not the *whole* story, rather than claiming that view-based theory is fundamentally and irreparably flawed. Similarly, how can you reconcile your strong claims with the evidence suggesting that face recognition is view based?

Reply. It is important to understand that the holistic representation in the Hummel and Stankiewicz model is not a stand-alone view-based model that is somehow "joined at the hip" to a structural description. Rather, the holistic representation is one *component* of that structural description. The Hummel and Stankiewicz model, like the Hummel and Biederman (1992) model that preceded it, represents structural descriptions as collections of activation vectors over units representing part attributes and spatial relations. In the Hummel and Stankiewicz model, the viewlike representation is just one part attribute (i.e., one component of the vector). It specifies the part's substructure (hence, it is called the substructure matrix or SSM) in terms of the coordinates of the part's categorical features (in a reference frame defined relative to the location and size of the part). The SSM represents the substructure of whatever part happens to be firing at the time[4] and serves to specify the object's hierarchical structure. If the "part" happens to be the whole object—as when all an object's features "accidentally" fire in synchrony (see Hummel & Stankiewicz, 1996a)—then the pattern of activation on the SSM is a holistic representation of the entire object (i.e., a view). This representation is sufficient for recognition provided the object is depicted in a familiar viewpoint. The purpose of the SSM is to permit recognition (in familiar viewpoints) when the dynamic binding of attributes and relations into parts-based sets fails (i.e., when multiple parts fire in synchrony with one another).

The point is that the SSM is neither a stand-alone route to recognition, nor is it intended to account for the findings that have been cited in support of view-based models. (To date, we have yet to even test the model for its ability to account for such findings.) Although the SSM is like a view-based model in the sense that it is coordinate based and holistic, it differs from a view-based model in that it uses a very coarse coordinate system. Extant view-based models require precise specification

---

[4]Recall that the Hummel and Stankiewicz model, like its predecessor JIM, binds part attributes into sets by synchrony of firing. Local interactions in the model's first two layers cause image features (e.g., lines and vertices) to fire in synchrony if they belong to the same part (geon) and out of synchrony if they belong to separate parts. This synchrony is carried forward into the model's intermediate layers and serves to bind part attributes and relations into parts-based sets. Once these interactions have established these parts-based synchrony relations, only one object part tends to fire at any given instant.

of the coordinates of an object's features for their alignment and view interpolation procedures. By contrast, the SSM distinguishes only 17 different locations (the center of the coordinate system, plus the 16 locations defined by eight orientations and two distances from the center). This representation is too coarse to serve as a basis for the alignment and interpolation operations performed by modern view-based models, but it is adequate in its role as one component of a structural description. Similarly, the SSM is not intended as an account of face recognition. The population of categorical features on which it is based and the imprecision with which those features' locations are specified make a very poor basis for the discrimination and recognition of individual faces.

Earlier in this chapter I claimed that very little of the interesting action in shape perception and common (nonface) object recognition is attributable to view-based representations. The SSM accounts for our ability to recognize objects in familiar views both rapidly and without attending to them, but it does little else. Importantly, it accounts for these phenomena only by virtue of the way it is integrated into the model's structural descriptions. The Hummel and Stankiewicz model is a structural description model that postulates a role for holistic representations to cope with the computational "cost" of generating a structural description (namely, the need for dynamic binding and the resultant need for both processing time and visual attention). As such, the model is a hybrid in important respects. But it is a particular kind of hybrid, and the role of its holistic representation is not to align or interpolate object views, but to generate "cost-effective" structural descriptions.

Objection 9. Structural descriptions cannot account for the metric precision of shape perception or the view dependence of object recognition.

Reply. Yes they can. Hummel and Stankiewicz (1998; Stankiewicz & Hummel, 1996) described a structural description model that accounts for both our ability to perceive metric properties (e.g., the degree of nonparallelism of a pair of lines) and the importance of categorical properties in shape perception and object recognition (such as the difference between parallel and nonparallel; see, e.g., Cooper & Biederman, 1993; Hummel & Stankiewicz, 1996b). In addition, this model makes novel predictions about the relations among visual attention, viewpoint sensitivity, and metric precision in shape perception. Structural description models can account for findings of viewpoint dependence in shape perception. Contrary to popular belief, structural descriptions are not strictly object-centered, view-invariant representations (Hummel, 1994; Hummel & Biederman, 1992; Hummel & Stankiewicz, 1998; Marr, 1982).

One (apparent) limitation of the structural description approach is that, as a general approach, it can account for anything: Structural descriptions are symbolic representations, so that as a general paradigm, the structural description approach is Turing complete. That is, for any (computable) pattern of behavioral data, there exists some structural description model that can account for it. The same cannot be said for the view-based approach. View-based models are holistic, and therefore nonsymbolic, so that the view-based approach is not Turing complete. As a general approach, view matching is more falsifiable than the structural description approach, and indeed it has been falsified. The important question is not, "Do structural descriptions mediate human object recognition?" but rather *"What kind* of structural description mediates human object recognition?"

SUMMARY AND CONCLUSIONS

It is currently popular to argue that evidence for view sensitivity in human object recognition indicates that object recognition is view based. In fact, the evidence indicates no such thing. There is some evidence for view sensitivity in human object recognition, but such findings do not imply that object recognition is literally view based. If shape perception and object recognition were really view based, then the world would look very different to us than it does. The core limitations of view-based theory derive directly from its foundational assumption that objects are represented as holistic views based on linear spatial coordinates. This assumption is indispensable to view-based theory because it is central to its account of our ability to recognize objects in novel viewpoints. The problem is that this assumption is deeply flawed. For the purposes of common object recognition and classification, the representation of shape is neither holistic nor based on linear spatial coordinates.

What is missing from the view-based account is any serious theory of representation. View-based theorists are typically open about the fact that they are more concerned with the operations that bring viewed images into register with stored views than with the vagaries of exactly how those views are represented, but this approach is a mistake. By ignoring the question of representation, view-based models answer the question of how we bring images into register with views in memory without asking the previous question of *do* we bring images into register with views in memory? In doing so, they provide some very elegant answers to a nonquestion. If visual representations were unstructured views, then such operations might be necessary, but visual representations are not unstructured views. They are highly structured, and it is impossible to understand object recognition (and other aspects of visual perception and cognition) without understanding *how* they are structured.

View-based theorists are not alone in their assumption that one can understand the mind without also understanding the structure of mental representations. It is currently popular to use recurrent back propagation and its relatives to model everything from hippocampal function (e.g., McClelland, McNaughton, & O'Reilly, 1995), to category learning (e.g., Noelle & Cotrell, 1996), to language (e.g., Elman et al., 1996). These models, like view-based models of object recognition, represent all knowledge holistically, as simple feature vectors. They lack—indeed, explicitly eschew—any basis for binding these vectors into compositional (i.e., symbolic) structures. Also like the view-based models, these models have an impressive list of accomplishments. It is not immediately apparent that they have lost anything by rejecting structured representations, but they have. For example, Marcus (1998) showed that such networks cannot generalize outside their training space. In essence, this means that, regardless of the number of examples on which such a network is trained, there are always some inferences that, although trivial for a person, are impossible for the network (see also chaps. 3 & 9, this volume). Like the limitations of view-based models, the limitations of these models become most apparent when they are required to generalize to new cases.

The reason for this limitation is that such networks cannot bind values to variables (in the same way that view-based models cannot bind elements to relations). As a result, they cannot execute a function in any truly general way (Marcus, 1998; see also chap. 9, this volume). Even the trivial identity function, $f(x) = x$, requires a capacity to represent the variable x and to bind arbitrary values to it. Models without the capacity for binding cannot execute even this trivial function.

Park and Cheng (1997) have shown that even causal reasoning—a task that is most often modeled with simple structure-free models (see Cheng, 1997, for a review)—depends on the capacity to explicitly bind values to variables. Fodor and Pylyshyn (1988) have noted similar fundamental problems stemming from the inability of traditional connectionist networks to represent and manipulate structured knowledge (see also Hummel & Biederman, 1992; Hummel & Holyoak, 1997; Shastri & Ajjanagadde, 1993).

Like human object recognition, human thinking is based on highly structured representations. Neither can be understood in terms of "smart" procedures (such as view interpolation or recurrent back propagation) operating on simple holistic representations.

APPENDIX

A linear coordinate system is a coordinate system in which the mapping from locations in the world (e.g., a retinal image) to values in the coordinate system is linear. In a linear coordinate system, any transformation,

t_i, on coordinates, c^w, in the world (e.g., as a result of moving a feature in an image) has a linear effect on the representation of those coordinates, c^r, in the coordinate system: The greater the effect of the transformation on the world, the greater its effect on a linear coordinate representation of that world. This is true for any linear coordinate system, regardless of the number of reference points on which it is based. The result is that all linear coordinate systems are formally equivalent in the sense that they generate the same ordinal similarity relations: If coordinate vector c_1^r (i.e., the representation of c_1^w) is more similar to vector c_2^r (the representation of c_2^w) than to c_3^r in one linear coordinate system, then c_1^r is more similar to c_2^r than to c_3^r in any other linear coordinate system (provided the systems have the same feature weightings, as discussed next).

For example, consider the coordinates of three points, a, b, and c in a retinal image: a is at location 1, 1, b is at 2, 2, and c is at 3, 3. That is, c_1^w is the vector [1 1 2 2 3 3]. Note that we can express any transformation on this vector as another vector, t_i, which we add to c^w. For example, we can move Feature c up (i.e., increase its coordinate in the vertical dimension) by one unit by setting t_1 to [0 0 0 0 0 1] and adding it to c_1^w. The resulting image, c_2^w, is the vector [1 1 2 2 3 4]. To move c up by two units, we add transformation t_2 ([0 0 0 0 0 2]) to c_1^w to get the image $c_3^w = $ [1 1 2 2 3 5]. Let us quantify the *effect*, $e(t_i, c_j^w)$, of transformation t_i on the image c_j^w as the sum of the differences between the original vector (c_j^w) and the transformed vector ($c_j^w + t_i$):

$$e(t_i, c_j^w) = \sum_j | c_j^w - c_j^w + t_i | . \tag{1}$$

(Equation 1 simplifies to the sum of vector entries in t_i.) Likewise, let us quantify the effect of t_i on the representation, c_j^r, of that image (c_j^w) as the sum of the differences between the representation (c_j^r) of the original image and the representation, $c_{j(t)}^r$, of the transformed image ($c_j^w + t_i$):

$$e(t_i, c_j^e) = \sum_j | c_j^r - c_{j(t)}^r | . \tag{2}$$

It is now straightforward to show that, in any linear coordinate system, if $e(t_2, c_j^w) > e(t_1, c_j^w)$, then $e(t_i, c_j^r) \geq e(t_i, c_j^r)$. That is, the greater the effect of a transformation of the coordinates in an image, the greater the effect of that transformation on any linear coordinate representation on that image. Consider two linear coordinate representations: s uses a single reference point, and in m the first feature (a) is related to the origin of the coordinate system, and every other feature is related to the previous feature (i.e., b to a, c to b, etc.). Representation m thus uses three reference points (one per feature). The most obvious version of s is simply to set s $= c^w$ (i.e., to adopt for the single reference point representation the same coordinates as used in the image), but in such an example, it is trivial that the effects on the representation scale with the effects on the image (because the two are identical). Therefore, to make the example less trivial, in s we use the first feature (a) as the origin of the coordinate system. The effects of transformations t_1 and t_2 on s and m are shown in the table here. As previously shown, c_2 is the result of transformation t_1 on image c_1, and c_3 is the result of transformation t_2 on c_1. An additional transformation, t_3, is included to illustrate the effect of moving a different feature.

Transformation	Image (c^w)	s (c^r)	m (c^r)
	$c_1 = [\,1\;1\;2\;2\;3\;3\,]$	$[\,0\;0\;1\;1\;2\;2\,]$	$[\,1\;1\;1\;1\;1\;1\,]$
$t_1 = [\,0\;0\;0\;0\;0\;1\,]$	$c_2 = [\,1\;1\;2\;2\;3\;4\,]$	$[\,0\;0\;1\;1\;2\;3\,]$	$[\,1\;1\;1\;1\;1\;2\,]$
$t_2 = [\,0\;0\;0\;0\;0\;2\,]$	$c_3 = [\,1\;1\;2\;2\;3\;5\,]$	$[\,0\;0\;1\;1\;2\;4\,]$	$[\,1\;1\;1\;1\;1\;3\,]$
$t_3 = [\,0\;0\;1\;0\;0\;0\,]$	$c_4 = [\,1\;1\;3\;2\;3\;3\,]$	$[\,0\;0\;2\;1\;2\;2\,]$	$[\,1\;1\;2\;1\;1\;1\,]$

In both the single reference point (s) and the multiple reference point (m) coordinate representations, the effect of t_1 on c_1 is 1.0, and the effect of t_2 on c_1 is 2.0. In these examples, the effects on the representations are identical to the effects on the original image, because both representations used the same scale as the image (i.e., a distance of 1.0 in the image maps to a distance of 1.0 in both representations). Changing the scales of the representations changes the absolute magnitudes of the effects of t_1 and t_2, but it does not change their ratio. The only way to change the ratio of the effects of various transformations is to assign different weights to different features (coordinates) in the representation (see Edelman & Poggio, 1991). For example, if all coordinates are given equal weight, then the effect of t_3 is equal to the effect of t_1 (namely, 1.0). If the weight on the x coordinate of Feature b (the third vector entry) is reduced to zero, then t_3 has no effect on either s or m. As long as s uses the same weights as m, the two representations always show identical effects of identical transformations. That is, s and m are formally equivalent.

It is important to emphasize that s and m are formally equivalent only because they are both linear. If m were based on nonlinear (e.g., categorical) relations (rather than linear relations), then s and m would not be formally equivalent (see Hummel & Stankiewicz, 1996b).

ACKNOWLEDGMENTS

Preparation of this chapter was supported by National Science Foundation Grant SBR-9511504. I am grateful to Steve Engel and Brad Love for their detailed and helpful comments on an earlier draft of the manuscript.

REFERENCES

Biederman, I. (1987). Recognition-by-components: A theory of human image understanding. *Psychological Review, 94* (2), 115–147.

Biederman, I., & Gerhardstein, P. C. (1993). Recognizing depth-rotated objects: Evidence and conditions for 3-dimensional viewpoint invariance. *Journal of Experimental Psychology: Human Perception and Performance, 19,* 1162–1182.

Biederman, I., & Gerhardstein, P. C. (1995). Viewpoint-dependent mechanisms in visual object recognition: A critical analysis. *Journal of Experimental Psychology: Human Perception and Performance, 21,* 1506–1514.

Bülthoff, H. H., & Edelman, S. (1992). Psychophysical support for a two-dimensional view interpolation theory of object recognition. *Proceedings of the National Academy of Science, 89,* 60–64.

Bülthoff, H. H., Edelman, S. Y., & Tarr, M. J. (1995). How are three-dimensional objects represented in the brain? *Cerebral Cortex, 3,* 247–260.

Cheng, P. W. (1997). From covariation to causation: A causal power theory. *Psychological Review, 104,* 367–405.

Clowes, M. B. (1967). Perception, picture processing and computers. In N. L. Collins & D. Michie (Eds.), *Machine intelligence* (Vol. 1, pp. 181–197). Edinburgh, Scotland: Oliver & Boyd.

Cooper, E. E., & Biederman, I. (1993, November). *Geon differences during object recognition are more salient than metric differences.* Poster presented at the annual meeting of the Psychonomic Society, Washington, DC.

Cooper, E. E., & Wojan, T. J. (in press). Differences in the coding of spatial relations in face and object identification. *Journal of Experimental Psychology: Learning, Memory, and Cognition.*

Dickinson, S. J., Pentland, A. P., & Rosenfeld, A. (1992). 3-D shape recovery using distributed aspect matching. *IEEE Transactions on Pattern Analysis and Machine Intelligence, 14,* 174–198.

Diwadkar, V. A., & McNamara, T. P. (1997). Viewpoint dependence in scene recognition. *Psychological Science, 8,* 302–307.

Edelman, S. (1998). Representation is representation of similarities. *Behavioral and Brain Sciences, 21,* 449–498.

Edelman, S., Cutzu, F., & Duvdevani-Bar, S. (1996). Similarity to reference shapes as a basis for shape representation. In G. Cottrell (Ed.) *Proceedings of the 18th annual conference of the Cognitive Science Society* (pp. 260–265). Mahwah, NJ: Lawrence Erlbaum Associates.

Edelman, S., & Poggio, T. (1991). *Bringing the grandmother back into the picture: A memory-based view of object recognition.* (A.I. Memo No. 1181). Cambridge, MA: Massachusetts Institute of Technology.

Edelman, S., & Weinshall, D. (1991). A self-organizing multiple-view representation of 3-D objects. *Biological Cybernetics, 64,* 209–219.

Ellis, R., & Allport, D. A. (1986). Multiple levels of representation for visual objects: A behavioral study. In A. G. Cohen & J. R. Thomas (Eds.), *Artificial intelligence and its applications* (pp. 245–257). New York: Wiley.

Ellis, R., Allport, D. A., Humphreys, G. W., & Collis, J. (1989). Varieties of object constancy. *Quarterly Journal of Experimental Psychology, 4,* 775–796.

Elman, J. L., Bates, E., Johnson, M. H., Karmaloff-Smith, A., Parisi, D., & Plunkett, K. (1996). *Rethinking inateness: A connectionist perspective on development.* Cambridge, MA: MIT Press.

Fodor, J. A. & Pylyshyn, Z. W. (1988). Connectionism and cognitive architecture: A critical analysis. In S. Pinker & J. Mehler (Eds.), *Connections and symbols* (pp. 3–71). Cambridge, MA: MIT Press.

Gallistel, C. R. (1990). *The organization of learning.* Cambridge, MA: MIT Press.

Garner, W. R. (1974). *The processing of information and structure.* Hillsdale, NJ: Lawrence Erlbaum Associates.

Goldstone, R. L., Medin, D. L., & Gentner, D. (1991). Relations, attributes, and the non-independence of features in similarity judgments. *Cognitive Psychology, 23,* 222–262.

Halford, G., Bain, J., Maybery, M., & Andrews, G. (1998). Induction of relational schemas: Common processes in reasoning and complex learning. *Cognitive Psychology, 35,* 201–245.

Hummel, J. E. (1994). Reference frames and relations in computational models of object recognition. *Current Directions in Psychological Science, 3,* 111–116.

Hummel, J. E., & Biederman, I. (1992). Dynamic binding in a neural network for shape recognition. *Psychological Review, 99,* 480–517.

Hummel, J. E., & Holyoak, K. J. (1997). Distributed representations of structure: A theory of analogical access and mapping. *Psychological Review, 104,* 427–466.

Hummel, J. E., & Kellman, P. K. (1998). Finding the pope in the pizza: Abstract invariants and cognitive constraints on perceptual learning. *Behavioral and Brain Sciences, 21,* 30.

Hummel, J. E., & Stankiewicz, B. J. (1996a). An architecture for rapid, hierarchical structural description. In T. Inui & J. McClelland (Eds.), *Attention and performance XVI: Information integration in perception and communication* (pp. 93–121). Cambridge, MA: MIT Press.

Hummel, J. E., & Stankiewicz, B. J. (1996b). Categorical relations in shape perception. *Spatial Vision, 10,* 201–236.

Hummel, J. E., & Stankiewicz, B. J. (1998). Two roles for attention in shape perception: A structural description model of visual scrutiny. *Visual Cognition, 5,* 49–79.

Jolicoeur, P. (1985). The time to name disoriented natural objects. *Memory and Cognition, 13,* 289–303.

Lawson, R., & Humphreys, G. W. (1996). View specificity in object processing: Evidence from picture matching. *Journal of Experimental Psychology: Human Perception and Performance, 22,* 395–416.

Lowe, D. G. (1987). The viewpoint consistency constraint. *International Journal of Computer Vision, 1,* 57–72.

Marcus, G. F. (1998). Rethinking eliminative connectionism. *Cognitive Psychology, 37,* 243–282.

Markman, A. B., & Gentner, D. (1993). Structural alignment during similarity comparisons. *Cognitive Psychology, 25,* 431–467.

Marr, D. (1982). *Vision.* San Francisco: Freeman.

Marr, D., & Nishihara, H. K. (1978). Representation and recognition of three dimensional shapes. *Proceedings of the Royal Society of London* (Series B. 200), 269–294.

McClelland, J. L., McNaughton, B. L., & O'Reilly, R. C. (1995). Why there are complementary learning systems in the hippocampus and neocortex: Insights from the successes and failures of connectionist models of learning and memory. *Psychological Review, 102,* 419–437.

Noelle, D. C. & Cottrell, G. W. (1996). Modeling interference effects in instructed category learning. In G. Cottrell (Ed.), *Proceedings of the 18th annual conference of the Cognitive Science Society* (pp. 475–480). Mahwah, NJ: Lawrence Erlbaum Associates.

Olshausen, B. A., Anderson, C. H., & Van Essen, D. C. (1993). A neurobiological model of visual attention and invariant pattern recognition based on dynamic routing of information. *Journal of Neuroscience, 13,* 4700–4719.

Palmer, S. E. (1978). Structural aspects of similarity. *Memory and Cognition, 6,* 91–97.

Park, J., & Cheng, P. W. (1997). *Boundary conditions for "overexpectation" in causal learning with discrete trials: A test of the Power PC theory.* Manuscript submitted for publication.

Poggio, T., & Edelman, S. (1990). A neural network that learns to recognize three-dimensional objects. *Nature, 343,* 263–266.

Poggio, T., & Vetter, T. (1992). Recognition and structure and from one 2D model view: Observations on prototypes, object classes, and symmetries. (AI Memo 1347). Cambridge, MA: Massachussetts Institute of Technology.

Quinlan, P. T. (1991). Differing approaches to two-dimensional shape recognition. *Psychological Bulletin, 109* (2), 224–241.

Rips, L. J. (1989). Similarity, typicality, and categorization. In S. Voisniadou & A. Ortony (Eds.), *Similarity, analogy, and thought* (pp. 21–59). New York: Cambridge University Press.

Saiki, J., & Hummel, J. E. (1998). Connectedness and part-relation integration in object category learning. *Memory and Cognition, 23*, 1138–1156.

Schacter, D. L., Cooper, L. A., & Delaney, S. M. (1990). Implicit memory for unfamiliar objects depends on access to structural descriptions. *Journal of Experimental Psychology: General, 119*, 5–24.

Shastri, L., & Ajjanagadde, V. (1993). From simple associations to systematic reasoning: A connectionist representation of rules, variables and dynamic bindings. *Behavioral and Brain Sciences, 16*, 417–494.

Stankiewicz, B. J., & Hummel, J. E. (1996). MetriCat: A representation for basic and subordinate-level classification. In G. Cottrell, (Ed.), *Proceedings of the 18th annual conference of the Cognitive Science Society* (pp. 254–259). Mahwah, NJ: Lawrence Erlbaum Associates.

Stankiewicz, B. J., Hummel J. E., & Cooper, E. E. (1998). The role of attention in priming for left-right reflections of object images: Evidence for a dual representation of object shape. *Journal of Experimental Psychology: Human Perception and Performance, 24*, 732–744.

Tanaka, K. (1993). Neuronal mechanisms of object recognition. *Science, 262*, 685–688.

Tanaka, J. W., & Farah, M. J. (1993). Parts and wholes in face recognition. *Quarterly Journal of Experimental Psychology: Human Experimental Psychology, 146A*, 225–245.

Tarr, M. J. (1995). Rotating objects to recognize them: A case study on the role of viewpoint dependency in the recognition of three-dimensional objects. *Psychonomic Bulletin & Review, 2*(1), 55–82.

Tarr, M. J., & Bülthoff, H. H. (1995). Is human object recognition better described by geon structural descriptions or by multiple views? *Journal of Experimental Psychology: Human Perception and Performance, 21*, 1494–1505.

Tarr, M. J., Bülthoff, H. H., Zabinski, M., & Blanz, V. (1997). To what extent do unique parts influence recognition across changes in viewpoint? *Psychological Science, 8*, 282–289.

Tarr, M. J., & Pinker, S. (1989). Mental rotation and orientation-dependence in shape recognition. *Cognitive Psychology, 21*, 233–282.

Tarr, M. J., & Pinker. S. (1990). When does human object recognition use a viewer-centered reference frame? *Psychological Science, 1* (4), 253–256.

Ullman, S. (1989). Aligning pictoral descriptions: An approach to object recognition. *Cognition, 32*, 193–254.

Ullman, S. (1996). *High-level vision: Object recognition and visual Cognition.* Cambridge MA: MIT Press.

Ullman, S., & Basri, R. (1991). Recognition by liner combinations of models. *IEEE Transactions on Pattern Analysis and Machine Intelligence, 13*, 992–1006.

Zerroug, M. (1994). *Segmentation and inference of 3-D descriptions from intensity images.* (Tech. Rep. IRIS-94-327). University of Southern California, Los Angeles.

III

CONCEPTS, CONCEPT USE, AND CONCEPTUAL CHANGE

This third and final part considers the role of dynamics in higher cognition, specifically in conceptual change in concept use and acquisition. In their chapter "Interactions Between Perceptual and Conceptual Learning," Robert L. Goldstone, Mark Steyvers, Jesse Spencer-Smith, and Alan Kersten argue that learned concepts can change perceptual representations and that because representations produced by our perceptual systems in turn ground our concepts, conceptual change of perceptual representations must be part of the explanation of human behavioral adaptability. Their argument has important consequences for the common methodology in cognitive science of using a small, fixed set of primitives from which all kinds of high-level representations and cognitive processes are constructed. It is well known that the fixed-feature-set approach does not work. Eventually two entities need to be discriminated but cannot be because they are built from the same subset of primitive features. The feature set is then allowed to grow, and the new feature set becomes ad hoc: Primitives are included only to draw rare distinctions that the experimenter or programmer knows ahead of time need to be drawn, and primitives that are never used are included. Goldstone, Steyvers, Spencer-Smith, and Kersten argue that the solution to this problem is for the cognitive system to develop in real time new primitives or features. Through this process of adding new features, perception becomes adapted to new environments and tasks. The claim then is that concept learning influences how, when, and which new features get added. In the experi-

187

ments they report here, they study the role of concept learning on sensitization to pre-existing and novel dimensions, the organization of objects into parts, and unitization, by which a single, functional unit is created for a complex pattern.

Next, Keith J. Holyoak and John E. Hummel, in "The Proper Treatment of Symbols in a Connectionist Architecture," consider the relation between the physical symbol system hypothesis (Newell & Simon, 1976) and connectionist architectures with their so-called subsymbolic representations. Specifically, Holyoak and Hummel consider the question "Can connectionist models eliminate physical symbol systems?" Their answer is "No." However, Holyoak and Hummel find connectionist architectures to be powerful and important models, and their task is to show how connectionist models can incorporate symbols and symbol systems. They call this project *symbolic connectionism*. They begin by discussing in detail the necessity in cognitive modeling for variables and values (variable binding). They raise a problem for the tensor product view of variable binding. They then discuss the notion of a symbol distributed over space and time. Here they present their theory of synchrony-based variable bindings and their computer model of this theory: learning and inference with schemas and analogies (LISA). Finally, they show that symbolic connectionism is not merely implementation.

Eric Dietrich next presents his proposal that analogical remindings change the concepts involved in the reminding. A famous example is the analogical reminding that happened to Rutherford. While experimenting on the structure of the atom, the trajectories of alpha particles shot at thin metallic foils reminded him of comets careening around the sun. From here, he and his students (most notably Bohr) went on to develop the nuclear model of the atom (sometimes depicted as the solar system model). Dietrich's claim is that this analogical reminding could not have happened to Rutherford unless his concepts representing comets, alpha particles, and atoms changed prior to having the analogy. It is well known that analogies and metaphors change concepts after the fact or as a result of having the analogy. Dietrich's claim is that conceptual change must occur *before* the analogy can be made in the first place, and both the retrieving concept and the concept retrieved during the reminding must change. He further analyzes the kind of change that must occur and argues that this change must occur to the high-level relational structure of the concepts involved. Lastly, his proposal about the mutability of concepts during analogical reminding puts some interesting constraints on the nature of concepts themselves. In particular, his proposal requires concepts to be malleable, and this malleability is most easily explained if concepts are viewed as representational processes rather than as static representations. Thus, the representational role (object, attribute, or relation) of a particular aspect of a situation to be represented cannot be determined in advance. Instead, representations are constructed in the process of retrieving items from memory and preparing them for comparisons.

Dedre Gentner and Phillip Wolff, in "Metaphor and Knowledge Change," present four specific forms of knowledge change (conceptual change), which occur as a result of understanding a given metaphor (metaphorical sentence). The four kinds are (a) knowledge selection, (b) projection of candidate inferences, (c) predicate rerepresentation, and (d) restructuring. The theoretical framework undergirding Gentner and Wolff's discussion of knowledge change is called *structure-mapping theory*. The fundamental claim of this theory is that the mental processes responsible for understanding metaphor and analogy result from aligning the relational structures of knowledge representations. The four kinds of knowledge change that Gentner and Wolff present actually alter the relational structure of knowledge representations. Gentner and Wolff also discuss metaphoric creativity, the idea that understanding a metaphor produces new knowledge, not just a rearrangement of old knowledge. The four kinds of knowledge change presented here go part of the way toward explaining the construction of such new knowledge.

The final chapter in the book, "Representation and the Construction of Preferences," by Arthur B. Markman, Shi Zhang, and C. Page Moreau, explicitly defends mental representations by arguing that dynamic representations are necessary to explain certain aspects of decision-making behavior. They begin by assuming that choice situations require a goal that needs to be satisfied. Thus, choices are dynamic, because options must be evaluated relative to the goal that sets up the choice. To demonstrate these dynamics, Markman, Zhang, and Moreau focus on consumer behavior and the preferences consumers construct in the process of picking among a set of choices to satisfy a goal. An important kind of information that consumers use to develop preferences is what the authors call *alignable differences.* Alignable differences are aspects of one option with a corresponding aspect in another option. For example, suppose that consumers are trying to decide between competing computer football games. They tend to give more weight to alignable differences among the games, such as one game having predefined plays and another game allowing users to create their own plays. Consumers tend to ignore properties that cannot be aligned in this way. For example, they likely ignore the fact that one game has practice sessions if the second game does not mention practice sessions at all (although if the second game explicitly says it does not have practice sessions, then this becomes an alignable difference again). Markman, Zhang, and Moreau argue that such alignable differences allow consumers to compare products and to see the products as in competition with each other. Without such differences, it is hard for consumers (or anyone) to make a choice (as between a toaster and new bookshelf). Importantly, alignable differences require representations.

Higher level cognitive processes like those described in this section are typically explained by using representations. Dynamics are usually less evident in theories of higher level cognitive processing than in theories of lower level cognitive processing. Thus, the chapters in this section are important, because they show that the dynamics that seem so central in perception and action also apply to more complex cognitive processes.

REFERENCES

Newell, A., & Simon, H. A. (1976). Computer science as empirical inquiry: Symbols Search. *Communications of the ACM, 19,* 113–126.

8

Interactions Between Perceptual and Conceptual Learning

Robert L. Goldstone
Mark Steyvers
Jesse Spencer-Smith
Alan Kersten
Indiana University, Bloomington

Confusions arise when *stable* is equated with *foundational*. Spurred on by the image of a house's foundation, we find it tempting to think that something provides effective support to the extent that it is rigid and stable. We argue that when considering the role of perception in grounding our concepts, exactly the opposite is true. Our perceptual system supports our ability to acquire new concepts by being flexibly tuned to these concepts. Whereas the concepts that we learn are certainly dependent on our perceptual representations, we argue that these perceptual representations are also influenced by the learned concepts. In keeping with one of the central themes of this book, behavioral adaptability is completely consistent with representationalism. In fact, the most straightforward account of our experimental results is that concept learning can produce changes in perceptual representations, the "vocabulary" of perceptual features used by subsequent tasks.

This chapter reviews theoretical and empirical evidence that perceptual vocabularies used to describe visual objects are flexibly adapted to the demands of their user. We extend arguments made elsewhere for adaptive perceptual representations (Goldstone, Schyns, & Medin, 1997; Schyns, Goldstone, & Thibaut, 1998) and discuss research from our laboratory illustrating specific interactions between perceptual and conceptual learning. We describe computer simulations that provide accounts of these interactions by using neural network models. These models have detectors that become increasingly tuned to the set of perceptual features that support concept learning. The bulk of the chapter is organized around mechanisms of human perceptual learning and computer simulations of these mechanisms.

FIXED AND FLEXIBLE FEATURE SETS

A dominant notion in cognitive science is the idea that cognition involves operations on a fixed set of hardwired primitive features. The fixed set of features provides the building blocks for representing objects. This idea has been highly productive because of its parsimony; a wide variety of objects can be represented by combining a small number of existing features in different arrangements. The field of linguistics saw one of the first feature set theories, in which phonemes are represented by the presence or absence of fewer than 12 features such as *voiced, nasal,* and *strident* (Jakobson, Fant, & Halle, 1963). Ascending in complexity, Schank (1972) proposed representing entire situations, such as ordering food in a restaurant, in terms of a set of 23 primitive concepts such as *physical-transfer, propel, grasp,* and *ingest.* In the field of object recognition, Biederman (1987) proposed a set of 36 geometric shapes such as *wedge* and *cylinder* to be used for representing objects such as telephones and flashlights. Wierzbicka (1992) proposed a set of 30 semantic primitives including *good, want, big,* and *time* to be composed together in structured phrases to generate all other words. Much of the work in concept learning, including the seminal work of Bruner, Goodnow, and Austin (1956), assumes that experimental participants come into the psychology laboratory already possessing the primitive features that they need to learn how to categorize objects. For example, participants know, before the categorization experiment begins, that a set of objects is to be described in terms of color, number, and shape. In short, a prevalent assumption in cognitive science is that cognition consists of combining the elements of a fixed set of *a priori* features.

Although appropriate and mandatory for answering many questions, this "fixed features" approach systematically overlooks situations in which the concept learner, in addition to learning an association between a set of features and a category, must also learn what counts as a feature. Perceptual features that are currently available constrain the concepts that are acquired (as in traditional concept learning systems), but we argue that the concepts to be acquired also influence the features that are developed. Thus, in contrast to theories that posit fixed features, the alternative pursued here is that the building blocks of cognition are neither fixed nor finite, but rather adapt to the requirements of the tasks for which they are employed (Schyns, Goldstone, & Thibaut, 1998; Schyns & Murphy, 1994). As argued by Gibson (1969), the perceptual interpretation of an entity depends on the observer's history, training, and acculturation.

These factors, together with psychophysical constraints, mold one's set of building blocks. There may be no single, unique set of perceptual primitives because the building blocks themselves are adaptive.

One of the notorious difficulties with representations based on a limited set of elements is that it is hard to choose exactly the right set of elements that suffices to accommodate all future entities that need to be represented.[1] On the one hand, if a small set of primitive elements is chosen, then it is likely that two entities that must be but cannot be distinguished with any combination of available primitives eventually arise. On the other hand, if a set of primitives is sufficiently large to construct all entities that might occur, then it likely includes many elements that lie unused, waiting for their moment of need to possibly arise (Schyns et al., 1998). By developing new elements as needed, newly important discriminations can cause the construction of building blocks that are tailored for the discrimination.

There is substantial neurological evidence for perceptual learning via imprinting of specific features in a stimulus. Weinberger (1993) reviewed evidence that cells in the auditory cortex become tuned to the frequency of often-repeated tones. Deeper in the cortex, cells in the inferior temporal area can be tuned by extended experience (over 600,000 trials) to particular views of three-dimensional (3D) objects (Logothetis, Pauls, & Poggio, 1995). Cells in the inferotemporal cortex can also be selective for particular faces, and this specificity is at least partially acquired given that it is especially pronounced for familiar faces (Perrett et al., 1984). There is neurological evidence that cortical areas involved with early perceptual processes are flexible, context sensitive, and tuned by training. For example, practice in discriminating small motions in different directions significantly alters electrical brain potentials that occur within 100 milliseconds of the stimulus onset (Fahle & Morgan, 1996). These electrical changes are centered over the primary visual cortex, which suggests plasticity in early visual processing. Karni and Sagi (1991) found evidence, based on the specificity of training to eye (interocular transfer does not occur) and retinal location, that is consistent with early, primary visual cortex adaptation in simple discrimination tasks. In fact, training in an auditory selective attention task may produce differential responses as early as the cochlea—the neural structure that is connected directly to the eardrum via three small bones (Hillyard & Kutas, 1983). In sum, there is an impressive amount of converging evidence that experimental training leads to changes in very early stages of information processing.

---

[1]One symptom of the difficulties associated with establishing a single set of features that suffices for representing a large set of objects might be called "feature creep." A historical examination of fixed feature theories often reveals a steady increase in the number of proposed fixed features. Early work by Schank in representing scenarios, by Wierzbicka in representing words, and by Biederman in representing objects proposed smaller sets of primitives than did their later work.

These theoretical and neurophysiological sources of evidence for experience producing perceptual changes parallel evidence from expert–novice differences. In many fields, including radiology (Myles-Worsley, Johnston, & Simons, 1988), gender discrimination of day-old chicks (Biederman & Shiffrar, 1987), and beer tasting (Peron & Allen, 1988) experts organize or parse the world differently than do novices. In these fields, part of what it means to be an expert is to have developed perceptual tools for analyzing the stimuli in a domain. In what follows, we explore some potential laboratory analogs of the development of perceptual expertise, albeit on a much shorter course of training. The experiments are organized in terms of particular mechanisms of interaction between perception and concept learning: sensitization of existing perceptual dimensions, sensitization of novel perceptual dimensions, perceptual reorganization, and unitization.

DIMENSION SENSITIZATION

One way in which perception becomes adapted to tasks and environments is by increasing the attention paid to perceptual dimensions that are important, by decreasing attention to irrelevant dimensions, or by both. Attention can be selectively directed toward important stimulus aspects at several different stages in information processing. Attention may be applied relatively late in information processing to strategically emphasize important dimensions (Nosofsky, 1986). Alternatively, attentional shifts may be perceptual, rather than strategic or judgmental, in nature. One source of evidence that shifts are not completely voluntary is that attentional highlighting of information occurs even if it is to the detriment of the observer. When a letter consistently serves as the target in a detection task and then later becomes a distracter—a stimulus to be ignored—it still automatically captures attention (Shiffrin & Schneider, 1977). The converse of this effect, negative priming, also occurs: Targets that were once distracters are responded to more slowly than never-before-seen targets (Tipper, 1992). Although most research has investigated the sensitization of relevant dimensions, perceptual learning can also involve the loss of an ability to discriminate along irrelevant dimensions. For example, Myles-Worsley et al. (1988) showed that expert radiologists have poorer recognition memory for x-rays that do not show disease than do less expert medical professionals. Also, Werker and Tees (1984) showed that adults have poorer discrimination abilities for certain non-native sounds than do infants.

In addition to entire dimensions becoming sensitized if relevant, particularly important regions in a dimension can also be sensitized. The largest body of empirical work showing an influence of categories on perception comes from work on categorical perception. According to this phenomenon, people are better able to distinguish between physically different stimuli when the stimuli come from different categories than when they come from the same category (Harnad, 1987). For example, Liberman, Harris, Hoffman, and Griffith (1957) generated a continuum of equally spaced consonant–vowel syllables changing continuously from /be/ to /de/. At a certain point on this continuum, people rather abruptly shift from identifying the sound as a /be/ phoneme to identifying it as a /de/. Moreover, people are better able to discriminate between two sounds that belong to different phonemic categories such as /be/ and /de/ than they are able to discriminate between two sounds that belong in the /be/ category, even when the physical differences between the pairs of sounds are equated. As such, perceptual sensitivity is at a peak at the boundary between phonemic categories.

There is an ongoing controversy about whether categorical perception effects are due to innate or learned categories. On the side of innateness, Infants as young as 4 months show categorical perception for speech sounds (Eimas, Siqueland, Jusczyk, & Vigorito, 1971). Furthermore, chinchillas show categorical perception effects for speech sounds akin to those produced by people (Kuhl & Miller, 1978), even though chinchillas presumably have little exposure to human language. On the side of experience, categorical perception in humans is modulated by the listener's native language and extended training. In general, a sound difference that crosses the boundary between phonemes in a language is more discriminable to speakers of that language than to speakers of a language in which the sound difference does not cross a phonemic boundary (Repp & Liberman, 1987). Laboratory training on the sound categories of a language can produce categorical perception among speakers of a language that does not intrinsically have these categories (Pisoni, Aslin, Perey, & Hennessy, 1982).

Work in our laboratory has found visual analogs to the trained categorical perception effects observed with speech. In Goldstone (1994), participants were first given categorization training involving the sizes or brightnesses of squares. On each trial of categorization training, a square appeared on the screen and participants were asked to categorize it into Category A or B. The "size categorizers" group received feedback indicating that the squares in the left and right two columns of Fig. 8.1 belonged to Category A and Category B, respectively. The "brightness categorizers" group received categorization training in which the squares in the upper and lower two rows of Fig. 8.1 belonged to Category A and Category B, respectively. The squares were calibrated so that the differences between adjacent squares were just barely detectable. Subsequent to 1.5 hours of categorization training, participants were transferred to a same/different judgment task in which horizontally or vertically adjacent squares from Fig. 8.1 were presented or the same square was repeated twice. Participants were required to respond as to whether the two squares were exactly identical on both their size and brightness or differed even slightly on either dimension. When a dimension was relevant for categorization, participants' same/different judgments along this dimension were more accurate (based on the d' measure from signal detection theory) than those from participants for whom the dimension was irrelevant and from control participants who did not undergo categorization training. This trend, found for both categorization groups, is shown in Figs. 8.2 and 8.3. The greatest sensitization of the categorization-relevant dimension was found along those particular dimension values that were the boundaries between the learned categories. However, the sensitization of the relevant dimension also extended to other values along the dimension even though these other values were originally placed in the same category. Thus, entire relevant dimensions are sensitized, but critical regions in those dimensions are also sensitized. In addition, Fig. 8.3 shows the one case of *acquired equivalence* that was found, in which a dimension that was *irrelevant* for categorization became desensitized relative to control participants. Compared with the control group of participants who were

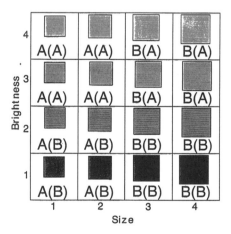

FIG. 8.1. Stimuli used by Goldstone (1994). Sixteen squares were constructed by factorially combining four values of brightness with four values of size. The letters outside the parentheses show the categorizations of the squares when size was relevant. The letters in the parentheses show the categorizations of the squares when brightness was relevant. Adapted from "Influences of Categorization on Perceptual Discrimination," by R. L. Goldstone, 1994, *Journal of Experimental Psychology: General, 123*, p. 183. Adapted with permission.

Size Relevant During Categorization

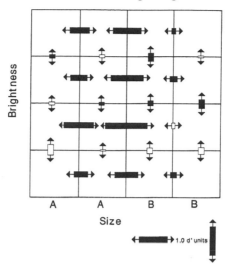

FIG. 8.2. This figure shows the change in perceptual sensitivity (measured in d' units) that is due to size categorization training. A black rectangle indicates a positive difference when the control groups' sensitivity is subtracted from the size categorizers' sensitivity. A white rectangle indicates a negative difference. The size of the rectangle indicates the absolute magnitude of the difference. Rectangles are placed between the two squares that are being discriminated. The greatest sensitization occurs at the boundary between the two size categories.

Brightness Relevant During Categorization

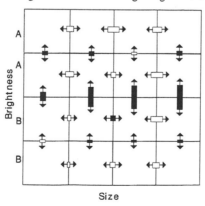

FIG. 8.3. This figure shows the change in perceptual sensitivity (measured in d' units) that is due to brightness categorization training. Each rectangle reflects the difference between the d' for brightness categorizers and the control group. The predominantly white, horizontal rectangles reflect a significant case of acquired equivalence whereby brightness categorizers are less adept than controls at making size discriminations.

given no categorization training, the desensitization that occurred for relevant dimensions was larger and more reliable than the desensitization that occurred for irrelevant dimensions.

SENSITIZATION OF NOVEL DIMENSIONS

Dimension sensitization following training provides evidence that not only do our perceptual encodings guide our categorizations, but that our categorizations also guide our perceptual encodings. However, shifts in dimensional attention do not necessarily require the postulation of new perceptual vocabulary elements. Existing elements may simply be emphasized or de-emphasized. From the same paradigm, we believe that we are also getting evidence for a second type of perceptual learning involving dimensionalization—the development of new dimensions. Size and brightness are easily distinguishable and are likely to be psychological dimensions for our participants before categorization training. We replicated the experiment just reported by using dimensions that people are less likely to register *as* dimensions (Goldstone, 1994). We used the brightness and saturation of colors, two dimensions that are often cited as the classic examples of integral dimensions (Garner, 1974). Dimensions are considered integral if it is difficult to attend to one dimension without also attending to the other dimension. However, after prolonged categorization experience in which brightness was relevant and saturation was irrelevant (or vice versa), we found that the relevant dimension became selectively sensitized. Thus, dimensions that were once fused can become more isolated with the proper categorization training. This result is consistent with evidence that color experts (art students and vision scientists) are better able to selectively attend to dimensions (e.g. hue, chroma, and value) that make up color than can nonexperts (Burns & Shepp, 1988). A large developmental literature suggests that people often shift from perceiving stimuli in terms of holistic, overall aspects to analytically decomposing objects into separate dimensions (Smith, 1989). This trend can be described as the construction of new perceptual vocabulary elements that are used to build object descriptions.

Sensitization of Entire Novel Dimensions

It has been argued that saturation and brightness, although they are integral dimensions for most people, are not genuinely arbitrary dimensions (Grau & Kemler-Nelson, 1988). To show the dimensionalization process for genuinely arbitrary dimensions, we have recently begun to explore situations where dimensions are generated by morphing between two pairs of arbitrarily chosen faces. One dimension is created by morphing between the top two faces shown in Fig. 8.4, and a second dimension

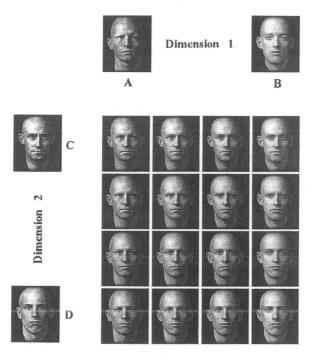

FIG. 8.4. Arbitrary dimensions can be created by generating a series of morphs between two randomly chosen faces. Dimension 1, running horizontally, morphs between Faces A and B. Dimension 2, running vertically, morphs between Faces C and D. Each of the faces in the 4 by 4 array possesses a unique set of coordinates on Dimensions 1 and 2.

is created by morphing between the two faces on the left. Using a technique described by Steyvers (1999), a four by four matrix of faces can be created from these two dimensions such that each face is defined one half by its value on Dimension 1 and one half by its value on Dimension 2. Arbitrary dimensions are thus generated by creating negative contingencies between two faces—the more of Face A that is present in a particular morphed face, the less of Face B there is. The horizontal dimension, Dimension 1, might be called the "The proportion of Face A relative to Face B" dimension. We refer to the vertical dimension as Dimension 2.

Just as in the previously described experiments, participants were initially given a categorization rule to learn that divided the four by four stimulus array of Fig. 8.4 either vertically or horizontally into equal halves. On each trial, participants saw a face and categorized it into one of two categories, with feedback from the computer indicating whether or not the participant was correct. Whereas Goldstone's (1994) participants were transferred to a same/different task, Goldstone and Steyvers' (1999) participants were transferred to another categorization task. The initial and transfer categorizations were related to each other by one of the seven ways shown in Table 8.1. In the representation used in Table 8.1 and Fig. 8.4, the dimension above the line is relevant, and the dimension below the line is irrelevant. Figure 8.4 would be represented as 1/2; Dimension 1 (morphing from Face A to B) is relevant, and Dimension 2 is irrelevant. Different faces were used as the anchoring end points for each of the four dimensions (one through four). Dimensions that were relevant during the first categorization could continue to be relevant during the second categorization, could become irrelevant, or could become absent altogether, and the same was true for irrelevant dimensions. For example, if the original categorization was 2/3 (Dimension 2 was relevant, and Dimension 3 was irrelevant) and the subsequent categorization was 1/2, then the dimension that was originally relevant becomes irrelevant and a new dimension becomes relevant for the final categorization.

Suggestive evidence of dimensionalization with these materials is that participants become increasingly adept at attending to one dimension while ignoring variation on irrelevant dimensions during the initial category learning. A more important measure is the categorization accuracy during the final categorization phase of the experiment, which was identical for all seven groups and involves the categorization 1/2 (Dimension 1 = relevant, 2 = irrelevant). As such, any systematic differences between conditions on final categorization performance must be due to differences in how the initial categorization prepared them for this final categoriza-

TABLE 8.1
Seven Conditions of an Experiment by
Goldstone and Steyvers (in preparation)

Initial Training	Subsequent Transfer	Relation Between Training and Transfer
1 Relevant 2 Irrelevant	1 Relevant 2 Irrelevant	Relevant and irrelevant dimensions are both preserved.
1 Relevant 3 Irrelevant	" "	Relevant dimension is preserved.
3 Relevant 2 Irrelevant	" "	Irrelevant dimension is preserved.
3 Relevant 1 Irrelevant	" "	Irrelevant dimension becomes relevant.
2 Relevant 3 Irrelevant	" "	Relevant dimension becomes irrelevant.
2 Relevant 1 Irrelevant	" "	Irrelevant dimension becomes relevant. Relevant dimension becomes irrelevant.
4 Relevant 3 Irrelevant	" "	Control—completely new dimensions.

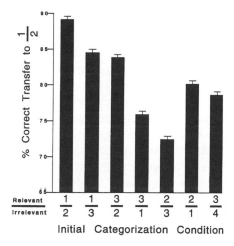

FIG. 8.5. Results from the transfer experiment. Each dimension is represented by the two faces that function as its end points. The dimension in the "numerator" was relevant during the initial categorization, and the dimension in the "denominator" was irrelevant. The bars show the overall percentage correct when each of seven initial categorization conditions was transferred to a 1/2 categorization, wherein Dimension 1 was relevant and 2 was irrelevant. The last bar shows the results from the control condition in which the initial and transfer categorization rules used completely different dimensions.

tion. The results, in Fig. 8.5, show several types of transfer based on the initial categorizations. The degree of transfer in a condition is best appraised by comparing it to the 3/4 control condition in which the initial and final categorizations involve completely different faces and dimensions. The categorization advantage of the first three conditions, 1/2, 1/3, and 3/2, over the control condition suggests that participants learn to selectively emphasize relevant dimensions and to de-emphasize irrelevant dimensions. That is, when intial and final categorizations share relevant or irrelevant dimensions, performance is better than in the control condition. This transfer is impressive because these conditions use completely new sets of faces in the final categorization. For example, none of the faces belonging to the 1/2 set is the same as faces from the 3/2 set. The only similarity between these sets is that Dimension 2 is irrelevant for both sets, and this similarity has a large beneficial effect on transfer.

The next two conditions of Fig. 8.5 demonstrate negative transfer effects owing to shared dimensions. Relative to the control condition (3/4), when irrelevant dimensions become relevant (3/1) and when relevant dimensions become irrelevant (2/3), performance suffers. The latter effect is particularly strong and is reminiscent of Shiffrin and Schneider's (1977) results that when participants are trained to respond to a particular letter as a target, performance is quite poor when that letter later becomes a distracter to be ignored. The results from the 2/1 condition seem surprising at first. In this condition, the relevant dimension becomes irrelevant *and* the irrelevant dimension becomes relevant, and yet performance is better than for the control condition. Our explanation for the beneficial transfer from 2/1 to 1/2 categorizations rests on the observation that both involve the same set of 16 faces. The categorization rules are orthogonal (separated by 90 degrees), splitting the stimuli horizontally or vertically. As such, both rules depend on separating the horizontal dimension from the vertical dimension to selectively attend to only one of these dimensions. Effective performance on the 2/1 categorization requires isolating Dimension 1 from Dimension 2. Once accomplished, this isolation may be useful in acquiring the 1/2 categorization because this categorization also requires the same differentiation of dimensions, albeit for opposite purposes.

This account is supported by additional experiments from our laboratory showing that transfer involving 90-degree rotations of a categorization boundary results in better final performance than does transfer involving 45-degree rotations. Although the 45-degree rotation might be expected to produce better performance because dimensions that are relevant in the final categorization are semirelevant during the initial categorization, this advantage is apparently overwhelmed by the incompatible, cross-cutting dimensionalizations that are required. In contrast, categorization boundaries that are separated by 90 degrees are compatible in promoting the same differentiation of one dimension from another. These results, in conjunction with the results shown in Fig 8.5, suggest that categorization learning involves not only allocating attention to existing dimensions, but also in isolating dimensions in the first place. In fact, it is possible to allocate attention to a dimension only if that dimension has previously been isolated. In some cases, early childhood experience or innate perceptual devices suffice to isolate dimensions, and category learning requires only attention weighting. However, in situations involving objects with dimensions that are initially integral for people, category learning also requires the construction of dimensional representations. Once constructed, these representations are employed for learning subsequent categorizations (for further evidence, see Schyns & Rodet, 1997).

Sensitization of Regions of Novel Dimensions

In addition to sensitizing entire dimensions, regions in novel dimensions can become sensitized, giving rise to categorical perception effects. Goldstone, Steyvers, and Larimer (1996) generated an arbitrary dimension by generating two random bezier curves and treating these objects as end points on a continuum. The values along the dimension were created by morphing from one random bezier to the other, similar to how the face dimensions were created. The stimuli were made by creating 60 linearly interpolated morphs between two random curves and selecting the 7 central curves as stimuli. During categorization training, participants learned one of two categorizations based on different cutoff values along this dimension. For the left-split group, the first three objects in Fig. 8.6 belonged to Category A, and the last four objects belonged to Category B. For the right-split group, the boundary between Categories A and B occurred between the fourth and fifth curves. A third control group learned a comparable categorization, but involving curves that were irrelevant for the subsequent task.

After categorization training, participants were transferred to a same/different judgment task. Participants were shown pairs of highly similar curves or the identical curve repeated twice and were instructed to say whether the curves had exactly the same shape or differed in any way.

The data of principal interest, shown in Fig. 8.7a, were participants' sensitivities at discriminating between pairs of adjacent curves, broken down as a function of their categorization condition. A d' measure of sensitivity was calculated based on participants' ability to correctly respond "same" and "different." Specifically, it is a function of the probability of responding "different" given that the curves were indeed different minus a function of the probability of incorrectly responding "different" given that the curves were the same. The d' values increase as participants' ability to correctly make discriminations increases.

One result of the experiment is that sensitivity is higher for the left- and right-split groups than for the group that was trained on an irrelevant categorization. This effect is consistent with previous work showing that pre-exposure to stimuli leads to their heightened discriminability (Gibson & Walk, 1956). More relevant to categorical perception, there was a significant difference between the pattern of sensitization for the left- and right-split groups. Although the effects of the two groups were not symmetric, the general effect of categorization training is that discriminability is relatively high for stimuli that fall near the category boundary. To

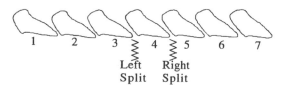

FIG. 8.6. These seven curves were constructed by morphing between arbitrary curves. The left-split and right-split groups saw the same seven curves, but the middle curve was categorized differently by the two groups.

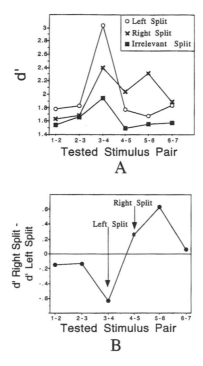

FIG. 8.7. The numbers on the horizontal axis reflect the numbers associated with the compared curves from Fig. 8.6. Fig. 8.7A shows participants' sensitivity (measured in d' units) at discriminating between adjacent curves. Fig. 8.7B plots the same data, but using a derived measure that is the difference between the right and left categorization groups. In general, the categorization condition with the categorization boundary closest to the tested pair had the highest sensitivity at discriminating the pair.

visualize this effect, Fig 8.7B plots a new measure derived from the data shown in Fig. 8.7A. In this figure, the sensitivity (d') of the left-split group is subtracted from the sensitivity of the right-split group. Thus, this measure is positive when the right-split group shows a greater sensitivity than the left-split group for a pair of curves. Figure 8.7B shows that the left-split group does relatively well when and only when the pair of tested curves lies closer to the left boundary than to the right boundary.

A Neural Network Model of Dimensional Sensitization

In developing a computational model for the observed categorical perception effects, we were drawn to neural networks that possess hidden units that intervene between inputs and outputs and are capable of creating internal representations. For our purposes, these hidden units can be interpreted as learned feature detectors and represent the organism's acquired perceptual vocabulary. The model consists of three processing stages, shown in Fig. 8.8. In the first stage, the input images are processed by a set of Gabor filters. In the second stage, a layer of hidden units learns to represent the perceptual dimensions along which the continuum of stimuli falls. The representation of the hidden units is changed by an unsupervised learning algorithm similar to Kohonen's self-organizing maps (e.g. Kohonen, 1995). In the last stage, a layer of category units classifies the input image based on the activity in the hidden unit layer. The weights from the hidden layer to the category units are learned in a supervised manner (Kruschke, 1992). The critical assumption of the model is that the input-to-hidden weights are influenced by the hidden-to-category weights. By unsupervised learning, the topology of the hidden detector units comes to reflect the morph-based dimension that underlies the experimentally created stimuli. By the category level supervision, the distribution of detectors is biased by the demands of the categorization.

The input patterns to the network are gray-scale, two-dimensional pictures of curves, and the categorization of the curve is supplied as a teacher signal for the category units. Twenty-eight curves are created by using the same technique of morphing between two arbitrary curves used in the experiment. The first stage of the network preprocesses these pictures by a set of Gabor filters (Daugman, 1985) with maximal sensitivities to line segments oriented at 0, 45, 90, or 135 degrees. The receptive fields of the filters are positioned at overlapping local regions of the image. The Gabor filters reduce the information contained in the original images to a manageable amount and capture some of the higher order shape invariants associated with a curve not captured by pixel-based representations. Figure 8.9 shows an example of the transduction of an image into Gabor

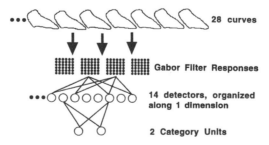

FIG. 8.8. An overview of the SOS network. The bezier curve images are passed through Gabor filters, and the resulting response patterns are presented to a one-dimensional set of detector units. These detectors adapt toward the filtered inputs, but are also influenced by the categorization of the inputs. Representative bezier curves, detector units, and connections are shown in this illustration.

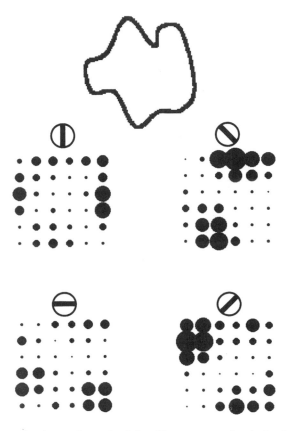

FIG. 8.9. This figure shows the Gabor filter responses for the bezier curve at the top. The activity of a filter is indicated by the magnitude of the black circle. For example, the large circles in the upper-left portion of the 45-degree-angle filter (the lower-right filter) indicate a strong 45-degree-angle component in the upper-left portion of the bezier curve.

filter responses. As a result of this process, each image is represented by 144 real numbers (36 image locations for each of four orientations).

The next processing stage involves the hidden layer consisting of 14 detector units. An individual detector becomes most active when an image leads to a Gabor filter activation pattern that matches the weights from the Gabor filters to the detector. The input-to-detector weight pattern can also be thought of as locations of the detector node in the space determined by the Gabor filters. At the start of learning, the detectors represent random activation patterns of these Gabor filters. By using a competitive learning rule, the hidden detector units become specialized for activation patterns caused by particular images or properties of these images. When a bezier curve is presented, the "winning" detector adjusts its weight vector toward the curve's Gabor filter representation. A detector wins by having input-to-detector weight values that are closest to the Gabor filter activation. The extent to which the nonwinning detector nodes update their weights is restricted by the topology that is imposed on the feature detectors; we used a one-dimensional lattice such that each detector (except at the two end points) has two neighbors. Far neighbors update their weights less than close neighbors of the winning detector unit. This imposed topology creates a dimensional representation such that neighboring detectors respond to similar images or images having similar properties. More globally, the positions of the 14 detectors come to reflect the arbitrary morph-based dimension.

For the purposes of this chapter, we only want to mention the learning equation for adjusting the weights from the Gabor filter responses to the detector units:

$$\Delta w_{ji}^{\text{det}} = ELN_{(j,winner)}(a_i^{in} - w_{ji}^{\text{det}}),$$

where $\Delta w_{ji}^{\text{det}}$ is the weight from the Gabor filter Response i to Detector j. L is a constant learning rate. The Function N is dependent on how far Detector j is from the winning detector; far neighbors to a winning detector give values close to 0, and close neighbors give values closer to 1, so that the most learning occurs for close neighbors of the winning unit. The $(a_i^{in} - w_{ji}^{\text{det}})$ factor adapts the detectors' weights toward the input activations; if the Gabor response is larger than the weight, then the input-to-detector weight increases to match it. So far, the description of the network conforms to a standard self-organizing map. A new factor is introduced with the term E, which is the total amount of error at the category units. The category unit activations depend on the weighted activation in the previous layer of hidden detector units. The category units learn in a supervised manner so that the errors in predicting category membership are used to update the weights to these category units. The term E is introduced in the learning equation of the hidden nodes to influence the rate of learning; if a stimulus leads to a miscategorization or a relatively undifferentiated response by the categorization units, the term E is high, which leads to an increased rate at which the winning detector unit and its neighbors move toward the current input activation. Stated more metaphorically, the network sends out an SOS to neighboring detector nodes to help handle the current miscategorized input. Because undifferentiated categorization responses or miscategorizations occur most frequently at or near the category boundary, the hidden detector units tend to migrate toward the categorization boundary. As a result, the region near the boundary is more densely populated by detector nodes.

In two separate runs of the SOS network, we chose two different locations for the category split, corresponding to left- and right-split groups.

Figure 8.10 shows the influence of category training on discrimination sensitivity. The activations for each of the 14 detector nodes are shown for each of the 28 curves presented to the network. As such, each of the 14 curves in Panel A (left split) and Panel C (right split) shows a response profile for one detector. The detectors are densely distributed around the categorization boundary as a result of the classification feedback in the learning rule for detectors. Importantly, the detectors are arranged topologically. As we move from left to right along the bank of detectors, we move along the arbitrary dimension that we experimentally formed. As such, the network has implicitly represented an abstract and arbitrary stimulus dimension through the topology of its detectors.

A sensitivity measure for same/different judgments was constructed by taking the Euclidean distance between the detector unit activation patterns for the two curves to be judged. Thus, the model tends to respond "different" to the extent that the two presented input patterns activate different detectors. As shown in Panels B and D of Fig. 8.10, the peak sensitivity occurs approximately at the category boundaries. This occurs because slightly different stimuli that occur near the category boundary cause quite different activation patterns on the detector units, given the dense concentration of detectors in this region.

The SOS network models categorical perception effects by creating relatively dense representations of items at the border between categories.

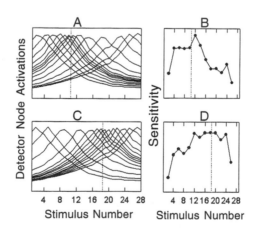

FIG. 8.10. The SOS network's simulation of the results shown in Fig. 8.7. The category boundaries are shown by dashed, vertical lines. The left panels show activation profiles for the 14 detector units when the categorization boundary was on the left (Panel A) or right (Panel C). In both cases, the categorization boundaries are densely populated with detectors, giving rise to the increase in sensitivity at the category boundaries shown in Panels B (left-split) and D (right-split).

This treatment of categorical perception differs from other neural network implementations. In Anderson, Silverstein, Ritz, and Jones' (1977) model, each category has its own attractor, and the stimuli that fall into one category are all propelled toward the category's attractor. In Harnad, Hanson, and Lubin (1994), the stimuli that fall into one category are repelled from the categorization boundary. One potential advantage of our account is that it explains how stimuli falling on the *same* side of a category boundary may also become more discriminable after categorization training, if they are sufficiently close to the category boundary. The results from our experiment suggest that this is the case for our participants, and this effect has been shown more persuasively by other researchers (Iverson & Kuhl, 1995). In networks that explain categorical perception by creating different attractors for different categories, unique items that are close to the boundary but fall in the same category become more similar with processing, not more distinctive. In general, developing detectors that both cover input patterns and are tailored to categorization requirements is a promising avenue for modeling perceptual learning phenomena related to categorical perception, stimulus pre-exposure, and discrimination learning.

THE SEGMENTATION OF OBJECTS INTO PARTS

People organize objects into parts, not simply by carving nature at the joints, but by carving joints into nature. It is more natural for us to think of an X as being broken down into a left slash and a right slash than as being composed of a *V* and an upside-down *V* intersecting at a point, even though both are possible decompositions (McGraw, Rehling, & Goldstone, 1994). Palmer conducted several studies on the naturalness of parts in whole objects, exploring factors that make certain parts more natural than others (Palmer, 1977, 1978). Palmer also developed a quantitative part goodness model that used a number of objective factors about the parts and whole: how close the line segments in a part were to each other, whether they formed closed objects, whether they had similar orientations, and whether the line segments of a part were similar to line segments in other parts. Palmer found that this objective measure of part naturalness correlated highly with empirical methods for assessing subjective part goodness, such as requesting people to rate the naturalness of a part or measuring participants' response times to confirm that a particular part is contained in the whole.

Pevtzow and Goldstone (1994) were interested in whether the naturalness of a part in a whole depends on not just the objective physical properties that Palmer considered, but also a person's subjective experience. In particular, we thought that how natural a part is might depend on whether it has been useful for categorization. In the same way that the world looks like a nail to the person who has a hammer, to the person who has learned that a particular feature is diagnostic for needed categorizations, the world may look like it is built from this feature. To test this conjecture, we gave participants a categorization task, followed by part/whole judgments. During categorization, participants were shown distortions of the four objects A, B, C, and D shown in Fig. 8.11. The objects were distorted by adding a random line segment that was connected to the segments already present. Using an experimental design that should now be familiar to the reader, we gave participants extended training with either a vertical or horizontal categorization rule. For participants who learned that A and C were in one category and B and D were in another, the two component parts at the bottom of Fig. 8.11 were diagnostic. For participants who learned that A and B belonged in one category and C and D belonged to the other, the components on the right were diagnostic. During part/whole judgments, participants were shown a whole and then a part and were asked whether the part was contained in the whole. As with Palmer's studies, it is assumed that the faster a person can correctly confirm the presence of a part, the more natural the part is. Participants were given both present and absent judgments. Participants were given trials with parts that were previously diagnostic or nondiagnostic and with complements of these category parts. A complement is what remains in a whole when a category part (one of the components shown in Fig. 8.11) is removed.

The major result to note from Fig. 8.12 is that participants were faster to correctly respond "present" when the part was diagnostic than when it was nondiagnostic. To the extent that one can find response time analogs of signal detection theory sensitivity and bias, this effect seems to be a sensitivity difference rather than a bias difference, because absent judgments also tended to be faster for diagnostic than nondiagnostic parts. Given that a category part that was diagnostic for one group was nondiagnostic for the other group, it is not simply the physical stimulus properties that determine how readily a person can segment an object into a particular set of parts; segmentation is also influenced by the learned categorical diagnosticity of the parts. The results for complements were unexpected; if a part was relevant during categorization, then participants were relatively slow to respond that the complement was present. One may have predicted the opposite because the part and its complement are consistent with the same segmentation of an object. However, the result is predicted if category parts attract attention to themselves when they are diagnostic, to the detriment of other parts in the display.

We have begun modeling the result from this experiment by using a competitive learning network. As with the experiment, the network is

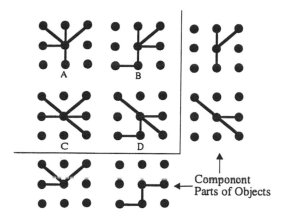

FIG. 8.11. Materials used by Pevtzow and Goldstone (1994). The four Objects A, B, C, and D were categorized into two groups. When A and B were placed in one group and C and D were placed in the other, the parts on the right were diagnostic. When A and C were placed in one group and B and D were placed in the other, then the parts on the bottom were diagnostic. Adapted from "Categorization and the Parsing of Objects," by R. Pevtzow and R. L. Goldstone, 1994, in *Proceedings of the 16th Annual Conference of the Cognitive Science Society* (Hillsdale, NJ: Lawrence Erlbaum Associates), p. 719. Copyright 1994. Adapted with permission

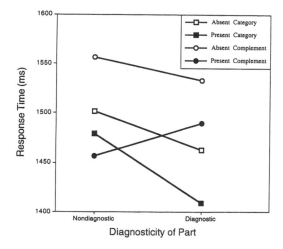

FIG. 8.12. It was easier to detect the presence or absence of a part in a whole object when the part was previously diagnostic for a categorization. The complement (the remaining line segments of the whole once the part has been removed) of a part was harder to find in a whole when the part was previously diagnostic for a categorization.

211

first given categorization training and then a subsequent segmentation task, using the same network weights. Similar to the simulation of acquired categorical perception, the network involves three layers: one representing the input patterns, one representing a bank of learned detectors, and one reflecting the category assignments of the inputs. Both the weights from the input patterns to the detectors and the weights from the detectors to categories are learned. The same network is used for categorizing and segmenting patterns, but the category units have an impact only during categorization. A schematic illustration of the network for the two tasks is shown in Fig. 8.13. The categorization task uses a standard unsupervised competitive learning algorithm (Rumelhart & Zipser, 1985), but includes a top-down influence of category labels incorporating supervised learning. The network begins with random weights from a 2D input array to a pair of detector units. When an input pattern is presented, the unit with the weight vector that is closest to the input pattern is the winner and selectively adjusts its weights to become even more specialized toward the input. By this mechanism, the originally homogenous detectors become differentiated over time, splitting the input patterns into two categories according to which detector is specialized for each pattern. Abstractly, the competitive learning algorithm, if supplied with jazz and classical pieces of music, automatically learns to group the pieces into these categories without feedback, because the pieces naturally cluster into these two groups. However, given that we want the detectors to reflect the experiment-supplied categories, we need to modify the standard unsupervised algorithm. This is done by including a mechanism

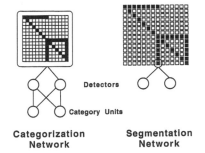

Categorization   **Segmentation**
Network   **Network**

FIG. 8.13. The categorization and segmentation network used to simulate the results shown in Fig. 8.10. The same input-to-detector weights are used for both the categorization and segmentation tasks. During categorization, an entire pattern is fed in as input at the same time, and one detector becomes specialized for the pattern. Effectively, detectors arise that sort the inputs into two categories according to their diagnostic line segments. During segmentation, a pattern is fed in one pixel at a time, and detectors learn to become specialized for pixels. Now, detectors sort the *parts* of one pattern into two segments.

such that detectors that are useful for categorizing an input pattern become more likely to win the competition to learn the pattern. The usefulness of a detector is assumed to be directly proportional to the weight from the detector to the presented category, which is provided as a label associated with an input pattern. The input-to-detector weights do not have to be set before the weights from detectors to categories are learned.

With this modified competitive learning algorithm, if we present the same four pictures but with different categorizations, then different detectors develop. Detectors emerge that tend to selectively represent the diagnostic, shared components of input patterns. If A and B of Fig. 8.11 are assigned to the same category, as are C and D, then detectors tend to emerge that respond preferentially to the component parts on the right side of Fig. 8.11. However, if we change the categorization, then detectors for the lower components are created.

Thus far, the category learning network has been described. The basic insight is that segmentation tasks can also be modeled by using competitive learning, and thus the two tasks can share the same network weights and consequently influence each other. Competitive learning for categorization sorts complete, whole input patterns into separate groups. Competitive learning for segmentation takes a single input pattern and sorts the pieces of the pattern into separate groups. For segmentation, instead of providing a whole pattern at once, we feed in the pattern one pixel at a time. Instead of grouping patterns, the network groups pixels together. With this technique, if the "original pattern" in Fig. 8.14 is presented to the network, the network might segment it in the fashion shown in the top decomposition. This figure shows the weights from the 2D input array to each of two detectors and reflects the specializations of the two detectors. The two segments are complements of each other—if one detector becomes specialized for a pixel, the other detector does not. This stems from the basic operation of the competitive learning algorithm by which the winning detector indirectly inhibits the other detector from learning to adapt to the input. Unfortunately, this segmentation is psychologically absurd; nobody would decompose the original figure into these parts. To create psychologically plausible segmentations, we modify the determination of winners. Topological constraints on detector creation are incorporated by two mechanisms: Input-to-detector weights "leak" to their neighbors in an amount proportional to a Gaussian function of their distance, and input-to-detector weights also spread to each other as a function of their orientation similarity, defined by the inner product of four Gabor filter responses. The first mechanism produces detectors that tend to respond to cohesive, contiguous regions of an input. The second mechanism produces detectors that follow the principle of good continuation, dividing X into two crossing lines rather than two kissing sideways

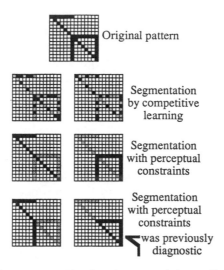

FIG. 8.14. When a competitive learning network is supplied the original pattern, the detectors specialize for different pixels. When the network is supplemented with perceptual biases to develop spatially coherent, smooth features, segmentations such as the one shown by the middle pair of detectors are obtained. When this latter network is run after it has already acquired a detector for a particular component during categorization training, then the segmentation shown by the last pair of detectors is typically found.

*V*s, because the two halves of a diagonal line are linked by their common orientation. Thus, if a detector wins for Pixel *X* (meaning that the detector receives the most activation when Pixel *X* is on), then the detector also tends to handle pixels that are close to, and have similar orientations to, Pixel *X*. With this modification and added dynamics that allow the network to escape local minima,[2] segmentations such as the middle decomposition occur. The segmentations now tend to break the object into whole line segments that are connected to each other. These two mechanisms are too simplistic to do justice to human perceptual biases on segmentation, but even in this simplistic form, they lead to segmentations that tend to obey the Gestalt laws of good continuation and closure. The segmentation network is a process-model alternative to Palmer's model of segmentation and produces roughly comparable results.

However, the segmentation network has a notable advantage over Palmer's model in explaining Pevtzow and Goldstone's results. The seg-

---

[2]Local minima were avoided by adding noise to input-to-detector weights and basing the magnitude of this noise on the strength of the input-to-detector weight.

mentation network, because it shares the same input-to-detector weights that were used for the categorization network, can be influenced by previous category learning. Detectors that were diagnostic for categorization are more likely used to segment a pattern because they are already primed. Thus, if a particular shape is diagnostic, the network segments the whole into this shape most of the time, as shown by the bottom decomposition in Fig 8.14. In short, category learning can alter the perceived organization of an object. By establishing multisegment features along a bank of detectors, the segmentation network is biased to parse objects in terms of these features. This application shows that two separate cognitive tasks can be viewed as mutually constraining self-organization processes. Categorization can be understood in terms of the specialization of perceptual detectors for particular input patterns, where specialization is influenced by categorization diagnosticity. Object segmentation can be viewed as specialization of detectors for particular parts in a single input pattern. Object segmentation can isolate an input pattern's single parts that are potentially useful for categorization, and categorization can suggest possible ways of parsing an object that would not otherwise have been considered.

THE UNITIZATION OF COMPONENTS FOR CATEGORIZATION

Thus far, we have described the influence of category learning on the sensitization of pre-existing and novel dimensions and the organization of objects into dimensions and parts. One final mechanism of perceptual learning is unitization. In unitization, a single functional unit is created for a complex pattern, and this functional unit can be identified without an analytic process of breaking it down into components and identifying the components. The letter A may originally be perceived by assembling evidence from independent feature detectors for oriented lines, but with prolonged practice, a single unitized chunk for the entire A image seems to emerge (LaBerge, 1973). Czerwinski, Lightfoot, and Shiffrin (1992; Shiffrin & Lightfoot, 1997) obtained evidence for such a unitization process, by finding large improvements in the speed and efficiency of detecting conjunctively defined targets in a feature search task. The current experiments, reported by Goldstone (in press), similarly explore unitization, but from a complementary perspective. First, our experiments are primarily concerned with the influence of category learning on unitization, under the hypothesis that a unit tends to be created if the parts that make up the unit frequently co-occur and if the unit is useful for determining a categorization. Second, we use a new method for analyzing response-time distributions to assess the presence of unitization.

Whenever the claim for the construction of new units is made, two objections must be addressed. First, perhaps the unit existed in people's vocabulary before categorization training. Our stimuli are designed to make this explanation unlikely. Each unit to be sensitized is constructed by connecting 5 randomly chosen curves. With 10 curves that can be sampled, there are 5^{10} possible different units. If it can be shown that any randomly selected unit can be sensitized, then an implausibly large number of vocabulary items are required under the constraint that all vocabulary items are fixed and *a priori*. The second objection is that no units need be formed; instead, people analytically integrate evidence from the five separate curves to make their categorizations. However, this objection is untenable if participants, at the end of extended training, are faster at categorizing the units than expected by the analytic approach. Quantifying what "faster than expected" means is the main task at hand.

The categorization task was designed so that evidence for five components must be received before certain categorization responses are made. As such, it was a conjunctive categorization task. The stimuli and their category memberships are shown in Fig. 8.15. Each of the letters refers to a particular segment of a "doodle." Each doodle was composed of five segments, with a semicircle below the segments added to create a closed figure. To correctly place the doodle labeled ABCDE into Category 1, all five components, A, B, C, D, and E, must be processed. For example, if the rightmost component was not attended, then ABCDE could not be distinguished from ABCDZ, which belongs in Category 2. Not only does no single component suffice for accurate categorization of ABCDE, but two-way, three-way, and four-way conjunctions of components also do

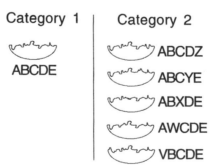

FIG. 8.15. Stimuli used by Goldstone (in press). Each letter represents a particular stimulus segment, and each stimulus is composed of five segments. To categorize the item represented by ABCDE as belonging to Category 1, it is necessary to process information associated with each of the segments.

not suffice. For example, the three-way conjunction C and D and E is possessed by the stimulus ABCDE, but this conjunction does not discriminate ABCDE from AWCDE or VBCDE. Only the complete five-way conjunction suffices to accurately categorize ABCDE.

If unitization occurs during categorization, then the stimulus ABCDE may become treated functionally like a single component with training. If this occurs, then participants should be able to quickly respond that this stimulus belongs to Category 1. A pronounced decrease in the time required to categorize the conjunctively defined stimulus ABCDE is taken as initial evidence of unitization.

For improvement in the conjunctive task to be taken as evidence for unitization, two important control conditions are necessary. First, it is important to show that tasks that do not require unitization do not show comparable speedups. To this end, a control task was included that allows participants to categorize the item ABCDE by attending to only a single component rather than a five-way conjunction. This was done by having Category 2 contain only one of the five Category 2 doodles shown in Fig. 8.15, randomly selected for each participant. This "One" (component) condition should not result in the same speedup as the "All" (components) condition where five components must be attended. If it does, then the speedup can be attributed to a simple practice effect rather than to unitization. Second, it is important to show that stimuli that cannot be unitized also do not show comparable speedups. For this control condition, it was necessary to attend to a five-way conjunction of components, but the ordering of the components in the stimulus was randomized. That is, ABCDE and CEBDA were treated as equivalent. In this "random" condition, a single template cannot serve to categorize the ABCDE stimulus, and unitization should therefore not be possible.

The results of the experiment were suggestive of unitization. The results in Fig. 8.16 reflect only the correct responses to the Category 1 doodle ABCDE because this is the only stimulus that requires the full five-component conjunction to be identified. The horizontal axis shows the amount of practice over a 2-hour experiment. The condition where all components were necessary for categorization, and where they were combined in a consistent manner to create a coherent image, showed far greater practice effects than did the others. This dramatic improvement suggests that the components are joined to create a single functional unit to serve categorization. Particularly impressive speedups were found when and only when unitization was possible and advantageous.

It is possible to get stronger evidence for unitization with this paradigm. The alternative to the unitization hypothesis is that responses in the All task are obtained by integrating evidence from five separate judgments of the type required in the One task. In arguing against this analytic

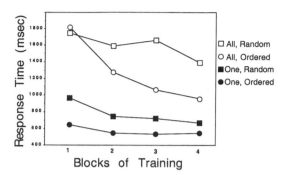

FIG. 8.16. Results from Goldstone (in press). The most pronounced improvement was observed when all components were required for a categorization, and the components were always in the same positions.

account, a highly efficient version of the analytic account was devised to observe whether it still predicted response times that were too slow. The first advantage given to the analytic model was fully parallel processing; All responses were made by combining five One responses, but evidence for these five One responses was assumed to be obtained simultaneously. Second, the model was given unlimited capacity; identifying one component was not slowed by the need to identify another component. In obtaining predictions from this charitably interpreted analytic model, it is important to remember that the All task is a conjunctive task. To categorize ABCDE as a Category 1 item with the required 95% categorization accuracy, all five components must be identified. Second, there is intrinsic variability in response times, even in the simple task where only one component must be identified. An analytic model of response times can be developed that predicts what the All task response-time distribution should be, based on the One task distribution. After training, a distribution of response times in the One task can be determined. To derive the analytic model's predictions, we can randomly sample five response times from this distribution. The *maximum* of these five times, rather than the average, is selected because no response can be made to the conjunction until all components have been recognized. We can repeat this selection process several times to create a distribution of the maximums, and this yields the predicted response-time distribution for the All task according to the analytic model. Fortunately, there is an easier way of obtaining the predicted distribution. The One task response-time distribution is converted to a cumulative response-time distribution, and each point on this distribution is raised to the fifth power. If the probability of one component's being recognized in less than 400 milliseconds

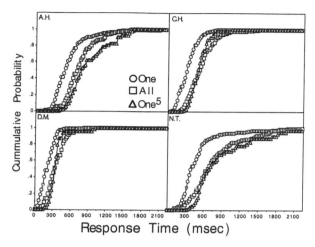

FIG. 8.17. The cumulative response time distributions for the four participants taken from the last session. The One and All distributions were empirically obtained. The One[5] distribution was obtained by raising each point along the One distribution to the fifth power and represents the analytic model's predicted cumulative distribution for the All task. Violations of this analytic model occur when the All task's distribution is shifted to the left of the analytic model's distribution. Such violations occur for the fastest half of response times for all four participants (significantly so for all participants except C. H.).

is .2, then the probability of all five components' being recognized in less than 400 milliseconds is .2 raised to the fifth power, assuming sampling independence.

A replication of the experiment shown in Fig. 8.16 was conducted that included the ordered All and One tasks. Only four research assistants participated as participants, but unlike the 2-hour experiment described previously, each participant was given eight 2-hour training sessions. The results, shown in Fig. 8.17, are only for Category 1 responses on the final day of the experiment. These results indicate violations of the analytic model. The cumulative response-time distributions show that the One task was naturally the fastest (most shifted to the left). The analytic model's predictions are shown by the curve labeled One[5], which is obtained simply by raising each point on the One curve to the fifth power. For two of the four participants, the actual All distribution was faster than the analytic models' predictions for all regions of the distribution. For all four participants, the fastest 30% of response times for the All task was faster than predicted by the analytic model, even though all participants were achieving accuracies greater than 95%. Although the advantage of the All over the One[5] distributions may not look impressive, they were significant by a Kolmogorov–Smirnoff test of distributions for all participants except C.H.[3] Thus, by the end of extended training, responses to the conjunctively defined ABCDE curve are faster than predicted by the analytic model, despite its charitable interpretation.

The conclusion we draw from these results is that category learning probably created new perceptual units. Large practice effects are found if and only if stimuli were unitizable (the first experiment), and responses after 14 hours of training were faster to conjunctively defined categories than predicted by a charitably interpreted analytic model. The results shown in Fig. 8.17 violate the analytic model only if negative dependencies or independence is assumed between the five sampled response times that make up one All judgment. Although it is beyond the scope of this chapter, we also have evidence for violations of the analytic model for classes of positive dependencies, using Fourier transformations to deconvolve shared input–output processes from the One task response-time distribution (Goldstone, in press; P. L. Smith, 1990).

One question still remains: Exactly how do people become so fast at categorizing ABCDE in the All task? Two qualitatively different mechanisms can account for the pronounced speedup of the conjunctive categorization: a genuinely holistic match process to a constructed unit, or an analytic model that incorporates interactive facilitation among the component detectors. In a holistic match process, a conjunctive categorization is made by comparing the image of the presented item with an image that has been stored over prolonged practice. The stored image may have parts, but these parts are either arbitrarily small or do not play a functional role in the recognition of the image. There is evidence supporting the gradual development of configural features. Neurophysiological findings suggest that some individual neurons represent familiar conjunctions of features (Perrett & Oram, 1993) and that prolonged training can produce neurons that respond to configural patterns (Logothetis et al., 1995). However, the results can also arise if detecting one component of ABCDE facilitates detection of other components. In either case, the process is appropriately labeled "unitization" in that the percepts associated with different components are closely coupled as a result of training. In fact, an interactive facilitation mechanism can be seen as the mechanism

---

[3]One may ask why the violations of the analytic model are restricted to, or at least maximized at, the fast response times. Most likely, a range of strategies was used for placing ABCDE into Category 1 in the All task. On some trials, an analytic strategy of combining evidence from separately detected components may have been used. On other trials, participants may have detected a single constructed unit. On average, the unit-based trials will be faster than the analytic trials. If the fast and slow response times tend to be based on single units and analytic integration, respectively, then we predict violations of the analytic model to be limited to, or more pronounced for, the fast response times.

that implements holistic unit detection at a higher functional level of description.

GENERAL REMARKS ON ADAPTIVE PERCEPTUAL VOCABULARIES

The general conclusions can be divided into empirical and theoretical ones. Empirically, evidence was found for several types of perceptual learning that accompanies concept learning. Concept learning can cause the perceptual sensitization of existing dimensions such as size and brightness and can cause sensitization of regions in a dimension, a finding suggesting that categorical perception can be due to learned categories. Not only can category learning lead to stretching and shrinking of existing dimensions, but it can also lead to selective sensitization along novel dimensions. These new dimensions may be created by breaking a fused dimension into subdimensions, as was the case with saturation and brightness, or by creating dimensions by morphing between arbitrary end points, as was the case with the bezier curves and bald heads. Finally, the object segmentation and unitization experiments indicate that concept learning can lead to the addition of new elements in a person's perceptual vocabulary. These new vocabulary elements change how objects are or ganized and can lead to responses that are more efficient than predicted by analytic models that do not develop new vocabularies.

The major theoretical contribution of the research has been to specify some possible ways in which perceptual and conceptual learning might interact. In both the neural networks described, feature detectors are developed that represent the network's set of acquired vocabulary elements. The networks begin with homogenous, undifferentiated detectors that become specialized for different inputs over time. Furthermore, both models have mechanisms by which detector-to-category associations modify the nature of the detectors. It is unnecessary to first develop detectors and then build associations between detectors and categories. These two types of learning can and should go on simultaneously.

Staking Out the Territory

It is worthwhile to step back and ask exactly what is entailed by the claim that perceptual vocabularies adapt to the demands of concept learning. What we mean by a perceptual vocabulary is the set of functional features used for describing objects. A functional feature, in turn, is defined as any object property that can be selectively attended to (for a similar claim, see Smith, Gasser, & Sandhofer, 1997). An organism shows evidence of using Feature X to describe an object if there is behavioral evidence that

X can be considered in isolation from other aspects of the object. Thus, a feature is a "chunk of object stuff" that has been individuated from the rest of the object. This definition explicitly denies that psychologically relevant features are objective properties of the external world. Even if a physicist can measure the illuminance of an object or a chemist can measure the tannin content of a Bordeaux wine, these stimulus properties are not psychological features unless the perceiving organism can isolate them as well. Tying featurehood to selective attention conforms to many empirical techniques for investigating features. Garner (1974) considered two features or dimensions to be separable if categorizations on the basis of one of the features are not slowed by irrelevant variation on the other. Treisman (e.g., Treisman & Gelade, 1980) argued that features are registered separately on different feature maps, which gives rise to efficient and parallel searches for individual features and the automatic splitting of different features that occupy the same object. Given this characterization of a feature, the claim for vocabulary creation seems less controversial than might be thought in view of the prevalence of fixed-vocabulary approaches. A substantial body of evidence from development (Smith, 1989) and expertise (Burns & Shepp, 1988) indicates that children and novices have a harder time selectively attending to stimulus aspects than do adults and experts. Claiming vocabulary creation does not necessitate that features are created *de novo* or that our perceptual system provides us with information that was not present *in any form* in the early stages of sensory processing. It is unclear whether these are even logically tenable positions. All that is required is that the organism shows behavioral evidence that stimulus elements come to be isolated with experience.

In some respects, our claim is similar to those made by theorists of dynamical systems in which an object is recognized if its processing follows the same trajectory as an object presented earlier, without requiring any decomposition of the objects into part representations (see, for example, Thelen & Smith, 1994). Both approaches stress the flexibility and plasticity of perceptual processing, and argue for powerful top-down and contextual influences on perception. However, a fundamental difference between the approaches is that we do posit a set of features that are used for describing objects. Radical versions of the dynamical systems approach have argued that objects are not represented by a set of elementary features at all. Thus, our approach is more closely tied to the traditional "fixed feature set" approach to cognition than it may initially appear. Our approach and the fixed feature set approach both assume that objects are represented in terms of a set of building blocks; the theories simply differ on whether this set is expandable.

In advocating building block representations over complete fluidity, we may be criticized on the same grounds of inflexibility that we used to criticize fixed feature set theories. In our approach, objects must be described in terms of a finite vocabulary of features that have been previously acquired. Still, we believe that the traditional advantages of building block theories compensate for this inflexibility. By building object descriptions from elements, we have a generative method for creating and accommodating novel objects. The advantages of propositional representations are accrued by establishing explicit relations between represented elements. Systematicities in the appearance, function, and influence of objects can be accounted for in terms of systematicities between their featural representations. Perhaps most important, decomposing objects into features provides an efficient and compressed representational code. Instead of coding objects in a raw, uncompressed manner, short codes can be used to token discrete features that can be associated with complex configurations. If a feature that represents the doodle ABCDE is built, then the large amount of information present in the rich doodle is compressed into a single feature. In the same way that a large data set can be reduced to a few major components (in principal component analysis) or dimensions (in multidimensional scaling), a marked information reduction can be achieved by establishing features that underlie systematic variation among a set of objects. This reduction is accomplished by identifying stimulus aspects that are highly correlated, isolating (differentiating) them from other aspects, and grouping (unitizing) them.

The empirical evidence that people execute such a feature-extraction process comes from transfer experiments. Features that were useful for an earlier categorization are more likely to be applied to a later categorization (see Fig. 8.5), are sensitized for subsequent same/different judgments (Figs. 8.2 and 8.3), are used as features for decomposing subsequent whole objects (Fig. 8.12), and can be detected without analytically composing them from smaller components (Fig. 8.17). The sum of this evidence suggests a feature development process that has a lasting impact on perceptual processing.[4] In dynamic models that recognize objects by pulling the raw object description toward an attractor state caused by a previous episode, there is little reason to expect prominent transfer on the basis of component, rather than overall, similarities.

In light of our commitment to (adaptive) building block representations of objects, our approach is perfectly consistent with evidence that people use particular sets of primitive elements. The geons, textons, or conceptual primitives of fixed feature set theories may be the end product of a general

---

[4]The influence on perception is lasting in the sense that it persists from training to transfer. However, it remains to be seen how permanent these influences are. In most cases, the endurance of a perceptual change is probably positively related to the amount of training required to produce the change.

perceptual learning strategy. Recent research in computer science has shown that sets of primitives, including Gabor filters, and size detectors can be created by a system provided naturalistic scenes (e.g. Miikkulainen, Bednar, Choe, & Sirosh, 1997). The advantages of learning, rather than simply positing, elements are that mechanisms are in place for acquiring slightly different primitives if the environment is modified, and specialized domains in the environment can have tailored sets of primitives designed for them (Edelman & Intrator, 1997).

Constraints on Computational Models of Perceptual and Conceptual Learning

We have been advocating systems that develop new perceptual vocabularies instead of relying on a fixed set of features. Some may object to this on grounds of computational plausibility. The argument is: With such a flexible system it takes too long to learn any category. Even with a fixed set of features, there may be a combinatorial explosion of complex rules involving these features, if we allow rules such as "white and (square or triangle)" (Bruner et al., 1956; Nosofsky, Palmeri, & McKinley, 1994). Moreover, the picture is much more grim if we allow the possibility of creating new features and entering these into Boolean expressions. In this case, there is a combinatorial explosion of potential features combined combinatorially with a combinatorial explosion of logical expressions. Our solution to the difficulties associated with finding good solutions in such an immense search space is to provide two sources of constraints. *Psychophysical constraints* enter in because not anything can be made into a feature. There is a heavy bias for features to be contiguous and coherent and to follow Gestalt laws of organization. In the segmentation network (see Fig. 8.14), these constraints were needed to create psychologically realistic segmentations. Mechanisms biased the acquired features to involve similarly oriented and positioned segments and served to constrain the number of features contemplated. Via *categorical constraints,* there is a bias to develop features that are diagnostic for relevant categories.

In the described networks, these two constraints act in parallel. There are problems with the flexibility and efficiency of either serial approach—starting with the set of candidate features admissible by psychophysical constraints such as topological coherence and then choosing the ones from this set that obey the categorical constraints, or vice versa (see also Wisniewski & Medin, 1994). In a serial approach that uses psychophysical constraints as a first filter on the feature selection, features that should be created if useful for a categorization are excluded. For example, segments that are separated by a pixel are probably eventually formed given enough training. These features can be accommodated by weakening the psychophysical constraint on connectedness, but only at the considerable cost of failing to sufficiently limit the search space of features generally. Parallel constraints allow the individual constraints to both strongly limit the search space of features but also to be relaxed if required by other constraints simultaneously being satisfied.

Finally, one possibility is that people may actually be quite poor at combining separate and distinct features into logical expressions. Creating categories such as "Large and (square or triangle)" may be rather unnatural, four decades of concept learning research not withstanding. At the same time, people seem to be adept at integrating components to create a single, coherent feature. Humans seem to be much more adept at creating coherent, useful features than they are at simultaneously attending to several unrelated sources of information. By providing mechanisms for the development of novel features, much of the need for searching through the space of logical rules is removed. In many cases, a single feature suffices if it can integrate many stimulus aspects.

Building Perceptual Vocabularies: A Reprise

Cognitive science researchers who have proposed particular fixed sets of primitives have cleverly designed primitives that are genuinely useful for representing words, objects, and events. Our point is simply that ordinary people may be almost as clever as these researchers and may come up with their own sets of tailored elements (Schyns et al., 1998). The advantage, of course, is that the elements can be tuned to the particular categories that are important. Fixed feature sets, no matter how cleverly constructed, cannot be perfectly tuned to the individual. Either the fixed feature sets have specific, special-purpose features, in which case the set is efficient at representing some things but incapable of representing other things, or the fixed feature set has a large number of general purpose, universal features, in which case it can represent everything, but not efficiently, taking advantage of the systematicities particular to a domain. Instead, if perceptual vocabularies are created, they are at least diagnostic for the category that they were created to accommodate. In sum, concepts certainly depend on perceptual encodings, but it is not viciously circular to claim that the perceptual encodings also depend on our concepts. In fact, our concepts seem to be able to "reach down" and influence the very features that compose the concepts.

ACKNOWLEDGMENTS

The research reported in this chapter has greatly benefited from comments and suggestions by Steven Harnad Arthur Markman, Douglas Medin, Richard Shiffrin, Philippe Schyns, Linda Smith, and Jean-Pierre Thibaut.

This research was supported by National Science Foundation Grant SBR–9409232, a James McKeen Cattell award, and a Jack Gill fellowship.

REFERENCES

Anderson, J. A., Silverstein, J. W., Ritz, S. A., & Jones, R. S. (1977). Distinctive features, categorical perception, and probability learning: Some applications of a neural model. *Psychological Review, 84*, 413–451.

Biederman, I. (1987). Recognition-by-components : A theory of human image understanding. *Psychological Review, 94*, 115–147.

Biederman, I., & Shiffrar, M. M. (1987). Sexing day-old chicks: A case study and expert systems analysis of a difficult perceptual-learning task. *Journal of Experimental Psychology: Learning, Memory, and Cognition, 13*, 640–645.

Bruner, J. S., Goodnow, J. J., & Austin, G. A. (1956). *A study of thinking.* New York: Wiley.

Burns, B., & Shepp, B. E. (1988). Dimensional interactions and the structure of psychological space: The representation of hue, saturation, and brightness. *Perception and Psychophysics, 43*, 494–507.

Czerwinski, M., Lightfoot, N., & Shiffrin, R. M. (1992). Automatization and training in visual search. *American Journal of Psychology, 105*, 271–315.

Daugman, J. G. (1985). Uncertainty relations for resolution in space, spatial frequency, and orientation optimized by two-dimensional visual cortical filters. *Journal of the Optical Society of America, 2*, 1160–1169.

Edelman, S., & Intrator, N. (in press). Learning as extraction of low-dimensional representations. In R. L. Goldstone, P. G. Schyns, & D. L. Medin (Eds.), *Psychology of learning and motivation* (Vol. 36, pp. 353–380). San Diego, CA: Academic Press.

Eimas, P. D., Siqueland, E. R., Jusczyk, P. W., & Vigorito, J. (1971). Speech perception in infants. *Science, 171*, 303–306.

Fahle, M., & Morgan, M. (1996). No transfer of perceptual learning between similar stimuli in the same retinal position. *Current Biology, 6*, 292–297.

Garner, W. R. (1974). *The processing of information and structure.* New York: Wiley.

Gibson, E. J. (1969). *Principles of perceptual learning and development.* New York: Appleton-Century–Crofts.

Gibson, E. J., & Walk, R. D. (1956). The effect of prolonged exposure to visually presented patterns on learning to discriminate them. *Journal of Comparative and Physiological Psychology, 49*, 239–242.

Goldstone, R. L. (1994). Influences of categorization on perceptual discrimination. *Journal of Experimental Psychology: General, 123*, 178–200.

Goldstone, R. L. (in press). Unitization during category learning. *Journal of Experimental Psychology: Human Perception and Performance.*

Goldstone, R. L., Schyns, P. G., & Medin, D. L. (1997). Learning to bridge between perception and cognition. In R. L. Goldstone, P. G. Schyns, & D. L. Medin (Eds.), *Psychology of learning and motivation* (Vol. 36, pp. 1–17). San Diego, CA: Academic Press.

Goldstone, R. L., & Steyvers. M. (1999). *Attention to novel face dimensions.* Manuscript in preparation.

Goldstone, R. L., Steyvers, M., & Larimer, K. (1996). Categorical perception of novel dimensions. In G. W. Cottrell (Ed.), *Proceedings of the 18th annual conference of the Cognitive Science Society* (pp 243–248). Hillsdale, NJ: Lawrence Erlbaum Associates.

Grau, J. W., & Kemler-Nelson, D. G. (1988). The distinction between integral and separable dimensions: Evidence for the integrality of pitch and loudness. *Journal of Experimental Psychology: General, 117,* 347–370.

Harnad, S. (1987). *Categorical perception.* Cambridge: Cambridge University Press.

Harnad, S., Hanson, S. J., & Lubin, J. (1995). Learned categorical perception in neural nets: Implications for symbol grounding. In V. Honavar & L. Uhr (Eds.), *Symbolic processors and connectionist network models in artificial intelligence and cognitive modelling: Steps toward principled integration* (pp. 191–206). Boston: Academic Press.

Hillyard, H. C., & Kutas, M. (1983). Electrophysiology of cognitive processes. *Annual Review of Psychology, 34,* 33–61.

Iverson, P., & Kuhl, P. K. (1995). Mapping the perceptual magnet effect for speech using signal detection theory and multidimensional scaling. *Journal of the Acoustical Society of America, 97,* 553–562.

Jakobson, R., Fant, G., & Halle, M. (1963). *Preliminaries to speech analysis: The distinctive features and their correlates.* Cambridge, MA: MIT Press.

Karni, A., & Sagi, D. (1991). Where practice makes perfect in texture discrimination: Evidence for primary visual cortex plasticity. *Proceedings of the National Academy of Sciences of the United States of America, 88,* 4966–4970.

Kohonen, T. (1995). *Self-organizing maps.* Berlin: Springer-Verlag.

Kruschke, J. K. (1992). ALCOVE: An exemplar-based connectionist model of category learning. *Psychological Review, 99,* 22–44.

Kuhl, P. K., & Miller, J. D. (1978). Speech perception by the chinchilla: Identification functions for synthetic VOT stimuli. *Journal of the Acoustical Society of America, 63,* 905–917.

LaBerge, D. (1973). Attention and the measurement of perceptual learning. *Memory and Cognition, 1,* 268–276.

Liberman, A. M., Harris, K. S., Hoffman, H. S., & Griffith, B. C. (1957). The discrimination of speech sounds within and across phoneme boundaries. *Journal of Experimental Psychology, 54,* 358–368.

Logothetis, N. K., Pauls, J., & Poggio, T. (1995). Shape representation in the inferior temporal cortex of monkeys. *Current Biology, 5,* 552–563.

McGraw, G., Rehling, J., & Goldstone, R. L. (1994). Letter perception: Toward a conceptual approach. In A. Ram & K. Eiselt (Eds.), *Proceedings of the 16th annual conference of the Cognitive Science Society* (pp. 613–618). Hillsdale, NJ: Lawrence Erlbaum Associates.

Miikkulainen, R., Bednar, J. A., Choe, Y., & Sirosh, J. (1997). Self-organization, plasticity, and low-level visual phenomena in a laterally connected map model of primary visual cortex. In R. L. Goldstone, P. G. Schyns, & D. L. Medin (Eds.), *Psychology of learning and motivation* (Vol. 36, pp. 257–308). San Diego, CA: Academic Press.

Myles-Worsley, M., Johnston, W. A., & Simons, M. A. (1988). The influence of expertise on x-ray image processing. *Journal of Experimental Psychology: Learning, Memory, and Cognition, 14,* 553–557.

Nosofsky, R. M. (1986). Attention, similarity, and the identification-categorization relationship. *Journal of Experimental Psychology: General, 115,* 39–57.

Nosofsky, R. M., Palmeri, T. J., & McKinley, S. C. (1994). Rule-plus-exception model of classification learning. *Psychological Review, 101,* 53–79.

Palmer, S. E. (1977). Hierarchical structure in perceptual representation. *Cognitive Psychology, 9,* 441–474.

Palmer, S. E. (1978). Structural aspects of visual similarity. *Memory & Cognition, 6,* 91–97.

Peron, R. M., & Allen, G. L. (1988). Attempts to train novices for beer flavor discrimination: A matter of taste. *Journal of General Psychology, 115,* 403–418.

Perrett, D. I., & Oram, M. W. (1993). Neurophysiology of shape processing. *Image and Vision Computing, 11,* 317–333.

Perrett, D. I., Smith, P. A. J., Potter, D. D., Mistlin, A. J., Head, A. D., & Jeeves, M. A. (1984). Neurones responsive to faces in the temporal cortex: Studies of functional organization, sensitivity to identity and relation to perception. *Human Neurobiology, 3,* 197–208.

Pevtzow, R., & Goldstone, R. L. (1994). Categorization and the parsing of objects. In A. Ram & K. Eiselt (Eds.), *Proceedings of the 16th annual conference of the Cognitive Science Society* (pp. 717–722). Hillsdale, NJ: Lawrence Erlbaum Associates.

Pisoni, D. B., Aslin, R. N., Perey, A. J., & Hennessy, B. L. (1982). Some effects of laboratory training on identification and discrimination of voicing contrasts in stop consonants. *Journal of Experimental Psychology: Human Perception and Performance, 8,* 297–314.

Repp, B. H., & Liberman, A. M. (1987). Phonetic category boundaries are flexible. In S. Harnad (Ed.), *Categorical perception* (pp. 89–112). Cambridge: Cambridge University Press.

Rumelhart, D. E., & Zipser, D. (1985). Feature discovery by competitive learning. *Cognitive Science, 9,* 75–112.

Schank, R. (1972). Conceptual dependency: A theory of natural language understanding. *Cognitive Psychology, 3,* 552–631.

Schyns, P. G., Goldstone, R. L., & Thibaut, J. (1998). Development of features in object concepts. *Behavioral and Brain Sciences, 21,* 1–54.

Schyns, P. G., & Murphy, G. L. (1994). The ontogeny of part representation in object concepts. In D. L. Medin (Ed.), *The psychology of learning and motivation* (Vol. 31, pp. 305–354). San Diego, CA: Academic Press.

Schyns, P. G., & Rodet, L. (1997). Categorization creates functional features. *Journal of Experimental Psychology: Learning, Memory, and Cognition, 23,* 681–696.

Shiffrin, R. M., & Lightfoot, N. (in press). Perceptual learning of alphanumeric-like characters. In R. L. Goldstone, P. G. Schyns, & D. L. Medin (Eds.), *Psychology of learning and motivation* (Vol. 36, pp. 45–82). San Diego, CA: Academic Press.

Shiffrin, R. M., & Schneider, W. (1977). Controlled and automatic human information processing, II: Perceptual learning, automatic attending and a general theory. *Psychological Review, 84,* 127–190.

Smith, L. B. (1989). From global similarity to kinds of similarity: The construction of dimensions in development. In S. Vosniadou & A. Ortony (Eds.), *Similarity and analogical reasoning* (pp. 146–178). Cambridge: Cambridge University Press.

Smith, L. B., Gasser, M., & Sandhofer, C. (in press). Learning to talk about the properties of objects: A network model of the development of dimensions. In R. L. Goldstone, P. G. Schyns, & D. L. Medin (Eds.), *Psychology of learning and motivation* (Vol. 36, pp. 219–256). San Diego, CA: Academic Press.

Smith, P. L. (1990). Obtaining meaningful results from Fourier deconvolution of reaction time data. *Psychological Bulletin, 108,* 533–550.

Steyvers, M. (1999). Morphing techniques for generating and manipulating face images. *Behavioral Research Methods, Instrumentation, and Computers, 31,* 359–369.

Thelen, E., & Smith, L. B. (1994). *A dynamic systems approach to the development of cognition and action.* Cambridge, MA: MIT Press.

Tipper, S. P. (1992). Selection for action: The role of inhibitory mechanisms. *Current Directions in Psychological Science, 1,* 105–109.

Treisman, A., & Gelade, G. (1980). A feature-integration theory of attention. *Cognitive Psychology, 12,* 97–136.

Weinberger, N. M. (1993). Learning-induced changes of auditory receptive fields. *Current Opinion in Neurobiology, 3,* 570–577.

Werker, J. F., & Tees, R. C. (1984). Cross-language speech perception: Evidence for perceptual reorganization during the first year of life. *Infant Behavior and Development, 7,* 49–63.

Wisniewski, E. J., & Medin, D. L. (1994). On the interaction of theory and data in concept learning. *Cognitive Science, 18,* 221–281.

9

The Proper Treatment of Symbols in a Connectionist Architecture

Keith J. Holyoak
John E. Hummel
University of California, Los Angeles

PHYSICAL SYMBOL SYSTEMS

A foundational principle of modern cognitive science is the physical symbol system hypothesis, which states simply that human cognition is the product of a physical symbol system (PSS). A symbol is a pattern that denotes something else; a symbol system is a set of symbols that can be composed into more complex structures by a set of relations. The term *physical* conveys that a symbol system can and must be realized in some physical way to create intelligence. The physical basis may be the circuits of an electronic computer, the neural substrate of a thinking biological organism, or in principle anything else that can implement a Turing machine-like computing device. Classical presentations of the PSS hypothesis include Newell and Simon (1976) and Newell (1980); more recent discussions include Newell (1990) and Vera and Simon (1993, 1994).

The PSS hypothesis, which implies that structured mental representations are central to human intelligence, was for some time uncontroversial, accepted by most cognitive scientists as an axiom of the field scarcely in need of either theoretical analysis or direct empirical support. In the mid-1980s, however, the hypothesis came under sharp attack from some proponents of connectionist models of cognition, particularly the advocates of models in the style of "parallel distributed processing," or PDP (Rumelhart, McClelland, & the PDP Research Group, 1986; more recently, Churchland, 1995; Elman, 1990; Elman et al., 1996; Seidenberg, 1994, 1997; and many others; see Marcus, 1998, for a review). The representations used in such models are often described as "subsymbolic" because the elementary units correspond to (relatively) low-level features, over which meaningful concepts are represented in a distributed fashion. Insofar as models based on "subsymbolic" representations are actually nonsymbolic yet adequate as accounts of human intelligence, the need for symbol systems is eliminated; hence models of this general class constitute "eliminative" connectionism (Pinker & Prince, 1988). Eliminative connectionism offers a direct challenge to the PSS hypothesis and thereby transforms the latter from an axiom of cognitive science into a controversial theoretical position, which has been vigorously defended by Fodor and Pylyshyn (1988), Pinker and Prince (1988), and Marcus (1998), among others.

Regardless of whether models based on distributed representations provide genuine alternatives to physical symbol systems, it is apparent that they have attractive properties as possible algorithmic accounts of cognition. Discrete symbols represent entities in an "all-or-none" fashion, thereby violating the principle of least commitment (e.g., using the presence or absence of the symbol *dog* to represent the presence or absence of a dog affords no direct basis for expressing inconclusive evidence that there may be a dog). Discrete symbols also fail to express the semantic content of the represented entities (e.g., the symbols *dog* and *cat* do not signify what dogs and cats have in common and how they differ). Distributed representations overcome both these limitations and capture some basic properties of human perception and thinking more effectively than do classical symbolic representations. By allowing similar inputs to elicit similar outputs, distributed representations capture broad regularities in human inductive inference and endow the system with error tolerance. They also support a variety of learning algorithms that can capture regularities in environmental inputs and that provide simple types of automatic generalization.

Another desirable property of connectionist architectures is that they are at least roughly consistent with neural architectures: Both consist of discrete computing elements that communicate in densely connected networks. In contrast to symbols in a traditional symbolic system, which can move around freely (e.g., from one function or role to another), nodes occupy fixed locations in connectionist networks, much as neurons occupy relatively fixed locations in the brain. As we see later, this difference between symbolic systems on the one hand and connectionist or neural systems on the other is important because it implies that nodes or neurons in a network need some special properties to bind fillers to roles or values to variables—the "binding problem" poses difficulties for the architecture of connectionist and neural networks. More generally, connectionist models provide a convenient language for linking cognitive phenomena to their possible neural substrates.[1]

Is it possible, or even desirable, for connectionist models to eliminate physical symbol systems? This question really has two parts. First, can distributed connectionist models eliminate *symbols?* The answer to this question hinges on a terminological issue about what a "symbol" is. If a symbol is narrowly defined as an atomic unit corresponding to a concept, then feature-based models may indeed be subsymbolic. If a symbol is defined more broadly as a representation that designates something, then distributed representations are as symbolic as the localist variety (see Touretzky & Pomerleau, 1994; Vera & Simon, 1994, for a debate that focuses on this definitional issue). We find the less restrictive definition to be more useful, but do not consider this part of the question further. The second part of the question is more substantive: Can distributed representations eliminate symbol *systems?* That is, is it possible to model the full scope of human cognition—including reasoning, relational generalization, language use, and complex object and scene recognition—with representations that do not allow the systematic composition of complex structures from simpler elements?

We argue that the answer is No. If this answer is accepted, then it follows that the PSS hypothesis is correct and the ultimate aim of eliminative connectionism is unattainable. However, the PSS hypothesis itself is an abstract description of the requirements for a cognitive architecture, rather than a prescription for any particular architecture. The core difference between the PSS hypothesis and the eliminative connectionist hypothesis is that the former postulates systematic, compositional mental representations, whereas the latter rejects them; hence the resolution of the debate hinges solely on the compositionality of human mental representations. The failure of eliminative connectionism (which founders on the compositionality of human mental representations) does not obviate the potential virtues of more realistic connectionist instantiations of the human cognitive architecture. What is required, then, is not eliminative connectionism, but rather a proper treatment of symbols in a connectionist architecture—an architecture that simultaneously retains the strengths of distributed representations and instantiates the PSS hypothesis—and hence constitutes *symbolic* connectionism (Holyoak, 1991; Hummel & Holyoak, 1998).

In the remainder of this chapter, we develop the case for symbolic connectionism. We first review evidence that central aspects of cognition

---

[1]At the same time, some apparent similarities between connectionist networks and neural networks—that nodes operate like neurons and connections operate like synapses—must be interpreted with caution. Neural processes are complex and not yet understood. The similarity of current connectionist models to actual neural networks lies more in their gross architectures than in the operation of their basic elements.

depend on compositional symbol systems. We then suggest certain requirements for a proper treatment of symbols in a connectionist network. Finally, we sketch an example of a connectionist architecture for reasoning and learning that meets these requirements.

ROLES AND FILLERS: THE NECESSITY
FOR VARIABLE BINDING

The best-known argument for the necessity of symbolic representations—the argument from systematicity—was made by Fodor and Pylyshyn (1988). They observed that knowledge is systematic in that the ability to think certain thoughts seems to imply the ability to think certain related thoughts. For example, a person who understands the meanings of the concepts *John*, *Mary*, and *loves* and can understand the proposition "John loves Mary" must surely understand the proposition "Mary loves John." Eliminative connectionist models do not ensure such systematicity. (In fact, as elaborated shortly, they ensure the *absence* of truly general systematicity.) A network of the PDP type can learn to respond in an appropriate fashion to an input representing any particular proposition; however, there is no assurance that learning one proposition enables a sensible response to a systematically related proposition (see Marcus, 1998).

Systematicity is the hallmark of a system in which complex symbols are composed in a regular fashion from simpler ones (see Halford, Wilson & Phillips, 1998). More primitive varieties of cognition can safely rely on specialized representational systems that do not require composition of complex symbols; instead, every significant stimulus configuration can be linked to appropriate responses, either innately or by associative learning. In this range, eliminative connectionist models may well be adequate. Strong evidence for systematicity has been found only for higher primates, most notably humans. Newell (1990) characterized the development of compositional symbol systems as the "Great Move" of evolution, triggered by the pressure to represent and manipulate increasingly diverse information about the physical and social environment. For example, humans can recognize scenes in which known or novel objects enter into varied spatial relations. Thus the relation *above (Object 1, Object 2)* can be instantiated by a triangle above a square, *above (triangle, square)*, or the reverse, *above (square, triangle)*. Human scene recognition is systematic with respect to a limited set of spatial relations and for this reason requires models based on composed symbols (i.e., structural descriptions; see chap. 7, this volume). Thinking and language require systematicity on a grander scale, because the pool of potential relations over which complex symbols can be composed is indefinitely large (e.g., *loves (lover, beloved), sells (seller, buyer, object), pretends (person (is [Object 1, Object 2])*, and so on). There is reason to think that the human ability to represent and manipulate domain-general relations is linked to evolutionary advances in prefrontal cortex (Robin & Holyoak, 1994).

As all these examples suggest, composability of symbols requires representations that distinguish variables from their values or, equivalently, roles from their fillers. "John loves Mary" is similar to "Mary loves John" in that both propositions involve the same relation and objects, but the two differ in that the assignments of objects as fillers of roles are reversed. It is this *combination of similarity and difference* between systematically related symbol structures that eliminative connectionist models fail to capture. Lacking any capacity to explicitly bind roles to their fillers, eliminative connectionist models must resort to various forms of conjunctive coding to bind fillers to roles (as elaborated shortly). For example, one node (or collection of nodes) may represent John in the agent role of the love relation (the conjunction *John + lover*), with a completely separate node (or pattern) representing John in the patient role (*John + beloved*). As a consequence, such models do not preserve object identities across relational contexts. This problem, already apparent with simple relational structures, becomes even more pernicious as the complexity of composed symbol structures increases. Eliminative connectionist models have only one basic resource for representing propositions: a fixed-length vector of units. This fixed vector thus becomes the procrustean bed into which all symbols must be forcibly fit. Because symbol structures can be of varying size and complexity, there is no way to guarantee that a given symbol is represented on the same (or even overlapping) set of units in two different structures. Thus, the units that code "Mary" in "John loves Mary" may not overlap with those that code "Mary" in "Mary loves John," much less with those that code "Mary" in "John believes that Peter's anger toward Mary caused him to write her a strongly worded letter."[2]

---

[2]Arguments (or roles) may suggest different shades of meaning as a function of the roles (or fillers) to which they are bound. For example, "loves" suggests a slightly different interpretation in *loves (John Mary)* than it does in *loves (John chocolate)*. However, such contextual variation does not imply in any general sense that the filler (or role) itself necessarily changes its identity as a function of the binding. For example, our ability to appreciate that the "John" in *loves (John Mary)* is the same person as the "John" in *bite (Rover John)* demands explanation in terms of John's invariance across the different bindings. If we assume invariance of identity with binding as the general phenomenon, then it is possible to explain contextual shadings in meaning when they occur (Hummel & Holyoak, 1997). However, if we assume lack of invariance of identity as the general rule, then it becomes impossible to explain how knowledge acquired about an individual in one context can be connected to knowledge about the same individual in other contexts.

The inadequacies of eliminative connectionist models are especially apparent in reasoning tasks that require placing roles and fillers into correspondence (Barnden, 1994). Consider a simple inference rule, "If Person 1 loves Person 2 and Person 2 loves Person 3, then Person 1 is jealous of Person 3." We can readily recognize a match between the antecedent ("if") portion of the rule and the propositions "John loves Mary" and "Mary loves George." The resulting inference, "John is jealous of George," requires carrying over the correspondences established for the "if" portion (John → Person 1, George → Person 3) to the "then" portion and using them to create the structurally appropriate inference (and not, for example, "George is jealous of John"). Such structural inferences require more than detecting some global similarity between the specific propositions and the "if" portion of the rule. The global similarity between the propositions and the antecedent of the rule is (at best) enough to suggest that someone is likely to be jealous of someone else; it is inadequate to indicate who is jealous of whom. Drawing this specific inference requires establishing, maintaining, and using a set of specific correspondences between roles and fillers (i.e., a set of variable bindings). No model that lacks the capacity to preserve object identities across roles can make systematic inferences of this type.

These problems are not limited to reasoning based on established general rules with explicit abstract variables, such as "Person 1." Fundamentally the same issues arise in reasoning by analogy to specific cases. Suppose the reasoner lacked the "jealousy rule" but had encountered a specific situation, "Alice loved Sam, and Sam loved Betty, so Alice was jealous of Betty." The reasoner now learns that John loves Mary and Mary loves George. Analogical mapping (e.g., Falkenhainer, Forbus & Gentner, 1989; Holyoak & Thagard, 1989) can readily establish the correspondences John → Alice, Mary → Sam, and George → Betty. When these correspondences are passed to an inference engine capable of "copying with substitution" (Falkenhainer et al., 1989; Holyoak, Novick, & Melz, 1994) from the source to the target analog, the conjecture "John is jealous of George" can be inferred. Moreover, once the target is extended by this inference, the full set of correspondences between the two analogs provides the basic ingredients for forming a new relational generalization. If the reasoner can take the structured intersection between the two analogs, keeping the commonalities while dropping the differences (i.e., generalizing over John the man and Alice the woman to construct a "person" variable), then the result is the "jealousy" rule. As has often been argued (Gick & Holyoak, 1983; Ross & Kennedy, 1990), analogical mapping sets the stage for relational generalization, which can yield abstract rules and schemas. None of this is possible, however, for models that lack the capacity to represent roles, fillers, and the bindings between them.

As these examples illustrate, both rule-based and analogical inferences depend on the capacity to detect and exploit *linking* relations between role assignments (or mappings). In the rule-based example, the binding John $\rightarrow$ Person 1 links the "if" portion of the rule to the "then" portion; in the analogical example, the mapping John $\rightarrow$ Alice links the initial mapping to the eventual inference. Marcus (1998; chap. 4, this volume) has shown that eliminative connectionist models lacking the capacity for variable binding are incapable of learning generalizations based on such linking relations. Instead, such models are inherently limited to learning the specific instantiations of linkages that hold for the set of examples on which they are trained. Although an eliminative connectionist model can then make "inferences" on which it has been directly trained (i.e., the model remembers particular associations that have been strengthened by learning), the acquired knowledge may not generalize *at all* to novel instantiations of the linking relations based on cases that lie outside the training set (also see Phillips & Halford, 1997).

These limitations can be illustrated by the performance of a particularly sophisticated example of an eliminative model, the Story Gestalt model of story comprehension developed by St. John (1992; St. John & McClelland, 1990). In one computational experiment (St. John, 1992, Simulation 1), the Story Gestalt model was first trained with 1,000,000 short texts consisting of propositions based on 136 different constituent concepts. Each story instantiated a script such as "<person> decided to go to <destination>; <person> drove <vehicle> to <destination>" (e.g., "John decided to go to a restaurant; John drove a jeep to the restaurant"; "Harry decided to go to the beach; Harry drove a Mercedes to the beach"). After learning a network of associative connections based on the 1,000,000 examples, the generalization ability of the model was tested by presenting it with a text containing a new proposition, such as "George decided to go to the airport," and having the model attempt to complete the "driving" script. St. John reported that when given a new proposition about deciding to go to the airport, the model typically activated the restaurant or the beach (i.e., the destinations in previous specific examples) as the destination, rather than making the contextually appropriate inference that the person would drive to the airport. This type of error (which appears unnatural in human text comprehension) results from the model's lack of a capacity to learn generalized linking relations (e.g., that if a person wants to go somewhere, that place is the person's destination). As St. John noted, "Developing a representation to handle role binding proved to be difficult for the model" (1992, p. 294).

A particularly simple example of a linking relation that reveals such generalization failures is the identity relation. Holyoak and Thagard (1995) argued that recognition of identity or sameness of one object to another is the most basic form of systematic analogical reasoning. The concept of identity appears to be in the cognitive capacity of both humans (including young children) and other primates. Both monkeys and chimpanzees are able to first learn to solve match-to-sample problems (e.g., picking a target object that is identical to a sample object) and then to successfully transfer to problems based on novel objects (e.g., D'Amato, Salmon, Loukas, & Tomie, 1985; Oden, Thompson & Premack, 1988). The ability to transfer to new objects suggests that these primates can recognize and respond to the identity relation in a way that goes beyond the training examples.

Marcus (1998) analysed the limitations of eliminative connectionist models in acquiring a function based on the identity relation. Suppose, for example, that a human reasoner was trained to respond with "1" to "1," "2" to "2," and "3" to "3." Even with just these three examples, the human is almost certain to respond to "4" with "4," without any direct feedback that this is the correct output for the new case. In contrast, an eliminative connectionist model (e.g., a feed-forward or recurrent network trained by back propagation[3]) is unable to make this obvious generalization. Such a model will have learned the specific input–output relations on which it was trained, but lacking the capacity to represent variables, generalization outside the training set is impossible. In other words, the model will simply have learned to associate "1" with "1," "2" with "2," and "3" with "3." A human, by contrast, will have learned to associate *input (number)* with *output (number)*, for any number; doing so requires the capacity to bind any new number (whether in the training space or not) to the variable *number*. Indeed, most people are willing to generalize even beyond the world of numbers. We leave it to readers to give the appropriate outputs in response to the following inputs: "A"; "B"; "flower"; "My ability to generate these responses indicates that I am binding values to variables."

The power of human reasoning and learning, then, is dependent on the capacity to represent roles and bind them to fillers. This is precisely the same capacity that permits composition of complex symbols from simpler ones. The human mind is the product of a physical symbol system; hence any model that succeeds in eliminating symbol systems ipso facto has succeeded in eliminating itself from contention as a model of the human cognitive architecture.

---

[3]Although eliminative models are often based on back propagation learning, their most basic limitations arise not from the learning algorithm per se, but rather from their lack of explicit role–filler representations. As we discuss later, models of this sort are unable to represent the knowledge necessary for true universal generalization and hence cannot succeed in modeling human relational generalization even if the modeler is allowed to hand-code the network.

THREE REQUIREMENTS FOR A
SYMBOLIC-CONNECTIONIST ARCHITECTURE

As we noted earlier, establishing the validity of the PSS hypothesis places broad constraints on the nature of the human cognitive architecture, but does not suffice to identify any specific architecture as psychologically real. Ultimately, the empirically correct model of the human cognitive architecture, as a *physical* symbol system, must specify the neural code for thought. A long road remains ahead before this goal is attained; little is yet known about the detailed neural substrate for propositional representation. Indeed, it appears in retrospect that the attraction of eliminative connectionism was in part due to premature and overly restrictive presumptions about "neural plausibility," according to which symbol systems (narrowly identified with specific "symbolic" architectures in the cognitive science literature) were viewed as inherently neurally implausible. The unknown often seems implausible. As Sherlock Holmes observed, however, once we have eliminated the impossible, what remains, however implausible, must be the truth. The human brain supports symbol systems; rather than pretending otherwise, we need to investigate how it does so.

There is nothing in the general notion of neural networks that precludes variable binding and composition of symbol structures. Indeed, many researchers in the connectionist tradition have seriously considered the question of how symbol systems can be embodied in a neural network (e.g., Feldman & Ballard, 1982; Hinton, 1990; Hummel & Holyoak, 1997; Plate, 1991; Pollack, 1990; Shastri & Ajjanagadde, 1993; Smolensky, 1990; Touretzky & Hinton, 1988). Given that the PSS hypothesis is accepted and that the brain is apparently a neural network (of some sort), the search for the human cognitive architecture leads in the direction of *symbolic* connectionism (Holyoak, 1991).

It is not our purpose here to describe and evaluate in detail the many proposed symbolic connectionist models. Some models perform rule-based inferences (e.g., Shastri & Ajjanagadde, 1993), and a few perform analogical mapping (e.g., Halford et al., 1994), but only our own model (Hummel & Holyoak, 1997) performs a wide range of the types of structured comparisons typical of human symbol processing. Here we state three apparent requirements for an adequate model of the human cognitive architecture, which have motivated our own theoretical tack (Hummel & Biederman, 1992; Hummel & Holyoak, 1993, 1996, 1997; Hummel & Stankiewicz, 1996), and which highlight limitations of alternative approaches (see also Hummel & Holyoak, 1998). Each of these requirements is motivated by a mix of computational considerations and empirical evidence about human cognition.

Independent, Dynamic Variable Binding

First, the cognitive architecture must be a symbol system: It must enable structured comparisons between complex symbol structures and allow the computation of systematic role–filler bindings, analogical mappings, and mapping of universal functions (see Holyoak & Thagard, 1995). This requirement implies that the model must provide mechanisms for the composition of symbol structures and therefore for variable binding. A variable binding espresses a role–filler or variable-value conjunction and has two essential properties.

Dynamic Binding

A variable binding is *dynamic* in the sense that it can be created and destroyed on the fly: *John* can be bound to the agent role of *love* $(x\ y)$ on one occasion and to some other role on another occasion.

Independent Binding

The binding must be *independent* of the entities it binds. Binding is something that a symbol system *does to* elemental units such as roles and fillers; it is not an intrinsic property of the units themselves, and it does not change the identities of those elements. For example, a propositional representation uses list position to express role–filler bindings: *John* is bound to the agent role of *loves* $(x\ y)$ by placing it in the first slot of that predicate. This is a "true" variable binding because list position is external to (i.e., independent of) the elements themselves, so that neither *John* nor *loves* $(x\ y)$ changes as a result of the binding. This independence is important because it allows the representation of John in the context of "John loves Mary" to overlap in a perspicuous manner with the representation of John in "Mary believes that Susan's anger toward John caused her to write him a strongly worded letter." The independence of binding and unit identity in human cognition is supported by the fact that people can effectively use constituents as retrieval cues to access larger structures stored in memory (e.g., Lesgold, 1972; Wanner, 1968). As discussed later, it is also supported by our ability to generalize rules universally.

It is important to distinguish independent binding from conjunctive coding, the dominant approach to binding in the connectionist literature. Conjunctive coding uses separate units (or patterns of activation) to represent separate bindings. For example, to represent *loves (John Mary)*, a conjunctive code would designate one unit or pattern, *A*, to represent the binding of *John* to the *lover* role, and a separate unit or pattern, *B*, to bind *Mary* to the *beloved* role; *loves (Mary John)* would be represented by two more patterns, *C* binding *Mary* to *lover*, and *D* binding *John* to *beloved*.

Critically, *A*, *B*, *C*, and *D* must differ from one another to unambiguously bind objects to their roles. As a result, John bound to lover (Unit *A*) differs from John bound to beloved (Unit *D*). Conjunctive coding is similar to variable binding in that it represents role–filler (or variable-value) conjunctions. It is also similar to variable binding in that it can be dynamic: It is possible to create and destroy conjunctive codes on the fly, as in the case of tensor product representations of binding (see Halford et al., 1994). It differs from true variable binding, however, because it carries binding information in the units themselves, rather than representing it independently of those units (i.e., conjunctive coding fails the requirement of independent binding): A unit that represents the conjunction *John + lover* is simply a symbol for that conjunction; it does not explicitly bind the symbol *John* to the role *lover*. As a result, conjunctive codes do not have the expressive power of symbolic representations based on independent dynamic variable binding (see also Hummel & Biederman, 1992).

Static Binding in Long-Term Memory

Second, although independent dynamic variable binding is a necessary prerequisite for symbolic representation, a cognitive architecture must also be able to establish static bindings—for example, by conjunctive coding—to code facts and rules in long-term memory (Hummel & Holyoak, 1993, 1997; Shastri, 1997). A code for independent dynamic binding based on temporal patterns (e.g., binding by synchrony of firing, as discussed shortly) is necessarily transient (hence naturally associated with working memory) and therefore must be supplemented by a static representation that stores bindings over extended periods. The static form of the binding must be capable of responding to the corresponding dynamic form (or a similar structure) when the latter enters working memory (recognition), and it must be able to reinstate the independent dynamic form when the structure (e.g., proposition) is called back into working memory (recall; Hummel & Holyoak, 1997).

It is interesting to consider whether something analogous to the distinction between dynamic and static binding arises in a traditional symbolic representation. For example, does the symbolic representation of a proposition on the hard drive of a computer differ—in a way analogous to the dynamic-static distinction—from the representation of that proposition in the computer's random-access memory? Although these representations certainly differ in some respects (for example, the latter is represented as a set of electronic currents in the registers that make up the computer's memory, whereas the former is a pattern of magnetic states on the computer's disk), it is unclear whether such differences map onto the dynamic-static distinction that arises for connectionist representations of symbolic structures. If not, then this requirement is unique to symbolic connectionist systems.

Distributed Representations of Propositional Content

Third, these representations and operations must be sufficiently robust to tolerate partial matches and imperfect correspondences. This capability is essential to rule-based and analogical inference, as well as to relational generalization. Therefore, concepts must have distributed representations of their meanings to provide simple mechanisms for error tolerance and similarity-based retrieval. In other words, symbols must be coded by distributed patterns, rather than by atomic elements. Requiring that symbols have distributed representations implies acceptance of the broader definition of "symbol" advocated by Vera and Simon (1994).

Numerous connectionist models have been proposed that satisfy the requirements for static binding for long-term storage and distributed representations. However, localist connectionist models (e.g., Feldman & Ballard, 1982; Shastri & Ajjanagadde, 1993) lack the benefits of distributed representations (see Hummel & Holyoak, 1993), as do traditional symbolic models (e.g., Anderson's [1993] ACT-R and its precursors; Rosenbloom, Laird, Newell, & McCarl's [1991] SOAR). Most distributed models do not satisfy the requirement for independent binding, in that the representation of a symbol in isolation (or as a constituent in one symbol structure) may have no overlap with the representation of the same symbol as a constituent in some other symbol structure. The models that exhibit this limitation include all eliminative models, as well as models based on tensor products (Smolensky, 1990) and their relatives, such as holographic reduced representations (HRR; Plate, 1991) and recursive autoassociative memories (the RAAM model of Pollack, 1990). This failure to satisfy the requirement for representing roles and fillers independently of their bindings is the direct consequence of relying solely on conjunctive bindings.

THE PROBLEM WITH TENSOR PRODUCTS FOR VARIABLE BINDING

The fact that models based solely on static bindings fail to represent roles and fillers independently of their bindings has generally been overlooked, and we sketch the reason for the problem. To a first approximation, tensor products and their relatives seem adequate as a solution to the variable binding problem (first requirement). However, inasmuch as satisfying this requirement entails satisfying the requirement for independent binding, tensor-based approaches are inadequate as a general solution to the binding problem. The limitations of tensor-based approaches—and the importance of the requirement for independent binding—are important but relatively subtle and so warrant detailed consideration.

A tensor product is an outer product of two or more vectors. For example, in the case of a tensor, **ab**, formed from vectors **a** and **b**, the ijth element of **ab** is simply the product of the ith element of **a** with the jth element of **b** (see Fig. 9.1):

$$\mathbf{ab}_{ij} = \mathbf{a}_i\mathbf{b}_j. \tag{1}$$

Tensors can be formed from any number of vectors in this way. For instance, a tensor can be formed from three vectors by setting the ijkth element of the tensor to the product of the ith element of the first vector, the jth element of the second, and the kth element of the third (see Fig. 9.2). Smolensky (1990), Halford et al. (1994), and others have shown that tensor products can be used to bind variables to values or fillers to roles. For example, as illustrated in Fig. 9.2, it is possible to represent the proposition

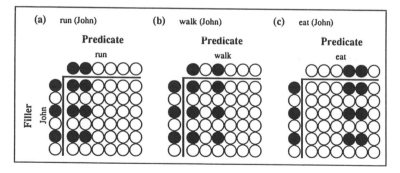

FIG. 9.1. A tensor product is an outer product of two or more vectors. (a) A tensor product representing a binding of the object *John* to the single-argument predicate *run (x)*. Black circles indicate values of 1 (active units), and circles indicate values of 0 (inactive units). *Run (x)* is represented by the vector [1, 1, 0, 0, 0, 0]. *John* is represented by the vector [0, 1, 0, 1, 0, 1]. The ijth element of the tensor *run (John)* is the product of the ith element of *run (x)* with the jth element of *John*. (b) A tensor product representing a binding of *John* to the predicate *walk (x)*. The vector for *walk (x)* shares active units with (but is not identical to) the vector for *run (x)*, so that the tensor for *walk (John)* shares active units with (but is not identical to) the vector for *run (John)*. (c) A tensor product representing a binding of *John* to the predicate *eat (x)*. The vector for *eat (x)* shares no active units with the vector for *run (x)*, so that the tensor for *eat (John)* shares no active units with the vector for *run (John)*.

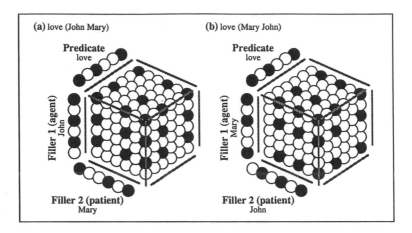

FIG. 9.2. (a) A tensor representation of the proposition *love (John Mary)*. Black circles indicate values of 1 (active units), and white circles indicate values of 0 (inactive units). (b) A tensor representation of *love (Mary John)*. Note that *John*, which is bound to different roles in the two propositions, is represented by different vectors in the two propositions: *John* is represented by the "vertical" (agent) vector in the first proposition and by the "horizontal" (patient) vector in the second.

loves (John Mary) with a three-dimensional tensor, **abc**, in which one vector (**a**) codes the predicate (loves), the second vector (**b**) codes the filler of the agent role (John), and the third vector (**c**) codes the filler of the patient role (Mary). Switching the roles to represent *loves (Mary John)* changes the assignment of John and Mary to role slots and thereby changes the tensor product. If *loves (John Mary)* is represented by **abc**, then *loves (Mary John)* is represented by **acb** (compare Figs. 9.2a and 9.2b).

A tensor product is analogous to a weight matrix between the simple vectors from which it is generated (the product rule for generating the tensor is precisely a Hebbian learning rule; Smolensky, 1990). As a result, it can be used to answer "questions" about the bindings of roles to fillers. For example, consider the tensor representation of "John runs" in Fig. 9.1a. Imagine activating the tensor and the vector for "run" and leaving the vector where John would be represented inactive. If the vector for "run" is treated as an input and the tensor is treated as a weight matrix, then the network activates John on the argument vector and effectively answers "John" to the question "Who is running?" In this sense, the tensor binds the argument "John" to the slot of the predicate "run" (see Halford et al., 1994; Smolensky, 1990).

However, tensor products do not adequately model role binding in human mental representation. Although a tensor can be used to *generate* one element of a binding given another element as a cue (as in the previous example), the tensor itself does not explicitly represent those elements and their bindings. As noted earlier, symbols in a symbol system are free to change bindings without changing their identities. That is, the identity of a symbol is invariant with whatever role bindings it happens to be participating in at any given time.

The tensor representation of a variable binding is not invariant in this way. Rather, the representation of a filler (or role) in a tensor changes as a function of the role (or filler) to which it happens to be bound. For example, consider the hypothetical tensor representations of *run (John)* in Fig. 9.1a and *walk (John)* in Fig. 9.1b. The representation of *run (x)* is similar but not identical to the representation of *walk (x)*, so that the tensor for *run (John)* is similar but not identical to the tensor for *walk (John)*. Predicates that do not overlap at all produce tensors that do not overlap. For example, the representation of *eat (John)* in Fig. 9.1c does not overlap at all with the representation of *run (John)* in Fig. 9.1a. The tensor thus captures the binding of John to these various roles, but it fails to capture the fact that John remains the same entity in each role. This point is somewhat subtle because *we* (the modeler or the reader of a modeling paper) know that John is the same in both cases; looking at the graphical representation of the tensor, we can "see" John in both cases—the fact that John is the argument in both cases is the reason that the first, third, and fifth units (but not the second, fourth, and sixth) are active in active columns of the tensor.

Although *we* know John is "in there," the tensor itself does not. To demonstrate this limitation more formally, let us define the similarity of two vectors, **a** and **b**, in terms of the cosine of the angle between them:

$$\cos(\mathbf{a}, \mathbf{b}) = \frac{\mathbf{a} \cdot \mathbf{b}}{\|\mathbf{a}\| \, \|\mathbf{b}\|}, \tag{2}$$

where $\|\mathbf{x}\|$ is the length of vector $\mathbf{x}$, and $\mathbf{a} \cdot \mathbf{b}$ is the inner product (or "dot product"):

$$\mathbf{a} \cdot \mathbf{b} = \Sigma_i a_i b_i. \tag{3}$$

The cosine is a measure of the similarity between two vectors. It is at a maximum (1.0) when the vectors are identical (i.e., when they point in the same direction, regardless of their lengths), zero when the vectors are unrelated (i.e., orthogonal), and at a minimum (–1.0) when the vectors are opposites (i.e., with positive values in one corresponding to negative values in the other; see Jordan, 1986). The cosine of the angle between any two tensors, **ab** and **a′b′** (i.e., their similarity), scales with the product of the similarities of the vectors from which they were created. For a tensor created from two vectors, **a** and **b**:

$$\cos(\mathbf{ab}, \mathbf{a'b'}) = \frac{\mathbf{a}\cdot\mathbf{a'} \times \mathbf{b}\cdot\mathbf{b'}}{\|\mathbf{ab}\| \, \|\mathbf{a'b'}\|}.$$
(4)

The cosine of the angle between two tensors goes to zero when either of the more basic similarities [$\cos(\mathbf{a}, \mathbf{a'})$ or $\cos(\mathbf{b}, \mathbf{b'})$] is zero and goes negative when either of the more basic similarities is negative. In a tensor representation, binding the same object to nonoverlapping roles results in nonoverlapping tensors.

It is tempting to reply that this is not a problem because the tensor really only needs to express binding information: The responsibility for expressing similarity lies not with the tensor, but with the simple vectors from which the tensor is generated. According to this reply, the preceding analysis actually reveals a strength of tensor-based representations because it shows that the tensor can, in principle, unambiguously express binding information.

This reply, however, fails for two reasons. The first is that tensors describing bindings of similar roles to similar fillers in fact are similar to one another (Equation 4). Thus, even if we wished to grant that it is not the tensor's responsibility to carry similarity information, the mathematics ensures that it inevitably is the tensor's burden. This problem is most extreme when the individual vectors ($\mathbf{a}$, $\mathbf{a'}$, $\mathbf{b}$, and $\mathbf{b'}$) are maximally dissimilar. If $\cos(\mathbf{a}, \mathbf{a'}) = -1$ (i.e., $\mathbf{a}$ and $\mathbf{a'}$ are opposites), and $\cos(\mathbf{b}, \mathbf{b'}) = -1$, then $\cos(\mathbf{ab}, \mathbf{a'b'})$ is *positive* 1.0 (see Equation 4): In this case, the dot products are maximimally *similar* precisely because their constituent roles and fillers are maximally *dissimilar!* A second and more serious problem is that even the simple vectors from which the tensor is constructed are not invariant across bindings, so that it does not help to assign the "responsibility" for similarity to them. Consider a predicate, such as *loves (x y)*, that takes more than one argument (Fig. 9.2). Bound to the agent role of such a relation, an object is represented in one vector space (i.e., collection of units); but bound to the patient role, the same object is represented in a completely different vector space. For example, as the agent of *loves (x y)*, John is represented on the "vertical" units (Fig. 9.2a); but as the patient, John is represented on the "horizontal" units (Fig. 9.2b). The representation of John in one role does not overlap at all with the representation of John in the other, even on the simple vectors.

The problems with tensor-based binding are compounded in schemes based on "compressed" tensors (e.g., Plate, 1991; Pollack, 1990). For example, in a holographic reduced representation (HRR) (Plate, 1991), a tensor is compressed (by summing over reverse diagonals) into a vector whose dimensionality is given by the diagonal of the original tensor. Because the HRR is derived from a tensor, it inherits the binding-identity tradeoff of the tensor; and because the dimensionality of the HRR is lower than the dimensionality of the tensor, the HRR encounters the additional problem that it underconstrains the tensor. That is, for any given HRR, multiple tensors can in principle produce it. The recovery of the tensor— that is, the recovery of the binding—is ill posed in an HRR. The same problems arise in other schemes for compressing tensors, including circular convolutions and recursive autoassociative memories (RAAMs; Pollack, 1990).

DISTRIBUTING A SYMBOL SYSTEM
OVER SPACE AND TIME

The problems with the tensor approach to binding stem from the fact that tensors are a brand of conjunctive coding: Each unit in a tensor represents a role–filler *conjunction* (see Hummel & Biederman, 1992). As a result, the representation of a role or filler is fundamentally in conflict with the representation of role–filler bindings (Hummel & Holyoak, 1993): To the extent that the tensor preserves one, it must sacrifice the other (Equation 4).

To satisfy the requirement for independent binding, a representational system needs a second degree of freedom—independent of the units' identities and their activations—to represent binding information: Units need a "tag" to express binding (i.e., such that units in the same group have the same value on their "tags"). The tag must be dynamic, so that units representing roles can be rapidly but temporarily bound to units representing the fillers of those roles. Recall that units in a connectionist network (like neurons) are not free to "move around," and list position (the binding tag used in propositional representations) is unavailable. In principle, however, many possible tagging systems are conceivable. For example, units that are bound together could be spray painted with a shared color; Mozer, Zemel, Behrmann, and Williams (1992) described a network that uses imaginary numbers as a binding tag. At present, however, the only proposed basis for tagging with any apparent neural plausibility is based on the use of *time*. In particular, it has been proposed that units fire in synchrony with one another when they are bound together and out of synchrony when they are not (Milner, 1974; von der Malsburg, 1981/1994; see Gray, 1994, for a review). For example, to represent *loves (John Mary)*, units representing "John" fire in synchrony with units for "lover," while units for "Mary" fire in synchrony with units for "beloved" (the John + lover set must fire out of synchrony with the Mary + beloved set); *loves (Mary John)* is represented by the very same units, but the units for "Mary" fire in synchrony with the units for "lover," while the units for "John" fire in synchrony with the units for "beloved" (Hummel & Holyoak, 1992).

There is some neurophysiological evidence for binding by synchrony in visual perception (e.g., in the striate cortex; Eckhorn et al., 1988; Gray

& Singer, 1989; König & Engel, 1995) and in higher level processing dependent on the frontal cortex (Desmedt & Tomberg, 1994; Vaadia et al., 1995). Numerous connectionist models use synchrony for binding. This mechanism has been applied in models of perceptual grouping (e.g., Eckhorn, Reitboeck, Arndt, & Dicke, 1990; von der Malsburg & Buhmann, 1992), object recognition (Hummel & Biederman, 1992; Hummel & Saiki, 1993; Hummel & Stankiewicz, 1996, 1998), rule-based reasoning (Love, 1999; Shastri & Ajjanaggade, 1993), episodic storage in the hippocampal memory system (Shastri, 1997), and analogical reasoning (Hummel & Holyoak, 1992, 1996, 1997).

Similarity in Dynamic Binding

Equation 4 characterizes how the similarity of different tensor products scales with the similarity of the simple vectors from which they are composed. It is possible to perform the same analysis on synchrony-based representations of binding, as illustrated in Fig. 9.3. In synchrony-based models, predicate roles and fillers occupy different regions of the same vector space, and—more important—a given role or filler always occupies the *same* part of the space (i.e., activates the same units) regardless of whatever else is bound to it. (Geometrically, this is what it means for role and filler identity to be invariant with binding.) Binding by synchrony corresponds to activating two or more vectors at the same time (one for the role and one for the filler); mathematically, binding by synchrony is vector addition (see Fig. 9.3). (By contrast, recall that tensor-based binding is vector multiplication: Equation 1.) As a consequence, the similarity of different bindings in a synchrony-based representation scales additively (rather than multiplicatively) with the similarity of the simple vectors (Hummel & Holyoak, 1998):

$$\cos(\mathbf{a} + \mathbf{b}, \mathbf{a}' + \mathbf{b}') = (\mathbf{a}\cdot\mathbf{a}' + \mathbf{a}\cdot\mathbf{b}' + \mathbf{b}\cdot\mathbf{a}' + \mathbf{b}\cdot\mathbf{b}')/\|\mathbf{a} + \mathbf{b}\| \ \|\mathbf{a}' + \mathbf{b}'\|, \qquad (5)$$

where $\mathbf{a} + \mathbf{b}$ is the vector generated by synchronizing $\mathbf{a}$ with $\mathbf{b}$ and $\mathbf{a}' + \mathbf{b}'$ is the vector generated by synchronizing $\mathbf{a}'$ with $\mathbf{b}'$. If roles ($\mathbf{a}$ and $\mathbf{a}'$) and fillers ($\mathbf{b}$ and $\mathbf{b}'$) are assumed to occupy nonoverlapping regions of vector space (i.e., assumed to share no units; see Hummel & Holyoak, 1997), then $\mathbf{a}\cdot\mathbf{b}'$ and $\mathbf{b}\cdot\mathbf{a}'$ go to zero, and Equation 5 simplifies to:

$$\cos(\mathbf{a} + \mathbf{b} \ \mathbf{a}' + \mathbf{b}') = (\mathbf{a}\cdot\mathbf{a}' + \mathbf{b}\cdot\mathbf{b}')/\|\mathbf{a} + \mathbf{b}\| \ \|\mathbf{a}' + \mathbf{b}'\|. \qquad (6)$$

Multiplication (as in the tensor scheme) corresponds to logical AND, whereas addition (as in the synchrony-based scheme) corresponds to logical OR. Tensor bindings are similar to the extent that their roles *and*

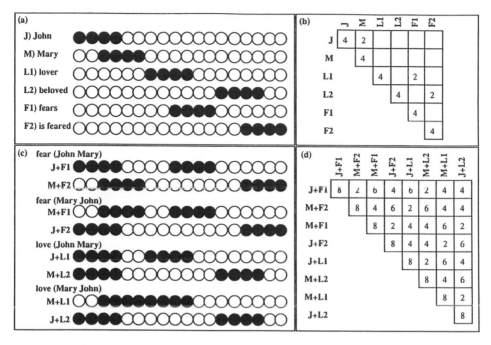

FIG. 9.3. (a) Hypothetical vector representations of *John*, *Mary*, the agent and patient roles of *love (x y)* (*lover* [L1] and *beloved* [L2], respectively) and the agent and patient roles of *fear (x y)* (*fearer* [F1] and *feared* [F2], respectively). Black circles indicate values of 1 (active units), and white circles indicate values of 0 (inactive units). (b) Matrix of dot products (similarities) of the vectors in (a). For example, the entry in Row J, column M is the dot product of the vector for *John* with the vector for *Mary*. Empty cells indicate values of zero. (c) Vectors formed by synchronizing (i.e., adding) each object vector in (a) with each role vector. For example, vector J + L1 is the vector produced by synchronizing (adding) the vector for *John* with the vector for *lover*. Pairs of vectors represent propositions. For example, J + L1 and M + L2 represent the role–filler bindings in *love (John Mary)* and jointly represent that proposition. (d) Matrix of dot products (similarities) of the (synchronized) vectors in (c). Note that the dot product for any pair of synchronized vectors (from c) is the sum of the dot products of the corresponding simple vectors (from a). For example, the dot product of J + L1 (*John + lover*) with M + F1 (*Mary + fearer*) (4) equals the dot product of *John* with *Mary* (2) plus the dot product of *lover* with *fearer* (2). The similarity of synchronized vectors scales with the sum of the similarities of the simple vectors from which they are composed.

fillers are similar (Equation 4), whereas synchrony-based bindings are similar to the extent that their roles *or* fillers (or both) are similar (Equation 6). The practical consequence of this property is that, in a synchrony-based scheme, *walk (Bill)* is guaranteed to be identical to *eat (Bill)* on the units representing Bill, even if *walk (x)* and *eat (x)* have nothing whatsoever in common. Moreover, because the numerator of Equation 6 is based on addition rather than multiplication, negative simple dot products (i.e., where $a \cdot a' < 0$ and $b \cdot b' < 0$) produces a negative value for $\cos(a + b, a' + b')$ (rather than a positive value, as in tensor-based schemes). That is, synchrony-based representations are similar precisely to the degree that they express similar concepts.

Using Synchrony to Form Symbolic Representations

It is one thing to show that synchrony-based bindings preserve the similarity structure of the entities they bind; it is another to show that the resulting bindings constitute useful symbolic representations. To count as symbolic, a knowledge representation must function as part of a system that can perform symbolic computations. We have recently developed a model that uses synchrony-based bindings to form representations that are meaningfully symbolic in this sense. This model, learning and inference with schemas and analogies (LISA), is a model of the major stages of analogical inference and relational generalization, namely, retrieval from long-term memory, mapping of structures in working memory, analogical inference, and schema induction (Hummel & Holyoak, 1996, 1997; for earlier versions of the model, see Hummel, Burns, & Holyoak, 1994; Hummel & Holyoak, 1992; Hummel, Melz, Thompson, & Holyoak, 1994). We describe LISA in only very general terms here. The details of LISA's operation as an analogical retrieval and mapping engine can be found in Hummel and Holyoak (1997), and the details of its operation as an inference and schema induction engine can be found in Hummel and Holyoak (1996).

LISA represents role–filler bindings in working memory as synchronized patterns of activation distributed over a collection of *semantic* units. For example, "John loves Mary" is represented by units for "John" firing in synchrony with units for the agent role of "loves," while units for "Mary" fire in synchrony with units for the patent role. Propositions are represented in LISA's long-term memory by a hierarchy of *structure units* (see Fig. 9.4). *Predicate units* (triangles in Fig. 9.4) bind semantic features into predicate roles, *object units* (circles) bind semantic features into objects, *subproposition (SP) units* (rectangles) bind roles to their fillers, and *proposition (P) units* (ovals) bind role–filler conjunctions into complete propositions. Note that all the bindings in LISA's long-term memory are static in that they are coded conjunctively (as dictated by the requirement for distributed representations). As such, these units do not directly represent the semantic content of a proposition; rather, they serve only to store that content in long-term memory and respond to it when it enters working memory (i.e., as patterns of activation on the semantic units). An analog

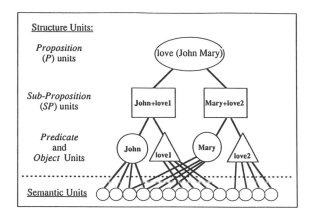

FIG. 9.4. Illustration of the representation of the proposition *love (John Mary)* in LISA's long-term memory. See text for details.

in LISA is represented as a collection of structure units coding the propositions in that analog. Separate analogs consist of nonoverlapping sets of structure units, but share the semantic units. Note that structure units are created as needed, rather than prestored; as we illustrate next, they can be learned by an algorithm for unsupervised learning.

Based on these representations, LISA performs analog retrieval and analogical mapping as a form of guided pattern recognition. When a proposition becomes active in one analog (a *driver* analog), it generates synchronized patterns of activation on the semantic units (one pattern for each role–filler binding). In turn, these patterns activate structure units in other *recipient* analogs. This process is analog retrieval: Patterns of activation generated by the driver activate (i.e., retrieve from long-term memory) units in other analogs. Mapping differs from retrieval solely by the addition of modifiable *mapping connections* between units of the same type in the driver and recipient analogs. During mapping, weights on the mapping connections grow larger when the units they link are active simultaneously and grow negative when one unit is active but the other is not. These connections permit LISA to learn the correspondences generated during retrieval. They also serve to constrain subsequent memory access and thus to constrain subsequent mappings. By the end of a simulation run, corresponding structure units have large positive weights on their mapping connections, and noncorresponding units have strong negative weights. Using these operations, LISA simulates a large body of findings in human analog retrieval and mapping and accounts for some complex asymmetries between retrieval and mapping (Hummel & Holyoak, 1997). These same operations also form the basis of LISA's capacity for schema induction, analogy-based inference (Hummel & Holyoak,

1996), and explicit rule-based inference. Let us consider analogy- and rule-based inference first.

Analogical Inference and Rule Use

Imagine that we give LISA an analog (henceforth *Analog 1*) containing the following two propositions (Fig. 9.5a):

$$P1 = input\ (X)$$
$$P2 = output\ (X),$$

where *P1* and *P2* are the names of the propositions, *input (x)* and *output (x)* are simple one-argument predicates (e.g., let *input* be connected to the semantic units *role* and *input*, and let *output* be connected to *role* and *output*), and X is a simple semantically empty object (e.g., let X connect either to the semantic unit *variable* or to no semantics at all; as we shall see, it does not matter which). Analog 1 is a typical analog in LISA notation (Hummel & Holyoak, 1997), and it can also be interpreted as a rule stating "X is *input*" and "X is *output*." That is, Analog 1 is LISA-ese for the identity function. Next, let us give LISA Analog 2 (Fig. 9.5b):

$$P1 = input\ (1),$$

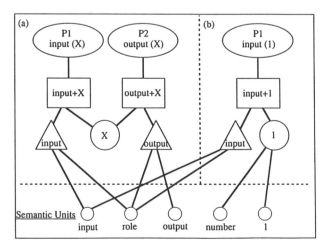

FIG. 9.5. (a) LISA representation of the rule, "X is input (proposition P1) and X is output (proposition P2)." (b) LISA representation of the question, "1 is input. What is output?" LISA "answers" the question in (b) by mapping the analog in (b) onto the analog in (a) (which binds the value 1 to the variable X) and then mapping back, creating the proposition P2 = "1 is output" in the analog in (b). See text for details.

where the predicate unit *input* is connected to the very same semantics as *input* in Analog 1 (but note that the predicate *input (x)* is represented by separate units in Analog 1 and Analog 2; Figs. 9.5a and 9.5b), and the object unit, *1*, is connected to semantics indicating that it is a number and that its value is one. Critically, *1* is connected to none of the same semantics as *X* in Analog 1, so that it bears no similarity whatsoever to that object (i.e., the variable *X* in the rule). As we shall see, this property distinguishes LISA from all eliminative connectionist approaches to modeling the identity function.

Now let us map Analog 2 onto Analog 1. *P1* (in Analog 2) is a single-place proposition and therefore has only one SP (namely, *input + 1*; Fig. 9.5b). When this SP fires, it activates the predicate unit *input* and the object unit *1*, which activate (in synchrony) their respective semantic units (*input*, *role*, *number*, and *1*). Although the semantics *number* and *1* excite nothing in Analog 1, *role* excites both *input* and *output* (in Analog 1), and *input* (the semantic unit) excites *input* (in Analog 1). Because the predicate *input* (in Analog 1) is receiving more bottom-up excitation than the predicate *output*, *input* "wins" the inhibitory competition, becomes fully active, and inhibits *output* to inactivity. The predicate unit *input* (in Analog 1) in turn excites the SP *input + X*, which excites the object *X*. As a consequence, *X* in Analog 1 is now active at the same time as *1* in Analog 2, so that the mapping connection between them grows: LISA has bound the value *1* to the variable *X* and stored this binding as a connection between them. Similarly, *input* (Analog 1) has learned an excitatory mapping connection to *input* (Analog 2) (because they were active at the same time). *Output* (Analog 1) was inactive while *input* (Analog 2) was active, so that *output* (Analog 1) has learned a *negative* (inhibitory) mapping connection to *input* (Analog 1).

Next let us make Analog 1 the driver and Analog 2 the recipient. When *P1* fires in Analog 1, it simply reinforces (i.e., strengthens) the mapping connections from *input* (in Analog 1) to *input* (in Analog 2) and from *X* to *1*. It also strengthens (i.e., makes more negative) the inhibitory connection between *output* (Analog 1) and *input* (Analog 2).

However, when *P2* fires, something more interesting happens. *P2* activates the SP *output + X*, activating *output* and *X*, which activates (in synchrony) the semantics *role* and *output*. At the same time, *X* activates *1* (in Analog 2) directly by way of the mapping connection between them. Meanwhile, the semantic unit *role* excites the predicate unit *input* (in Analog 2), but *output* (in Analog 1) inhibits *input* (in Analog 2) owing to the negative mapping connection between them. In fact, although the object *1* is receiving excitatory input over its mapping connection, all the predicates in Analog 2 (all one of "them") are receiving inhibitory input over their mapping connections, a situation that indicates that no predicates in Analog 2 correspond to the currently active predicate in Analog 1. This situation serves as a cue that it is necessary to "invent" a new predicate corresponding to whatever predicate is currently active in Analog 1 (a variety of "copy with substitution and generation"; Holyoak et al., 1994). LISA invents a new predicate (call it *output, where the "*" indicates that LISA invented it, and "output" indicates that it corresponds to output in Analog 1) and connects it to whatever semantic units (corresponding to predicates) are currently active (in this case, output and role).

The predicate *output is now coactive (in synchrony) with the object unit 1 in Analog 2. For the same reason input was inhibited by output, the SP input + 1 (in Analog 2) is inhibited by the SP output + X (Analog 2), and P1 is inhibited by P2. As a consequence, LISA invents the SP *output + 1 and the P unit *P2 (in Analog 2), connects them to each other, and connects *output + 1 to the predicate *output and the object 1. (LISA knows what to connect to what on the basis of the units' co-activity. It simply connects all the active units.) Together, these operations—mapping from Analog 2 to Analog 1, mapping back from Analog 1 to Analog 2, and filling in the gaps in Analog 2—cause LISA to infer the proposition P2 = output (1). That is, given the identity function (Analog 1) and the question input (1), LISA answers output (1) (i.e., "the output of the identity function run on the input 1 is 1").

We ran LISA on exactly this problem and on several others like it (Hummel & Holyoak, 1998). In each case, it gave the right answer as output: input (1) → output (1), input (2) → output (2), input (3) → output (3). We also ran it on the non-numerical problems input (flower) and input (Mary). Not surprisingly, it also gave the correct responses to these problems. It is important to emphasize that LISA was able to solve the identity problem in spite of the fact that there was no semantic overlap whatsoever between the object (X) in the rule (i.e., Analog 1) and the objects in the problems on which it was tested (1, 2, 3, flower, and Mary). Like a human reasoner, but unlike any eliminative connectionist model (see chap. 4, this volume), LISA generalized the identity function universally. Its ability to do so stems directly from its ability to bind values (such as 1, flower, and Mary) to variables (such as X).

Note also that LISA would have been far less successful in solving this problem had it represented variable-value (or role–filler) bindings with tensors (or their variants) rather than with synchrony. The ease with which LISA maps the identity function hinges on the fact that the predicate input (x) is represented in exactly the same way regardless of what its argument happens to be (the requirement for independent binding and Equation 6): It is the mapping of input (in Analog 2) to input (in Analog 1) that binds the value (1, 2, etc.) to the variable (X) and bootstraps the solution to the problem. Had LISA bound input (x) to its argument (the object X) by using tensor products, then the resulting tensor would depend on both the predicate (*input [x]*) and its argument (X), so that there would be no guarantee that the tensor representing *input (X)* (in Analog 1) would overlap at all with the tensor representing *input (y)* (where y denotes any arbitrary object) in Analog 2 (recall Equation 4). This is not to say that tensor-based models might not solve the identity function in a different way, for example, by treating the tensor as a weight matrix, as discussed previously. Mapping the identity function in this way, however, is formally equivalent to the approach of the eliminative connectionist models (inputs are represented by one vector, outputs by another, and the function is mapped by the weights between). As such, this version of the tensor-based approach is subject to all the same limitations as traditional eliminative connectionist models (discussed next; see also Marcus, 1997).

Analogy-Based Rule Induction

It might be objected that our demonstration of identity mapping in LISA—and especially our comparison of LISA with traditional eliminative models—is misleading. After all, the eliminative models *learn* to solve the identity function by example; we simply *gave* LISA the rule. Granted the rule, it is no surprise that LISA solved the problem.

This objection fails for two reasons. The first is that the eliminative model could not solve the identity function even if we gave it the rule (or more accurately, *tried* to give it the rule). "Giving" an eliminative model the identity rule is a matter of giving it N input units and N output units and connecting the ith input unit to the ith output unit (for all $i = 1 \ldots N$). In such an arrangement, the network simply copies to the output units whatever it is given on the input units. Voilà—we have given the eliminative model the identity function—or have we? Note that even this model does not generalize universally because there are a finite number of inputs it can represent in the first place (given by the dimensionality, N, of the input and output vectors). That is, this model expects—indeed, demands—its inputs and outputs to be representable in a *particular* feature space, as given by N (see chap. 4, this volume). LISA, by contrast, does not care how its inputs are represented. (Recall that it maps the function even though there is no semantic overlap between X and any value bound to X.) LISA's solution to the identity function hinges instead on the predicate *input (x)*; once Analog 1 is established, LISA can then map the identity function on any argument bound to *input (x)*. We have indeed given LISA a *rule*, in the true sense of a function that binds values to variables. The trouble is not that we gave LISA the rule, but that there is *no way* to give the eliminative model such a rule, even if we wanted to.

The second answer to the objection is that, although the previous demonstration assumes the pre-existence of the rule, LISA is capable of learning the rule by example. Moreover, as we show, LISA can learn to generalize universally from only one or two examples. Whereas the eliminative model requires a number of examples that scale with the number of problems it is eventually asked to solve, LISA can solve *any* problem (i.e., an infinity of them) after just one or two examples. LISA induces the identity rule in the same way as it induces any schema—by unsupervised learning (of the kind that allows it to "invent" structure units, as in the previous example) along with *intersection discovery* (see Hummel & Holyoak, 1996).

Imagine that we give LISA the following example:

> *Analog 1*   Analog 2
> *P1 = input (1)*   *P1 = input (2)*
> *P2 = output (1)*   *P2 = output (2),*

and have it map Analog 1 onto Analog 2 as in the previous example. The predicate unit *input* in Analog 1 maps to *input* in Analog 2, *output* maps to *output*, *1* maps to 2, and the corresponding SPs and *P* units likewise map to one another. Because every structure unit in Analog 1 has a corresponding unit in Analog 2, this mapping does not require LISA to invent (i.e., learn or infer) any new structures in Analog 2.

Now let us create a third analog, Analog 3, which initially contains no structure units at all. Once *P1* in Analog 1 maps to *P1* in Analog 2, these units excite one another directly via their mapping connection. Analog 3 contains no units; there is no unit to develop positive mapping connections to *P1* in Analog 1 (or *P1* in Analog 2). That is, nothing in Analog 3 maps to *P1* in Analog 1. Recall that this lack of mapping is LISA's cue to invent new structure units. In Analog 3, LISA invents the *P* unit *P1, the SP **input + 1*, the predicate *input, and the object **1* (let us assume that Analog 1 is the driver and that the names of invented units are taken from the driver; hence, the new object is **1* rather than **2* or *number). The principles underlying learning in Analog 3 are so far just the same as those underlying the "copy with substitution and generation" (i.e., inference) in the previous example.

However, analogs that are learning to be schemas, such as Analog 3, are subject to one additional constraint: The object and predicate units in these analogs have a connection-level threshold that prevents them from learning connections to any semantic units with activations below a certain value, Θ (Hummel & Holyoak, 1996). Otherwise, these units update their connections in the "usual" fashion (i.e., via a modified Hebbian rule; see Hummel & Holyoak, 1996). In addition, predicate and object units in the recipient (Analog 2, if Analog 1 is the driver) send activation back to the semantic units. As a result, semantic units that are connected to active units in both the driver and the recipient tend to have about twice as much input as semantic units that are connected to one but not the other. For example, the semantic unit *number* is connected both to the object *1* (in Analog 1) and to the object *2* (in Analog 2). When *P1* in Analog 1 maps to *P1* in Analog 2, *number* therefore has two sources of input. By contrast, the semantic unit *1* is connected to the object *1* in Analog 1, but is not connected to anything in Analog 2; the semantic unit *2* is connected to the object *2* in Analog 2, but to nothing in Analog 1. The semantic unit *number* thus receives about twice as much excitatory input as either *1* or *2* and therefore becomes more active.

In combination with the threshold, Θ, on the predicate and object units in the schema (Analog 3), this feedback from recipient analogs to semantics causes Analog 3 to perform a kind of intersection discovery. Units in Analog 3 learn connections to only highly active semantic units—that is, semantics that are common to the driver and the recipient. In the case of Analog 3, this means that the object unit **1* in Analog 3 learns only a connection to the semantic unit *number*. **1* represents numbers *generally*, not just the numbers *1* and *2*, from which it was induced by example. The same process operates on the predicate unit **input* in Analog 3. In this case, *input* in Analog 1 has all the same semantics as *input* in Analog 2; all their semantic units receive two sources of input. Therefore, **input* in Analog 3 learns connections to all those semantic units and ends up connected to exactly the same units as both examples from which it was induced. Once these operations have run on both *P1* and *P2* (in Analogs 1 and 2), Analog 3 is the equivalent of:

$$P1 = input \ (number)$$
$$P2 = output \ (number).$$

Based on Analog 3, LISA can now map the identity function for any number. In fact, Analog 3 is prepared to generalize much more universally than that. Let Analog 4 be *P1 input (flower)*, where *flower* is assumed to have no semantic overlap whatsoever with *number* in Analog 3. Our first example showed that LISA can map the identify function even when the object (1, 2, flower, etc.) has no semantic overlap with the variable in the function (*X* in the previous example). Because *flower* has no semantic overlap with *number*, mapping Analog 4 onto Analog 3 is just a repeat of that first example: LISA infers **P2 = *output (flower)* in Analog 4. (Hummel & Holyoak, 1998, ran these simulations, and this is exactly what it does.) Hence, after just one training example (mapping Analog 1 onto Analog 2 and inducing Analog 3), LISA can generalize universally. If, while Analog 3 is being mapped onto Analog 4, a new empty analog, Analog 5, is allowed to learn a schema (rule) from their intersection, then Analog 5 ends up being the equivalent of:

$$P1 = input\ (X)$$
$$P2 = output\ (X)$$

where X is semantically empty (it connects to the intersection of *flower* and *number*, which is the empty set). LISA has now induced the rule we gave it in the very first example.

Not only is LISA's rule learning blindingly fast compared with back propagation learning (as used in many eliminative connectionist models), but the results are also much more general. After just one example, LISA knows how to "play the identity function game" and can play it with any new input. The learning trials required by people—and their subsequent ability to generalize universally—are much more on the scale of LISA than on the scale of an eliminative connectionist model or a model based on tensor binding. The difference between LISA and both these alternative approaches is that LISA can bind values to variables and arguments to roles while preserving the similarity relations among the constituent concepts. As a result, LISA is a connectionist implementation of a symbol system that can map and learn symbolic functions (such as the identity function). Tensor product models attempt to bind values to variables, but fall short of the mark; as a result, their ability to generalize also falls short of the mark. Eliminative connectionist models do not even attempt to bind values to variables, and as a result, their performance falls far below the mark. After hundreds or thousands (or even millions) of iterations through its training set, a back propagation model is still just as guaranteed to fail to generalize universally as it was before training started. Universal generalization is *in principle* out of reach for any model that cannot bind values to variables; it does not matter how long one trains the back propagation model—it never truly learns the identity function (Marcus, 1998).

A more important criticism of LISA's ability to learn the identity function is that we gave it the predicates *input (X)* and *output (X)* in the examples from which the rule was induced. The question of how a human reasoner discovers these predicates in the first place is an important one for which we cannot yet offer a complete answer. However, it is safe to assume that at least for trivial problems such as the identity function, adult reasoners come armed with predicates corresponding to *input (X)* (e.g., "This is the example on which I am being tested") and *output (X)* ("This is the response I am supposed to give"). Even if we assume the existence of these predicates, it is not a trivial matter to specify how the reasoner can use them to solve the problem. Eliminative connectionists would also be willing to postulate concepts such as "input" and "output," but their models are nonetheless incapable of using those concepts to perform useful work. It is this capacity that requires symbol processing and that the preceeding simulations are intended to demonstrate.

WHY SYMBOLIC CONNECTIONISM IS NOT "MERE" IMPLEMENTATION

Fodor and Pylyshyn (1988) observed that a connectionist model might, in principle, capture the systematicity (compositionality) of human cognition, but that in so doing, the resulting model would simply implement a (traditional-style) symbolic model. The "invited inference" was that nothing is to be gained from the exercise of implementing symbol processing in a connectionist framework. Is symbolic connectionism just a roundabout way of getting "back where we started"?

The answer is a resounding No. The issue of whether the mind is a physical symbol system is a question at the level of computational theory (Marr, 1982): What function is the mind computing? In the most abstract terms, the answer is that the mind is performing symbol manipulation. This question and its answer are very important, as the failings of eliminative connectionist models attest, but the answer does not tell us *how* the mind is doing symbol manipulation, which is a question at Marr's level of representation and algorithm. It is here that symbolic connectionism represents a striking advance over traditional symbolic architectures of cognition (e.g., Anderson, 1993; Rosenbloom et al., 1991).

One advantage of symbolic connectionism derives from an apparent weakness: It is *hard* to do symbol manipulation in a connectionist architecture. This is because symbol manipulation requires dynamic binding, and dynamic binding is difficult to perform in a connectionist architecture (see Hummel & Stankiewicz, 1996, 1998). In the case of dynamic binding by synchrony of firing, some mechanism has to get the right units into synchrony with one another and (even more difficult) keep them *out* of synchrony with all the other units. It takes *work* to establish synchrony and (especially) asynchrony, and some process must perform this work. By contrast, dynamic binding in a symbolic model is trivially easy: The correct bindings are simply *given*. By definition, placing the symbol "John" into the first slot of the predicate *loves (x y)* binds John to the agent role of that predicate. There is nothing else to say and no other work to do. If we then want to bind "John" to some other role, we can do it, as many times as we want, with as many predicates as we want, and as many other objects as we want.

In a traditional symbol architecture, bindings are free, so we can have as many as we need. Of course, a theorist may opt to impose some limit on binding, in deference to the glaring fact that people have limited capacity to make and break role bindings, but this is simply an ad hoc "add-on" rather than a deep implication of the proposed symbolic architecture. It is here that the computational weakness of symbolic connectionism becomes a psychological virtue. A model that represents bindings with synchrony (such as LISA, and related models such as JIM; Hummel & Biederman, 1992; Hummel & Stankiewicz, 1996) is *inherently* limited in the number of things it may simultaneously have active and mutually *out* of synchrony with one another (although there is no theoretical limit to the number of entities in any one synchronized group). That is, there is a limit on the number of distinct bindings such a model may have in working memory at any one time (Hummel & Holyoak, 1997; Shastri & Ajjanaggade, 1993). Humans, too, have limited working memory and limited attention. Thus Hummel and Stankiewicz (1996, 1998) argued that a primary function of visual attention is to keep the separate elements of a visual display out of synchrony with one another. Symbolic connectionism—as an *algorithmic* theory of symbol systems—provides a natural account of the fact that humans have a limited working memory capacity. Similar symbolic-connectionist considerations predict various other limitations of human symbolic reasoning as well (see Hummel & Holyoak, 1997). One thing to be gained by asking *how* the human cognitive architecture implements symbols (rather than simply assuming *that* it does, as in the traditional symbolic approach) is an understanding of some of the limitations of that architecture.

Symbolic connectionism also explains some strengths of the human cognitive architecture, connections that are equally mysterious from the traditional symbolic perspective. One is the capacity to map semantically related predicates that take different numbers of arguments, for example, mapping *taller (A B)* and *taller (B C)* onto *tallest-to-shortest (D E F)*. LISA can solve this mapping (Hummel & Holyoak, 1997). Traditional symbolic models, by contrast, must enforce an inviolable "N-ary restriction" (whereby a predicate with N arguments may map only to another predicate with N arguments), which precludes such mappings (see Hummel & Holyoak, 1997). Other strengths of symbolic connectionism derive from the value of distributed representations of semantic content (see Hummel & Holyoak, 1997). The early connectionists were right about the value of distributed representations, and symbolic connectionism is just as able to exploit those strengths as "traditional" (eliminative) connectionism. In fact, it is *better* able to do so, because symbolic connectionism embeds these representations into systematic structures. Armed with dynamic binding, LISA can implement fast inductive learning of universal generalizations by using a simple variant of the Hebbian algorithm for unsupervised learning. As an aside, it is interesting to note that LISA's learning by analogy is a variety of learning by example—a property that it shares with back propagation. It is thus more constrained than traditional algorithms for unsupervised learning (e.g., Kohonen, 1982; Marshall, 1995; von der Malsburg, 1973). At the same time, it is less "heavy-handed"—and much more psychologically plausible—than the explicit error-correction algorithm of back propagation. In LISA, the "teacher" is just a familiar example (i.e., a source analog), not an all-knowing external device.

A further advantage of symbolic connectionism over either traditional symbolic modeling or eliminative connectionist modeling is that it provides a vocabulary for talking about the relation between truly associative, nonsymbolic processes and more complex symbolic processes. In symbolic connectionism, these are all part of the same system: Take symbolic connectionism, strip away dynamic variable binding, and the result is simple (connectionist-style) associationism.

Finally, symbolic connectionism maintains the basic architecture of earlier connectionist models (densely connected networks of local computing elements) while adding a more fine-grained use of the informational capacity of time. As compared with the elements of traditional symbolic models (lists of localist symbols, which can be constructed and modified by explicit list operations), the elements of symbolic connectionism provide more direct links to neural architecture and hence set the stage for addressing questions at Marr's (1982) implementation level. A *physical* symbol system, as embodied in a human or other biological organism, is realized in the brain. There is a neural code for thought, and symbolic connectionism—the proper treatment of symbols—may guide us in cracking the code.

ACKNOWLEDGMENTS

Preparation of this chapter was supported by National Science Foundation Grant SBR–9729023. Eric Dietrich, Arthur Markman, and Jay McClelland provided valuable comments on an earlier draft.

REFERENCES

Anderson, J. R. (1993). *Rules of the mind.* Hillsdale, NJ: Lawrence Erlbaum Associates.
Barnden, J. A. (1994). On the connectionist implementation of analogy and working memory matching. In J. A. Barnden & K. J. Holyoak (Eds.), *Advances in connectionist and neural*

computation theory, Vol. 3: Analogy, metaphor, and reminding (pp. 327–374). Norwood, NJ: Ablex.

Churchland, P. (1995). The engine of reason, the seat of the soul: A philosophical journey into the brain. Cambridge MA: MIT Press.

D'Amato, M. R., Salmon, D. P., Loukas, E., & Tomie, A. (1985). Symmetry and transitivity of conditional relations in monkeys (Cebus apella) and pigeons (Columba livia). Journal of the Experimental Analysis of Behavior, 44, 365–373.

Desmedt, J., & Tomberg, C. (1994). Transient phase-locking of 40 Hz electrical oscillations in prefrontal and parietal human cortex reflects the process of conscious somatic perception. Neuroscience Letters, 168, 126–129.

Eckhorn, R., Bauer, R., Jordan, W., Brish, M., Kruse, W. Munk, M., & Reitboeck, H. J. (1988). Coherent oscillations: A mechanism of feature linking in the visual cortex? Multiple electrode and correlation analysis in the cat. Biological Cybernetics, 60, 121–130.

Eckhorn, R., Reitboeck, H., Arndt, M., & Dicke, P. (1990). Feature linking via synchronization among distributed assemblies: Simulations of results from cat visual cortex. Neural Computation, 2, 293–307.

Elman, J. L. (1990). Finding structure in time. Cognitive Science, 14, 179–212.

Elman, J. L., Bates, E. A., Johnson, M. K., Karmiloff-Smith, A., Parisi, D., & Plunkett, K. (1996). Rethinking innateness: A connectionist perspective on development. Cambridge, MA: MIT Press.

Falkenhainer, B., Forbus, K. D., & Gentner, D. (1989). The structure-mapping engine: Algorithm and examples. Artificial Intelligence, 41, 1–63.

Feldman, J. A., & Ballard, D. H. (1982). Connectionist models and their properties. Cognitive Science, 6, 205–254.

Fodor, J. A., & Pylyshyn, Z. (1988). Connectionism and cognitive architecture: A critical analysis. Cognition, 28, 3–71.

Gick, M. L., & Holyoak, K. J. (1983). Schema induction and analogical transfer. Cognitive Psychology, 15, 1–38.

Gray, C. M. (1994). Synchronous oscillations in neuronal systems: Mechanisms and functions. Journal of Computational Neuroscience, 1, 11–38.

Gray, C. M., & Singer, W. (1989). Stimulus specific neuronal oscillations in orientation columns of cat visual cortex. Proceedings of the National Academy of Sciences, USA, 86, 1698–1702.

Halford, G. S., Wilson, W. H., Guo, J., Gayler, R. W., Wiles, J., & Stewart, J. E. M. (1994). Connectionist implications for processing capacity limitations in analogies. In K. J. Holyoak & J. A. Barnden (Eds.), Advances in connectionist and neural computation theory, Vol. 2: Analogical connections (pp. 363–415). Norwood, NJ: Ablex.

Halford, G. S., Wilson, W. H., & Phillips, S. (1998). Processing capacity defined by relational complexity: Implications for comparative, developmental, and cognitive psychology. Brain and Behavioral Sciences, 21, 803–864.

Hinton, G. E. (Ed.). (1990). Connectionist symbol processing. Cambridge, MA: MIT Press.

Holyoak, K. J. (1991). Symbolic connectionism: Toward third-generation theories of expertise. In K. A. Ericsson & J. Smith (Eds.), Toward a general theory of expertise: Prospects and limits (pp. 301–335). Cambridge: Cambridge University Press.

Holyoak, K. J., Novick, L. R., & Melz, E. R. (1994). Component processes in analogical transfer: Mapping, pattern completion, and adaptation. In K. J. Holyoak & J. A. Barnden (Eds.), Advances in connectionist and neural computation theory, Vol. 2: Analogical connections (pp. 130–180). Norwood, NJ: Ablex.

Holyoak, K. J., & Thagard, P. (1989). Analogical mapping by constraint satisfaction. Cognitive Science, 13, 295–355.

Holyoak, K. J., & Thagard, P. (1995). Mental leaps: Analogy in creative thought. Cambridge, MA: MIT Press.

Hummel, J. E., & Biederman, I. (1992). Dynamic binding in a neural network for shape recognition. *Psychological Review, 99*, 480–517.

Hummel, J. E., Burns, B., & Holyoak, K. J. (1994). Analogical mapping by dynamic binding: Preliminary investigations. In K. J. Holyoak & J. A. Barnden (Eds.), *Advances in connectionist and neural computation theory, Vol. 2: Analogical connections* (pp. 416–445). Norwood, NJ: Ablex.

Hummel, J. E., & Holyoak, K. J. (1992). Indirect analogical mapping. *In Proceedings of the 14th annual conference of the Cognitive Science Society* (pp. 516–521). Hillsdale, NJ: Lawrence Erlbaum Associates.

Hummel, J. E., & Holyoak, K. J. (1993). Distributing structure over time. *Behavioral and Brain Sciences, 16*, 464.

Hummel, J. E., & Holyoak, K. J. (1996). LISA: A computational model of analogical inference and schema induction. In C. W. Cottrell (Ed.), *Proceedings of the 18th annual conference of the Cognitive Science Society* (pp. 352–357). Hillsdale, NJ: Lawrence Erlbaum Associates.

Hummel, J. E., & Holyoak, K. J. (1997). Distributed representations of structure: A theory of analogical access and mapping. *Psychological Review, 104*, 427–466.

Hummel, J. E., Melz, E. R., Thompson, J., & Holyoak, K. J. (1994). Mapping hierarchical structures with synchrony for binding: Preliminary investigations. In A. Ram & K. Eiselt (Eds.), *Proceedings of the 16th annual conference of the Cognitive Science Society* (pp. 433–438). Hillsdale, NJ: Lawrence Erlbaum Associates.

Hummel, J. E., & Saiki, J. (1993). Rapid unsupervised learning of object structural descriptions. *Proceedings of the 15th annual conference of the Cognitive Science Society* (pp. 569–574). Hillsdale, NJ: Lawrence Erlbaum Associates.

Hummel, J. E., & Stankiewicz, B. J. (1996). An architecture for rapid, hierarchical structural description. In T. Inui & J. McClelland (Eds.), *Attention and performance, XVI: Information integration in perception and communication* (pp. 93–121). Cambridge, MA: MIT Press.

Hummel, J. E., & Stankiewicz, B. J. (1998). Two roles for attention in shape perception: A structural description model of visual scrutiny. *Visual Cognition, 5*, 49–79.

Jordan, M. I. (1986). An introduction to linear algebra in parallel distributed processing. In D. E. Rumelhart, J. L. McClelland, & the PDP Research Group, *Parallel distribute processing: Explorations in the microstructures of cognition* (Vol. 1, pp. 365–422). Cambridge, MA: MIT Press.

Kohonen, T. (1982). Self-organized formation of topologically correct feature maps. *Biological Cybernetics, 43*, 59–69.

König, P., & Engel, A. K. (1995). Correlated firing in sensory-motor systems. *Current Opinion in Neurobiology, 5*, 511–519.

Lesgold, A. M. (1972). Pronominalization: A device for unifying sentences in memory. *Journal of Verbal Learning and Verbal Behavior, 11*, 316–323.

Love, B. C. (1999). Utilizing time: Asynchronous binding. In M. S. Kearns, S. A. Solla, & D. A. Cohn (Eds.), *Advances in neural information processing systems* (Vol. 11). Cambridge, MA: MIT Press.

Marcus, G. F. (1998). Rethinking eliminative connectionism. *Cognitive Psychology, 37*, 243–282.

Marr, D. (1982). *Vision*. San Francisco: Freeman.

Marshall, J. A. (1995). Adaptive pattern recognition by self-organizing neural networks: Context, uncertainty, multiplicity, and scale. *Neural Networks, 8*(3), 335–362.

Milner, P. M. (1974). A model for visual shape recognition. *Psychological Review, 81*, 521–535.

Mozer, M. C., Zemel, R. S., Behrmann, M., & Williams, C. K. (1992). Learning to segment images using dynamic feature binding. *Neural Computation, 4*, 650–665.

Newell, A. (1980). Physical symbol systems. *Cognitive Science, 4*, 135–183.

Newell, A. (1990). *Unified theories of cognition*. Cambridge, MA: Harvard University Press.

Newell, A., & Simon, H. A. (1976). Computer science as empirical inquiry: Symbols and search. *Communications of the ACM, 19*, 113–126.

Oden, D. L., Thompson, R. K. R., & Premack, D. (1988). Spontaneous transfer of matching by infant chimpanzees (*Pan troglodytes*). *Animal Behavior Processes, 14,* 140–145.

Phillips, S., & Halford, G. S. (1997). Systematicity: Psychological evidence with connectionist implications. In M. G. Shafto & P. Langley (Eds.), *Proceedings of the 19th conference of the Cognitive Science Society* (pp. 614–619). Mahwah, NJ: Lawrence Erlbaum Associates.

Pinker, S., & Prince, A. (1988). On language and connectionism: Analysis of a parallel distributed processing model. *Cognition, 28,* 73–193.

Plate, T. (1991). Holographic reduced representations: Convolution algebra for compositional distributed representations. In J. Mylopoulos & R. Reiter (Eds.), *Proceedings of the 12th International Joint Conference on Artificial Intelligence* (pp. 30–35). San Mateo, CA: Morgan Kaufmann.

Pollack, J. B. (1990). Recursive distributed representations. *Artificial Intelligence, 46,* 77–106.

Robin, N., & Holyoak, K. J. (1994). Relational complexity and the functions of prefrontal cortex. In M. S. Gazzaniga (Ed.), *The cognitive neurosciences* (pp. 987–997). Cambridge, MA: MIT Press.

Rosenbloom, P. S., Laird, J. E., Newell, A., & McCarl, R. (1991). A preliminary analysis of the Soar architecture as a basis for general intelligence. *Artificial Intelligence, 47,* 289–325.

Ross, B. H., & Kennedy, P. T. (1990). Generalizing from the use of earlier examples in problem solving. *Journal of Experimental Psychology: Learning, Memory, and Cognition, 16,* 42–55.

Rumelhart, D. E., McClelland, J. L., & the PDP Research Group. (1986). *Parallel distributed processing, Vol. 1: Foundations.* Cambridge, MA: MIT Press.

Seidenberg, M. S. (1994). Language and connectionism: The developing interface. *Cognition, 50,* 385–401.

Seidenberg, M. S. (1997). Language acquisition and use: Learning and applying probabilistic constraints. *Science, 275,* 1599–1603.

Shastri, L. (1997). A model of rapid memory formation in the hippocampal system. In M. G. Shafto & P. Langley (Eds.), *Proceedings of the 19th conference of the Cognitive Science Society* (pp. 680–685). Mahwah, NJ: Lawrence Erlbaum Associates.

Shastri, L., & Ajjanagadde, V. (1993). From simple associations to systematic reasoning: A connectionist representation of rules, variables and dynamic bindings using temporal synchrony. *Behavioral and Brain Sciences, 16,* 417–494.

Smolensky, P. (1990). Tensor product variable binding and the representation of symbolic structures in connectionist systems. *Artificial Intelligence, 46,* 159–216.

St. John, M. F. (1992). The Story Gestalt: A model of knowledge-intensive processes in text comprehension. *Cognitive Science, 16,* 271–302.

St. John, M. F., & McClelland, J. L. (1990). Learning and applying contextual constraints in sentence comprehension. *Artificial Intelligence, 46,* 217–257.

Touretzky, D., & Hinton, G. (1988). A distributed production system. *Cognitive Science, 12,* 423–466.

Touretzky, D., & Pomerleau, D. A. (1994). Reconstructing physical symbol systems. *Cognitive Science, 18,* 345–353.

Vaadia, E., Haalman, I., Abeles, M., Bergman, H., Prut, Y., Slovin, H., & Aertsen, A. (1995). Dynamics of neuronal interactions in monkey cortex in relation to behavioural events. *Nature, 373,* 515–518.

Vera, A. H., & Simon, H. A. (1993). Situated action: A symbolic interpretation. *Cognitive Science, 17,* 7–48.

Vera, A. H., & Simon, H. A. (1994). Reply to Touretzky and Pomerleau: Reconstructing physical symbol systems. *Cognitive Science, 18,* 355–360.

von der Malsburg, C. (1973). Self-organization of orientation selective cells in the striate cortex. *Kybernetik, 14,* 85–100.

von der Malsburg, C. (1981/1994). The correlation theory of brain function (1994 reprint of a report originally published in 1981). In E. Domany, J. L. van Hemmen, & K. Schulten (Eds.), *Models of neural networks II* (pp. 95–119). Berlin: Springer.

von der Malsburg, C., & Buhmann, J. (1992). Sensory segmentation with coupled neural oscillators. *Biological Cybernetics, 67,* 233–242.

Wanner, H. E. (1968). *On remembering, forgetting, and understanding sentences: A study of the deep structure hypothesis.* Unpublished doctoral dissertation, Harvard University.

10

Analogy and Conceptual Change, or You Can't Step Into the Same Mind Twice

Eric Dietrich
Binghamton University

Sometimes analogy researchers talk as if the freshness of an experience of analogy resides solely in seeing that something is like something else—seeing that the atom is like a solar system, that heat is like flowing water, that paintbrushes work like pumps, or that electricity is like a teeming crowd. Analogy is more than this, however. Analogy is not just seeing that the atom is like a solar system; rather, it is seeing something *new* about the atom, an observation enabled by "looking" at atoms from the perspective of one's understanding of solar systems. The question for analogy researchers then is: Where does this new knowledge about atoms come from? How can an analogy provide new knowledge and new understanding?

My answer is that having an analogy *changes* the concepts involved in the analogy. More specifically, merely having an analogy changes one's concepts. I call this answer the *analogical conceptual change hypothesis*. In this chapter, I argue for this hypothesis and explain some of its implications. I must argue for this hypothesis more or less from first principles, because, as a psychologist colleague pointed out to me, it is not clear how to test the hypothesis experimentally, at least not right now. This is unfortunate, not just because it means the hypothesis remains untested, but because psychologists have a tendency to lose interest in ideas that are not subject to experimental verification or refutation. So, for better or worse, this chapter is about what we might call *theoretical psychology*.[1]

The next two sections of this chapter present needed background, first on analogy and analogical reminding and then on conceptual change and its dynamics. As I lay out this background, I use it to elaborate the analogical conceptual change hypothesis and specify the kind of concept change that I think must occur to have analogies (more specifically, to have analogical remindings). Then, in the next three sections, I use the traditional tools available to us theoretical types—logic, plausible assumptions, and others' data—to argue (a) that probability assessments indicate that the specified conceptual change must occur *before* one can experience an analogy, (b) that the notion of mapping crucial to the theory analogy (defined later) camouflages a serious unpaid theoretical debt, and (c) that paying the debt of (b) while obeying the probability assessments of (a) requires a view of concepts where the types of constituents that make up concepts are not fixed, but can rapidly be transformed into one another, especially during analogical reminding.[2]

ANALOGY AND ANALOGICAL REMINDING

The General Picture and Definitions of Terms

The cognitive phenomenon I am primarily interested in is reminding: specifically, *analogical reminding*. (Sometimes researchers, e.g., Hummel & Holyoak, 1997, include analogical reminding as part of the general definition of analogical thinking.) Analogical reminding is common; it occurs any time some concept or percept in one domain recalls, in the right way for an analogy, another concept in another domain. For example, imagine that while walking down a sidewalk one night, one sees a jumble of garbage cans, some standing upright, some lying on their sides or against one another, and one is suddenly reminded of Stonehenge on the Salisbury Plain in England. Here is another example. I was cross-country skiing with a colleague. We paused to rest and drink some water. Although it was cold, we were warm, and she, being mindful of hypothermia, took

---

[1]The phrase *theoretical psychology* makes some cognitive scientists shudder. I think this is because researchers are worried about lapsing into the kind of speculation that eventually led to behaviorism in the mid-20th century. Nevertheless, I think theoretical psychology is important and has a place in modern cognitive science; we should not avoid it.

[2]To dispel any misconceptions, it does not follow from (a) to (c) that the computational hypothesis fundamental to cognitive science is false or that there are no such things as mental representations. I am arguing that one of the computational processes in our heads, analogy, is a representation construction process.

off one glove to cool down. She then quipped: "My hand is like a dog's tongue when he's panting in the summer."

Such occurrences are the sorts of the phenomena I am concerned with. I am not here interested in the phenomenon of a hearer's understanding an analogy spoken to her. I am not primarily interested in linguistic analogies, but rather the analogies that occur spontaneously in one's head during cases of reminding. I am also concerned with long-term and working memory.

A fair amount is known about analogical reminding and the broader class of *similarity-based retrieval* to which analogical remindings belong. Analogical reminding comprises at least two processes: *access* and *mapping* (Forbus, Gentner, & Law, 1995; Hummel & Holyoak, 1997). Access (also simply called "retrieval") is the process of retrieving some memory item (which I call the *retrieved item*) from long-term memory based on some other item in working memory (which I call the *retrieving item*). After retrieval the retrieved item and the retrieving item coexist in working memory.

Before defining mapping, I need to say a few words about my terminology. Generally, I use the term *item* to refer to anything in either long-term or working memory. This gets around the problem of worrying about when a memory element is a concept and when it is not. I still use the term *concept* when the item referred to is obviously, or traditionally treated as, a concept. This situation most frequently happens when the item is in working memory. However, unlike some psychologists, notably Barsalou (1989), I do not adhere to the restriction of using "concept" exclusively to refer to items in working memory.

I also assume that concepts and, in general, items, are *representations* of some sort. For example, in the garbage cans/Stonehenge case, the perceptually based representation of the garbage cans in working memory accessed the Stonehenge representation in long-term memory. The representation of the garbage cans is the retrieving item, and the representation of Stonehenge the retrieved item. The item in working memory can be perceptual, like the representation of the garbage cans, or it can be an item previously retrieved from long-term memory, as in the stream-of-consciousness phenomenon (for example, once the memory item representing Stonehenge was in working memory, it might have then accessed the memory of the stone faces on Easter Island).

Mapping is the process of matching constituents of the two items now in working memory. Mapping is essentially a process of finding *functional counterparts* between concepts (see, e.g., Gentner, 1983, 1989; Hummel & Holyoak, 1997). The mapping process locates which *object nodes* (or more simply, *objects*) in one concept are the functional counterparts of object nodes in the other concept. For example, in garbage-henge, the representations of the cans are the object nodes, and they map onto the representations of the stone monoliths. In the ungloved-tongue case, the representation of the ungloved hand maps onto the representation of a dog's panting tongue. What makes these objects functional counterparts of each other is the role they are represented as playing in the concept or representation. These roles are represented by *structural relations* among the objects making up the concept. The mapping process ignores *attributes* of objects. Attributes are representations of *properties*, which occur in the external world. For example, dog tongues are wet. Being wet is the property in the world, and internally it is represented by an attribute designated by something like "being wet."

From this preliminary discussion of mapping, we can see the three main constituents making up memory items: objects (object nodes), attributes, and structural relations. These three represent three different parts or aspects of the world: physical or nonphysical things, the properties of these things, and the functional roles these things can partake in. Mapping is a very important notion; I return to it shortly when I discuss the nature of analogy in more detail. Later, I discuss an interesting and important problem with the notion.

Analogical remindings are individually generated, occurring in the heads of most humans past a certain young age (there is evidence that very young children can recognize analogies provided that their knowledge is manipulated and changed in the appropriate way, see Gentner, Ratterman, Markman, & Kotovsky, 1995; Kotovsky & Gentner, 1996). Analogical remindings are frequently creative and therefore are implicated in theories of creativity (Finke, Warde, & Smith, 1992; Hofstadter, 1995).

Gentner and her colleagues pointed out that, broadly speaking, there seem to be three large types of remindings: (1) analogical remindings (e.g., Rutherford noticing that the alpha particles in his experiments were like comets), (2) superficial remindings (as when a yellow balloon reminds us of the sun—sometimes called "mere appearance" or "attribute-similarity remindings"), and (3) mundane remindings (as when garbage cans remind one of other garbage cans or of putting out the garbage for tomorrow morning's pickup—sometimes called "literal similarity remindings"; Forbus et al., 1995; Gentner, 1989). Gentner et al.'s theory explains, in part, the relative frequencies of these three kinds of reminding. According to the experimental evidence, superficial and mundane remindings are the most common; analogical remindings are rarer. I do not think that these remindings are as rare as the Rutherford case might lead us to believe. One does not need an insight into particle physics to experience a creative, if quirky, analogical reminding: The garbage-henge and ungloved-tongue cases are just such examples. (Gentner and her colleagues might categorize the garbage-henge case as a superficial reminding, rather than a true case of analogical reminding, but I do not think this is right. I return to this later when I discuss the properties of true analogies.)

I can fine-tune the analogical conceptual change hypothesis a bit, now. The hypothesis predicts that analogical remindings alter one or both the items involved in the episode of reminding. (It is worth considering the extent to which the other types of remindings alter concepts and other memory items, but that is a task for another paper.)

Analogy and Structure Mapping

What makes a reminding an *analogical* reminding is simply that it is a retrieval of an item from long-term memory resulting in an analogy with the item doing the retrieving. Analogy is the cognitive process whereby one thing is seen as resembling another. What does it mean for two concepts to resemble each other, to be similar? This is a deep question. Answering it requires having a theory of analogy and at least the beginnings of a theory of concepts. My answer to this question is derived from Gentner's structure-mapping theory (1983, 1989). I assume her theory for two related reasons. First, as I said, it is impossible to define analogy beyond a sort of folk definition without appealing to some theory or other, and, second, her theory, at least its central part, has more or less achieved the status of "the received view."

On Gentner's structure-mapping theory of analogy, two memory items (concepts) are analogous when one is *mappable* to the other (e.g., if the working memory item *maps* onto the item retrieved from long-term memory). Mapping, as I said, is a process of finding functional counterparts between the two concepts. This process has three parts. First, the objects of one item must map onto the objects of the other item. Consider the well-known analogy of the atom and a solar system (see Fig. 10.1). The analogy maps representations for planets onto representations for electrons and a representation of the sun onto a representation of the nucleus. Second, the two memory items must have the same *structure* for an analogous mapping to be successful. Having the same structure means that their higher order relations are *identical*. In Fig. 10.1, this identical structure is realized by the two-place predicates "attracts," "more massive than," and "revolves around." In an analogy, it is these relational structures of the concepts that matter, not the lower level properties or attributes of the objects. Third, low-level properties or attributes must be discarded for purposes of the analogy. For example, that the sun is yellow and hot is irrelevant to the analogy, and so the mental representations of these attributes are not part of the mapping. The analogous concepts need

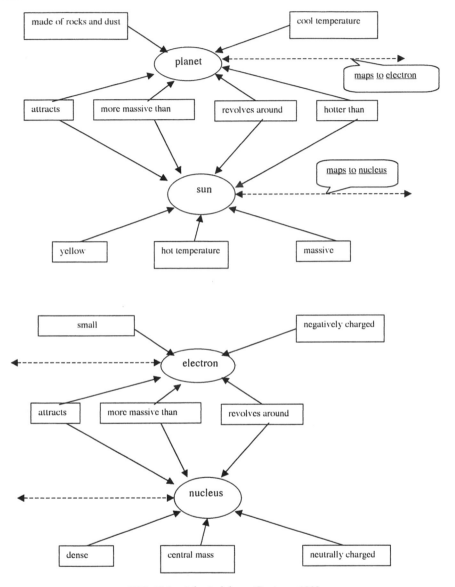

FIG. 10.1. Adapted from Gentner, 1983.

not share object attributes and usually do not share any substantive attributes, that is, attributes beyond things like "physical object." Together, these three parts mean that objects in analogous concepts are represented as *purely* functional counterparts.

In analogy, both high-level structures and objects are mapped; attributes or properties are not. There is an infelicity, however, in this use of the term *mapping*. When analogy researchers speak of mapping structures, the structures must be identical (at some level). When they speak of mapping objects, the objects *cannot* be identical—otherwise what is the point of the analogy? Mapped objects are not identical, but mapped structures are. This infelicity is not important in itself, but it does indicate that mapping tends to be underspecified and treated rather loosely in theories of analogy. I discuss mapping and these problems in a later section. Because the term *mapping* is the accepted technical term for both kinds of matching, I use it for both, but the difference between the two should definitely be borne in mind. When it matters to the discussion, I flag the difference.

At this point, it is beneficial to step through some simple examples. Thinking that a yellow balloon is like the sun is not an analogy (but a similarity comparison) because the similarity of the two (the balloon and the sun) is based on the property of being yellow. Being yellow is not a relation ("yellower than" is a relation, but it is not operative in this case). Thinking that an ungloved hand is like a dog's tongue is an analogy because the similarity between the two is based on the complex relation: "Exposed body part causes heat dissipation." Not only is this a relation, but it is a *higher order* relation between a property (being an exposed body part—a tongue or a hand) and an event or process (losing or giving off heat). (The fact that a flat hand also resembles a flat tongue was probably important for the retrieval, too, but not for the analogy; see Forbus, et al., 1995). Garbage-henge is arguably an analogy (a case of analogy reminding) and not a case of mere superficial similarity reminding because the similarity between the garbage cans and the monoliths of Stonehenge was based on relations such as "lies next to," "stands next to," "lies athwart," and "is leaning on" and not merely on simple properties describing the whole collection of objects, such as "lies in a semicircle."

It is clear from these examples that concepts can match or be similar in three ways that correspond directly to the three classes of remindings (see earlier). The three kinds of similarity are analogical similarity, superficial or mere-appearance similarity, and literal similarity. Analogical similarity, as we have seen, results from structural and object matches, but not attribute matches. Superficial similarity results from object and attribute matches only. Literal similarity matches result from structural, attribute, and object matches.

Structure mapping theory also postulates conceptual change. After the analogy between the two analogues has been made, information can be imported from the retrieved item to the retrieving item. This is usually the order because the retrieved item is the one the individual "knows best"; it is the richer one from which knowledge can be imported to the retrieving item. This process is called *projection of candidate inferences* (Gentner, 1983,

1989; see chap. 11, this volume). The wider theory also postulates three other kinds of conceptual change (for a total of four kinds):

1. Progressive alignment, whereby children's knowledge becomes more abstract so that more high-order similarities can be recognized (this is also sometimes called "unpacking" and "gentrification of knowledge"; Gentner et al., 1995; Kotovsky & Gentner, 1990, 1996).[3]
2. Highlighting, whereby less salient conceptual properties are made more salient (chap. 11, this volume).
3. Restructuring, whereby whole systems of knowledge get changed (chap. 11, this volume).

It is important to note that all these changes happen *because* of analogy. In contrast, the analogical conceptual change hypothesis claims that analogy happens *because of* conceptual change (of a certain sort, to be explained later). The analogical conceptual change hypothesis does not deny that there are the sort of postanalogy conceptual changes hypothesized by Gentner. My hypothesis agrees with Gentner on this point: Her four kinds of change happen *after* an analogy has been made. Rather, my hypothesis claims that a specific kind of change occurs before the analogy and that the analogy happens because of this change.

Analogical Reminding and MAC/FAC

In addition to their theory of analogy, Gentner and her colleagues have a theory and computer model of similarity-based retrieval called MAC/FAC. MAC/FAC stands for "Many are called but few are chosen." (When there is no chance of confusion, I use the term *MAC/FAC* to refer both to their computer program and their theory of analogical reminding.) The program MAC/FAC incorporates a computer model of Gentner's structure mapping theory called the structure mapping engine (SME; see Falkenhainer, Forbus, & Gentner, 1989). MAC/FAC is not intended as a model of reminding in general. It is strictly a model of similarity-based remindings. (It is not the only such model. See, e.g., Hummel & Holyoak, 1997, and Thagard, Holyoak, Nelson, & Gochfield, 1990.)

MAC/FAC explains three interesting facts.

Fact one: It explains the observed ratios of the three types of remindings that people experience. As I mentioned earlier, Type 1 is rarer than both Type 2 and Type 3, with Type 3 being the most common.

---

[3]Perhaps another name could be *Gentnerfication* because the process produces increasingly mappable structures of the kind postulated by structure mapping theory.

Fact two: It explains why similarity-based retrieval is strongly sensitive to superficial similarity and only weakly sensitive to structural similarity.

Fact three: It explains why high-level relational similarity is a better predictor than surface similarity of how useful a reminding is in terms of making further inferences. This means that analogical remindings are more useful than mere appearance remindings for making inferences. (Mundane remindings are quite useful too, but, importantly, since they are literally similar, they do not usually generate *new* knowledge. Analogies are best for that.)

Briefly, here is MAC/FAC's explanation of these three facts. As we noted earlier, Type 3, the mundane remindings, are retrievals based on literal similarity between the retrieving item and the retrieved item. That is, these remindings are based on matches of both relational structures and attributes. Type 3 remindings are based on the highest quantity and quality of matches. This is why garbage cans tend to remind one of other garbage cans. Type 2 remindings, the superficial ones, are the second most common. This is because they are the easiest to make. Matching attributes and other low-level features requires computationally simple operations, like taking the dot product of feature vectors. Finally, analogical remindings (Type 1) do occur from time to time because (in part), although they are expensive, they are the most useful in terms of making analogical inferences, and importing and creating new knowledge.

All of this suggests that similarity-based reminding is a two-staged process. Stage 1, the MAC stage, is primarily sensitive to surface similarities. Retrieval based on surface similarities is easy and cheap, so the MAC stage is relatively fast. On the other hand, the MAC stage is relatively *insensitive* to high-level, relational similarities. This is not so good because relational similarities, not surface similarities, between memory items are the foundation of good inferences and new knowledge. What is needed is another stage that *is* sensitive to relational similarities. The MAC stage functions as a wide filter producing a set of potential remindings as output, which get passed to the FAC stage (which is where SME is located in the MAC/FAC program). The FAC stage is slower and more computationally expensive because it is sensitive to high-level relational structure. This is not a problem because, thanks to the MAC stage, it works over a much smaller set than all the system's memory.

The interaction of the two stages tends to produce remindings based on both high-level and superficial matches—Type 3 remindings. This accords with the experimental data. Although the FAC stage uses SME, it is not a stage just for analogy matching. If it were, then MAC/FAC would produce mostly analogical remindings, which would not fit the data. Rather, SME is designed so that, while running in MAC/FAC, it tends to produce mostly mundane remindings (based on matches of both relational structure and attributes), yet it still retrieves analogies from time to time (based on relational matches only).[4]

I do *not* assume Gentner's MAC/FAC theory of reminding for the reason that my analogical conceptual change hypothesis is incompatible with it (although I pay attention to the data MAC/FAC are meant to explain).

My hypothesis, to refine it further, claims that *access* (or retrieval) changes the items involved. *The change is to the relational structure of the analogous items.* I call this change *retrieval-based structural change.* It is part of my hypothesis that by the time both items are in working memory, one or both have been changed structurally (if only slightly), and this change funds the analogy—or better, this change *is* the analogy.

Retrieval-based structural change simply does not happen in MAC/FAC. It does seem that such conceptual change runs counter to some rather deep architectural features in the MAC stage. However, it is not clear to me that retrieval-based structural change is *inconsistent* with the central feature of MAC/FAC: that memory retrieval is a two-stage process, one fast and insensitive and the other slow but sensitive. True, MAC/FAC is a model based on collected psychological data, but the data I discuss here—the garbage-cans/Stonehenge case—are data over and beyond what MAC/FAC was intended to model. It seems to me that, if my hypothesis is correct and there is such a thing as retrieval-based structural change, MAC/FAC can be slightly altered and augmented without radically altering the general MAC/FAC approach to reminding. Some of the detailed architecture of MAC/FAC must be changed if I am right, but nothing central to it.

THE MUTABILITY OF CONCEPTS

The general idea that concepts change over time is not new. It has been explored by many. Indeed, the idea is venerable. Henri Poincaré and

---

[4]This is an interesting feature of SME: although it is primarily thought of as an analogy engine (in fact, as an implementation of structure mapping theory) in MAC/FAC, SME nevertheless produces mostly mundane remindings. Briefly, this is primarily due to the MAC stage: SME produces mundane remindings because that is mostly what the MAC stage gives it. SME can run in one of three different modes: analogy mode, literal similarity mode, and mere appearance mode. In MAC/FAC, SME is run in literal similarity mode. Yet, in MAC/FAC, it still produces analogies and mere appearance matches from time to time. Indeed, SME is almost always run in literal similarity mode, and still it produces analogies and mere appearance matches. SME works by coalescing initial local matches into global matches. Apparently, the ratios of the three types of remindings depend on which local matches are produced and how successfully they combine into global matches. For the technical details of SME's architecture, see Falkenhainer et al. (1989). The details for the way SME works in MAC/FAC can be found in Forbus et al. (1995).

William James both hypothesized that concepts were active and nonstatic (Poincaré, 1908/1952; James, 1890/1950). In fact, the thread of the idea that concepts are fluid and constructed goes back through the Roman materialist philosopher, Lucretius (55 BCE/trans. 1951), to the Greek philosopher Heraclitus, who said "[T]he moving world can only be known by what is in motion" (Wheelwright, 1964, p. 58).[5]

To a first approximation, the cognitive dynamics of retrieval-based structural change depend on *interacting concepts*. The interaction produces the change. Because concepts are the way we conceive things, this squares nicely with the analogical conceptual change hypothesis: The reason the atom–solar system analogy shows us something new about atoms is that

---

[5]Many psychologists have discussed conceptual change and the constructive processes involved in analogy and related processes, and there are several hypotheses in psychology about analogy and conceptual change. For example, see Barsalou (1983, 1987, 1989); Camac and Glucksberg (1984); Gentner (1983, 1989); Gentner and Markman (1995); Glenberg, Kruley, and Langston (1994), Glucksberg and Keysar (1990); Kelly and Keil (1987); Markman and Medin (1995); and chapter 11, this volume. See also Black (1979). For a good synopsis of the field of analogy and some interesting speculation on its future direction, see Hoffman (1995).

Intuition-based artificial intelligence has also contributed a fair number of intriguing hypotheses about the nature of analogical conceptual change. For example, see French (1995); Hofstadter, (1995); Mitchell (1993); Indurkhya (1997); and Schank (1982).

Some psychologists are now beginning to explore *how* some of the changes are produced in humans, that is, what the detailed mental processes are that result in conceptual change. See Gentner et al. (1995), Kotovsky and Gentner (1996), and chapter 11.

In artificial intelligence (AI), the "how" question takes on complicated empirical and methodological baggage. For an AI program that implements a model or hypothesis about analogical conceptual change, we definitely know how the change occurs: we cannot write code without specifying the details of a process. But does the process in the machine of changing knowledge representations have anything to do with the process in humans of conceptual change? This is the empirical/methodological question. Unfortunately, for a variety of reasons, including the fact that we still do not know all that much about how concepts change in humans, many AI modelers to date have had to invent their own processes by relying on introspection and intuitions of what is plausible. I think, by and large, such speculation is a good thing simply because it widens the pool of what we consider possible, but it should be remembered that it is speculation, and speculation based on data derived from introspection.

Not all AI programs, however, are based on introspective data. Some robust and highly suggestive computer models of analogy and conceptual change are based on psychological data collected in experiments. Moreover, the performance of these models has also been experimentally compared with human performance. In many ways, these programs and their ties to psychological experimental represent one of cognitive science's real success stories (Forbus, Gentner, Markman, & Ferguson, 1998). See ACME and its associated model of memory access, ARCS (Holyoak & Thagard, 1989; Thagard et al., 1990), IAM (Keane & Brayshaw, 1988; Keane, Ledgeway, & Duff, 1994), LISA (Hummel & Holyoak, 1997), Phineas (Falkenhainer, 1990a, 1990b), and the structure mapping engine (SME) and its associated model of memory access and retrieval MAC/FAC (Falkenhainer et al., 1989; Forbus et al., 1995).

it changes the concept representing atoms. Care must be taken here because the interacting concept view suggests that concepts exist ahead of time in long-term memory as static memory items, and it is not obvious that this is true—to put it mildly (see, e.g., Barsalou, 1989).

There is a fair amount of agreement, at least among psychologists, that long-term memory items are not at all like classical data structures, inertly sitting in one's head waiting to be read or updated. Beyond this, however, there is not much agreement. How stable are the items in long-term memory? Are items in long-term memory retrieved as units? Does an organism retrieve an item from long-term memory, or does it construct the item from something "subconceptual" in long-term memory? When an organism retrieves information (to use a neutral term) from long-term memory at one time and retrieves the same information (in some sense) at another time, is the resultant working-memory item the same both times? If not, what influences the change? (Many cognitive scientists have wrestled with these questions. Barsalou [1983, 1987, 1989] has done an especially interesting job. The questions I asked are derived from Barsalou, 1989). I have only partial answers to some of these questions. I encapsulate my answers in the following three assumptions, which seem plausible given the data.

> Assumption 1: The items in long-term memory are more or less stable (but not static). Think of them as "chunks of knowledge," which might be either conceptual or something subconceptual from which concepts are built. (We do not have enough information at this time to decide this issue.)

> Assumption 2: Items in working memory that come from long-term memory do *not* get there via simple retrieval, like getting a book off a shelf. Instead, some sort of construction process occurs. (This seems to me to be the minimal assumption need to explain data on concept flexibility such as Barsalou's.[6])

It is important to note that Assumption 2 does *not* imply that items in long-term memory are subconceptual, although they might be, in fact. The construction process I refer to is one *from* long-term to working memory. For example, both working-memory and long-term memory items can be something we reasonably regard as concepts, but the work-

---

[6]For example, Barsalou has shown that what counts as the typical member of a category, e.g., the category of birds, can change depending on context and that such changes are reflected by changes in representation. Also, he has shown that different individuals in the same population produce different examples of what counts as a typical member of a category. Finally, some of his data contravenes the more or less traditional view of how we represent categories (like birds). This view assumes category representations have a stable, definitional core. In some of Barsalou's experiments, subjects explicitly relying on definitions of categories did not exhibit the expected conceptual stability. See Barsalou, 1985, 1987, and 1989.

ing-memory concepts may be assembled from a variety of different long-term memory concepts. In other words, how we conceptualize the world in working memory need not be how we remember the world in long-term memory. I still continue to use the term *retrieval* to describe getting information from long-term to working memory, but this process should not be understood as a simple find-and-fetch.

Assumption 3: Items (concepts) in working memory can interact with one another and thereby change one another.[7] However, this is not the kind of conceptual change hypothesized by the analogical conceptual change hypothesis.

Together with the above three assumptions, the analogical conceptual change hypothesis makes the following three claims.

Claim 1: The very process of analogical reminding alters our concepts. Specifically, it alters their high-level structure in some way—perhaps by constructing new abstractions. (Further research is needed to figure out the details of this structural change.) In any case, how we conceive of the world is thereby altered (however slightly, and perhaps only temporarily). Either item, the retrieving item or the retrieved item or both, may be changed. This is what I called retrieval-based structural change. This conceptual change is arguably the central reason that analogical reminding is an important cognitive process and why it is creative.

Claim 2: The kind of conceptual change hypothesized in Claim 1 happens at the time of retrieval.

Claim 3: The order of events is this: (a) During an episode of reminding, an item in working memory (a concept, usually) interacts with items in long-term memory (chunks of knowledge) by attempting to retrieve at least one of them; (b) during the interaction one (or both) changes in some way; (c) in most cases, mundane remindings occur, but if the change is of the right sort (i.e., if it allows for a mapping of high-level relational structure, which may be new), an analogy results; (d) the

---

[7]One can discern two views in the literature: First, concepts exist ahead of time in long-term memory, and in working memory they interact with and change each other; second, concepts do not exist ahead of time in long-term memory but are constructed from more or less stable chunks of knowledge, and once in working memory the items interact and change. Because we currently lack enough information to decide how long-term memory items are stored, the point of these two views is the same for our purposes: Concepts in working memory interact and change one another. I am not going to choose between these two views. Besides, it is not clear one *can* pick between these two views. It is possible to set up these two views so that it is *logically* impossible to distinguish between them, just as with the two claims that the world was created 5 minutes ago complete with memories and the world was not created 5 minutes ago and past events really did happen.

person who had the analogy sees something new that he or she did not before because the memory items have changed, if only a little; (e) events can now proceed as described in structure mapping theory; for example, projection of candidate inferences can now take place.

These claims center around *when* a certain kind of conceptual change occurs. The change I am interested in occurs before the analogy is formed and in fact leads to the analogy's being formed. In the next section, I give my argument for this conclusion.

THE LOW-PROBABILITY ARGUMENT

Analogy is mapping objects and relational structures. Analogical remind-ing is retrieving items with the requisite mappable structures. Two ques-tions need answering: (a) Why do the structures match each other? (b) What is mapping? In this section, I address the first question; in the next section, I address the second.

Question (a) is really a question about timing. It can be re-asked this way: Do the two structures match *before* the analogy, or do they match *after* (and because of) the reminding? There are, accordingly, two answers to this question: The structures match before the analogy; and the struc-tures do not match ahead of time but are somehow built by the process of analogical reminding itself.[8] MAC/FAC and structure mapping theory (as well as several other theories of analogy and analogical reminding), assume the first answer—the structures are there ahead of time (e.g., see Falkenhainer, 1988 [e.g., p. 59], Gentner, 1989, p. 213, 1983, p. 158; Hummel & Holyoak, 1997; Kotovsky & Gentner, 1990; chap. 11, this volume). For

---

[8]Readers might think there is a third answer: The structures *partially* match at the beginning, before the analogy, and then match more completely in the way required for analogy after the reminding and because of the reminding. I have no doubt that this sometimes occurs and may even be the usual case, but it is important to notice that this is a variant of the second answer. I favor the second answer. It says that the relevant conceptual structures do not match *in the way required for an analogy* before the analogy (except rarely, perhaps). According to structure mapping theory, analogies are *isomorphisms* between high-level structure. In an important sense, the two concepts simply share the one structure that funds their being analogous. (There is a fair amount of agreement on this point, although it is not universally accepted. As I said, I assume it is true because I am assuming structure mapping theory.) A partial match, by definition, is not an isomorphism. A partial match may get the analogy process started, but the question remains, where do the isomorphic structures come from? Where does the unifying structure funding the analogy come from? The second answer just says that the structures were not there ahead of time—they are not part of the concept and are not stored in some generalization or ISA hierarchy (as in Falkenhainer, 1988). From this fact, I infer that the relevant structures were constructed in real time. This is simply a restatement of the analogical conceptual change hypothesis.

example, the reason atoms remind one of solar systems is that the mental representations for each have the same high-level structure, and both representations had that structure before the analogy occurred. I argue that the second answer is the better answer by arguing that first answer is implausible.

Before I get to my argument, I must discuss a couple of matters. The first is that if MAC/FAC assumes that structures are mapped because they match ahead of time, then is MAC/FAC committed to the view that long-term memory items are fixed, static things retrieved via a simple find-and-fetch operation? As a matter of fact, MAC/FAC does assume just this. The MAC stage specifically assumes that long-term memory items are basically concepts that are simply retrieved and placed in working memory (Forbus et al., 1995). However, it is not clear to me that MAC/FAC has to assume this. The essence of MAC/FAC seems to be compatible with the three assumptions about memory I made earlier.

The second matter is a possible source of confusion. One may suppose that any theory that adopts the first answer is bedeviled by the question: "If the representation for atom already looks like the one for solar system, what is the point of the analogy in the first place?" It is a mistake to suppose this. For example, in structure mapping theory and MAC/FAC, an analogy allows information, in the form of other predicates, to transfer from one analogue to the other (from the retrieved item to the retrieving item). These are called candidate inferences and were discussed previously. Also, merely knowing that, for instance, atoms are like solar systems, is itself useful. For example, one can construct a new category by describing them both by using a unifying notion such as "central force systems" or some such. Moreover, as we also noted earlier, one source for the emergence of structure *is* explained in an extension of structure mapping theory. This extension explains the emergence of relational structure across developmental time from a younger child to an older one and postulates a process called progressive alignment (Gentner et al., 1995; Kotovsky & Gentner, 1996). So even if the structures match ahead of time, there is still something for analogy and analogical reminding to do.

Nevertheless, the first answer should be abandoned. What are the chances that the structures of the two memory items resemble each other ahead of time, before the analogy has occurred? They must be quite low—too low to explain the quantity of analogical remindings that occur in each of us. In short, it seems completely implausible, in the usual case, that the relational structures of the analogues antecedently match. For example, again suppose one sees some overturned, jumbled garbage cans at the curb and is reminded of Stonehenge. Note first that it is highly unlikely that the jumble of cans matches the jumble of monoliths on the Salisbury Plain. This means that it is highly unlikely that the percept formed by seeing the cans matches the part of the concept of Stonehenge representing the pattern of the stones seen from a certain perspective. In fact, it is unlikely that the perception of the jumble of the cans antecedently matches even a decayed, partial memory of how the stones are arranged at Stonehenge.

If this is right, then because the high-level, relational structures of the two analogues do not antecedently match (except in very rare cases) but they do match at the time the analogy is made, it must be that the high-level structures are constructed at the time of the reminding.

I call this the low-probability argument. It is a plausibility argument; it is not intended to have the force of a theorem in mathematics. I now turn to defending it against some objections. Doing this also allows me to elaborate it.

Objection 1. The probability of analogues antecedently matching is not that low. There are constraints on perception and memory such that the way we perceive and store information guarantees that some items are bound to match other items.

Reply. This objection amounts to a bare assertion that what seems to me to be *im*plausible is in fact plausible. It is unclear what these constraints appealed to might be, and without a good story about them, we have dueling assertions based on dueling intuitions. The low-probability argument is crucial to my claim that retrieval causes changes in concepts or memory items. Hence, I am willing to give up the low-probability argument only if a good explanation is offered as why the analogues have antecedently mappable structures. Because no compelling explanation is currently on the table and because my intuition still seems the most plausible, I will stick with it.

The objection also clashes with another intuition that several cognitive scientists have (me included): Concepts are, in many ways, plastic and malleable; we can see analogies between all kinds of things. It seems implausible therefore that perception and memory can both support that kind of plasticity while maintaining relational structures that match ahead of time. There are just too many ways two things can be analogous. That we store all those ways ahead of time seems unlikely. It seems more likely, and even more efficient, that reminding produces the changes in real time.

Objection 2. I have focused on the wrong probability. Consider garbage-henge again. Although the probability is low that the current perceptual image of the garbage cans *identically* matches the imperfectly remembered perceptual image of Stonehenge, this is not the relevant probability. The relevant probability is the one measuring the likelihood that the garbage can percept was *merely similar* to the Stonehenge concept. This probability may be quite high, high enough to explain the common occurrence of analogical remindings.

Reply. What does "merely similar" mean? Unless one reduces similarity to identity at some point, one gets an infinite regress of similarities: X is similar to Y because a feature or aspect of X is similar to a feature of Y, and these features are similar because their features in turn are similar, and so on. This explains nothing. The notion of similarity without identity in some form is vacuous. (Gentner [1983, fn. 6] was the first to make this point in this context. In fact, this objection amounts to rejecting structure mapping theory.)

Consider five strings of characters:

1. a s d f g h j k l.   2. q w e r t y u i o.
3. q w e r x y u i o p. 4. z c v b n m.
5.

Letterwise, String 1 is not similar to any other string. Strings 2 and 3 are similar because they have some identical substrings. However, one can say that Strings 1 and 2 are similar because they have the same number of letters (a bit of information about both strings that is implicitly represented—to draw it out requires abstracting). This is perfectly legitimate but requires that the two strings have *identical* cardinalities. String 4 is not similar to any of the others preceding it (even using cardinality) unless one says that it, like the others, is made up of letters from the English alphabet: a perfectly legitimate move, but one that requires saying that Strings 1, 2, 3, and 4 were all drawn from *identical* alphabets. Finally, try to imagine what it means to say that a string was similar to one of the first four strings without some feature of it being identical to one of their features. Imagine a fifth string, String 5. Suppose that it shares no identical features with any of the other four strings, but that it is nevertheless similar to, say, String 1. Neither its subparts nor any of its abstractions is identical to String 1; nevertheless it is similar to 1. What does String 5 look like? I cannot think of such a string, and I believe this is because there is no such string.

These observations illustrate a general principle: Similarity must reduce to identity of some aspect or other. If this is right, then there is no such thing as analogical retrieval based exclusively on the two items being "merely similar." The retrieving item and the retrieved item may in fact be similar, but that is because some feature of the two is identical. In analogy, this feature is the relational structure of the objects.

Objection 3. There is empirical evidence that retrieval is governed primarily by surface similarity or commonality. This evidence is in fact one of the reasons for the MAC stage in MAC/FAC. Retrieval *is* based on similarity and not identity.

Reply. The MAC stage of MAC/FAC assumes identity. It assumes that two memory items are candidates for analogical mapping based on an estimate of their structural similarity. This estimate is the dot product of their content vectors. The dot product multiplies identically matching vector components. So identity is crucial to MAC/FAC.

This objection is actually based on an ambiguity in the word *similarity*. When Gentner and her colleagues used the term, they did not mean "similarity without identity"; rather they meant "similarity because of identity."

Objection 4. If we concede then that the relevant high-level structures probably do not match ahead of time, why does the conceptual change happen at the time of the *reminding*? It is more plausible that it is not the reminding that causes the construction of the matching high-level structures, but rather the analogy itself.

Reply. Analogical remindings happen very quickly. This objection requires that the reminding occur, then the change associated with the analogy, and then the analogy, that is, the mapping. It seems implausible that there is enough time for this to occur. It seems more plausible that the very process of retrieving items from long-term memory alters the items retrieved. The alteration or change may be very slight; nevertheless, it does seem likely that such change occurs.

However, because the nature of mapping is up in the air, I concede that the mapping process itself might include a process responsible for changing memory items. This complicates the analogy process, but it might be correct, and it is certainly worth exploring. If this objection is correct, my central point remains however: High-level structures do not antecedently match and are changed at some point during the process of analogical reminding.

Objection 5. Am I ignoring the data that gave rise to MAC/FAC?

Reply. No. The data are that retrieval is most sensitive to surface matches, relatively insensitive to high-level structure, but that analogies are nevertheless based on matching and mapping high-level structure. The analogical conceptual change hypothesis, retrieval-based structural change, and the low-probability argument are all compatible with these data. My hypothesis is *not* the claim that an item in working memory can retrieve just any item it wants from long-term memory merely by transforming the latter's high-level structure. It seems likely that making such changes costs in energy, time, and/or space. Analogical reminding can therefore be relatively expensive—more expensive than mundane and mere-appearance remindings (even though mundane remindings match at the structural level, too, there is not much to change here because the structures literally match). Retrieval can be a process of probing long-term memory, attempting to construct several different items in parallel based on the retrieving item, and then retrieving the one that is most easily changed to match the retrieving item. It can often be the case that changing a long-term memory item is too expensive relative to retrieving some item that amounts to surface reminding or mundane reminding. This seems even more likely if goals for accessing long-term memory are factored into the retrieving process.

Here's where we are. I have used the low-probability argument to argue that it is unlikely that the retrieving item and the retrieved item have matching high-level, relational structures before the reminding. Assuming this is correct, then because an analogical reminding includes some sort of identity mapping between the structures of the retrieving item and the retrieved item, the process of analogical reminding must itself change the structure of one or both of the two items involved. I have argued that it is the retrieval process itself that is responsible for the changes, but it can be the mapping process provided that the mapping process is made more complicated. The changes involved may be slight, not permanent, and in the usual case too expensive to complete before a more ordinary reminding is completed, but once in a while the changes are completed and we experience an analogy, which can be either quirky or sublime, but is always interesting.

MAPPING AND THE PARADOX OF ANALOGY

The analogical conceptual change hypothesis amounts to the claim that retrieval-based structural change must occur if reminding is to produce analogies from time to time, which it clearly does. The argument for this claim is based on plausibility assessments that the probability of memory items matching antecedently is too low—at least in the general case. Conceptual changes, therefore, must occur as part of the reminding process, and therefore, reminding is constructive and concepts are quite mutable.

We know *why* the changes occur, but we do not yet know in detail *what* changes (beyond saying it is structure). To work toward an understanding of what changes, in this section, I argue that a natural interpretation of the notion of mapping leads to the conclusion that analogy is *impossible*. In the following section, I offer some changes to our notion of concepts and analogical reminding that solve this problem.

The important question of *how* the changes are produced is left for another time, mainly because I do not know how they are produced (but see Oshima [1996] for some interesting speculation on this question). Also, although we do know why the changes occur—the memory items do not match ahead of time—we know the answer to this question only in a proximal, shallow way. A deeper question is: Why do retrieving items try to transform retrieved items in the first place? That is, why do analogical remindings occur at all? I suspect the answer to this question lies in the realm of the evolution of cognition, and must appeal to the notions of exaptation, situated action, and the fact that our ancestors could not draw as many distinctions as we do. Briefly, the explanation may go something like this. If situated action is the best explanation for low-level perceptual and motor abilities (a big assumption), it is reasonable to infer that the question of how to explain higher cognition can also benefit from a situated action approach. This requires postulating that concepts interact with one another because that is all that is available for any organism capable of higher cognition. The move here amounts to modeling conceptual interaction as a sort of *perspective shift*—an *inner* perspective shift. Because, in general, it is in our survival interest to see such relations in the world as there are, the most advantageous way for concepts to interact is to attempt to change one another to highlight their similarities. Voilà, analogy. Of course, this is pure speculation at this point, but it does make a certain amount of sense. (For more details see Dietrich & Fields [1996] and Dietrich, Morrison, & Oshima [1996].)

Now to the paradox. Imagine once again walking down the street at night and seeing some garbage cans strewn about. Suddenly you *see* Stonehenge right there on the curb and spilling out into the street. Such things rarely occur, which is good, because Stonehenge is on a plain in Salisbury, England, and not on your curb. Why don't such weird things occur? On a plausible interpretation of the mapping operation (explained below), you ought to see Stonehenge on the curb, but you do not. I call this the *paradox of analogy*. It needs to be explained away.

I phrased the paradox in terms of *seeing* Stonehenge on the curb for dramatic effect. Of course, retrieving the Stonehenge memory fully is not enough to get us to see Stonehenge on the curb. Retrieving memories does not usually produce hallucinations. The technical point is this: On a natural interpretation of the notion of mapping (that it is activation), the entire Stonehenge memory—objects, relations, *and* attributes—ought to be retrieved and activated in a case of "analogical" reminding, but it is not. Why? Any memory retrieval involving mapping always ought to result in *complete* retrieval of a concept. There ought to be no such thing as analogy, but there is. This is our paradox, and this is the matter to which I now turn.

The usual response to the paradox is to reinvoke the notion of mapping and to say that in an analogy only objects and structures get mapped. Mapping, as we know, is defined as a structure-sensitive comparison. Mapping finds the invariant relational structure between the object nodes of two memory items (refer once again to Fig. 10.1.) Given this, the paradox is dissolved: Because the lower level properties of the memory item do not get mapped, it follows that the whole memory is not part of the analogy. For example, in garbage-henge, "is-made-of-stone" is an attribute predicate that does not get mapped, and so is not part of the analogy. So of course you wouldn't see Stonehenge on your curb. (Or put correctly: so of course all of your Stonehenge memory would not get retrieved and activated.)

But what is a structure-sensitive comparison, really? What does mapping two memory items onto each other amount to in the brain? The simplest and most natural neural interpretation of the term *mapping* is to say that mapping is *activation*. If mapping is activation, then the above answer to the paradox will not do. Here's why.

Think in terms of a network of nodes and activation arcs between them. Activation usually *spreads*. So, given that the object nodes and the structure nodes of the retrieved item get activated, why does the activation not spread from these two areas to activate the attribute nodes of the retrieved item, too? In garbage-henge, the high-level structure got activated and the object nodes got activated (cans mapped onto monoliths, "lies-next-to" in the garbage-can percept mapped onto "lies-next-to" in the Stonehenge memory, etc.), and presumably activation spreads both from the objects and from components making up the high-level structure. So the attribute nodes ought to have been activated. For example, "is-made-of-stone" ought to have been activated. Activation ought to have spread to it. But we know that this is not what happened. If "is-made-of-stone" and other attribute nodes were activated, then because the object and high-level structure nodes were already active, the entire memory of Stonehenge would have become active, and hence retrieved. But this is not what happened. By assumption, only the object nodes and high-level nodes got activated and retrieved because an analogy was made, not a mundane or some other kind of reminding. Therefore, something is still wrong. On the assumption that mapping is activation, we predict a phenomenon that simply doesn't occur, namely the retrieval and activation of entire memory items which instead ought to be only analogous. The paradox makes the phenomenon of analogy disappear. Yet analogy clearly exists.

One answer that works, but seems a tad desperate on the face of it, is that attributes do not get activated because then you would not get an analogy! This answer requires that the system (or organism) know ahead of time that it was constructing an analogy and not an ordinary, veridical reminding. Consider Rutherford. The behavior of alpha particles in his experiments reminded him of comets in their orbits around the sun. The proposed solution here is that his brain analogically retrieved comets because it was searching for an analogy in the first place. Because it was searching for an analogy in the first place, the retrieval process did not activate the attribute or property nodes of his comet concept. Hence only the structure and object nodes were available for mapping (activation), and hence the behavior of alpha particles in his experiments analogically reminded Rutherford of comets. That is how he had his analogy.

Note that there is no logical problem with this answer. The answer is *not* the claim that the system knows ahead of time which analogy it wants. That *is* impossible. The claim here is that the system knows ahead of time that it wants an analogy of some sort. A system can know this ahead of time. Still, I do not think this solution to the paradox, in its current form, can be right for three reasons. First, it breaks up memory retrieval into at least two disjoint processes, one for analogical retrieval and one for ordinary (both mundane and superficial?) remindings. Although this may be correct, it seems ad hoc. One should postulate multiple process only if one has to. It is frequently better science to try to unify processes under one framework if possible. This is in fact what MAC/FAC does and is one of its principal advantages: MAC/FAC is a *single* process with two stages. Second, this solution makes it difficult to explain the data that support MAC/FAC. Indeed, the alleged two separate processes (one for analogical retrieval and one for mundane retrieval, say) must interact to have a chance of explaining the MAC/FAC data, and if they interact, this solution reduces to MAC/FAC. Third, this solution seems to make what is a property or an attribute in a concept fixed and unchangeable; indeed, it seems to fix all three components of memory items: attributes, relational structures, and object nodes. For the analogical retrieval process to look for an analogy, it has to ignore attributes and map everything else. It can do that only if attributes are there to ignore and everything else is there to map. For example, if "is-made-of-stone" or "is-made-mostly-of-ice" are attribute nodes in one's concept of the Stonehenge monoliths and comets, respectively, then this solution fixes them as attributes permanently, because only that way can the analogical retrieval process know to ignore them. They can never be rendered as relational structures, for example. However, memory items seem more plastic than this.

Another solution to the paradox of analogy, where mapping is assumed to be activation, advocates a sort of general demotion of properties. On this solution, properties in the world are not that important; in turn, the attributes in a concept simply do not matter much for purposes of retrieval and inference. This solution seems incorrect because sometimes representing properties is important and thus attributes are important in reminding.

Still another solution is to say that mapping is not activation. But activation must occur anyway; that is arguably what retrieval amounts to. Certainly activation is a necessary part of retrieval. Hence the paradox remains (it depends on activation). And now mapping is something over and above activation. What can that be? Not only does this solution not work, it leaves mapping undefined.

Nevertheless, having objected to all three solutions, I still think there is something worth exploring in them, especially the first two: Analogical reminding is a separate, independent process, and properties are, in general, less important than relational structure. The first two solutions become more palatable if one assumes that memory items are malleable in a certain way and that working-memory items are constructed during reminding. In the next section I consider detailed variants of all three solutions.

So here is where we are. On a natural interpretation of mapping—it is activation—we are stuck with the vexed question: Why does retrieval not always retrieve a whole item from long-term memory? Why does retrieval not activate the object nodes, the structural relation nodes, *and* the attribute nodes of a given item? In short, why is there any such thing as analogy? Why don't you *see* Stonehenge on the curb?[9]

WHAT IS A CONCEPT THAT A HUMAN
MAY MAKE ANALOGIES WITH IT?

The low-probability argument is a constraint on reminding. It entails that during analogical reminding, the relational structure of one or both the analogous items are changed by the retrieval. The paradox is a constraint on analogy. It entails that the crucial notion of mapping cannot be simple spreading activation. We can satisfy these two constraints by assuming that *reminding includes a process of constructing mappable structures*. This

---

[9]This is a version of a general problem. The question of where to stop the activation is a problem in *every* case of reminding and hence in every case of thinking. Think of cats. Not everything you know about cats is activated when you do this. Although it would be bad to design an intelligent system that always retrieved everything it knew about any subject when it was reminded of that subject, how do we design a system so that it retrieves what it needs without retrieving everything, given that, in the general case, it does not know ahead of time what it needs? I think this problem is quite interesting and requires for its solution a marriage between heuristic-driven retrieval (most of the time, an intelligent system need only retrieve the "standard" information for a concept), a theory of conceptual boundaries, i.e., a theory of where one concept ends and another begins, and a theory of how concepts coalesce to form the larger structures we call knowledge.

assumption ramifies, giving us a novel picture of concepts, conceptual change, and analogical reminding.

There are actually two pictures: a simpler one and one that is complex and more speculative. Each picture corresponds to a way of dissolving the paradox of analogy, and both pictures assume that the low-probability argument is correct. I discuss both pictures in this section.

Dissolving the Paradox: The Simple Solution

The low-probability argument requires that structures be built during analogical reminding. The simplest way to do that is to assume that constructed structures are made from other structures and that the construction process is really one of *altering existing structures*. So, the relational structures of (at least one of) the retriever and the retrieved item are altered slightly during reminding.

The simplest way to dissolve the paradox, then, is to say that the mapping process occurs during the retrieval process—and not afterward—and that the mapping process *is* the structure-altering process, altering the existing relational structure of one (or both) of the analogous items. To see that this dissolves the paradox, we need only note that on this solution the mapping process is *not* a process of spreading activation, but rather one of structure altering. The reason attributes do not get activated is that activation is not being passed to them. Relational structures are being altered, but activation is a separate process. In fact, memory item activation, on this solution, is left unspecified.

For example, my representation of Stonehenge has a structural component specifying how I remember the monoliths being arranged. On the Salisbury Plain, the monoliths are in an open circle, and the circle is incomplete now because several of the monoliths have fallen over or tilted. Suppose there are some garbage cans arranged (by accident) in a kind of semicircle, and they too are a jumble—some upright, some tilted, some fallen over. The configuration of the monoliths is not exactly the same as the configuration of the garbage cans. This much is certain. But consider my representations of the cans and of Stonehenge, especially the structural components representing the configurations of the two groups of things. If we assume that these structural components are not identical before the reminding, and after the analogical reminding they are identical (at least at some level—a quite abstract level, perhaps), then we are led to conclude that the reminding process aligned the structural relation components of the representations (i.e., the representations of the configurations of the stones and the cans) and that this aligning process had to *alter* the structural relations in (at least) my perceptual representation of the cans. The first assumption is just the low-probability argument, and the second assumption is just Gentner's prevailing theory of analogy. We can safely conclude that viewing mapping as a purely structure-altering process (i.e., as a *nonactivating*, structure-altering process) that occurs during reminding dissolves the paradox.

On this solution, the reason that whole memory items are not retrieved is that analogical reminding is first and foremost a structure-altering process. Because structures are defined over object nodes, object nodes come along for the ride. Activating the entire memory item (i.e., the attributes, too) is never a problem. Analogy occurs, therefore, because of a split between activation and representation construction.

This solution to the paradox is like the third one discussed earlier. Accordingly, it has the main problem of that one: Its explanation for why attributes do not get activated during analogical retrieval is too ad hoc, because activation is not incorporated into this solution and is left as a problem for another day. It would be nice to have a solution that incorporated activation. The next one does that. But it also requires a much more complicated view of concepts.

Dissolving the Paradox: The Speculative Solution

This solution does not leave the problem of activation dangling. The general framework for this solution is this: Replace the traditional, tripartite view of concepts, which sees them as comprising objects, attributes (properties), and structural relations, with a more process-oriented view in which none of the three components is fixed, but rather changes (or can change) during analogical remindings. Nothing is essentially a property or an object, but rather takes on that role in certain contexts. (If this is right, then it is possible that other [all?] cognitive processes result in this sort of conceptual change, but here I am concerned only with analogical reminding.)

The key to this second solution is that *analogical reminding can change what counts as relational structures in memory items.*

The second solution uses the following four premises:

1. Representing the relations things in the world can partake in is crucial to an organism's survival—much more important than merely representing the things themselves together with (or as the nexus of) their properties or attributes.
2. Mapping is activation, and activation spreads. (In the first solution, mapping had to be purely structure altering.)
3. There is no such thing as reminding, in general. Rather, there are different kinds of reminding. Analogical reminding is just one species of reminding. Analogical reminding exists to highlight and

categorize the relations between things the cognitive organism finds in the world.

4. People can transform information represented by attributes into logically similar information represented as relational structures. That is, they can represent the color of an apple as *red (apple)* at one time and then at another represent the color of the apple as *color-of (apple, red)*.

Premise 1 does *not* imply that we do not store information about the attributes of things in the world. We clearly do, but Premise 1 does suggest that attributes are important in mental representing only in certain contexts; they can be ignored in other contexts. Premise 1 seems plausible on inductive grounds, once it is noted that relations represent functional roles (in general, to say $R[A, B]$ is to say that A functions in a certain R way relative to B). It is very rare for a thing-in-itself to be important to us. Usually what matters is the role the thing plays, and several things can usually play that role. Think about the two major things in life—food and sex—all that matters is whether something is edible or able to be mated with, and both are relations. In fact, it seems plausible that most of our categories are functionally defined. If so, then relations tell us what types of things there are in the world. Even knowledge of particulars (*this* coffee cup; *that* green mechanical pencil) is arguably functional, at least in part: Successfully referring to this particular coffee cup in the world requires using the nexus of a collection of (internally represented) properties (white, thick, heavy) together with a collection of functional relations (holds coffee, reminds me of the University of West Florida).[10]

On a deeper, more philosophical level, Premise 1 is plausible because we live in a universe that is a vast collection of processes; nothing is just a static object. Heraclitus was right: All is change, and we cannot step into the same river twice. Relations are just a way of representing processes (on the *situated action* way of viewing things, *all* relations [even "greener-than"] really amount to representing a process of some sort; see Bickhard & Terveen, 1995).

Premise 2 is simply the best way to fold activation into a solution to the paradox.

Premise 3 is quite controversial, but it makes sense, especially if Premise 1 is true. Here is an argument for it. Recall that relational structure is the functional organization of objects (object nodes in mental representations). To represent a dog's panting tongue as releasing heat to the surrounding

---

[10]This claim has a strong Berkeleyan flavor to it, but only a flavor. I am not saying that things *in the world* are only collections of perceived properties. They may be, but I am not committed to that view here.

air is to represent that tongue as playing a role in a certain process. That role is the tongue's function at that time. To represent an ungloved hand as releasing heat to the surrounding cold air is to represent that hand as playing the same role. That is the foundation of the analogy between the two. But it is unlikely that that role, the representation of a dog's tongue and the representation of the ungloved hand, identically matched between the two items before the analogy. It is unlikely that that role was salient or highlighted in each item in the same way and to the same extent before the analogy occurred. Indeed the *point* of the analogy, it seems, was to highlight or make salient the relevant heat-dissipation role (represented by some structure) that became common between the two items. Because this structure was not there ahead of time, constructing and matching this structure must have occurred with the construction of the analogy. This makes analogical reminding unlike other forms of reminding— analogical reminding is the type of reminding used for the special purpose of constructing and aligning structure. Hence, analogical reminding is just one species of reminding.[11]

(I want to stress again that I am not assuming that the matching structure was created from nothing. Nor am I assuming that any two memory items can be made analogous. The relevant matching structure was no doubt created from already existing structures and attributes specific to each of the two items, which might have been *similar* to each other before the analogy occurred. Remember, merely being similar is not good enough. The structures, or least some aspect of them, must be able to be made identical.)

For Premise 4, it is well known that people can represent the same information in different ways—the color of an apple, for example. Can people transform, for instance, *red (apple)* into *color-of (apple, red)*? Gentner and her colleagues provided evidence that such changes occur *during development* (Gentner et al., 1995; Kotovsky & Gentner, 1990, 1996). The leap we have to make here is that such changes can occur very quickly—

---

[11]The form of highlighting I mentioned *seems* very similar to Gentner and Wolff's notion in chapter 11, this volume. I am not sure of this because in her theory of analogy, Gentner also seems committed to the view that analogies happen because the relevant structures antecedently match. It is quite clear that Gentner thinks analogy is responsible for interesting conceptual change. However, throughout her many papers, Gentner tries to have it both ways: Analogous structures are there ahead of time, *and* analogous structures (or parts of structures) are constructed at some time around the analogy. I have struggled with this antinomy in her theory, and my considered opinion now is that it is really an unresolved issue with structure mapping theory. If this right, then structure mapping theory could be changed to accommodate my retrieval-based structural change and indeed the whole of my analogical conceptual change hypothesis without doing it serious damage and, I suggest, improving it slightly by making it better able to handle concepts' robust capacity for change.

during reminding, in fact. It is this that makes the second solution appear radical.

Now, the second solution is this. Creatures with robust cognitive abilities need to be able to represent and compare relations (Premise 1). Analogical reminding is a process that focuses on structure (Premise 3). It can alter and rearrange existing structure to meet this need, but analogical reminding can also change what counts as relational structures in memory items. In particular, it can change attributes into relational structures (Premise 4). The reason attributes do not get activated during the mapping process on the second solution (Premise 2) is that with respect to analogical reminding attributes qua attributes *do not exist*. The second solution dissolves the paradox because attributes are not activated *qua attributes* (i.e., qua single-place predicates). This, however, does not sideline *the information* that attributes contain because attributes and structures can slide back and forth, each changing into the other. Attribute-hood is a relative thing and not fixed.

This completes the second solution to the paradox.

CONCLUSION

The second solution is my favorite because it hypothesizes mental representations that are malleable and that change and alter owing to cognitive pressures. It seems to me that only such malleable mental representations have a chance of explaining the robustness and creativity of human cognition. Furthermore, if the analogical change hypothesis is right, then, because analogical reminding is a very common psychological process, we can conclude that the constituents of the mind, the constituents of thought, change rather frequently.

The picture of the human mind (and indeed other animal minds) that emerges from the second solution is exciting to contemplate, for it is a picture of a dynamic and fluid mind. This it seems to me is a welcome result for many reasons, not least of which is that everything in the analogical change hypothesis is compatible with computationalism. A robust cognitive dynamics can be had in the computational paradigm, which is good, because it is the best paradigm we have. We can now rigorously start exploring the plasticity and malleability of concepts and memories; this is the key to how we create new knowledge from old and see what we had not seen before.

ACKNOWLEDGMENTS

I thank Doug Beyer, Robert Davidson, and Art Markman for good comments on an earlier draft. I thank Chris Fields, Ken Forbus, Bob French,

Dedre Gentner, Celia Klin, and Art Markman for discussing these matters with me. I thank my graduate research group—Jon Beskin, Doug Beyer, Phil Gross, Lewis Loren, Clay Morrison, and Michiharu Oshima—for helping me formulate these ideas.

REFERENCES

Barsalou, L. (1983). Ad hoc categories. *Memory and Cognition, 11*, 211–227.

Barsalou, L. (1985). Ideals, central tendency, and frequency of instantiation as determinants of graded structure in categories. *Journal of Experimental Psychology: Learning, Memory, and Cognition, 11*, 629–654.

Barsalou, L. (1987). The instability of graded structure: Implications for the nature of concepts. In U. Neisser (Ed.), *Concepts and conceptual development: Ecological and intellectual factors in categorization* (pp. 101–140). Cambridge: Cambridge University Press.

Barsalou, L. (1989). Intraconcept similarity and its implications for interconcept similarity. In S. Vosniadou & A. Ortony (Eds.), *Similarity and analogical reasoning* (pp. 76–121). Cambridge: Cambridge University Press.

Black, M. (1979). More about metaphor. In A. Ortony (Ed.), *Metaphor and thought* (pp. 19–41). Cambridge: Cambridge University Press.

Camac, M., & Glucksberg, S. (1984). Metaphors do not use assoiations between concepts, they are used to create them. *Journal of Psycholinguistic Research, 13*, 443–455.

Dietrich, E., & Fields, C. (1996). The role of the frame problem in Fodor's modularity thesis: A case study of rationalist cognitive science. In K. Ford & Z. Pylyshyn (Eds.), *The robot's dilemma revisited: The frame problem in artificial intelligence* (pp. 9–24). Norwood, NJ: Ablex.

Dietrich, E., Morrison, C., & Oshima, M. (1996). Conceptual change as change of inner perspective. In *Embodied cogntion and action: Proceedings from the 1996 AAAI Fall Symposium* (pp. 37–41). Menlo Park, CA: AAAI Press.

Falkenhainer, B. (1988). *Learning from physical analogies: A study in analogy and the explanation of process* (Rep. No. UIUCDCS-R-88-1479). Unpublished doctoral dissertation, University of Illinois at Urbana-Champaign.

Falkenhainer, B. (1990a). Analogical interpretation in context. In *Proceedings of the 12th annual conference of the Cognitive Science Society*. Hillsdale, NJ: Lawrence Erlbaum Associates.

Falkenhainer, B. (1990b). A unified approach to explanation and theory formation. In J. Shrager & P. Langley (Eds.), *Computational models of scientific discovery and theory formation* (pp. 157–196). San Mateo, CA: Morgan Kaufmann.

Falkenhainer, B., Forbus, K., & Gentner, D., (1989). The structure-mapping engine: Algorithm and examples. *Artificial Intelligence, 41*(1), 1–63.

Finke, R., Ward, T., & Smith, S. (1992). *Creative cognition*. Cambridge, MA: MIT Press.

Forbus, K., Gentner, D., & Law, K. (1995). MAC/FAC: A model of similarity-based retrieval. *Cognitive Science, 19*, 141–205.

Forbus, K., Gentner, D., Markman, A., & Ferguson, R. (1998). Analogy just looks like high-level perception: Why a domain-general approach to analogical mapping is right. *Journal of Experimental and Theoretical AI, 10*(2), 231–257.

French, R. (1995). *The subtlety of sameness*. Cambridge, MA: MIT Press.

Gentner, D. (1983). Structure-mapping: A theoretical framework for analogy. *Cognitive Science, 7*, 155–170.

Gentner, D. (1989). The mechanisms of analogical learning. In S. Vosniadou & A. Ortony (Eds.), *Similarity and analogical reasoning* (pp. 199–241). Cambridge: Cambridge University Press.

Gentner, D., & Markman, A. (1995). Similarity is like analogy: Structural alignment in comparison. In C. Cacciari (Ed.), *Similarity* (pp. 111–148). Brussels, Belgium: BREPOLS.

Gentner, D., Rattermann, M. J., Markman, A., & Kotovsky, L. (1995). Two forces in the development of relational similarity. In T. J. Simon & G. S. Halford (Eds.), *Developing cognitive competence: New approaches to process modeling* (pp. 263–313). Hillsdale, NJ: Lawrence Erlbaum Associates.

Glenberg, A., Kruley, P., & Langston, W. (1994). Analogical processes in comprehension. In M. A. Gernbacher (Ed.), *Handbook of psycholinguistics* (pp. 609–640). New York: Academic Press.

Glucksberg, S. & Keysar, B. (1990). Understanding metaphorical comparisons: Beyond similarity. *Psychological Review, 97*, 3–18.

Hoffman, R. (1995). Monster analogies. *AI Magazine, 16*(3), 11–35.

Hofstadter, D. R. (1995). *Fluid concepts and creative analogies.* New York: Basic Books.

Holyoak, K., & Thagard, P. (1989). Analogical mapping by constrain satisfaction. *Cognitive Science, 13*(3), 295–355.

Hummel, J., & Holyoak, K. (1997). Distributed representations of structure: A theory of analogical mapping. *Psychological Review.*

Indurkhya, B. (1997). Metaphor as change of representation. *Journal of Experimental and Theoretical AI, 9*(1), 1–36.

James, W. (1950). *The prinicples of psychology* (Vol. 1). New York: Dover. (Original work published 1890)

Keane. M., & Brayshaw. M., (1988). The incremental analogy machine: A computational model of analogy. In D. Sleeman (Ed.), *Third European working session on machine learning.* London: Pitman.

Keane, M., Ledgeway, T., & Duff, S. (1994). Constaints on analogical mapping: A comparison of three models. *Cognitive Science, 18*, 387–438.

Kelly, M., & Keil, F. (1987). Metaphor comprehension and knowledge of semantic domains. *Metahpor and Symbolic Activity, 2*, 35–51.

Kotovsky, L., & Gentner, D., (1990). Pack light: You will go farther. In *Proceedings of the second midwest Artificial Intelligence and Cognitive Science Society Conference* (pp. 60–72). Carbondale, Illinois.

Kotovsky, L., & Gentner, D., (1996). Comparison and categorization in the development of relational similarity. *Child Development, 67*, 2797–2822.

Lucretius, Titus. (55 BCE/1951 trans.). *On the nature of the universe.* (R. E. Latham, Trans.). New York: Penguin Books.

Markman, A., & Medin, D. (1955). Similarity and alignment in choice. *Organizational Behavior and Human Decision Processes, 63*, 117–130.

Mitchell, M. (1993). *Analogy-making as perception .* Cambridge, MA: MIT Press.

Oshima, M. (1996). Analogy as a creative process. Unpublished master's thesis, State University of New York, Binghamton, Binghamton, NY.

Poincaré, H. (1952). *Science and method.* New York: Dover. (Original work published 1908, Paris; English version 1914, London)

Schank, R. (1982). *Dynamic memory.* Cambridge, England: Cambridge University Press.

Thagard, P., Holyoak, K., Nelson, G., & Gochfield, D. (1990). Analog retrieval by constraint satisfaction. *Artificial Intelligence, 46*, 259–310.

Wheelwright, Philip (Trans.). (1964). *Heraclitus* [with commentary]. New York: Antheum. (Original work published by Princeton University Press, 1959)

Metaphor and Knowledge Change

Dedre Gentner
Phillip Wolff
Northwestern University, Evanston

> *The tiger roaring like a fire, the fire roaring like a tiger, are metaphors by which both fire and tiger are made clear.*
>
> —Litt

In a recent magazine article, the issue of government control of research agendas was explored by using the metaphor "Science is a flashlight." Science, like a flashlight, is bounded in its scope: Only areas directly under its beam are visible. So far, the metaphor may seem obvious, but a further implication is that because of this boundedness, decisions about the direction of the beam are crucial. Until recently, the article pointed out, scientists have had the major say in where the flashlight was aimed, but increasingly it is government agencies, not scientists, who control the direction of search. The notion of controlling the direction of science was presumably not a new issue to readers. Nevertheless, the metaphor contributed a new connection: The fact that vision is limited makes it crucial who controls its direction.

There is broad consensus that metaphors can lead to change of knowledge. In some cases, the change seems one of enrichment: New concepts, connections, or perspectives are added to the underlying representations. In other cases, the change involves the re-representation of old concepts and/or the restructuring of the conceptual systems.

Yet despite this agreement, there is little consensus on *how* such change might occur: that is, on what processes might bring about knowledge change. Black (1979) asserted that metaphor may lead to emphasizing, suppressing, or reorganizing features of the terms, especially those of the primary subject (the target) (see also Verbrugge & McCarrell, 1977). He suggested that these changes may follow from the construction of a "parallel implication-complex," but the details of this process were left unspecified. Comparison models figure largely in the current approach to metaphor, yet, as noted by Glucksberg and Keysar (1990), pure comparison models do not offer a means by which knowledge change can be achieved. For example, Ortony's (1979a) salience imbalance model is relatively explicit as to which existing features are incorporated into a metaphor's interpretation—namely, those that are high-salient in the base and low-salient in the target. However, although Ortony noted that metaphors sometimes convey that features from the base (vehicle) should be attributed to the target (tenor), the salience imbalance framework does not provide a mechanism by which attempted predications can come about. Glucksberg and Keysar (1990) proposed that the process of understanding a metaphor may prompt generation of a new category and from this category the attribution of novel inferences (see also Glucksberg & Keysar, 1990; Keysar, 1989; Shen 1992; Way, 1991).

Some accounts have explained metaphor comprehension in terms of mappings between dimensional spaces (as in Rumelhart & Abrahamson's [1973] model of analogy). For example, Tourangeau and Sternberg (1981, 1982) proposed that metaphor understanding follows from the identification of dimensional mappings that contribute to high in-domain similarity and low between-domain similarity. Kittay and Lehrer (1981) discussed the domain-interaction view in terms of semantic field theory. When lexical items from one semantic field are transferred to another semantic field, the donor field provides structure for the second field. For metaphors that are "alive," Kittay and Lehrer predicted changes in the semantic relations governing the fields because typically the fields in such metaphors are structured differently. Kelly and Keil (1987) suggested that change of knowledge may occur at the level of the domains or semantic fields from which the target and base terms are drawn. They found evidence that metaphor comprehension could affect domain organization. Pairs of concepts that could form appropriate metaphors increased in rated similarity after subjects read other metaphors relating their domains. But although domain-interaction accounts help to specify the conditions under which change may occur, they do not specify how it occurs: by what processes semantic fields are aligned, especially when the attributes of the target (tenor) and base (vehicle) do not match perfectly. Ortony (1979a) called this problem "domain incongruence." Furthermore, any model of metaphoric change of meaning must deal with the fact that not just any adaptation can occur: People are quite selective in interpreting nonliteral comparisons.

In this chapter, we set forth four mechanisms of change of knowledge: *knowledge selection, projection, re-representation,* and *restructuring.* We also discuss two specific representational outcomes that may follow from application of these mechanisms: *stored categories* and *stored mappings.* We discuss research relevant to these mechanisms and outcomes and offer our own approach to metaphor, one based on considering metaphor as akin to analogy. Our perspective draws on distinctions outlined in Falkenhainer, Forbus, and Gentner (1986, 1989), Gentner (1983, 1989), Gentner and Markman (1993, 1995), and Medin, Goldstone, and Gentner (1993), in which comparison is viewed as a process of alignment and mapping between pairs of structured representations. As we show, this view of metaphoric comparison allows us to escape many of the limitations inherent in pure comparison accounts.

Finally, although our proposals are aimed at addressing metaphorically driven change of knowledge, we think their scope may be broader. As noted by Pylyshyn (1979) and Fodor (1975), there is an inherent paradox in the cognitive approach to knowledge acquisition. If existing concepts and schemas are the medium of our thinking, then how can something new be expressed or comprehended? Does not what is needed for the acquisition of a new idea presume the prior presence of the idea itself? Nowhere is this paradox encountered more squarely than in the arena of metaphor and analogy.

THE STRUCTURE-MAPPING ACCOUNT: METAPHOR AS ALIGNMENT AND MAPPING

Representational Assumptions

We assume representations that include explicit labeled relations and arguments, including higher-order relations that can take whole assertions as their arguments. The representational system must also be able to capture rich perceptual information, including detailed object descriptions and dimensional information. Formally, the representational elements are objects (or *entities*), object descriptors (called *attributes*), functions (which express dimensional information), and *relations* between representational elements. Attributes and relations are predicates with truth values. Functions differ from predicates in that they map from a set of arguments onto values other than truth values. For example, the assertion that the ball is red can be represented by using *red* as an attribute, as in (1) or by using *color* as a relation, as in (2) or by using *color* as a function, as in (3):

(1) *Red* (ball).

(2) *Color* (ball, red).

(3) *Color* (ball) = red.

These three representations reflect different construals, which we take to be psychologically meaningful. In Representation 1, redness is expressed as an independent attributional property of the ball. Representation 2 focuses on the *color* relation—redness is expressed as one of a set of alternative arguments to the *color* relation. In Representation 3, *color* is represented as a dimension with *red* as one of its values. As noted previously, whereas 1 and 2 can take truth values, 3 cannot. Computationally, this functional notation is convenient for expressing statements when the exact value of the quantity is not of immediate interest. For example, color (ball 1) = color (ball 2) states that the balls are the same color without having to specify *which* color. Functions are useful for representing dimensions. Our psychological assumption here is that physical quantities like height and weight, numerical quantities, and eventually many abstract qualities—such as wealth or status—are often represented as dimensions.

Structure Mapping

In our account of metaphor comprehension, we make two fundamental assumptions: (a) that metaphor comprehension typically involves a comparison process, and (b) that the comparison process is structure sensitive. This second assumption is drawn from structure-mapping theory. We first lay out this framework as it applies to analogy and similarity and then discuss its application to metaphor.

A central characteristic of this account is that analogy and other comparison processes involve an alignment of relational structure (Gentner, 1982, 1983, 1989). This alignment process finds matches that are *structurally consistent*: that is, that observe *parallel connectivity* and *one-to-one correspondence*. *Parallel connectivity* means that if two predicates correspond then their arguments must also correspond. *One-to-one correspondence* means that any element in one representation can correspond to at most one matching element in the other representation (Falkenhainer, Forbus, & Gentner, 1986, 1989; Gentner, 1983, 1989; Holyoak & Thagard, 1989). For example, when comparing the atom (the *target* domain) to the solar system (the *base* domain), if *revolve* (planet, sun) is matched to *revolve* (electron, nucleus), then by parallel connectivity the sun must correspond to the nucleus and the planet to the electron, because they play the same role in the common relational structure. By one-to-one correspondence, these object bindings must be unique.[1]

A central claim is that in understanding analogies we seek matching *connected systems of relations*. A matching set of relations interconnected by higher-order constraining relations makes a better analogical match than do an equal number of matching relations that are unconnected to one another. To put it another way, an individual match matters more, and is more likely to be included in the final interpretation of the comparison, if it is connected via higher-order relations to other relations that also match. We call this tendency to align and map interconnected systems of predicates the *systematicity principle* (Gentner, 1983, 1989). This preference for connected systems is also what drives new inferences from a comparison. When the alignment process has resulted in a "best" interpretation,[2] then any predicates that exist in the base but not the target and that are *connected to the common system* that constitutes the comparison's interpretation can be imported into the target as *candidate inferences*. The systematicity principle thus represents a tacit preference for coherence and inferential potential in interpreting comparisons.

We suggest that structure mapping provides a framework for other comparison types as well as for analogy. Indeed, process models of structural alignment and mapping have proved fruitful in the study of overall similarity (literal similarity) comparisons (Bowdle & Gentner, 1997; Falkenhainer, Forbus, & Gentner, 1989; Gentner, 1989; Gentner & Markman, 1993, 1994, 1995, 1997; Goldstone, 1994; Goldstone, Gentner, & Medin, 1989; Goldstone & Medin, 1994; Goldstone, Medin, & Gentner, 1991; Markman & Gentner, 1993a, 1993b, 1996; Medin, Goldstone, & Gentner, 1990, 1993). Analogy differs from overall similarity in that in literal similarity, the corresponding objects are similar to one another. In contrast, analogy is characterized by *relational focus*: Objects correspond by virtue of playing like roles in the relational structure rather than by any inherent object similarity. For instance, the nucleus need not be hot and gaseous like the sun. A particularly striking example of this sort of structural dominance is a *cross-mapping* (Gentner & Toupin, 1986), in which similar objects play different relational roles in two analogous scenarios (see also Gentner & Rattermann, 1991; Ross, 1989), for instance, grandmother is to mother as mother is to daughter.

---

[1]The nine planets, because they are relationally equivalent, can be treated as one generic planet.

[2]The best interpretation is determined by a number of factors, including whether it is structurally consistent and maximal in size and depth (Falkenhainer, Forbus, & Gentner, 1989; Gentner, Rattermann, & Forbus, 1993) and whether it is contextually relevant (Forbus & Oblinger, 1990; Holyoak & Thagard, 1989; Spellman & Holyoak, 1996).

There is considerable evidence supporting the general assumptions of the structure-mapping theory of comparison, as well as its application to metaphor. A central idea of this model is that processing comparisons involves the matching of structured representations (as opposed to lists of independent features), an assumption that is in line with a substantial amount of research in cognitive psychology (e.g., Biederman, 1987; Gentner & Stevens, 1983; Johnson-Laird, 1983; Lassaline & Murphy, 1996; Lockhead & King, 1977; Markman, 1999; Murphy, 1996; Murphy & Medin, 1985; Norman, Rumelhart, & the LNR Group, 1975; Palmer, 1977, 1978; Pomerantz, Sager, & Stoever, 1977; Rumelhart & Ortony, 1977; Schank & Abelson, 1977). One way to observe the effects of structure in comparison is to use cross-mappings to put structural commonalities in conflict with other kinds of similarities (e.g., of features or objects; Gentner & Toupin, 1986; Goldstone & Medin, 1994; Markman & Gentner, 1993b; Rattermann, Gentner, & DeLoache, 1989, 1999; Ross, 1987). For example, Markman and Gentner (1993b) showed people two scenes. In one, a women was shown *giving* food to a squirrel; in the other, the women was shown *receiving* food from a man. One group of subjects rated how similar the two scenes were to each other, while another group simply rated the two scenes' aesthetic value (to control for time spent looking at the pictures). All subjects were then asked to say which thing in the second picture best corresponded to the *woman* in the first picture. Subjects who first rated the similarity of the scenes made significantly more relational mappings (i.e., woman to squirrel) ($M = 69\%$) than subjects who did not ($M = 42\%$). These findings suggest that the act of carrying out a similarity comparison induced a structural alignment and increased people's likelihood of making matches on the basis of shared relational roles over simple object similarities. (See Fig. 11.1.)

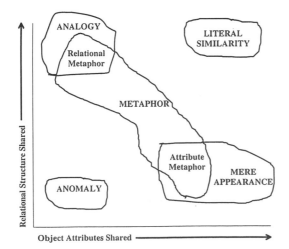

FIG. 11.1. Similarity space.

Metaphor

Now let us apply structure-mapping theory to metaphor. It must be admitted at the outset that metaphor is a protean phenomenon. Metaphors, like analogies, are nonliteral comparisons, but whereas analogies are used for explanatory-predictive purposes, metaphors can also be used in expressive-affective contexts (for longer discussions, see Boyd, 1979; Fauconnier, 1990; Gentner, 1982; Gentner, Falkenhainer & Skorstad, 1988; Steen, 1991). Figure 11.1 illustrates a similarity space showing the continuum from analogy (common relational structure) to literal similarity (common relational structure plus common object descriptions) and from literal similarity to mere-appearance matches (common object descriptions). Metaphor spans the range from attributional comparisons like (1) through relational comparisons like (2):

1. For the black bat, night, has flown (Tennyson).
2. A novel is a mirror carried along a main road (Stendhal).

Indeed, metaphor is even more polymorphous than Fig. 11.1 can portray, for in certain literary contexts metaphors can escape the constraints of structural consistency, as in Example 3.

3. On a star of faith pure as the drifting bread, / As the food and flames of the snow (Dylan Thomas).

This permissiveness follows from the communicative emphasis on capturing affect in metaphor. An unresolvable mapping is irritating in an analogy, because the comparison is responsible for conveying clear inferences based on common structure. It can be pleasing in metaphor, where the sense of rich intermeshing can be part of the experience.

The bulk of the metaphors used in psychology experiments are explanatory-predictive metaphors and are structurally well behaved, if somewhat on the lifeless side. There are occasional attribute comparisons such as:

4. Her hair was spaghetti.

However, relational comparisons (analogies) like (5) form by far the most frequent category:

5. Cigarettes are time bombs.

We will focus our discussion on explanatory-predictive metaphors. These are almost always relational, and most can be analyzed in the same manner as analogies. For example, consider A. E. Housman's metaphorical comparison: "A poet can no more define poetry than a terrier can define a rat." Although not a cross-mapping, this metaphor involves a set of unlikely object correspondences. Clearly, the correspondences between *poet* and *terrier* and between *poetry* and *rat* are not meant to reflect pairwise object similarity. The poet is not seen as a dog, much less poetry as vermin, except with respect to the relation between them—the unthinking avidity of the pursuit.[3]

In this metaphor, the intended meaning conveys a highly specific relational structure. Some metaphors go even further and invite the application of an extended domain mapping. For example, consider Shakespeare's metaphor:

I have ventured,
Like little wanton boys that swim on bladders,
This many summers in a sea of glory;
But far beyond my depth: my high-blown pride
At length broke under me; and now has left me,
Weary and old with service, to the mercy
Of a rude stream, that must forever hide me.

This extended mapping between swimming boys and the arena of political intrigue preserves perfect structural consistency throughout, deepening as the further implications of the parallel are developed. Here the very incongruity of the object-level correspondence between the adventuring boys and the aging and defeated man is part of its effectiveness.

As these examples suggest, much of metaphoric comprehension can be seen as analogical mapping.[4] As we review in the following sections, there is considerable evidence that the process of comparison is sensitive to relational structure (Clement & Gentner, 1991; Gentner & Clement, 1988; Goldstone, Gentner, & Medin, 1989; Markman & Gentner, 1993a, 1993b) and that comprehension of metaphors involves an alignment process (Gentner, Imai, & Boroditsky, 1999; Gentner & Wolff, 1997; Wolff & Gentner, 1992, in press). In the following sections we amplify the structural

---

[3]Consider the hopelessness of trying to capture this meaning if one were restricted to parameter space representations. By mapping a multidimensional space of animal dimensions onto the multidimensional space or spaces for poets and poetry, one can convey that poets are more fierce than poetry, but not the specific relation of pursuit between them.

[4]We do not attempt to deal here with metaphors that are radical departures from structural consistency. Fauconnier's (1990) research on complex metaphor and blending processes provides a good framework for these extensions.

alignment model and provide more evidence focusing on the issue of how metaphors and analogies can lead to change of knowledge.

MECHANISMS OF CHANGE

Knowledge Selection

In the richness of our representations, knowledge can often get buried. When two concepts are compared, aspects that typically remain unconsidered can be picked out and made the focus of attention. For example, in thinking about televisions, certain properties easily come to mind: that they are medium-sized appliances, that they display pictures, that they have antennae, and so on. Given the metaphor "Television is bubble gum for the mind," however, the shared idea of mindless activity comes to the fore. The power of knowledge selection is perhaps most evident when this *highlighting* mechanism is used to pick out knowledge that is not normally salient. Highlighting or knowledge selection is one of the major ways that analogies and metaphors illuminate their targets (Black, 1962, 1979; Clement & Gentner, 1991; Elio & Anderson, 1981; Hayes-Roth & McDermott, 1978; Indurkhya, 1991; Kuhn, 1979; Way, 1991; Winner, 1988). (See Fig. 11.2.)

A process model of knowledge selection and highlighting must account for the generativity of metaphor comprehension. For example, consider the metaphor: "If we do not plant knowledge when young, it will give us no shade when we are old" (Chesterfield). You were probably able to infer the base domain of a growing tree and the intended image of something that begins small and grows slowly but that, properly cared for, eventually becomes an immense and rewarding presence. Yet you had no way of anticipating this meaning from the foregoing text; it had to emerge from the metaphorical comparison. This example demonstrates that modeling metaphor comprehension as the process of verifying expected patterns (whether derived from external context or from the person's current goal state) is overly restrictive (See Carbonell, 1981, 1982; Holyoak, 1985, for arguments on the other side). Instead, we need a

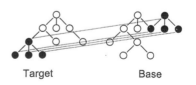

Target　　　　　　Base

FIG. 11.2. Knowledge selection.　*TV is chewing gum for the mind.*

process model that can derive a plausible meaning de novo from the juxtaposition of two representations.

In the structure-mapping engine (SME; Falkenhainer, Forbus, & Gentner, 1989), structural alignment is performed by using a local-to-global algorithm that can arrive at unanticipated matches.[5] Initially, matches are made between all pairs of identical elements.[6] This initial set of local matches is typically inconsistent and many to one. In the next phase, SME imposes the structural constraints of *one-to-one correspondence* and *parallel connectivity* to coalesce the local matches into (typically) several structurally consistent subsystems (kernels), which in turn are joined into one or a few maximal structurally consistent interpretations. SME produces a structural evaluation of each of its possible final interpretations by using an algorithm that favors systems that are large (i.e., have many matching predicates) and *deep* (i.e., with higher-order relational connections, rather than large sets of independent matches).[7] Finally, predicates connected to the common structure in the base, but not initially present in the target, are proposed as *candidate inferences* in the target. As we discuss in the next section, in this way structural alignment and mapping can lead to the projection of unplanned inferences.

The systematicity assumption is crucial to our account of metaphor comprehension. The assumption that people prefer to match predicates belonging to interconnected systems of knowledge rather than isolated independent components has several implications. First, not all matching predicates should enter into an interpretation: only information tied to the maximal common structure. Thus the structural alignment model does not fall prey to the problem that besets simple comparison models, that of predicting inclusion of all matching information (Camac & Glucksberg, 1984; Glucksberg & Keysar, 1990; Goodman, 1970; Rips, 1989; Tourangeau & Rips, 1991; Tourangeau & Sternberg, 1981). Evidence for the selective power of systematicity was found in an experiment by Clement and Gentner (1991). In their study, subjects read two analogous passages. The target and base contained two clearly matched pairs of facts. In one case, the key matching facts were connected to larger causal systems that also

---

[5]The initial representations must contain between them the relations that are matched, but the process is nontrivial all the same, because the representations can be sufficiently rich that the outcome of a mapping process cannot be determined by simply importing "the" base structure to the target.

[6]This initial search for identities means that SME does not need to solve the (computationally intractable) general graph-matching problem, contrary to Hummel and Holyoak's (1997) claim. Semantic similarity between predicates is captured through a decomposition into partial identities; we return to this later.

[7]See Forbus and Gentner (1989) and Forbus and Oblinger (1990) for the details of how the smaller kernal structures are combined into larger structures and evaluated.

matched between base and target. Specifically, each fact was the consequent of another matching pair of facts. In the other case, the pair of key facts was matched equally well locally, but each was the consequent of a different (nonmatching) antecedent. Thus, the two did not belong to matching systems, even though they matched perfectly well locally. According to the systematicity principle, only facts that are connected to *corresponding relational systems* should get included in the interpretation. Consistent with this prediction, when asked which matching pair contributed more to the analogy, subjects selected the pair that was connected to a matching antecedent. Thus, the feature selection problem is dealt with by using systematicity as a selection constraint.

A second implication of the systematicity assumption is that it predicts that, on the whole, people should have a preference for relational information over attribute information in their interpretations. This result is predicted because relations, to a greater degree than attributes, serve to make knowledge more connected and systematic. Studies by Gentner (1988) and Gentner and Clement (1988) are consistent with this prediction: Adult subjects' interpretations of metaphors were found to contain predominantly relational rather than attributional information. In contrast, their descriptions of the individual concepts that entered into the metaphor contained approximately the same amount of relational and attributional information. Furthermore, subjects' aptness ratings were correlated with the relationality, but not the attributionality, of their interpretations (Gentner, 1988). Tourangeau and Rips (1991) found a similar emphasis on relational commonalties in a metaphor-interpretation task. Their subjects rated the degree to which interpretations (from another group of subjects) specified relations rather than simple attributes. They found that relationality ratings for assertions used in interpretations were higher than for those not included in the interpretation but included in the target and base descriptions.

A final example of metaphoric highlighting comes from an unpublished study by Gentner and Koenig. They asked whether comparison processes would induce an abstract schema that would permit subsequent relational retrieval, instead of surface-based retrieval as is typically found in reminding studies (Gentner, Rattermann, & Forbus, 1993; Gick & Holyoak, 1983; Holyoak & Koh, 1987; Keane, 1988; Ross, 1987). Subjects rated the similarity of pairs of proverbs. The pairs were either relationally similar— "You can't tell a book by its cover" and "All that glitters is not gold"—or object similar—"Don't look a gift horse in the mouth" and "You can lead a horse to water but you can't make it drink." Subjects who rated the similarity of relationally related pairs were much better able to recall the original items when given another relationally similar proverb than were subjects who rated the similarity of dissimilar or surface-similar pairs. In contrast, although surface-based retrieval (i.e., retrieval given a surface-similar cue) was generally high, it was not much improved by rating the similarity of surface-similar pairs. This result suggests that the similarity comparison highlighted the common relational structure.

A second study assessed whether the schemas derived would carry forward. Subjects rated the similarity of pairs of proverbs and afterward wrote out interpretations for new proverbs, some of which were relationally similar to the originals. Subjects who gave similarity ratings for relationally similar pairs wrote abstract interpretations of the new proverbs by using the schema consistent with that embedded in the original pair. In contrast, subjects who rated surface similar pairs and control subjects who merely rated the importance of the original proverbs instead of comparing them tended to write concrete, idiosyncratic interpretations of the new proverbs. These results suggest that the act of comparison led to a highlighting of common structure, resulting in a more abstract representation of the proverbs' meaning.

Knowledge selection is an important aspect of metaphorical insight. It is true that by itself it suffers from the classic problem of traditional comparison models: It is limited to information contained in the initial representations of the terms (Glucksberg & Keysar, 1990; Tourangeau & Rips, 1991; Way, 1991). Nonetheless, if we assume that human knowledge is typically rich and situationally embedded, then the metaphoric selection and extraction of smaller subsystems from the thicket of knowledge serve a valuable function. Furthermore, when alignment and highlighting identify common structure, they provide a basis for processes that add or alter knowledge, such as *projection*.

Projection

Linguists and rhetoricians have often asserted that metaphor involves a transfer of meaning from the base to the target. The Greek ancestor of the term *metaphor* means "to transfer or carry over" (Verbrugge & McCarrell, 1977; Wheelwright, 1962). We refer to this sort of transfer as *projection of candidate inferences*. It is also called *property introduction* (Glucksberg & Keysar, 1990; Ortony, 1979a), or *attribution*.

This process of transferring inferences from one domain to another is well illustrated in the history of scientific discovery (Boyd, 1979; Dreistadt, 1968; Gentner, 1982; Gentner & Jeziorski, 1993; Hesse, 1966; Kuhn, 1979; Nersessian, 1992; Oppenheimer, 1956; Thagard & Holyoak, 1985). The discovery of mesons offers an apt example (Oppenheimer, 1956). In the late 1940s, the Japanese physicist Hideki Yukawa proposed that the electrical and nuclear forces might be analogous (Yukawa, 1982). It was already known that for the electric force, interactions between electrically charged bodies were mediated by electrical fields. Using arguments from relativity and quantum theory, Yukawa speculated that corresponding fields and particles might exist for nuclear forces. These particles—mesons—were eventually found in cosmic rays. In this instance, as in most instances of scientific invention, the projection depended on a previous partial alignment. A comparison and partial alignment led to a further inference.

A similar kind of reasoning may occur in more mundane metaphors. For example, "My surgeon is a butcher" suggests a clumsy, brutal surgeon. Common structure between surgeons and butchers emerges in this juxtaposition: Both cut flesh with specialized implements. The normal manner and purpose of the cutting are quite different for surgeons and butchers, however. In this metaphor, the cutting structures are easily aligned, permitting a transfer of information from the base term (*butcher*) to the target term (*surgeon*). The resulting candidate inference is that the surgeon cuts in the manner of a butcher, crudely and without regard for the well-being of the organism. Thus, in the structure-mapping framework, projection is a structural completion process that follows the initial structural alignment (see Fig. 11.3). As discussed earlier, candidate inferences are formed by mapping across parts of the relational structure of the base that are connected to the base's matching structure, but for which there is not yet corresponding structure in the target. Once such potential inferences are identified, they are brought over from the base and inserted into the target structure, subject to verification of their validity in the target domain.

Projection represents an important way in which metaphor can lead to knowledge change: by the carryover of information from one concept to another. Because the structure-mapping account involves both alignment and projection, it does not suffer from the criticism leveled at pure comparison models, namely that they are inherently incapable of explaining how information found in only one of the terms can enter into an interpretation (Glucksberg & Keysar, 1990; Way, 1991). In addition, projection offers a way of explaining the phenomenon of *metaphorical directionality:* that is, for people's preference for one ordering of the terms over another. Because projection occurs directionally, from the more systematic

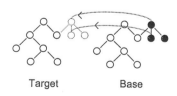

Target   Base

FIG. 11.3. Projection.   *That surgeon is a butcher.*

of the two aligned structures—which, in a felicitous metaphor, will be the base domain—people implicitly prefer orderings that result in the greatest amount of transfer (Bowdle & Gentner, 1997). Bowdle and Gentner found that asymmetries in the preferred direction of a comparison can be predicted by the degree to which one term possesses more systematic relational structure than the other. People prefer to place the more relationally coherent structure in the base position and are more likely to draw inferences in this direction (Bowdle & Gentner, 1997; Gentner & Bowdle, 1994).

Findings from Clement and Gentner (1991) supported the view that projection is constrained by common relational structure. Subjects read two analogous passages and then made predictions about one of the passages (the target) on the basis of information contained in the other (the base). The base passage contained two facts for which there were no corresponding facts in the target. One of these facts was the consequent of a fact that matched a target fact: That is, it was part of a relational structure in the base that matched relational structure in the target. The other fact was the consequent of a fact that did not match anything in the target. As predicted, subjects' willingness to make a particular inference depended on whether it was tied to the common relational structure.

Evidence for projection has also been found in children. In a study by Gentner (1977), children were asked to say where on a mountain or tree a body part, such as a knee, would be found. Importantly, the place on a tree where a knee might be expected to be was not marked; the task thus required projection on the basis of a partial mapping of the objects. Four-year-old children performed very well. Their high level of performance held even when the trees or mountains were put on their sides or upside down. Chen and Daehler (1989) showed that 6-year-olds can transfer a solution from a story to a physical apparatus, provided that the elements are easily aligned. In another study, Gentner and Toupin (1986) investigated the role of higher-order relations in children's mappings. They asked children 4 to 6 and 8 to 10 years of age to transfer a story plot from one group of characters to another Half the children were given simple sequential plots; the other half (the systematic condition) received the same plots but with added beginning and ending sentences that expressed a causal or moral summary. In addition, the transparency of the mapping was manipulated by varying the similarity of corresponding characters. For both ages, transfer accuracy was nearly perfect with highly similar corresponding characters (e.g., *chipmunk* → *squirrel* and *moose* → *elk*), lower when corresponding characters were quite different (e.g., *chipmunk* → *lion* and *moose* → *trout*), and lower still in the cross-mapped condition in which similar looking characters played different roles (e.g., *chipmunk* → *elk* and *moose* → *squirrel*). For the older group, but not the younger group, systematicity also had strong effects: 9-year-olds could map virtually perfectly even in cross-mappings as long as they had systematic relational structure. However, when given stories that lacked systematicity, they were at the mercy of the object similarities; their accuracy was low in the cross-mapped condition. These results show that processes of alignment and mapping are present from early in development and that they become more fluent and more independent of surface similarity as children acquire higher-order connecting relations to guide their projections.

We have argued that in general alignment precedes and guides projection. However, there are exceptions. As discussed below, highly conventional 'stock' metaphoric bases have stored metaphorical senses: for instance, 'jail' as a confining institution). Further, some metaphors involve a more complex interplay of alignment with other processes of blending (Fauconnier, 1990). For example, consider Alexander Pope's couplet:

"Satire or sense, alas! can Sporus feel?
Who breaks a butterfly upon a wheel."

The reader is invited to imagine stretching a butterfly on a rack; the very difficulty of doing so invites the image of one so insubstantial as to be unworthy of torture.

In summary, the mechanism of projection provides a way of importing knowledge that is initially present in the base but not in the target. In this case, change of knowledge occurs in the target. We now consider cases in which change of knowledge applies to *both* domains. In the next section we discuss mechanisms for re-representing initially mismatching predicates to reveal common structure.

Predicate Re-Representation

The evolution of plants and animals has been compared to the growth pattern of a great tree. In *On the Origin of Species,* Darwin extended this metaphor in several interesting ways (Dreistadt, 1968). Just as the competition between spatially close twigs can be especially intense, so can competition between animal species at the same ecological niche. The winning twigs may grow into great branches that spread out and bear other branches and twigs. Likewise, animal species that survive can become the progenitors of other species.

The Great Tree metaphor is grounded in similarities between two large systems of relations. However, the precise way in which competition occurs among animals is markedly different from the way in which it occurs among branches in a tree. Animals often compete by physically fighting for food, territory, and mates, whereas twigs compete in a less dramatic manner, by gaining or losing resources rather than by aiming direct injury at one another. As another example, when it is said that one animal species *comes from* another, the relation is one of genealogy over time, whereas when the same thing is said of twigs, the relation seems to be spatial in addition to (or instead of) temporal. The question is, how do we align such nonidentical structures? Competition differs across animals and plants, but not so much so that the similarities cannot be perceived.

The issue of nonidentical correspondences is an important problem for models based on similarity (Black, 1962, 1979; Hesse, 1966; Miller, 1979; Ortony, 1979a, 1979b; Ortony, Vondruska, Foss, & Jones, 1985; Tourangeau & Sternberg, 1981, 1982; Way, 1991). If meaning components (predicates) that should correspond in order to fit a larger mapping do not match exactly, by what mechanism can their correspondences be known?

In computational models of analogy, several proposals have been made as to how this problem might be solved. The *taxonomic re-representation* approach employs abstraction hierarchies. According to Burstein (1986), when the relations in the base and target differ, a "virtual relation" can be formed in the target that is a sibling or ancestor of the corresponding base relation. In a similar fashion, Winston (1980) suggested that ancestors for predicates like KILL can be found with subroutines that generate predicates like HURT or HAS-CONFLICT-WITH. Falkenhainer (1990) incorporated a notion of *minimal ascension* into his contextual structure-mapping engine (*Phineas*). In cases where two consequents match identically but the antecedents do not, Phineas attempts to match the antecedents by climbing the taxonomic hierarchy until the minimal common ancestor is found: DESTROY and STAB might have the common superordinate of HARM. This approach seems psychologically plausible in cases where a firm taxonomic hierarchy can be assumed. However, this assumption may be unwarranted for verbs (Gentner, 1981; Graesser & Hopkinton, 1987; Huttenlocher & Lui, 1979).

Another way in which nonidentical predicates can be matched is by performing *decompositional re-representation* (Gentner & Rattermann, 1991; Gentner, Rattermann, Markman, & Kotovsky, 1995; Kotovsky & Gentner, 1996). (See Fig. 11.4.) In re-representation, predicates are decomposed into subpredicate structures, much as in lexical decomposition. This allows similarities between predicates to be manifest as identities in (some of the) subcomponents. For example, in a metaphor like "The hotter the anger the sooner quenched," there is an implicit comparison between anger and

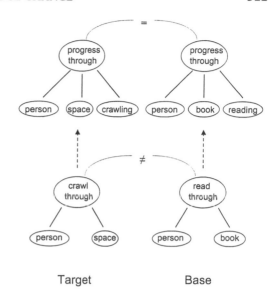

Target   Base

FIG. 11.4. Re-representation.   *He crawled his way through the book.*

fire. To align these structures, the initial representation[8] of the assertion HOTTER-THAN (f_1, f_2) can be re-represented to form the equivalent subpredicate structure GREATER-THAN (*temperature* f_1, *temperature* f_2). Similarly, the relational predicate ANGRIER-THAN (s_1, s_2) can be re-represented as GREATER-THAN (*anger* s_1, *anger* s_2). The mapping problem now reduces to placing the nonidentical dimensional functions of *anger* and *temperature* in correspondence.[9] Once the original comparative assertions are re-represented, their similarity becomes apparent: Both involve a notion of comparative magnitude, albeit along different dimensions.

Re-representation provides a means by which matches between nonidentical predicates can be made, but unrestrained re-representation would be computationally expensive and, worse, could lead to profligate matching. The decision to re-represent must be constrained. One way to accomplish this is by limiting re-representation to just those cases in which neighboring predicates already match. This approach to the nonidenticality problem is the one used in Falkenhainer's (1990) Phineas and in Keane

---

[8]These representations are assumed to be conceptual rather than specifically verbal. That is, we assume a conceptual level of representation that is not modality specific.

[9]SME can match nonidentical functions and entities but requires identity to set up a correspondence between relations and attributes (truth-bearing predicates). Thus re-representing specific relations in terms of abstract relations over specific functions allows us to capture the sense that the same structures hold across different specific domains.

and Brayshaw's (1988) incremental analogy machine (IAM) model of analogical reasoning.

A second issue is whether there is a set of standard processes for re-representation and whether this is influenced by experience. One plausible scenario is that people first check an abstraction hierarchy before matching nonidentical features. If a common abstraction does not exist, as would be the case when a particular pair of nonidentical predicates is encountered for the first time, people may then perform re-representation. If such a re-representation is used repeatedly, it may come to be added to the abstraction hierarchy. Another possibility is that the underlying predicate formats become more available so that in future matches their similarity can be more easily identified. Over the course of many comparisons, this process of format change can have the effect of making mental representations more unified and therefore easier to work with (Gentner & Rattermann, 1991). Such a process may lead to the kind of *representational redescriptions* envisioned by Karmiloff-Smith (1991). She argued that in conceptual development children move through stages of understanding in which representations in one phase are redescribed in the next (e.g., procedural to declarative), with the result that the child's representations become increasingly more flexible and context independent. We suggest that alignment and re-representation mechanisms may contribute to this redescription process.

The process of re-representation is important in cross-domain metaphor, in which people must match descriptions across disparate dimensions. For example, Asch (1955) explored how predicates used to describe physical objects can be used to describe qualities about people. Like physical objects, people can be described as deep or shallow, narrow or wide, hard or soft, bright or dull. In several instances, Asch found that many metaphorical usages had the same meaning across cultures (see also Greenberg, 1966; Lakoff & Johnson, 1980; Osgood, 1949). For instance, the morpheme for "straight" is used to designate honesty, righteousness, and correct understanding. However, in some cases, there is considerable cultural variation: For example, "hot" can stand for a wide range of meanings, including wrath (Hebrew), enthusiasm (Chinese), sexual arousal (Thai), worry (Thai), energy (Hausa), and nervousness (Shilba). In some sense, these are all alike in being positive ends of some generalized energy dimension, but the variety of specific dimensions used suggests that these dimensional relations are at least partly culturally selected or constructed.

How do children learn such systems of dimensional correspondences? Kotovsky and Gentner (1996) asked whether re-representation might contribute to children's learning about cross-dimensional matches. Their study focused on children's ability to perceive similarity solely on the basis of common perceptual higher-order relations such as monotonicity and symmetry. They gave children a forced-choice triads task in which they were shown a standard embodying some relational structure—say, *symmetry* (e.g., XoX)—and asked to say which of two other figures it was most similar to: another instance of symmetry (HiH) or a second figure that lacked the symmetry relation (iHH). One of the choices (HiH) preserved the relational structure of the standard while changing the specific object attributes (e.g., shape). The other choice (iHH) was created by rearranging the components of the relational choice. Thus, both choices were equally dissimilar to the standard in terms of object attributes, but only the relational choice shared the higher-order relational structure of the standard. The key variable was the degree of concrete lower-order similarity between the standard and the relational choice. In some instances, the relational choice had the same dimension of change (either size or darkness) as the standard. In other instances, the dimension of change was different.

When children were given mixed sets of these similarity triads (without feedback), 4-year-olds chose randomly except in the close-similarity case when both the dimension of change (size or shading) and the polarity of change were the same. They could match XoX/HiH but not xOx/HiH. Kotovsky and Gentner then investigated ways of teaching 4-year-olds to perceive the cross-dimensional match. In one study, they attempted to induce re-representation by teaching 4-year-olds names for the higher-order relations: for instance, *even* for symmetry. Learning to label and sort cards according to these higher-order labels improved children's performance on subsequent cross-dimensional similarity matches. Perhaps more surprisingly, simple juxtaposition of several concrete "easy" matches also seemed to induce re-representation. When 4-year-olds received a set of in-dimension pairs first, followed by a set of cross-dimensional pairs, they performed much better on the cross-dimensional pairs than children who received the same set in mixed order. A similar benefit occurred for children who received blocks of same-polarity matches—such as xOx/iVi—before blocks of opposite-polarity matches—such as xOx/IvI. Kotovsky and Gentner interpreted these findings as indicating that initial concrete matches between the standard and relational choice helped children form more abstract representations of monotonic increase and decrease (cf. Gentner et al., 1995). This finding that close literal similarity matches facilitate subsequent analogical matches that embody the same relational structure appears to be quite general in learning and development (Gentner & Medina, 1998).

Why should close similarity matches facilitate subsequent abstract matches involving the same relational structure? Gentner and Kotovsky suggested a mechanism of *progressive alignment*. Four specific assumptions were made. First, children initially represent the relations in a dimension-specific manner (e.g., *darker than* and *bigger than*). That is, for young children, the representation of a difference in magnitude is bound up with the dimension of difference. Second, close matches are easy to perceive—in a sense, they are automatically aligned. Third, alignment results in a slight highlighting of the common relational structure. After repeated such alignments, the higher-order relational structure—such as *symmetry* or *monotonic change*—is strong enough so that a partial match can be made even in a cross-dimensional pairing. Fourth, this partial match invites a re-representation: a decomposition that further brings out and clarifies the likeness. In this case, a re-represention that separates the *greater-than* relation from the specific dimension—for instance, *greater* [*darkness* (a), *darkness* (b)])—will reveal an identical system of relations expressed across different dimensions. The common higher-order symmetry pattern can then be perceived.

Research by Smith and Sera (1992) provides another possible example of re-representation over the course of learning and development. In their experiments, children were asked to say "which is *more*" for pairs of mice of different size, loudness, or darkness. Even 2-year-olds showed a consistent mapping between *more* and *bigger*. However, the mapping between *more* and *louder* was not firmly present at 2 years and became more consistent with age and experience. The mapping between magnitude and darkness showed yet another pattern. Two-year-olds had a consistent mapping from *more* to *darker* and from *bigger* to *darker*: Big mice were paired with dark mice and little mice with light mice. However, 4-year-olds were random on the mapping from size to darkness. Adults were split: Half assigned *large* to *dark*; the other half, *large* to *light*. Smith and Sera speculated that the shift from consistent to random to split mappings between size and darkness may be related to the onset of words for the darkness dimension. The English language is ambiguous as to the polarity of the *light/dark* dimension. Both *light* and *dark* can occupy the positive pole in different contexts. Perhaps an initial consistent perceptual mapping is set aside as children try to integrate language and perception.

A study by Vosniadou, Ortony, Reynolds, and Wilson (1984) examined re-representation developmentally. In one of their experiments, children listened to seven short stories that ended with a concluding sentence that was either literal or metaphoric. A metaphoric ending was something like "Sally was a bird flying to her nest"; a literal counterpart to this was "Sally was a girl running to her home." Comprehension was measured by children's ability to act out the stories with toys. First graders tended to act out the test sentence literally. For example, in demonstrating how "Sally flew to her nest," they moved the doll through the air. Third graders, on the other hand, reinterpreted (re-represented) the verb to mean "run" and thus had the doll move quickly across the ground. These children apparently could re-represent two events to reveal common structure. This re-representation potential contributes to making nonliteral comparison a potent developmental force. However, the results also show that re-representation is not automatic. Juxtaposition does not guarantee an illuminating alignment.

One result of re-representation can be an increase in the uniformity with which the relations are encoded. We hypothesize that such representational uniformity can increase the likelihood of relational remindings (Forbus, Gentner, & Law, 1995). Clement, Mawby, and Giles (1994) explored the effect of relational predicate similarity on analogical access and mapping between disparate domains. They used materials in which similar relations were expressed either in terms of the same predicates (so that the likeness was manifest) or else in terms of merely similar predicates (so that the likeness was latent, requiring re-representation to be aligned). Analogical access (that is, being reminded of a past situation given a current analogous situation) was better with manifest similarity. In contrast, analogical mapping (that is, the alignment and projection between two current situations) was relatively unaffected by the latent-manifest distinction. In analogical reminding, with only the current situation in working memory, success depends on the degree of match of the pre-existing representations, whereas during mapping, with both situations present in working memory, there is opportunity for re-representation.

This is a good point to step back and consider the issue of identicality in matching predicates. The structural alignment process we propose has a tiered identicality requirement. Three distinct patterns occur vis à vis identity. First, some conceptual identities are necessary to begin the alignment process. Second, these initial identities license other nonidentical correspondences: In particular, identical relations license matches between nonidentical functions and identities. Third, given a partial alignment, the process of re-representation finds new identities. From this perspective, identical relations are as much an *output* constraint as an input requirement in the structure-mapping model. Processes of re-representation can be modeled by adopting processes like those discussed earlier, capable of initiating and constraining re-representational activity. However, re-representation is still relatively unexplored in computational models.

Restructuring

Knowledge change can occur not only at the level of individual concepts, but also at the level of systems. The notion that analogy and metaphor prompt change at the system level has a long history in cognitive science (Black, 1979; Gentner, 1982; Gentner et al., 1997; Indurkhya, 1991; Nersessian, 1992; Schön, 1979; Verbrugge & McCarrell, 1977). In the following sections, we discuss how this sort of change may occur. To do so, we explore in some depth a historical example of restructuring by use of metaphor.

At the turn of the century, physicists were trying to conceptualize the atom (Wilson, 1983). One early proposal, made by J. J. Thomson, was that the atom was a sphere of positive electricity in which negatively charged electrons were stuck like plums in a pudding. The plum-pudding model was supported by a number of major scientists. Soon, however, the model was challenged by Thomson's own student, Earnest Rutherford. Rutherford's atom was a serious departure from Thomson's. How did this departure come about?

In the first decade of the century, Rutherford was working on determining the characteristics of alpha particles (helium atoms stripped of their electrons: i.e., two protons and two neutrons). Rutherford and Hans Geiger (of the Geiger counter), then Rutherford's lab manager, used a technique of aiming a beam of alpha particles at a thin piece of metal foil. By placing a zinc-sulfide screen behind the foil, the researchers could count the number of alpha particles passing through at various angles. Rutherford recognized that these experiments could bear on the structure of the atom. A discovery occurred in 1909 when Rutherford looked for scattering of alpha particles at large angles of deflection. The results were extraordinary. A small but significant number of screen marks indicated that a few of the alpha particles had been scattered backward, deflected through an angle of more than 90 degrees. As Rutherford noted: "It was as though you had fired a fifteen-inch shell at a piece of tissue paper and it had bounced back and hit you." The number of large-angle deflections was far greater than predicted from the simple accumulation of many small deflections.

As Wilson (1983) described it, for the next 18 months Rutherford pondered the finding. Thomson's atom was clearly incapable of predicting the severe change in direction. Sometime in December 1910, Rutherford appears to have settled on a model of the atom (Wilson, 1983) as containing a massively charged, very minute center (later to be called the nucleus) that was surrounded, at relatively great distances, by even smaller electrons distributed throughout a sphere. What led Rutherford to this model? A visit made by the Japanese physicist Nagaoka, which preceded Rutherford's announcement by several weeks, may have had an effect on his thinking. In 1904, Nagaoka had proposed a "Saturnian" model of the atom, a disk-shaped atom with a large, heavy center surrounded by rings of electrons. Another intriguing possibility is hinted at by the fact that in Rutherford's copy of Newton's *Principia* there are copious notes in the margins next to the sections on the inverse square law and the hyperbola (Wilson, 1983). These are sections where Newton described the mathematics underlying the paths of comets and other heavenly bodies around central masses like the sun. As has been suggested by several biographers (e.g., Andrade, 1964; Eve, 1939; Wilson, 1983), Rutherford probably recognized that the path of the alpha particle, being hyperbolic, was like the path of a comet. Strengthening the connection was the observation made by Rutherford and his colleagues that the severity of the alpha particles' deflection increased with the atomic weight (and therefore the charge) of the metal in the foil, as would be expected by analogy with a comet being defected from a star of varying mass. Rutherford may have pursued the parallels and asked whether the path of an alpha particle is caused by a central force, like the comet's path with respect to the sun. The central force idea then perhaps invited a further mapping of electrons to planets. Electrons in the atom might be distributed around some central attractor like planets around the sun. The relative distances between the nucleus and the electrons might be large, like the relative distances between the sun and the planets. In a letter to Nagaoka in 1911, Rutherford wrote that the alpha particles must be considered as passing "right through the atomic system" and noted the similarities (and some differences) between his spherical atom and Nagaoka's Saturnian disk.

The shift from Thomson's plum-pudding model to Rutherford's solar-system model is an example of restructuring via a series of implicit or explicit analogical comparisons. It resulted in a fundamental rearrangement of already known elements. According to Thomson, negatively charged electrons were surrounded by a sphere of positively charged electricity. According to Rutherford, it was nearly the other way around: the element being surrounded was now a positively charged nucleus. Besides this spatial reversal, there was also a fundamental change in how the positive charge was carried; rather than being distributed throughout a sphere, the positive charge was now carried by an entity with mass, a nucleus (see Fig. 11.5).

On the analysis, Rutherford's restructuring began with an alignment between the path of an alpha particle and the path of a comet. Given this local alignment, the structural mapping begins to take on a life of its own. Predicate structures not present in the target but connected to the matching predicate structure in the base are projected as a candidate inference (here, a comet's relation to the sun). New elements (a central object) or relations (attraction or repulsion between the central object and orbiting elements) may be postulated to exist in the target system. These new structures may be incompatible with pre-existing structures; a charged central object cannot be added to the plum-pudding atom without disturbing the balance between the sphere of positive electricity and the negative electrons. Conflicts may be resolved in a number of ways; structures may be eliminated from the target system (e.g., the distribution of

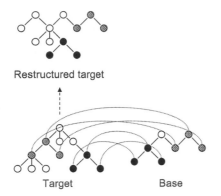

Restructured target

Target   Base

*The plum-pudding atom is like the solar-
system atom.*   FIG. 11.5. Restructuring.

positive charge), or new structures may be induced from other sources
of knowledge (e.g., incorporation of orbits as in the Bohr atom). Either
way, the overall effect is a rearrangement of the system's basic elements.
Rutherford's discovery (as constructed by Wilson) is a classic example of
restructuring. It goes beyond candidate inferences and local re-representation and involves reorganization and revision of the previous representational structure.

A Little Restructuring Is a Dangerous Thing. Apart from their role in
scientific creativity, we may ask whether metaphoric comparisons influence ordinary learning and reasoning about science. Gentner and Gentner
(1983) carried out empirical studies to test whether people's conceptual
inferences in a problem domain follow predictably from their metaphors
for the domain. The domain they considered was electricity. One common
metaphor for this domain compares electricity to water flow: electricity
is water, wires are pipes, batteries are reservoirs, current is flowing water,
voltage is pressure, and resistors are narrow constrictions in pipes. Another common metaphor involves comparing electricity to a crowd moving through a long hall. Here the correspondences are that electricity is
a crowd, wires are paths, current is the number of entities that pass a
point per unit time, voltage is how forcefully they push each other along,
and resistors are narrow gates. Each of these models has its strengths and
weaknesses. The "electricity is water" metaphor captures well how batteries combine to affect voltage. This is because the difference between
serial and parallel reservoirs can be understood in terms of height of fluid,
a relatively accessible distinction that can then map into electricity. However, this metaphor does not capture resistance well; people do not seem

to reason fluently about how serial and parallel narrow constrictions affect flow rate in a water system. The moving crowd metaphor captures resistance much more naturally: In the moving crowd metaphor, resistance corresponds to gates, and people find it easy to simulate the movement of a crowd through various gate configurations.

Gentner and Gentner asked subjects which metaphor they used for electricity and then tested subjects for their ability to solve various circuit problems. As predicted, subjects using the water metaphor performed better on battery problems than on resistor problems, and subjects using the moving-crowd metaphor showed the reverse ordering.

Encouraged by these results, Gentner and Gentner asked whether teaching a new model could help people remedy deficiencies in their existing mental models (unpublished analysis). Subjects were first assessed as to their initial mental models of electricity. Then they were taught to use a particular metaphor, with half receiving the metaphor consistent with their view and half the other (inconsistent) metaphor. Thus, for subjects whose initial model was to view electricity as a teeming crowd, half were told more about these correspondences, and half were taught the metaphor that views electricity as water. The prediction was that this new metaphor would help subjects to solve problems that were hard to solve using their existing model. For example, we expected former *crowd* modelers to improve on battery problems when given the *water* model. However, subjects instead performed *worse* when asked to switch models than did the subjects in the consistent conditions. One interpretation is that the new model led to partial restructuring, leaving the learner with no consistent framework. Possibly matters would have improved had retraining continued over a long period; in this case, it would have been interesting to know whether subjects who learned the new models well showed a decline in performance on the problems supported by their original models. Learning in complex domains may be especially vulnerable to these sorts of transition costs (Spiro, Feltovich, Coulson, & Anderson, 1989; Wiser, 1986).

PRODUCTS OF ALIGNMENT AND MAPPING

In the previous sections, we have reviewed four kinds of change that can result from structural alignment and mapping: knowledge selection, projection, re-representation, and restructuring. Sometimes these changes in knowledge representation are temporary. They serve to get us through the moment—to afford a fleetingly interesting perspective. Sometimes the changes are lasting. Metaphor use may result in a new category or in a conventionalized extended mapping between two conceptual systems.

Metaphors Can Create New Categories

A classic example of metaphoric category creation occurred in the formulation of the scientific notion of *wave* (Hesse, 1966; Oppenheimer, 1956). Initially, the concept was based on the regular, rhythmic movements of water. More generally, it was recognized that these movements had regular relations: When two waves collide, they can either reinforce each other (constructive interference), or cancel each other out (destructive interference). Waves can be dispersed by going through an orifice (diffraction). These properties were found to be true with sound as for water waves. In extending beyond liquids to sound, however, wave phenomena were extended to encompass air as a possible medium through which waves could travel. Once abstracted this far, the concept of a wave was available for further extensions. Light was found to possess the abstract commonalities of constructive and destructive interference and diffraction as well as a major difference: Propagation was possible (indeed, more efficient) in a vacuum. (Like subatomic particles, to which the wave notion was also extended, light is not completely subsumed under the wave rubric; some of its properties are best explained in terms of quanta.) As the extension of the *wave* category broadened, its intension became more abstract.

Glucksberg and Keysar (1990) suggested that the connection between metaphors and categories is fundamental to the nature of metaphor. They suggested that categories are invoked or created in the comprehension of metaphor. Kennedy (1990) and Shen (1992) made similar arguments. As Glucksberg and Keysar pointed out, this view is consonant with the fact that metaphors can be phrased as class-inclusion statements—"Encyclopedias are gold mines"—but literal comparisons cannot—(*) "Encyclopedias are dictionaries." It also offers an explanation for why many metaphors, like class-inclusion statements, are highly asymmetric. Just as the class-inclusion statement "Leeches are parasites" cannot be turned around to make "Parasites are leeches," metaphors like "Suburbs are parasites" resist being turned around to form "Parasites are suburbs."

The claim that metaphors and categories are intimately related can be taken in different ways. The first is that metaphors may be used to *create categories*. The second is that metaphors are *processed by applying categories as opposed to through comparison*. We agree with the first claim, but not the second.

The first view, that metaphor can create categories, has been persuasively argued by Glucksberg and Keysar (1990, 1993) and Shen (1992), among others. Examples such as "He's a real Caligula" demonstrate that even an individual's description can give rise to a category via metaphor. Glucksberg and Keysar noted that metaphorical categories can become conventionalized into ordinary categories. For example, in American Sign Language the concept *furniture* is conveyed by a set of specific instances: bed, chair, and so on. As with the concept of *wave*, the new concept is often an abstraction or extension of the normal meaning of the base term of the metaphor. For example, one sense of the term *sanctuary* refers to a religious edifice; the other, to any location of safety. This second sense may be an extension of "a holy place where one is safe from persecution" to "any place of safety." Similarly, Miller (1993) suggested that "leg of a table" was once understood as a metaphorical comparison between the support of a table and the leg of an animal, but that "leg" has since acquired a secondary meaning. Category creation may also come about through use of a compound noun (Levi, 1978): For instance, "soldier ant" formed from the comparison of certain ants to soldiers. (See Wisniewski [1996] and Wisniewski & Gentner [1991] for evidence of structural alignment in noun–noun compounding.) Such concept creation from metaphors may extend to terms that do not normally strike us as metaphorically derived: for example, "antidote," "bait," "cannibal," "home," "parasite," "scavenger," "shield," and "trap." At one time, such uses as "Her sarcasm was a shield" might have seemed metaphoric. Now, however, these relational terms can apply widely across ontological boundaries. To the extent that metaphors provide mechanisms for concept extension, they offer a means of explaining not only the formation of metaphorical categories but also some aspects of polysemy in word meaning (Bowdle & Gentner, 1999; Gentner & Wolff, 1997; Lehrer, 1990; Miller, 1993).

We next turn to the second possible claim, that metaphors are understood not through comparison but through accessing (or creating) a category associated with the base. Comprehension through categories instead of comparison is an intriguing idea, but we suspect its application is limited to cases where a metaphorical category already exists. For example, if we hear "My boss is a pig," it seems likely that comprehension can proceed by inheritance from this conventional category; we do not have to infer the metaphor's meaning by comparing *pigs* and *bosses* anew (Bowdle & Gentner, 1995, 1999a, b; Gentner & Wolff, 1997; Glucksberg, Gildea, & Bookin, 1982; Wolff & Gentner, 1990, in press). When the metaphor to be understood is novel, however, category models face a critical selection problem: How is the correct category created? According to Glucksberg and Keysar (1990), an ad hoc category is formed of which the base is the prototypical member, and this category is applied to the target. Such a category must reflect both terms of the metaphor (Medin, Goldstone, & Gentner, 1993). We clearly do not derive the same interpretation (or apply the same category) for "My surgeon is a butcher" and "Ghenghis Khan is a butcher." Glucksberg, McGlone, and Manfredi (1997) noted this point and acknowledged that there must be some influence of the target as well as the base. We suggest that the easiest and most natural way to model the joint influence of the two concepts is by assuming a process of comparison via alignment and mapping (see Fig. 11.6). In other words, we suggest that for novel metaphors, the common structure— which may eventually become a category—*arises from* the comparison.

We have carried out several studies aimed at revealing the processing mechanisms for metaphor. The results suggest that novel metaphors are processed through structural alignment rather than through accessing a category associated with the base (Bowdle & Gentner, 1995, 1999a, b; Gentner & Wolff, 1997; Wolff & Gentner, 1992, in press). Our method was to prime metaphors with either the base or the target and then to ask which most facilitated metaphor comprehension. We reasoned as follows. If metaphors are interpreted in terms of base-derived categories rather than by comparison, then processing should begin with the base. For instance, given a base term like *jail*, a category like "situations that oppress" may be derived. Once a category is established, an interpretation of the metaphor would proceed by the application of this category to the target, *job*. If this is the underlying process, then we should see a base advantage. People should be faster to interpret a metaphor when it is preceded by the base rather than by the target.

In contrast, according to the structural alignment model, processing begins with alignment; the directional projection of features from the base term to the target occurs later in processing. Because this initial matching process requires simultaneous access to both the terms, there should be no base advantage. Thus, the structure-mapping model predicts that preceding a metaphor with its base should be no more facilitative than preceding a metaphor with its target.

Across a series of experiments we failed to find evidence for a base advantage. Seeing the base term in advance was no more advantageous than seeing the target in advance. However, seeing both terms consistently

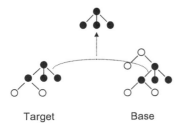

Target   Base

You're no John F. Kennedy.   FIG. 11.6. Category creation.

resulted in faster metaphor comprehension than did seeing either of the terms alone.[10] Additional support for the structural alignment model comes from the fact that metaphors rated high in relational similarity were processed faster than metaphors rated low in relational similarity. These findings suggest that metaphor comprehension occurs by means of comparison and alignment.

However, there was one interesting exception: We found some evidence for a base advantage when highly conventional metaphoric bases were used (provided that the relational similarity between the terms was low). Further studies have confirmed this shift from novel to conventional metaphors (Bowdle & Gentner, 1999; in press; Wolff & Gentner, 1999). This suggests that the normal interpretation process for metaphors, as for analogies, is alignment and mapping. But when a metaphoric meaning becomes highly conventional, interpretation may proceed by directly accessing this stored meaning.

Conventionalizing Metaphoric Meanings. When two representations are aligned, common relational structure can emerge. When the same category is derived repeatedly from a given metaphoric base, it may come to be stored along with the base term. In this way, a conventionalized or "stock" metaphor may develop through schema abstraction (Brown, Kane, & Echols, 1986; Elio & Anderson, 1981; Forbus & Gentner, 1986; Gick & Holyoak, 1980, 1983; Hayes-Roth & McDermott, 1978; Medin & Ross, 1989). Processing can then take place by accessing the category abstraction rather than by comparing the normal full meanings of the terms.

These considerations lead to the suggestion of a "career of metaphor" (Bowdle & Gentner, 1995, 1999; in press; Gentner & Wolff, 1997; Wolff & Gentner, 1999): If conventionalization results in stored schema, then processing may change as the metaphor base becomes more associated with a conventionalized concept. As mentioned earlier, Wolff and Gentner found that processing could begin with the base if the base was associated with a conventionalized meaning. That is, the process of understanding a metaphor appeared to be one of structural alignment between the two literal meanings except when base conventionality was high, in which case the category associated with the base was accessed early in the process.

Other research is consistent with the claim that conventionalization results in a shift in processing from online active interpretation to retrieval of stored meanings (Cacciari, 1993; Cacciari & Tabossi, 1988; Clark &

---

[10]This result is strongly predicted by the structure-mapping model, but not by an initial pure category-projection model, in which any early advantage should reside in accessing the base term's category. However, Glucksberg et al.'s (1997) extension of the class-inclusion model, the *attributive category* model, postulates initial (differential) processing of *both* base and target, and thus can predict the obtained priming results.

Lucy, 1975; Gentner & Wolff, 1997; Gibbs, 1979, 1980; Hoffman & Kemper, 1987; Wolff & Gentner, 1992). For example, Blank (1988) found evidence that conventional metaphors are processed faster than those for which the structural alignments must be made online. He found that metaphorical targets from highly familiar conceptual families (*Time is money*) were responded to as quickly as literal controls. When the metaphorical mapping was less familiar (e.g., *Love is a sickness*), responses were slower to metaphorical targets than to literal controls. Likewise, Blasko and Connine (1993) found that subjects responded to metaphorically related targets from familiar metaphors as quickly as they responded to literally related targets. However, when the metaphors were low in familiarity, subjects responded more slowly to metaphorically related targets than to literally related targets.

The effect of conventionality on processing has been studied with other kinds of tropes, with similar results (Cacciari, 1993; Hoffman & Kemper, 1987). Studies by Clark and Lucy (1975) and Gibbs (1979) found that people were faster to verify pictures and paragraphs consistent with the nonliteral meaning of an indirect request than with the literal meaning. Studying idioms, Gibbs (1980) showed subjects paragraphs that could induce an idiom's literal or nonliteral meaning. The task was to say whether a paraphrase immediately following an idiom was consistent with the meaning of the idiom. Subjects were much faster to confirm conventional nonliteral uses of the idioms than literal ones. These studies suggest that conventional meanings are accessed and comprehended quickly[11] (see also Cacciari & Tabossi, 1988; Swinney & Cutler, 1979). These results are consistent with the claim that metaphor comprehension leads to the creation of conventionalized interpretations.

Metaphors: The Creation of Domains. Some writers (e.g., Boyd, 1979) have argued that when disciplines (e.g., physics) mature, their reliance on metaphors decreases. Others have argued that metaphors remain important (e.g. Campbell, 1920; Kuhn, 1979; Oppenheimer, 1956). Gentner and Grudin (1985) found support for the latter possibility. They examined metaphors for the mind that appeared across nearly a century (1891–1981) in the journal *Psychological Review*. Two interesting findings emerged. In terms of frequency, the number of metaphors used across the decades

---

[11]However, alignment processes may occur even in this case. In Gentner and Wolff's studies, a base advantage was found only when (a) the conventionality the base's metaphorical meaning was high and (b) the relational similarity between the target and base was low. When the terms were of high relational similarity, processing seemed to proceed in terms of comparison, even if base conventionality was high. Gentner and Wolff suggested a race model between direct comparison of the literal meaning and access to the stock meaning of the base. Wolff and Gentner (1999) also found evidence for initial alignment even for conventional metaphors.

was U shaped, with the bottom of the U occurring roughly when behaviorism was dominant. The use of metaphors for mental processes (like all discussion of mental processes) dwindled to a trickle. The other finding was that whereas the number of metaphors was approximately the same at the beginning and ending periods, the kinds of metaphors used were different. In the early decades, *animate* and *spatial* metaphors were by far the most usual. In the later decades, spatial metaphors continued to be frequent, but system metaphors (especially computer metaphors) became the most frequent class, reflecting the greater attention to mechanisms in current theories.

A related question is how metaphors fare across the development of expertise in an individual. Cooke and Bartha (1992) found that metaphor use actually increased with expertise. Participants in their study were asked to explain the results of several hypothetical experiments. The ratio of psychological metaphors to the total number of ideas was higher for subjects experienced in psychology than for inexperienced subjects. When compared with respect to everyday metaphors, the two groups were the same. Both these results suggest that even though any particular metaphor may become "bleached" and conventionalized, overall metaphor use may not diminish over the development of knowledge.

An interesting instance of metaphorically created categories occurs in our own field. Many technical terms in psychology have at least partial metaphorical status. Gentner (1982) noted that we have "reverberating circuits," "mental distance," "perceptual defense," "memory capacity," "mental image," and "depth of processing." In their historical survey, Gentner and Grudin (1985) noted the usage of such terms as "associative force" (Woodworth), "goal gradient" (Dennis), and "ego defenses" (Minard). As these examples suggest, the elements of a metaphoric mapping are often interconnected in ways that reveal domain relations. As we noted before, analogical mapping is implicitly oriented toward connected systems rather than toward isolated matches. The systematicity bias is a means by which structure-mapping processes bridge the gap between concepts and theories. If we think of theories as the domain structures in which the local concepts are embedded, then analogy and metaphor on this account are ideally suited to transfer such theories.

Consistent with this emphasis, we often find metaphorical categories forming an interrelated system. For example, one common conceptualization of the mind is that it is a physical space (Roediger, 1980). Two important correspondences in this metaphor are that memories are objects in this space and that recall involves spatial search. Metaphors like this derive their force not from a local mapping between the base concept of physical objects to the target concept of memories but rather from mapping the *system* of spatial relations in which these objects are embedded. As cognitive theories evolved (and as technological advances created a greater set of potential bases), Gentner and Grudin's historical trace shows a shift from such general spatial metaphors to more complex systems metaphors that yield more specific inferences about mental processes: telephone switchboard metaphors, circuitry metaphors, and most prominent of all, computer metaphors. Boyd (1979) identified a number of terms formed from the "mind is a computer" metaphor, including "information processing," "encoding," "decoding," "indexing," "feedback," and "memory stores." We now turn to systems of metaphoric mappings.

Global Domain Mappings

So far we have focused on metaphor as creating new categories. A more profound way that analogies and metaphors can lead to change in knowledge is through extended systems of mappings. Lakoff and his colleagues have suggested that a rich set of stored metaphoric mappings pervades our language (Gibbs, 1992; Lakoff, 1988, 1990; Lakoff & Johnson, 1980; Lakoff & Turner, 1989; Turner, 1988). They argue that many everyday expressions imply metaphorical parallels between abstract structures and structures grounded in our experience with the physical world. By correspondence with spatial orientation, for example, we can explain some of the meaning behind expressions like "She fell into disgrace" and "He rose in prominence" (Nagy, 1974). Other metaphorical mappings appeal to culturally grounded systems such as objects in motion, possession, and growth of plants, such as "He stole my idea" (*ideas are objects*), "I can't swallow your proposal" (*ideas are food*), or "The seeds of her great ideas were planted in her youth" (*ideas are plants*). The striking thing about these metaphors is that they involve large, coherent systems of related mappings. For example, Lakoff and Johnson (1980, pp. 90, 91) list examples of the *An argument is a journey* metaphor:

- *We have set out to prove that bats are birds.*
- *So far, we have seen that no current theories will work.*
- *We will proceed in a step-by-step fashion.*
- *This observation points the way to an elegant solution.*
- *He strayed from the line of argument.*
- *Do you follow my argument?*
- *I am lost.*
- *We have covered a lot of ground in our argument.*
- *You are getting off the subject.*

Lakoff and his colleagues have made a persuasive case for the importance of these conventional metaphors. However, two key issues are as yet unresolved: First, what is their psychological status, and second, how do they arise? We begin with the second question and then turn to the first.

How do metaphoric systems come into being? Clearly, no process that operates simply by finding local commonalities or common categories between pairs of concepts compared is adequate, for the essence of these mappings is in large-scale mappings between entire systems of concepts. We propose that these metaphors are processed initially as structural alignments (Murphy, 1996). The structural alignment model explains large-scale domain mappings in terms of correspondences between structured systems. The mechanisms of highlighting, projection, re-representation, and restructuring can be applied to large-scale metaphors.

We now come to the issue of the psychological status of metaphoric systems. Lakoff claimed that conceptual metaphors—including highly conventional metaphors—are psychologically real, enduring mappings that are used in thinking and argued for the invariance hypothesis: that schemas from the base domain are imported into the target. Both claims have been sharply challenged in recent times. Glucksberg, Brown, and McGlone (1993) offered evidence that people do not access the *anger is heat* metaphor when processing conventional metaphoric phrases like "lose one's cool." Murphy (1996) argued that conceptual metaphors are better accounted for as structural alignments between semantically parallel domains than as projective mappings from a base domain, which create meaning in the target domain.

Keysar and Bly (1995) convincingly showed that the seeming semantic transparency of a metaphoric or idiomatic system may be illusory. They asked English speakers to interpret "dead" English idioms such as "The goose hangs high" and found that interpretations were strongly driven by contextual information, rather than by the idiom itself. For example, subjects thought "The goose hangs high" conveyed good news in a happy story and bad news in a sad story. Worse, subjects were convinced that the idioms themselves were transparent. They maintained that they would have arrived at the same interpretation had they seen the idiom in isolation and furthermore, that any other English speaker would arrive at the same interpretation. Keysar and Bly's results, and the points raised by Murphy and by Glucksberg et al., make it clear that we cannot assume that metaphoric language necessarily implies a psychologically real domain mapping.

Gentner and Boronat (1992, 1999) conducted an empirical test of the domain-mapping hypothesis (Boronat, 1990; Gentner, et al., in press). If metaphors are processed by structural alignment, then extended metaphorical mappings should be processed fluently as long as they preserve the domain mapping. If an alignment and mapping process is actively guiding comprehension of "live" metaphors in discourse, people should be more fluent at reading sentences that consistently extend the existing structural alignment than at reading sentences based on a different mapping. For example, after reading Sentence 1, people should read Sentence 2a faster than Sentence 2b:

1.   Her anger had been simmering all afternoon.
2a. When Harry got home, she was boiling over.
2b. When Harry got home, she was glacially cool.

Gentner and Boronat (1992, 1999) gave people passages containing extended metaphors such as *anger is a beast*. In four experiments, subjects were timed as they read passages containing these extended metaphors. The last sentence of each passage was always a metaphorical comparison. In some cases, this last metaphor was consistent with the metaphoric mapping underlying the passage. In other cases, the last sentence was based on a different metaphor from the mapping that informed the passage. As predicted, subjects read the last sentence significantly faster when it extended the existing mapping than when it drew on a new metaphoric mapping. This finding supports the basic tenet that metaphors are processed by alignment and mapping and suggests that people find it natural to incrementally extend such mappings. (See Forbus, Ferguson, & Gentner, 1994, for a computational extension of SME that performs such incremental mappings.) These findings are crucial to the claim that large-scale domain metaphors are psychologically real.

However, if conventionalization gradually results in metaphorical meanings coming to be stored with the base term, then we should see a very different pattern for highly conventional metaphors. For extremely conventional metaphors, the abstract metaphorical interpretation may simply be an alternative word sense. In this case, there should be no particular cost for switching metaphors, because comprehension in any case simply involves finding the appropriate word sense. On this account, in the extended metaphor task described earlier, we would predict no advantage in reading time for last sentences whose metaphors are consistent with their passages over those that are inconsistent. Indeed, Gentner and Boronat found that when the passages used highly conventional metaphors (Experiments 1 and 2), subjects were not significantly slowed by a shift in the metaphor.

This finding is convergent with the research on metaphors and idioms (discussed previously) that suggests that conventionalization results in a shift in processing from online active interpretation to retrieval of stored meanings (Blank, 1988; Bowdle & Gentner, 1995, 1999; Cacciari, 1993; Cacciari & Tabossi, 1988; Clark & Lucy , 1975; Gentner & Wolff, 1997; Gibbs, 1979, 1980; Hoffman & Kemper, 1987; Wolff & Gentner, 1992, in press). There is also supporting evidence for the claim that some metaphors are processed as large-scale conceptual systems. Allbritton, McKoon, and Gerrig (1995) found that large-scale conceptual metaphor schemas facilitate recognition judgments for schema-related sentences in text (see also Gibbs, 1990, 1994; Nayak & Gibbs, 1990; but see Glucksberg, Brown, & McGlone, 1993, for contradictory evidence). Further evidence comes from studies of metaphors from space to time (Gentner & Imai, 1992; Gentner, Imai, & Boroditsky, 1999; McGlone & Harding, 1998). This research capitalized on the existence of two English metaphoric *space* → *time* systems: the *ego-moving* metaphor, wherein the observer's context progresses along the timeline toward the future, and the *time-moving* metaphor, wherein time is conceived of as a river or conveyor belt on which events are moving from the future to the past. For example, Gentner and Imai (1992) asked subjects to process statements about time, stated in terms of spatial metaphors, such as "Joe's birthday is approaching" (*time-moving*) or "We are approaching the holidays" (*ego-moving*). As in the Gentner and Boronat studies, people's processing of the metaphors was slowed by a shift from one space–time metaphor to the other.

Metaphoric Mappings in the Creation of a Domain. We noted earlier that analogical mappings can be formative in the development of a new domain, as in the Rutherford atom example. The metaphors used in cognitive psychology vary in their systematicity. Pylyshyn (1989) contrasted coherent system-mapping metaphors, such as the computer metaphor for cognition, with other metaphors that lack systematicity, offering as examples of the latter Freud's hydraulic metaphor for the unconscious and the "mind's eye" metaphor of visual imagery. Such metaphors, he argued, are deceptive; they provide a spurious sense of comfort but not a clear theory. Gentner (1982) made a related point about Freud's theory of anal eroticism, with its claims that feces, money, gift, baby, and penis are often unconsciously treated as equivalent in dreams. This kind of many-to-many mapping places few constraints on the interpretations possible for a given dream.

The trouble with such metaphoric collections in theory building is that, lacking a systematic base and a structurally consistent mapping, they cannot support clear candidate inferences. Figure 11.7, adopted from Gentner (1982) and Markman and Gentner (1999), shows the inferential indeterminacy that arises from $n - 1$ correspondences (a particularly clear case of structural inconsistency).

It must be noted that although we have distinguished local metaphors from systematic metaphorical mappings, there is a continuum between them. Some cases seem purely local: "He's a real pig" seems relatively unconnected to any larger system (indeed, it is not even self-consistent, in that this same metaphor can mean that someone is a male chauvinist, that

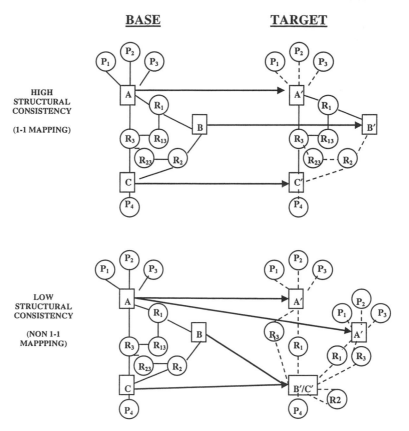

FIG. 11.7. Structural consistency and inference projection.

he eats too much, or that he is a policeman). Other cases seem to be global mappings, such as mapping from vertical dimension to emotions like sadness ("His spirits sank"; "He had never felt so low") or the computer metaphor for cognitive processing just discussed.

Still other metaphors seem intermediate between local categories and global system mappings. For example, Turner (1987) noted in his discussion of kinship metaphors that *mother* is often used to convey that one thing is the source or cause of another, as in "Necessity is the mother of invention." This entails a fairly local mapping—two base elements (mother and child) and some relations between them. Turner (p. 156) also cites examples that draw on a larger portion of the base: "Aristotle sayeth that the erthe is moder and the sonne fader of trees." Here the base elements include *mother, father,* and *child,* together with a relational system that is sufficiently elaborated to invite different father–child relations from mother–child relations and even perhaps a father–mother relation. Here *mother* participates in a system metaphor.

METAPHORIC CREATIVITY

Metaphors have always been associated with creativity. Recently, this aspect of metaphor has received increased attention. In a study by Tourangeau and Rips (1991), subjects wrote down interpretations for a series of metaphors and listed properties for each of the terms on which the metaphor was based. When interpretations were broken down by type, a majority of properties listed for the interpretations were not listed in either the target or base object descriptions. Many of the features listed for the interpretations were thus "emergent": that is, features that were not apparent in either the base or target representations. Similar results were obtained by Gentner and Clement (1988). The emergent nature of interpretations has implications for metaphor processing. To the extent that the properties of an interpretation are constructed or discovered online, then even for perfectly acceptable metaphors, there is no necessary pre-existing relation between the two words. One term of a metaphor need not prime the other. This prediction was tested by Camac and Glucksberg (1984). Subjects were shown a pair of letter strings and asked to decide whether one or both the strings were words. The word pairs were either preassociated, metaphorically associated, or nonassociated. Word pairs that were preassociated were responded to quickly. However, metaphorical pairs were responded to no faster than nonassociated pairs. The degree of preassociation for metaphorically related word pairs can therefore be quite low, supporting the constructive or emergent nature of metaphor interpretation.

Additional evidence for the existence of emergent features comes from a study by Blasko and Connine (1993). Subjects were instructed to make a lexical decision about a visually present word after hearing either the base or the target of a metaphorical sentence. Half the words to be verified were related to the meaning of the metaphor formed by the base and target. The other half were unrelated to the metaphor's meaning. The main result was that test words related to the meaning of the metaphor were verified no faster than unrelated words. In contrast, metaphorically related test words were facilitated when subjects heard both the target and base together. (See also Verbrugge & McCarrell, 1977.) These results suggest that the meaning emerges from combining the two forms and does not simply pre-exist in one of the individual terms. In sum, the results from these studies indicate that metaphor is most deeply and fruitfully understood when both terms are simultaneously present. These findings fit with the evidence offered earlier that a novel metaphor is first and foremost an alignment of representations (Gentner & Wolff, 1997; Wolff & Gentner, 1992, in press). Juxtaposing two terms invites a process of structural alignment and mapping that result in highlighting, candidate inferences, and re-representation. We suggest that comparison is crucial to creativity in metaphor.

These mechanisms and products are not unique to metaphor. On this account, metaphor is highly related to literal similarity—that is, to comparisons with substantial relational and object-attributional commonalties. To put it another way, we have argued here that novel metaphors are like analogies and elsewhere that similarity is like analogy (Gentner & Markman, 1995, 1997); to complete the pattern, we now suggest that metaphor is like similarity. The claim that metaphoric processing is like literal processing has a long history in the field (Gentner, 1983, 1989; Gibbs, 1984; Gibbs & Gerrig, 1989; Ortony, Vondruska, Foss, & Jones, 1985; Rumelhart, 1979).

We suggest that the processes of knowledge change discussed here apply to mundane literal similarity as well as to analogy and metaphor. Why then are the results so much more noticeable with analogy and metaphor? At least two factors enter into whether or not one concept is capable of changing another. One is the possibility of a good alignment. The other is the presence of some differences—in effect, some reason to change. Literal similarity has the advantage on the first factor; metaphor, on the second. In literal similarity, the concepts are already so close that the resulting adjustments to the representations are small. With metaphors, however, there are sufficient differences to permit substantial change.

The notion that differences are critical to metaphor comprehension may seem to fly in the face of common sense. According to Glucksberg and Keysar (1990), differences play little or no role in metaphor comprehension; if metaphors did focus on differences, their illuminatory effect would surely be overwhelmed by the vast number of differences. In the same vein, Ortony (1979a) suggested that both the difference weights in Tversky's (1977) contrast model equation for similarity might best be set to zero, to reflect the lack of relevance of differences in metaphor. Although this intuition is appealing, it leads to a conundrum: If differences between base and target are ignored, then how can the base transform the target? We suggest that *some* differences are important. Research by Markman and Gentner suggests that in carrying out comparisons people focus on *alignable differences*—differences connected to the common structure in the same way, such as the fact that cars have four wheels while motorcycles have only two. People discount *nonalignable differences*—differences unconnected to the common structure, or connected differently, such as the fact that motorcycles are popular with gangs and cars have steering wheels (Gentner & Markman, 1994, 1995; Markman & Gentner, 1993a). However, alignable differences are not only noticed, but are a prime source of new inferences. Bowdle and Gentner (1997) gave people pairs of stories varying in their alignability and relative systematicity and asked them to make inferences in either direction they chose. People strongly preferred to make inferences from the more systematic to the less systematic story, if the scenarios were alignable. (Nonalignable pairs yielded no directional preference, as predicted.) Furthermore, the inferences were typically based on alignable differences between the scenarios.

CONCLUSIONS

We have discussed the ways in which metaphors can change knowledge. Metaphors can highlight, project, re-represent, and, occasionally perhaps, restructure. These processes can lead to metaphorical categories and stored mappings. We have argued that these mechanisms are ways by which metaphors can lead to change of knowledge.

How have we fared with respect to Fodor's challenge that one can learn only what is already present? On the minus side, our proposals do not solve the problem of where the original predicates come from. Still, there are some kinds of knowledge change that we can account for:

- Candidate inference projection: A predicate P—previously expressed in the assertion $P(b_1, b_2)$—is mapped from base to target, so that the combination $P(t_1, t_2)$ is expressed for the first time.
- Re-representation: A predicate K is aligned with a predicate L, resulting in a re-representation that creates a slightly new predicate, M—for instance, *trail* $(b1, b2)$ and *chase* $(t1, t2)$ may result in *pursue* $(x1, x2)$.
- Schema abstraction: A system of assertions common to both base and target is abstracted and stored as a schema, resulting in a new predicate—sometimes with the invitation of a relational label: for example, learning the term *symmetric*.

We suggest that these changes are psychologically significant. They offer a means of attaining a conceptual system richer than the initial system. Candidate inference projection, although its effects are modest on each application, is a generative mechanism. For every new application of a given analog, new inferences can occur, resulting in an indefinite number of potential new combinations of predicates and arguments. Schema abstraction—abstracting and storing a higher-order pattern—can facilitate noticing the same pattern in the future. After sufficient in-domain experience or after learning a word for *symmetric*, Kotovsky and Gentner's 4-year-olds could see cross-dimensional similarity patterns they had previously missed. If this is not learning, it is a good facsimile. Eventually, these processes can reveal ideas more general and powerful than their original instantiations suggested. As Bertrand Russell put it, "It must have required many ages to discover that a brace of pheasants and a couple of days were both instances of the number two."

ACKNOWLEDGMENTS

This work was supported by National Science Foundation grant SBR-95-11757 and ONR grant N00014-92-J-1098 to the first author. We thank Arthur Markman, Ron Ferguson, Ken Forbus, Sarah Brem, Brian Bowdle, and the rest of the Similarity and Analogy group for discussions during the evolution of this work.

REFERENCES

Allbritton, D. W., McKoon, G., & Gerrig, R. (1995). Metaphor-based schemas and text representations: Making connections through conceptual metaphors. *Journal of Experimental Psychology: Learning, Memory, and Cognition, 21*, 1–14.

Andrade, E. N. Da C. (1964). *Rutherford and the nature of the atom.* New York: Doubleday.

Asch, S. E. (1955). On the use of metaphor in the description of persons. In H. Werner (Ed.), *On expressive language* (pp. 29–38). Worcester, MA: Clark University Press.

Biederman, I. (1987). Recognition-by-components: A theory of human image understanding. *Psychological Review, 94*, 115–147.

Black, M. (1962). *Models and metaphors.* Ithaca: Cornell University Press.

Black, M. (1979). More about metaphor. In A. Ortony (Ed.), *Metaphor and thought* (pp. 19–43). Cambridge: Cambridge University Press.

Blank, G. D. (1988). Metaphors in the lexicon. *Metaphor and Symbolic Activity, 3*, 21–36.

Blasko, D. G., & Connine, C. M. (1993). Effects of familiarity and aptness on metaphor processing. *Journal of Experimental Psychology: Learning, Memory, and Cognition, 12*, 205–308.

Boronat, C. B. (1990). *Effects of base shift and frequency in extended metaphor processing.* Unpublished master's thesis, University of Illinois at Urbana-Champaign.

Bowdle, B., & Gentner, D. (1995, November). *The career of metaphor.* Paper presented at the meeting of the Psychonomics Society, Los Angeles, CA.

Bowdle, B., & Gentner, D. (1997). Informativity and asymmetry in comparisons. *Cognitive Psychology, 34*(3), 244–286.

Bowdle, B., & Gentner, D. (1999a). Metaphor comprehension: From comparison to categorization. *Proceedings of the twenty-first annual conference of the Cognitive Science Society.* Mahwah, NJ: Lawrence Erlbaum Associates.

Bowdle, B., & Gentner, D. (1999b). *The career of metaphor.* Manuscript in preparation.

Boyd, R. (1979). Metaphor and theory change: What is "metaphor" a metaphor for? In A. Ortony (Ed.), *Metaphor and thought* (pp. 186–201). Cambridge, England: Cambridge University Press.

Brown, A. L., Kane, M. J., & Echols, C. H. (1986). Young children's mental models determine analogical transfer across problems with a common goal structure. *Cognitive Development, 1*, 103–121.

Burstein, M. H. (1986). Concept formation by incremental analogical reasoning and debugging. In R. S. Michalski, J. G. Carbonell, & T. M. Mitchell (Eds.), *Machine learning: An artificial intelligence approach* (Vol. 2, pp. 351–369). Los Altos, CA: Morgan Kaufmann.

Cacciari, C. (1993). The place of idioms in a literal and metaphorical world. In C. Cacciari & P. Tabossi (Eds.), *Idioms: Processing, structure, and interpretation* (pp. 27–55). Hillsdale, NJ: Lawrence Erlbaum Associates.

Cacciari, C., & Tabossi, P. (1988). The comprehension of idioms. *Journal of Memory and Language, 27*, 668–683.

Camac, M. K., & Glucksberg, S. (1984). Metaphors do not use associations between concepts, they are used to create them. *Journal of Psycholinguistic Research, 13*, 443–455.

Campbell, N. R. (1920). *Physics, the elements.* Cambridge, England: Cambridge University Press.

Carbonell, J. G. (1981). Invariance hierarchies in metaphor interpretation. *Proceedings of the third annual conference of the Cognitive Science Society* (pp. 292–295). Hillsdale, NJ: Lawrence Erlbaum Associates.

Carbonell, J. G. (1982). Metaphor: An inescapable phenomenon in natural language comprehension. In W. G. Lehnert & M. H. Ringle (Eds.), *Strategies for natural language processing* (pp. 415–435). Hillsdale, NJ: Lawrence Erlbaum Associates.

Chen, Z., & Daehler, M. W. (1989). Positive and negative transfer in analogical problem solving by 6-year-old children. *Cognitive Development, 4*, 327–344.

Clark, H., & Lucy, P. (1975). Understanding what is meant from what is said: A study in conversationally conveyed requests. *Journal of Verbal Learning and Verbal Behavior, 14*, 56–72.

Clement, C. A., & Gentner, D. (1991). Systematicity as a selection constraint in analogical mapping. *Cognitive Science, 15*, 89–132.

Clement, C. A., Mawby, R., & Giles, D. E. (1994). The effects of manifest relational similarity on analog retrieval. *Journal of Memory and Language, 33*, 396–420.

Cooke, N. J., & Bartha, M. C. (1992). An empirical investigation of psychological metaphor. *Metaphor and Symbolic Activity, 7*, 215–235.

Dreistadt, R. (1968). An analysis of the use of analogies and metaphors in science. *Journal of Psychology, 68*, 97–116.

Elio, R., & Anderson, J. R. (1981). The effect of category generalizations and instance similarity on schema abstraction. *Journal of Experimental Psychology: Human Learning and Memory, 7*, 397–417.

Eve, A. S. (1939). *Rutherford.* Cambridge, England: Cambridge University Press.

Falkenhainer, B. (1990). A unified approach to explanation and theory formation. In J. Shrager & P. Langley (Eds.), *Computational models of scientific discovery and theory formation* (pp. 157–196). Los Altos, CA: Morgan Kaufmann.

Falkenhainer, B., Forbus, K. D., & Gentner, D. (1986). The structure-mapping engine. *Proceedings of the fifth national conference on Artificial Intelligence* (pp. 272–277). Los Altos, CA: Morgan Kaufmann.

Falkenhainer, B., Forbus, K. D., & Gentner, D. (1989). The structure-mapping engine: An algorithm and examples. *Artificial Intelligence, 41*, 1–63.

Fauconnier, G. (1990). Domains and connections. *Cognitive Linguistics, 1*(1), 151–174.

Fodor, J. A. (1975). *The language of thought.* New York: Random House.

Forbus, K. D., Ferguson, R. W., & Gentner, D. (1994). Incremental structure-mapping. *Proceedings of the 16th annual conference of the Cognitive Science Society* (pp. 313–318). Hillsdale, NJ: Lawrence Erlbaum Associates.

Forbus, K. D., & Gentner, D. (1986). Learning physical domains: Toward a theoretical framework. In R. S. Michalski, J. G. Carbonell, & T. M. Mitchell (Eds.), *Machine learning: An artificial intelligence approach* (Vol. 2, pp. 311–348). Los Altos, CA: Morgan Kaufmann.

Forbus, K. D., & Gentner, D. (1989). Structural evaluation of analogies: What counts? *Proceedings of the 11th annual conference of the Cognitive Science Society* (pp. 341–348). Hillsdale, NJ: Lawrence Erlbaum Associates.

Forbus, K. D., Gentner, D., & Law, K. (1995). MAC/FAC: A model of similarity-based retrieval. *Cognitive Science, 19,* 141–205.

Forbus, K. D., & Oblinger, D. (1990). Making SME greedy and pragmatic. *Proceedings of the 12th annual conference of the Cognitive Science Society* (pp. 61–68). Hillsdale, NJ: Lawrence Erlbaum Associates.

Gentner, D. (1977). Children's performance on a spatial analogies task. *Child Development, 48,* 1034–1039.

Gentner, D. (1981). Some interesting differences between nouns and verbs. *Cognition and Brain Theory, 4*(2), 161–178.

Gentner, D. (1982). Are scientific analogies metaphors? In D. S. Miall (Ed.), *Metaphor: Problems and perspectives* (pp. 106–132). Brighton, England: Harvester.

Gentner, D. (1983). Structure-mapping: A theoretical framework for analogy. *Cognitive Science, 7,* 155–170.

Gentner, D. (1988). Metaphor as structure mapping: The relational shift. *Child Development, 59,* 47–59.

Gentner, D. (1989). The mechanisms of analogical learning. In S. Vosniadou & A. Ortony (Eds.), *Similarity and analogical reasoning.* New York: Cambridge University Press.

Gentner, D., & Boronat, C. B. (1992, May). *Metaphor as mapping.* Paper presented at the Workshop on Metaphor, Tel Aviv, Israel.

Gentner, D., & Boronat, C. (in preparation). *Novel metaphors are processed as generative domain-mappings.*

Gentner, D., & Bowdle, B. (1994). The coherence imbalance hypothesis: A functional approach to asymmetry in comparison. In *Proceedings of the 16th annual meeting of the Cognitive Science Society.* Hillsdale, NJ: Lawrence Erlbaum Associates.

Gentner, D., Bowdle, B., Wolff, P., & Boronat, C. (in press). Metaphor is like analogy. In D. Gentner, K. J. Holyoak, & B. Kokinov (Eds.), *Analogy: Theory and phenomena.* Cambridge, MA: MIT Press.

Gentner, D., Brem, S., Ferguson, R. W., Markman, A. B., Levidow, B. B., Wolff, P., & Forbus, K. D. (1997). Analogical reasoning and conceptual change: A case study of Johannes Kepler. *Journal of the Learning Sciences, 6*(1), 3–40.

Gentner, D., & Clement, C. A. (1988). Evidence for relational selectivity in the interpretation of analogy and metaphor. In G. H. Bower, (Ed.), *The psychology of learning and motivation, advances in research and theory* (Vol. 22, pp. 307–358). New York: Academic Press.

Gentner, D., Falkenhainer, B., & Skorstad, J. (1988). Viewing metaphor as analogy. In D. H. Helman (Ed.), *Analogical reasoning: Perspectives of artificial intelligence, cognitive science, and philosophy* (pp. 171–177). Dordrecht, The Netherlands: Kluwer.

Gentner, D., & Gentner, D. R. (1983). Flowing waters or teeming crowds: Mental models of electricity. In D. Gentner & A. L. Stevens (Eds.), *Mental models* (pp. 99–129). Hillsdale, NJ: Lawrence Erlbaum Associates. (Reprinted in *Cognitive functions: Classic readings in representation and reasoning,* M. J. Brosnan, Ed., Eltham, London: Greenwich University Press)

Gentner, D., & Grudin, J. (1985). The evolution of mental metaphors in psychology: A 90-year retrospective. *American Psychologist, 40*(2), 181–192.

Gentner, D., & Imai, M. (1992). Is the future always ahead? Evidence for system-mappings in understanding space-time metaphors. *Proceedings of the 14th annual meeting of the Cognitive Science Society* (pp. 510–515).

Gentner, D., Imai, M., & Boroditsky, L. (1999). *As time goes by: Evidence for two systems in processing space–time metaphors.* Manuscript submitted for publication.

Gentner, D., & Jeziorski, M. (1993). The shift from metaphor to analogy in western science. In A. Ortony (Ed.), *Metaphor and thought* (2nd ed., pp. 447–480). Cambridge, England: Cambridge University Press.

Gentner, D., & Markman. A. B. (1993). Analogy—Watershed or Waterloo? Structural alignment and the development of connectionist models of cognition. In S. J. Hanson, J. D. Cowan, & C. L. Giles (Eds.), *Advances in neural information processing systems* (Vol. 5, pp. 855–862). San Mateo, CA: Morgan Kauffman.

Gentner, D., & Markman, A. B. (1994). Structural alignment in comparison: No difference without similarity. *Psychological Science, 5(3)*, 152–158.

Gentner, D., & Markman, A. B. (1995). Similarity is like analogy: Structural alignment in comparison. In C. Cacciari (Ed.), *Similarity in language, thought and perception* (pp. 111–147). Brussels, Belgium: BREPOLS.

Gentner, D., & Markman, A. B. (1997, January). Structure mapping in analogy and similarity. *American Psychologist, 52*, 45–56.

Gentner, D., & Medina, J. (1998). Similarity and the development of rules. *Cognition, 65*, 263–297.

Gentner, D., & Rattermann, M. J. (1991). Language and the career of similarity. In S. A. Gelman & J. P. Byrnes, (Eds.), *Perspectives on language and thought interrelations in development* (pp. 225–277). Cambridge, England: Cambridge University Press.

Gentner, D., Rattermann, M. J., & Forbus, K. D. (1993). The roles of similarity in transfer: Separating retrievability and inferential soundness. *Cognitive Psychology, 25*, 524–575.

Gentner, D., Rattermann, M. J., Markman, A. B., & Kotovsky, L. (1995). Two forces in the development of relational similarity. In T. J. Simon & G. S. Halford (Eds.), *Developing cognitive competence: New approaches to process modeling* (pp. 263–313). Hillsdale, NJ: Lawrence Erlbaum Associates.

Gentner, D., & Stevens, A. L. (Eds.). (1983). *Mental models.* Hillsdale, NJ: Lawrence Erlbaum Associates.

Gentner, D., & Toupin, C. (1986). Systematicity and surface similarity in the development of analogy. *Cognitive Science, 10*, 277–300.

Gentner, D., & Wolff, P. (1997). Alignment in the processing of metaphor. *Journal of Memory and Language, 37*, 331–355.

Gibbs, R. W., Jr. (1979). Contextual effects in understanding indirect requests. *Discourse Processes, 2*, 149–156.

Gibbs, R. W., Jr. (1980). Spilling the beans on understanding and memory for idioms in conversations. *Memory and Cognition, 8*, 449–456.

Gibbs, R. W., Jr. (1984). Literal meaning and psychological theory. *Cognitive Science, 8*, 275–304.

Gibbs, R. W., Jr. (1990). Psycholinguistic studies on the conceptual biases of idiomaticity. *Cognitive Linguistics, 1*, 417–451.

Gibbs, R. W., Jr. (1992). Categorization and metaphor understanding. *Psychological Review, 99(3)*, 572–577.

Gibbs, R. W., Jr. (1994). *Poetics of mind: Figurative thought: Language and understanding.* Cambridge: Cambridge University Press.

Gibbs, R. W., Jr., & Gerrig, R. J. (1989). How context makes metaphor comprehension seem "special." *Metaphor and Symbolic Activity, 4*, 145–158.

Gick, M., & Holyoak, K. J. (1980). Analogical problem solving. *Cognitive Psychology, 12*, 306–355.

Gick, M., & Holyoak, K. J. (1983). Schema induction and analogical transfer. *Cognitive Psychology, 15,* 1–38.

Glucksberg, S., Brown, M., & McGlone, M. S. (1993). Conceptual analogies are not automatically accessed during idiom comprehension. *Memory and Cognition, 21,* 711–719.

Glucksberg, S., Gildea, P., & Bookin, H. (1982). On understanding non-literal speech: Can people ignore metaphors? *Journal of Verbal Learning and Verbal Behavior, 1,* 85–96.

Glucksberg, S., & Keysar, B. (1990). Understanding metaphorical comparisons: Beyond similarity. *Psychological Review, 97,* 3–18.

Glucksberg, S., & Keysar, B. (1993). How metaphors work. In A. Ortony (Ed.), *Metaphor and thought* (2nd ed., pp. 401–424). New York: Cambridge University Press.

Glucksberg, S., McGlone, M. S., & Manfredi, D. (1997). Property attribution in metaphor comprehension. *Journal of Memory and Language, 36*(1), 50–67.

Goldstone, R. L. (1994). Similarity, interactive activation, and mapping. *Journal of Experimental Psychology: Learning, Memory, and Cognition, 20*(1), 3–28.

Goldstone, R. L., Gentner, D., & Medin, D. L. (1989). Relations relating relations. *Proceedings of the 11th annual conference of the Cognitive Science Society* (pp. 131–138). Hillsdale, NJ: Lawrence Erlbaum Associates.

Goldstone, R. L., & Medin, D. L. (1994). Time course of comparison. *Journal of Experimental Psychology: Learning, Memory, and Cognition, 20*(1), 29–50.

Goldstone, R. L., Medin, D. L., & Gentner, D. (1991). Relational similarity and the nonindependence of features in similarity judgments. *Cognitive Psychology, 23,* 222–262.

Goodman, N. (1972). Seven strictures on similarity. In N. Goodman (Ed.), *Problems and projects* (pp. 437–447). New York: Bobbs-Merrill. (Reprinted from *Experience and theory,* L. Foster & J. W. Swanson, Eds., 1970, University of Massachusetts Press)

Graesser, A., & Hopkinson, P. (1987). Differences in interconcept organization between nouns and verbs. *Journal of Memory and Language, 26,* 242–253.

Greenberg, J. H. (1966). *Language universals.* The Hague, The Netherlands: Mouton.

Hayes-Roth, F., & McDermott, J. (1978). An interference matching technique for inducing abstractions. *Communications of the ACM, 21*(5), 401–411.

Hesse, M. B. (1966). *Models and analogies in science.* Notre Dame, IN: University of Notre Dame Press.

Hoffman, R. R., & Kemper, S. (1987). What could reaction-time studies be telling us about metaphor comprehension? *Metaphor and Symbolic Activity, 2,* 149–186.

Holyoak, K. J. (1985). The pragmatics of analogical transfer. In G. H. Bower (Ed.), *The psychology of learning and motivation: Advances in research and theory* (Vol. 19, pp. 59–87). New York: Academic Press.

Holyoak, K. J., & Koh, K. (1987). Surface and structural similarity in analogical transfer. *Memory & Cognition, 15,* 332–340.

Holyoak, K. J., & Thagard, P. (1989). Analogical mapping by constraint satisfaction. *Cognitive Science, 13,* 295–355.

Hummel, J. E., & Holyoak, K. J. (1997). Distributed representations of structure: A theory of analogical access and mapping. *Psychological Review, 104*(3), 427–466.

Huttenlocher, J., & Lui, F. (1979). The semantic organization of some simple nouns and verbs. *Journal of Verbal Learning and Verbal Behavior, 18,* 141–162.

Indurkhya, B. (1991). Models in metaphor. *Metaphor and Symbolic Activity, 6,* 1–27.

Johnson-Laird, P. N. (1983). *Mental models: Towards a cognitive science of language, inference, and consciousness.* Cambridge, MA: Harvard University Press.

Karmiloff-Smith, A. (1991). *Beyond modularity: A developmental perspective on cognitive science.* Cambridge, MA: The MIT Press.

Keane, M. T. (1988). Analogical mechanisms. *Artificial Intelligence Review, 2,* 229–250.

Keane, M. T., & Brayshaw, M. (1988). The incremental analogical machine: A computational model of analogy. In D. Sleeman (Ed.), *Third European Working Session on Machine Learning* (pp. 53–62). San Mateo, CA: Kaufmann.

Kelly, M. H., & Keil, F. C. (1987). Metaphor comprehension and knowledge of semantic domains. *Metaphor and Symbolic Activity, 2,* 35–51.

Kennedy, J. M. (1990). Metaphor—Its intellectual basis. *Metaphor and Symbolic Activity, 5,* 115–123.

Keysar, B. (1989). On the functional equivalence of literal and metaphorical interpretations in discourse. *Journal of Memory and Language, 28,* 375–385.

Keysar, B., & Bly, B. (1995). Intuitions of the transparency of idioms: Can one keep a secret by spilling the beans? *Journal of Memory and Language, 34*(1), 89–109.

Kittay, E. F., & Lehrer, A. (1981). Semantic fields and the structure of metaphor. *Studies in Language, 5,* 31–63.

Kotovsky, L., & Gentner, D. (1996). Comparison and categorization in the development of relational similarity. *Child Development, 67,* 2797–2822.

Kuhn, T. S. (1979). Metaphor in science. In A. Ortony (Ed.), *Metaphor and thought* (pp. 186–201). Cambridge, England: Cambridge University Press.

Lakoff, G. (1988). Conventional metaphor as the basis for analogical reasoning. In D. H. Helman (Ed.), *Analogical reasoning: Perspectives of artificial intelligence.* Boston: D. Reidel.

Lakoff, G. (1990). The invariance hypothesis: Is abstract reason based on image-schemas? *Cognitive Linguistics, 1*(1), 39–74.

Lakoff, G., & Johnson, M. (1980). *Metaphors we live by.* Chicago: University of Chicago Press.

Lakoff, G., & Turner, M. (1989). *More than cool reason: A field guide to poetic metaphor.* Chicago: University of Chicago Press.

Lassaline, M. E., & Murphy, G. L. (1996). Induction and category coherence. *Psychonomic Bulletin and Review, 3*(1), 95–99.

Lehrer, A., (1990). Polysemy, conventionality, and the structure of the lexicon. *Cognitive Linguistics, 1–2,* 207–246.

Levi, J. N. (1978). *The syntax and semantics of complex nominals.* New York: Academic Press.

Lockhead, G. R., & King, M. C. (1977). Classifying integral stimuli. *Journal of Experimental Psychology: Human Perception and Performance, 3*(3) 436–443.

Markman, A. B. (1999). *Knowledge representation.* Mahwah, NJ: Lawrence Erlbaum Associates.

Markman, A. B., & Gentner, D. (1993a). Splitting the differences: A structural alignment view of similarity. *Journal of Memory and Language, 32,* 517–535.

Markman, A. B., & Gentner, D. (1993b). Structural alignment during similarity comparisons. *Cognitive Psychology, 25,* 431–467.

Markman, A. B., & Gentner, D. (1996). Commonalities and differences in similarity comparisons. *Memory & Cognition, 24*(2), 235–249.

Markman, A. B., & Gentner, D. (in press). Structure-mapping in analogy and similarity: The importance of being connected. *American Journal of Psychology.*

McGlone, M. S., & Harding, J. (1998). Back (or forward?) to the future: The role of perspective in temporal language comprehension. *Journal of Experimental Psychology: Learning, Memory, and Cognition, 24*(5), 1211–1223.

Medin, D. L., Goldstone, R. L., & Gentner, D. (1990). Similarity involving attributes and relations: Judgments of similarity and difference are not inverses. *Psychological Science, 1,* 64–69.

Medin, D. L., Goldstone, R. L., & Gentner, D. (1993). Respects for similarity. *Psychological Review, 100*(2), 254–278.

Medin, D. L., & Ross, B. H. (1989). The specific character of abstract thought: Categorization, problem-solving, and induction. In R. J. Sternberg (Ed.), *Advances in the psychology of human intelligence* (Vol. 5, pp. 189–223). Hillsdale, NJ: Lawrence Erlbaum Associates.

Miller, G. A. (1979). Images and models, similes and metaphors. In A. Ortony (Ed.), *Metaphor and thought* (pp. 202–250). Cambridge, England: Cambridge University Press.

Miller, G. A. (1993). Images and models, similes and metaphors. In A. Ortony (Ed.), *Metaphor and thought* (2nd ed., pp. 357–400). Cambridge, England: Cambridge University Press.

Murphy, G. L. (1996). On metaphoric representation. *Cognition, 60*(2), 173–204.

Murphy, G. L., & Medin, D. L. (1985). The role of theories in conceptual coherence. *Psychological Review, 92,* 289–316.

Nagy, W. (1974). *Figurative patterns and the redundancy in lexicon.* Unpublished doctoral dissertation, University of California, San Diego.

Nayak, N. P., & Gibbs, R. W. (1990). Conceptual knowledge in the interpretation of idioms. *Journal of Experimental Psychology, 119*(3), 315–330.

Nersessian, N. J. (1992). How do scientists think? Capturing the dynamics of conceptual change in science. In R. N. Giere, & H. Feigl (Eds.), *Minnesota studies in the philosophy of science* (pp. 3–44). Minneapolis: University of Minnesota Press.

Norman, D. A., Rumelhart, D. E., & the LNR Research Group. (1975). *Explorations in cognition.* San Francisco: Freeman.

Oppenheimer, R. (1956) . Analogy in science. *American Psychologist, 11,* 127–135.

Ortony, A. (1979a). Beyond literal similarity. *Psychological Review, 86,* 161–180.

Ortony, A. (1979b). The role of similarity in similes and metaphors. In A. Ortony (Ed.), *Metaphor and thought* (pp. 1–16). Cambridge, England: Cambridge University Press.

Ortony, A., Vondruska, R. J., Foss, M. A., & Jones, L. E. (1985). Salience, similes, and the asymmetry of similarity. *Journal of Memory and Language, 24,* 569–594.

Osgood, C. E. (1949). The similarity paradox in human learning: A resolution. *Psychological Review, 56,* 132–143.

Palmer, S. E. (1977). Hierarchical structure in perceptual representation. *Cognitive Psychology, 9,* 441–474.

Palmer, S. E. (1978). Fundamental aspects of cognitive representation. In E. Rosch & B. B. Lloyd (Eds.), *Cognition and categorization* (pp. 259–303). Hillsdale, NJ: Lawrence Erlbaum Associates.

Pomerantz, J. R., Sager, L. C., & Stoever, R. J. (1977). Perception of wholes and their component parts: Some configural superiority effects. *Journal of Experimental Psychology: Human Perception and Performance, 3,* 422–435.

Pylyshyn, Z. W. (1979). Metaphorical imprecision and the "top-down" research strategy. In A. Ortony (Ed.), *Metaphor and thought* (pp. 186–201). Cambridge, England: Cambridge University Press.

Pylyshyn, Z. (1989). The role of location indexes in spatial perception: A sketch of the FINST spatial-index model. *Cognition, 32*(1), 65–97.

Rattermann, M. J., Gentner, D., & DeLoache, J. (1989). *Effects of competing surface similarity on children's performance in an analogical task.* Poster presented at the biennial meeting of the Society for Research in Child Development, Kansas City, MO.

Rattermann, M. J., Gentner, D., & DeLoache, J. (1999). *Effects of relational and object similarity on children's performance in a mapping task.* Manuscript in preparation.

Rips, L. (1989). Similarity, typicality, and categorization. In S. Vosniadou, & A. Ortony (Eds.), *Similarity and analogical reasoning* (pp. 21–59). New York: Cambridge University Press.

Roediger, H. L., III. (1980). Memory metaphors in cognitive psychology. *Memory & Cognition, 8,* 231–246.

Ross, B. H. (1987). This is like that: The use of earlier problems and the separation of similarity effects. *Journal of Experimental Psychology: Learning, Memory, and Cognition, 13*(4) 629–639.

Ross, B. H. (1989). Remindings in learning and instruction. In S. Vosniadou & A. Ortony (Eds.), *Similarity and analogical reasoning* (pp. 438–469). New York: Cambridge University Press.

Rumelhart, D. (1979). Some problems with the notion of literal meanings. In A. Ortony (Ed.), *Metaphor and thought* (pp. 186–201). Cambridge, England: Cambridge University Press.

Rumelhart, D. E., & Abrahamson, A. A. (1973). A model for analogical reasoning. *Cognitive Psychology, 5,* 1–28.

Rumelhart, D. E., & Ortony, A. (1977). Representation of knowledge in memory. In R. C. Anderson, R. J. Spiro, & W. E. Montague (Eds.), *Schooling and the acquisition of knowledge.* Hillsdale, NJ: Lawrence Erlbaum Associates.

Schank, R. C., & Abelson, R. (1977). *Scripts, plans, goals, and understanding: An inquiry into human knowledge structures.* Hillsdale, NJ: Lawrence Erlbaum Associates.

Schön, D. A. (1979). Generative metaphor: A perspective on problem-setting in social policy. In A. Ortony (Ed.), *Metaphor and thought* (pp. 186–201). Cambridge, England: Cambridge University Press.

Shen, Y. (1992). Metaphors and categories. *Poetics Today, 13,* 771–794.

Smith, L. B., & Sera, M. D. (1992). A developmental analysis of the polar structure of dimensions. *Cognitive Psychology, 24,* 99–142.

Spellman, B. A., & Holyoak, K. J. (1996). Pragmatics in analogical mapping. *Cognitive Psychology, 31,* 307–346.

Spiro, R. J., Feltovich, P. J., Coulson, R. L., & Anderson, D. K. (1989). Multiple analogies for complex concepts: Antidotes for analogy-induced misconception in advanced knowledge acquisition. In S. Vosniadou & A. Ortony (Eds.), *Similarity and analogical reasoning* (pp. 498–531). New York: Cambridge University Press.

Steen, G. J. (1991). The empirical study of literary reading: Methods of data collection. *Poetics Today, 13.*

Swinney, D., & Cutler, A. (1979). The access and processing of idiomatic expressions. *Journal of Verbal Learning and Verbal Behavior, 18,* 523–534.

Thagard, P., & Holyoak, K. (1985). Discovering the wave theory of sound: Inductive inference in the context of problem solving. *Proceedings of the ninth international joint conference on Artificial Intelligence* (pp. 610–612). Los Altos, CA: Morgan Kaufmann.

Tourangeau, R., & Rips, L. (1991). Interpreting and evaluating metaphors. *Journal of Memory and Language, 30,* 452–472.

Tourangeau, R., & Sternberg, R. J. (1981). Aptness in metaphor. *Cognitive Psychology, 13,* 27–55.

Tourangeau, R., & Sternberg, R. J. (1982). Understanding and appreciating metaphors. *Cognition, 11,* 203–244.

Turner, M. (1987). *Death is the mother of beauty: Mind, metaphor, and criticism.* Chicago: University of Chicago Press.

Turner, M. (1988). Categories and analogies. In D. H. Helman (Ed.), *Analogical reasoning: Perspectives of artificial intelligence, cognitive science, and philosophy* (pp. 3–24). Dordrecht, The Netherlands: Kluwer.

Tversky, A. (1977). Features of similarity. *Psychological Review, 84,* 327–352.

Verbrugge, R. R., & McCarrell, N. S. (1977). *Metaphoric comprehension: Studies in reminding and resembling.*

Vosniadou, S., Ortony, A., Reynolds, R. E., & Wilson, P. T. (1984). Sources of difficulty in the young child's understanding of metaphorical language. *Child Development, 55,* 1588–1606.

Way, E. C. (1991). *Knowledge representation and metaphor.* Dordrecht, The Netherlands: Kluwer.

Wheelwright, P. (1962). *Metaphor and reality,* Bloomington: Indiana University Press.

Wilson, D. (1983). *Rutherford: Simple genius.* Cambridge, MA: MIT Press.

Winner, E. (1988). *The point of words: Children's understanding of metaphor and irony.* Cambridge, MA: Harvard University Press.

Winston, P. H. (1980). Learning and reasoning by analogy. *Communications of the ACM, 23*(12), 689–703.

Wiser, M. (1986). *Learning about heat and temperature: A context-based historically inspired approach to a novice-expert shift*. Paper presented at the National Science Foundation Conference on the Psychology of Physics Problem Solving: Theory and Practice, New York.

Wisniewski, E. J. (1996). Construal and similarity in conceptual combination. *Journal of Memory and Language, 35,* 434–453.

Wisniewski, E. J., & Gentner, D. (1991). On the combinatorial semantics of noun pairs: Minor and major adjustments to meaning. In G. B. Simpson (Ed.), *Understanding word and sentence* (pp. 241–284). Amsterdam: Elsevier.

Wolff, P., & Gentner, D. (1992). The time course of metaphor comprehension. *Proceedings of the 14th annual conference of the Cognitive Science Society* (pp. 504–509). Bloomington.

Wolff, P., & Gentner, D. (1999). From symmetric to asymmetric processing: Two stages in the comprehension of metaphors.

Wolff, P., & Gentner, D. (in press). Evidence for role-neutral initial processing of metaphors. *Journal of Experimental Psychology: Learning, Memory and Cognition.*

Yukawa, H. (1982). *Tabibito* (L. Brown & R. Yoshida, Trans.). Singapore: National Printers.

12

Representation and the Construction of Preferences

Arthur B. Markman
University of Texas

Shi Zhang
University of California, Los Angeles

C. Page Moreau
Southern Methodist University

Research at the intersection of psychology, economics, and marketing has focused on how people make choices. This problem is important to psychologists, because decision making is a fundamental part of our cognitive existence, and the decisions we make influence the direction of our lives. Economists have a stake in the psychology of decision making, because many economic models make assumptions about the inherent rationality of decision makers. Finally, research in marketing focuses on practical aspects of the decision-making process to best understand how to present products to consumers and to influence their preferences.

Much research in this area has been influenced by subjective expected utility models and variations on this theme. These models suggest that people faced with a set of options can evaluate these options by breaking them down into their components, determining the goodness (or utility) of the components, and then combining the goodness of different components by weighting them as a function of their importance. Models may permit subtle (although important) modifications of this general process by varying the shape of the function that determines the importance of options or by allowing options to be compared with some reference point rather than requiring that some absolute judgment about preference be made (Coombs & Avrunin, 1988; Kahneman & Tversky, 1979). However, these models still retain the basic notion that preference is some function of goodness and importance (see Goldstein & Weber, 1995).

Although significant research has questioned whether people's choices are governed by the bonds of utility models, this work has typically assumed that standard economic models provide a good computational-level description of how choices ought to be carried out. This work has suggested that people often pursue alternative choice strategies that combine importance and goodness information in less complete ways that respect the limitations of human cognitive capacity at the risk of leading to suboptimal choices (Kahneman & Tversky, 1984; Payne, Bettman, & Johnson, 1993; Tversky & Kahneman, 1986).

Finally, there is research that has focused on the construction of preferences (see also Mellars & Cooke, 1996; Slovic, 1995). This work suggests that preferences are dynamic. According to this view, components of choice options may not always have an inherent level of importance or a predefined degree of goodness. Instead, people make use of information such as goals, reasons, and motivational states to build their preferences. In this chapter, we focus on dynamic aspects of preferences. Consistent with this view, we suggest that the importance of features of choice options is determined by the dynamics of the way people learn about options as well as by the information that is activated during the choice situation. We further suggest that the goodness of components of options is strongly influenced by the decision maker's active goals.

Although we believe that preferences evolve dynamically and that they are often constructed at the time of choice, we do not believe that these dynamics obviate the need to think about how choice options, background knowledge, and goals are represented. Instead, we think that representation is critical for understanding the dynamics of preferences. In this chapter, we focus primarily on evidence that choice is dynamic. We discuss this evidence in the context of cognitive models that are explicit about the importance of representation in cognitive processing.

We focus primarily on evidence for dyamics in choice, because we believe that the discussion about the need for representation in cognitive science has focused primarily on conceptual discussions of what representations can and cannot do. The purpose of this chapter is to provide data that bear on the dynamics of choice, which we believe require sophisticated representations and processes to explain. The data are drawn largely from studies of consumer behavior. In consumer behavior, there are a number of established methods that bring to light key aspects of the dynamics of choice. This evidence needs to be explained by any theory of decision making. Thus, it serves as a challenge to those who want to eliminate discussions of representation from models of cognitive processing. Consumer behavior is also a good domain for research, because the work in this area goes beyond the materials frequently used in psychological studies of choice like gambles and objects described by features on a small number of obvious dimensions. Furthermore, consumer choices are an important part of daily life, so that participants in studies of consumer choice are able to bring to bear frequently used strategies in a familiar setting.

THE CONSTRUCTION OF PREFERENCE

As we embark on a discussion of the dynamics of preference, it is important to point out the boundaries of these dynamics. Research on dynamics is often motivated by the inherent variability of the details of cognitive processing. For example, Thelen and Smith (1994; Thelen, 1995) suggested that cognitive science should dispense with representation, because models based on representation are often too rigid to account for the fine details of processing. In particular, Thelen (1995) presented compelling examples of individual differences in motor development not well explained by rule-based models of motor processing that assume rigid representational structure.

The primary focus of this chapter is the dynamics of choice. Nonetheless, a considerable number of consumer choices are not constructive. Instead, they consist of repeating a previous course of action. For example, consumer choice studies have analyzed "scanner data." Scanner data studies involve tracking the shopping habits of consumers for a set of frequently purchased package goods by using the data from universal product code (UPC) scanners at the supermarket. Mathematical models have shown that consumer brand choices exhibit remarkable stability across purchase occasions (e.g. Guadagni & Little 1983; Keane 1977). Intuitively, this brand loyalty makes sense. On a trip to the supermarket, it is easier to pick the brand of tomato sauce chosen in the past than to evaluate all the brands for their quality and price.

It is important not to lose sight of the importance of brand loyalty in consumer choice. When people are faced with a decision, the most common course of action is simply to retrieve a previous choice from memory and to use it. This retrieval suggests that an enduring representation of past choices in memory can be used in a new situation. Thus, any model of choice must explain not only how choices are constructed dynamically (as we discuss in the rest of this chapter), but also how choices are made based on past experience. Furthermore, choice models must ultimately distinguish between cases where people use the results of previous choices and cases where they construct a new preference. The importance of stored evaluations is an important component of other research as well, such as work suggesting that stereotypes and other evaluative judgments are activated and used automatically (Bargh, 1997). The relative contribution of automatic and constructive evaluation ultimately requires an understanding of the ways that representation is used in choice situations. For now, however, we leave this issue in favor of an examination of the dynamics of preference construction.

STAGES OF CHOICE

If we talk about the dynamic aspects of a choice, it is helpful to begin with a description of the choice situation. Such a definition may seem trivial. Most psychological studies present participants with a set of options and ask them to select the one they prefer. Thus, a decision seems to involve selecting an item from among a set of options. There are two problems with this view. First, it is not clear that there must be an explicit set of options available at the beginning of a choice setting. Although it is handy for the purposes of experimental control to present someone with a set of options, the set of options can itself be constructed during choice. Second, this definition neglects the importance of the decision maker's goals in making a choice. Why must the decision maker make a choice in the first place? In the case of consumer choice, there must be some goal that is not currently satisfied for the consumer that the choice can satisfy. When buying tomato sauce, for example, the choice may be made in service of the broader goal of making spaghetti and meatballs. In other choices, the overall goal may be more diffuse, as when a 45-year-old man buys a red convertible to alleviate midlife angst. Thus, the choice situation is fundamentally connected to the satisfaction of some set of goals. Models of choice must provide information about how the goals relevant to a choice are determined and how they influence preference.

We are hardly the first to recognize the importance of goals in choice. Lewin (1935) conceptualized goals as involving fields of force that either attracted (approach goals) or repelled (avoidance goals). On his view, people's actions exist in a state of flux that is influenced by these forces. The importance of approach and avoidance motivations in choice situations has been incorporated into more recent approaches to choice such as Busemeyer and Townshend's (1993; Townshend & Busemeyer, 1995) decision field theory and Crowe and Higgins' (1997) work on strategy choice. However, whereas Lewin viewed behavior as driven by goals, more recent work has not defined the choice situation by the need to satisfy a goal, but has rather assumed that goals play some role in determining how the choice is carried out.

In the context of decision making, goals can be conceptualized as cognitive structures that describe states of the world that the individual wants to achieve. In keeping with previous work, these goals can be desired states of the world to be attained (i.e., approach goals) or undesired states of the world to be avoided (i.e., avoidance goals). It is important to recognize that goals in this setting are representational structures. Simple drives, like attaining food, are relatively direct in their action. On the basis of physiological signals, an individual may seek food. There is still important additional information that must be used, even in this case, as the individual must know what kinds of things are considered to be food. For many goals, however, the relation between the goal and the states of the world is more indirect. People must be able to translate their goals into specific aspects of a choice setting. Wanting a safe car is an abstract description that requires knowing how properties like the weight and speed of the car influence its safety. The relation between the goals of a decision maker and the specific attributes of the choice setting is one for which representations seem critical for understanding.

Thus, we view the choice situation as one in which someone has an unsatisfied goal and for which some action is required to satisfy it. The choice involves determining the course of action that satisfies the goal. Given this definition, choices involve determining a set of options that are relevant and establishing preferences for them. In the next section we review some previous research on the construction of a choice set. Then, we discuss factors that influence the importance of features of the options given a set of options. Finally, we discuss how the goodness of particular aspects of options can be determined. Our goal in this discussion is to describe important phenomena in the construction of preference. Although we do not yet have a complete model of how preference is constructed, we believe that the evidence described here demonstrates the importance of representation in choice.

CONSTRUCTING THE CHOICE SET

Research on consumer behavior has acknowledged that the consumer may have a goal to satisfy when making a choice, but not have a specific set of options in mind to satisfy that goal. Thus, the consumer's first task when faced with a new choice is to construct the set of options. This set of options is typically called the *consideration set* (Lilien, Kotler, & Moorthy, 1992; Roberts & Lattin, 1997). Understanding the way consideration sets are formed is of particular practical significance for marketers, because the objects in the consideration set determine what is ultimately selected. From a theoretical standpoint, consideration sets are important, because they emphasize that it is not straightforward to generalize the results of studies that assume people select from among a predetermined set of options to more general cases.

Many studies have suggested that consideration sets include between two and eight different brands (Hauser & Wernerfelt, 1989). The size of the particular set established by a consumer reflects a trade-off between the cognitive effort required to evaluate the option and the benefit of having an additional option in the set. On this view, the more difficult it is to evaluate each option, the smaller the size of the consideration set. When the brands in a set differ widely on their attributes and on the ease of determining the properties of the options, then the consideration set is small. In contrast, when the brands share many attributes and when the information is easy to extract, then the consideration set can be larger, because less effort is required to extend the set of items being considered (Bettman, Johnson, & Payne, 1991). The degree of risk associated with the product (including psychological and financial risk as well as the possibility that the product will not satisfy the consumer's goals) also influences the size of the consideration set. Consideration sets tend to get larger as the risk associated with the choice grows. Thus, for low-risk choices (like selecting a tomato sauce for a family dinner) the size of the consideration set may be very small indeed (perhaps including only the brand purchased last).

Another factor that influences the formation of consideration sets is memory. In laboratory studies, most choices are *stimulus based*. That is, the set of options is presented and is available throughout the choice. In contrast, many consumer choices are *memory based*. In a memory-based choice, consumers must first recall the items from memory, and only then can they make a choice. Nedungadi (1990) demonstrated this point by showing that priming procedures that increase the recall of brands can influence the number of brands considered during a choice. Thus, factors that influence the accessibility of brands in memory increase their likelihood of being selected by ensuring that they are entered into consumers' consideration set.

The composition of the consideration set can have two primary influences on choice. The most straightforward influence is that options in the consideration set are the ones likely to be selected, as a consumer is not likely to choose a brand he or she is not considering. However, a second more subtle influence of the composition of the consideration set is that the presence of one item can influence the evaluation of another. One prominent example of this phenomenon is the *attraction effect* (Huber, Payne, & Puto, 1982; Huber & Puto, 1983; Simonson, 1989). As an illustration of the attraction effect, imagine two brands of beer. Brand A is great tasting, but is expensive. Brand B does not taste as good as Brand A, but is cheaper. Imagine further that given the choice between brands A and B, the consumer is indifferent. In the case of the attraction effect, the consideration set also includes a third brand (Brand C) that is more expensive than Brand A and tastes slightly worse than Brand A, although it tastes better than Brand B. Brand C is asymmetrically dominated by Brand A, because it is worse than Brand A on both dimensions, although the choice between Brands B and C still involves some trade-offs. Given a consideration set like this, people select Brand A at a high rate (even though they were indifferent between Brands A and B in a consideration set including only those two brands). This effect is called the attraction effect, because the presence of the dominated alternative attracts market share to the dominating alternative. As this effect demonstrates, the relative preference of a pair of brands is influenced by the composition of the consideration set.

In sum, the set of options is not always given at the start of a choice. Instead, people must determine which objects are relevant to a decision. The formation of consideration sets is influenced both by the importance of the decision and by the difficulty of extracting information about the options. The formation of consideration sets is important, however, both because it determines the options that can possibly be selected and also because it can affect the relative preference for objects in the consideration set.

DETERMINING THE IMPORTANCE OF ATTRIBUTE INFORMATION

Given a set of choice options, the decision maker must find some way to evaluate the members of that set to determine which is preferred. This is an important part of the process that is examined by most research on decision making, as the participants in studies are typically given a set of choice options and are asked to select the one they prefer. A central component of this aspect of choice is the process that determines what information about the options is important for the decision. Two aspects of this process that we describe here are the comparability of the choice options and the relation between the choice options and active goals.

Comparability and Importance

When given a set of options (particularly a small set), it is natural to compare the options to one another. The differences between options are particularly important, because a choice cannot be based on the aspects that a set of options have in common. Thus, if the comparison process promotes particular kinds of differences, these differences are likely to be important in choice.

Research on the way people make comparisons assumes that items being compared are represented by using structured relational representations and that comparison involves the alignment of pairs of these representations (Gentner & Markman, 1994, 1995, 1997; Goldstone, 1994; Holyoak & Thagard, 1989; Hummel & Holyoak, 1997; Markman & Gentner, 1993, 1996; Medin, Goldstone, & Gentner, 1993, chap. 11, this volume). Although a complete review of the alignment process is beyond the scope of this chapter, we must describe a few basic principles. First, the structural alignment view of comparison assumes that mental representations consist of objects, attributes that describe objects, and relations that relate two or more objects, attributes, or other relations. Pairs of relational representations are compared by placing identical relations and attributes in correspondence and also by placing the arguments of matching relations (i.e., the things related) into correspondence. For example, a person's representation for one brand of electronic organizer may have the relation *input device (Brand A, keyboard)*, and the representation of Brand B may have the relation *input device (Brand B, computer connection)*. Placing these two relations in correspondence leads Brand A to be matched to Brand B and keyboard to be matched to computer connection.

This analysis of comparison suggests that the output of a comparison consists of correspondences between the representations of the objects. Some of the elements placed in correspondence are identical (e.g., *input device(X,Y)*). These identical correspondences are commonalities of the pair. Other corresponding pieces of information are not identical (e.g., *keyboard* matching to *computer connection*). These nonidentical correspondences are called *alignable differences*, because they are seen as similar as a result of the way the representations were aligned. Not all differences between a pair are alignable differences. It is possible that one item has properties that do not correspond to any aspect of the other item. These differences are called *nonalignable differences*. For example, one electronic organizer may come with a leather carrying case, while the other does not.

In the domain of similarity, there is ample evidence that alignable differences are a focal output of comparison and nonalignable differences are not. Given pairs of nouns or verbs, people tend to list more alignable differences than nonalignable differences (Markman & Gentner, 1993; Markman & Wisniewski, 1997; Pavlicic & Markman, 1997). Alignable differences tend to be listed more fluently than nonalignable differences when people are asked to list only a single difference of a pair (Gentner & Markman, 1994). When people rate the similarity of pairs of pictures, changes in objects that are alignable differences have a greater influence on rated similarity than do changes in objects that are nonalignable differences (Markman & Gentner, 1996). Finally, objects that are alignable differences of a pair are better retrieval cues for the original item than are objects that are nonalignable differences (Markman & Gentner, 1997). Taken together, these data suggest that the comparison process focuses people selectively on alignable differences, particularly in complex comparisons, where there is a lot of information to which a person can attend.

Structure in Simple Judgment and Choice. This promotion of alignable differences is also evident in studies of judgment and choice. In an early study, Slovic and MacPhillamy (1974) showed people descriptions of pairs of students and asked them to determine which one would have a higher grade-point average. The students were each described by two test scores. Each student had a score from one test that both of the pair had taken (i.e., an alignable difference) and one score from a test unique to that student (i.e., a nonalignable difference). Participants in this study systematically gave more weight to the score from the shared test, suggesting that alignable differences were particularly important.

In a study of choice, Markman and Medin (1995) showed people pairs of paragraph descriptions of video games and asked them to decide which game was likely to sell best and to justify their decision. Half the properties of each game had a corresponding property in the other game, thereby forming an alignable difference. For example, one computer football game was described as having predefined plays, whereas the other was described as allowing players to create their own plays. The other half of the properties of each game had no correspondence with the properties of the other game. For example, one football game was described as having a practice session, whereas the other did not have any information about a practice session. The descriptions were designed so that features that were alignable differences for some subjects were nonalignable differences for others. An analysis of the justifications revealed that people discussed the alignable differences more often than the nonalignable differences.

This finding was extended by Lindemann and Markman (1996). In this study, the choice options were colleges, and the participants had to recommend a college for a younger sibling to visit. Two extensions to the methodology are important for this discussion. First, ratings of the perceived importance of the attributes were obtained from one group of participants (who did not take part in the decision task). Second, some participants were asked to make a decision and justify it, while others were asked to think aloud while making a decision. In both the justification and protocol tasks, people were more likely to mention alignable differences than nonalignable differences, a finding suggesting that the results of the earlier study were not a reflection of what people believe makes a good justification. Furthermore, analysis of the individual properties suggested that people used features that were rated as being important more often when they were part of an alignable difference than when they were part of a nonalignable difference. Thus, people systematically ignored features that were objectively important when those features were not alignable with the properties of other options.

The ease with which options can be compared has also been demonstrated to influence the type of information that is used to make a choice (Johnson, 1984, 1988). When the options are easy to compare (e.g., two toasters), then the choice tends to focus on specific aspects of the choice options (e.g., the number of slots). When the options are hard to compare (e.g., a toaster and a smoke alarm), then the choice tends to focus on more abstract properties such as the relative quality of the options or the amount they are needed. This focus on abstract properties reflects the fact that as options get more dissimilar, the information about them that can be placed in correspondence (i.e, their commonalities and alignable differences) also gets more abstract.

There are two components of this reliance on alignable differences in these choice tasks. First, as discussed earlier, the comparison process favors alignable differences over nonalignable differences. Because the paragraph descriptions were moderately difficult to process, people may have used the most accessible properties to make their decisions. Second, even if people considered both the alignable and nonalignable differences, it is more difficult to evaluate a nonalignable difference than to evaluate an alignable difference (see Hsee, 1996, for a discussion of the effects of evaluability on choice). To evaluate an alignable difference, one value can be compared directly with another. Only the relative preference of one value to another is needed to decide which option is best for that alignable property. In contrast, for nonalignable differences, the decision maker must be able to construct an absolute level of preference for the feature, because the feature cannot simply be evaluated against a corresponding feature of some other option. Consistent with this latter aspect, research on consumer choice suggests that novices in a domain are more strongly swayed by information that is phrased as a comparative benefit of a product (e.g., that a computer is the fastest in its class) than by information that is phrased in terms of its absolute properties (e.g., that a computer has a 220 MHz PowerPC 604 processor) (Conover, 1982; Maheswaren & Sternthal, 1990; Maheswaren, Sternthal, & Gürhan, 1996).

Structure in Memory and Choice. Further evidence suggests that comparisons need not take place between options presented simultaneously (Zhang & Markman, 1998). In one study, participants were shown 10 features of a fictitious brand of microwave popcorn and were asked to evaluate the brand on three scales as an encoding task.[1] In a second session 1 week later, the participants were shown the same brand again followed by descriptions of two new brands. Each of these brands was also described by 10 features. Of these 10 features, 4 were commonalities across the set of three brands, 3 were alignable differences, and 3 were nonalignable differences. Furthermore, one of the brands presented only in the second session was given attributes that were rated by other participants as superior to those of the first brand. Thus, this *enhanced late entrant* was objectively superior to the other two entrants. After evaluating all three brands on the same scales, participants were asked to recall as many features as possible for all three brands and to allocate 100 points across the brands in proportion to their preference.

If people compare the brands presented in Session 2 with those presented in Session 1, then we would expect that the commonalities and alignable differences of the three brands would be reasonably well recalled but that the nonalignable differences of the later brands would not be well recalled. Consistent with this finding, more alignable differences than nonalignable differences were recalled for both the later entrants. Furthermore, the data from the points allocation task suggested that the objectively superior entrant presented in Session 2 was preferred to the first entrant. A third session was held one week after Session 2, and only the recall and points allocation tasks were given. The same pattern of data was also obtained in this third session. Thus, people were able to use this accessible information to form a preference for the brands.

What kind of information is needed to achieve a focus on alignable differences? The structural alignment view of comparison suggests that people must know the structure of the domain to allow elements to be placed in correspondence. Without this underlying relational knowledge, there can be no corresponding elements that differ. For example, if people are learning about a new product like electronic organizers, which allow people to store information about their schedule as well as phone numbers and memos, then they can place properties in correspondence only if they know which elements play the same role in different models of that product. For example, electronic organizers must have some way of entering information into the system. Most have small keyboards, but some allow the user to write information directly on a touch-sensitive screen by using a special pencil. Unless a consumer understands that information must be entered into the device, they do not recognize that the keyboard, numeric keypad, and touch-sensitive screen all serve the

---

[1]This methodology was derived from earlier studies by Kardes and Kalyanaram (1992), who were interested in the impact of the order of the entry of products in the market on the memorability of the features of those entrants.

same function. Not all information is structural, however. Preference information—information about the relative goodness of particular properties—does not provide information about how the information in a domain is structured.

If the focus on alignable differences observed in the study described previously requires people to understand the structure of the familiar product class of microwave popcorn, then we would not expect an advantage in recall for alignable differences in an unfamiliar domain like electronic organizers. To test this possibility, a group of undergraduates was surveyed by using a methodology similar to the one employed in the study with microwave popcorn except that the materials described three brands of electronic organizers (Zhang & Markman, 1999). People in this study were also asked whether they had ever used an electronic organizer before. As we would expect if structural knowledge is important for the alignment process, those people who had never used an electronic organizer before found it difficult to recall the distinctive features of brands presented only in Session 2, and they showed no preference for the objectively superior brand presented in Session 2. In contrast, people who indicated that they had used an electronic organizer before were able to recall the alignable differences of the late entrants, and they indicated a preference for the superior late entrant.

To demonstrate that this effect is due to the presence of structural information, three other groups of participants were tested. One group was given a passage that provided structural information about electronic organizers. This passage included information such as the fact that organizers need to have information entered and that there are three different ways to enter information: large keyboards, touch-sensitive screens, and standard numeric keypads. A second group was given a passage that provided preference information about the product, but not structural information. In this passage, people were told whether experts liked particular features that an electronic organizer might have. Finally, a third group was given a passage that included both structural and preference information.

Consistent with the claim that structural information is crucial for allowing features that play the same role to be placed in correspondence, participants given passages that contained structural information were able to recall many of the alignable differences of all of the brands, and they demonstrated a preference for the objectively superior late entrant. In contrast, participants who were given only preference information did not recall the alignable differences of the brands presented only in the second session as well as they recalled the alignable differences of the brand presented in the first session. These participants showed no overall preference for the superior later entrant. Thus, for the distinctive properties of late entrants to be recalled, the attributes must be alignable differences with those of the earlier entrants in the market, but the consumer must also have enough knowledge about the product to be able to determine which properties in the new brand correspond to those in the brands already known.

Goals, Representativeness, and Importance

The previous sections discussed examples of how the structure of people's knowledge about options influenced what properties were perceived to be important. A second important determinant of what information is important in choice is the relation of that information to a decision maker's active goals. A central way that goals influence choice processing is by allowing people to filter the information they consider in a choice with respect to active goals (Huffman & Houston, 1993). We discuss this process in more detail in this section.

People may consider a potentially limitless amount of information when they approach a choice. Thus, it is important for people to have strategies for paring the amount of information that they have to consider. One thing that people can do is to use only the information relevant to the active goals in the choice situation. This point was demonstrated by using a process-tracing method (Shen, Markman, & Krantz, 1999). The process-tracing technique was a variant of the Mouselab system (Bettman, Johnson, & Payne, 1990; Payne, Bettman, & Johnson, 1988, 1993). In Mouselab, people are presented with an information board like that shown in Fig. 12.1. The information board has a matrix with a different option in each row and a different attribute in each column. Initially, all the information is hidden. If the participant puts the mouse cursor over a box and presses the mouse button, the information in that box is revealed. When the mouse button is released, the information is covered again. In this way, Mouselab allows us to track what information is accessed and the order in which it is examined.

In one study, participants were shown four options, each described by six attributes (Shen, Markman & Krantz, 1999, Experiment 1). The options were all cars. The attributes were properties of cars that were related to one of three abstract properties—comfort, safety, or power/performance. For example, the time to accelerate from 0 to 60 miles per hour, the horsepower, and a rating of road holding were all attributes related to the abstract property of power/performance. Because not all participants were expected to know enough about cars to know which specific attributes were related to abstract properties, all of them were given a reference sheet that described the attributes and related them to the abstract properties. Given this set of attributes, each option was described by three

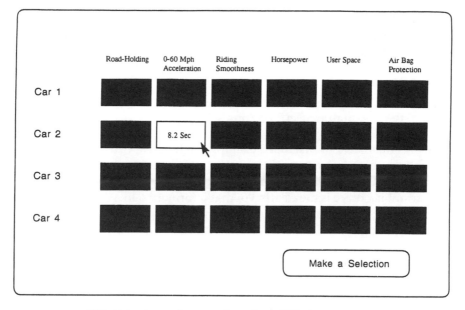

FIG. 12.1.   A sample screen from the MOUSELAB program.

attributes related to one of the abstract properties, two attributes related to a second of the abstract properties, and one attribute related to the remaining abstract property.

At the beginning of each trial, participants were given a goal scenario that described a person shopping for a car and listed a goal for the purchase (e.g., maximizing the safety of the car). Then, the information board was shown, and participants were able to access the information. At any time, they could stop looking at information and make a decision by clicking the mouse in the decision button at the bottom of the screen and typing the number of the row containing the option they preferred.

A clear result from this study was that people looked almost exclusively at information about attributes that were relevant to the active goal rather than about attributes not relevant to the goal. In addition, the mean time that people spent looking at a piece of information was much longer when it was relevant to the active goal (m = 552 ms) than when it was not relevant to the active goal (m = 194 ms). These results suggest that people use the active goal to determine what information is relevant in making a choice. Similar results were obtained by Huffman (1996).

Goals also influenced the way that information was processed after it was deemed relevant. Studies using the Mouselab methodology have demonstrated that there are two central modes of decision processing (Johnson, 1984; Payne et al., 1988, 1993): *attribute-based processing*, which involves looking at values of the same attribute for different choice options (i.e., looking in a column of the matrix), and *alternative-based processing*, which involves looking at different attributes in a single option (i.e., looking across the rows of the matrix). In our studies, attribute-based processing was generally more common than alternative-based processing. That is, people preferred to compare the values of specific attributes rather than to evaluate the information in an option. However, when alternative-based processing did occur, it tended to involve clusters of attributes, all of which were relevant to the same active goal. This finding suggests that when people integrate information about different attributes of an option, they do so relative to active goals. That is, people do not seem to integrate information to make a highly abstract evaluation like a determination of utility. Instead, they appear to evaluate how well particular options satisfy active goals.

DETERMINING THE GOODNESS OF INFORMATION

Goals are critical for evaluating choice options. We suggest that a choice situation inherently involves an active goal that must be satisfied. On this view, a choice cannot be made in the absence of a goal. This claim is compatible with studies by Tversky and Shafir (1992). They told participants to imagine that it was the end of the semester and they had just taken a difficult examination. They were not sure whether they passed or failed the exam. They then saw a special offer for a vacation package that was going to expire that day. They were asked whether they would go on the trip, not go on the trip, or would pay a small fee to hold the price in the offer to the following day when they would find out the results of the exam. In this case, 61% of participants chose to pay the fee to hold the price. Two other groups of participants were also tested. One group was told to imagine they had taken the exam, found out they had failed, and then saw the offer for the vacation package. A second group was told that they had taken the exam, found out they had passed, and then they saw the offer for the vacation package. Interestingly, 54% of the participants told to imagine they failed the exam and 57% of the participants told to imagine they passed the exam elected to go on the vacation. This finding suggests that a number of the people in the original scenario elected to pay a fee to defer their decision to obtain a piece of information that *would not have affected their decision*. That is, these participants would have gone on the trip regardless of whether they passed or failed.

   Although some of these participants would have gone on the trip regardless of the outcome of the exam, their goals for taking the trip are likely to be different in each case. If they passed the exam, then the trip was a celebration or reward, and if they failed the exam, the trip was a consolation. Thus, the goals for taking the trip were different. On the view we are espousing here, the decision could not be made without knowing the outcome of the test, because without an active goal, the choice options cannot be evaluated. Only after a goal has been established can the participants evaluate the options.[2]

In this case, the active goals were determined by an interaction between the recent context and the encounter with a choice option. When students complete an exam at the end of a term, it is not clear that they immediately begin to think of trips they can take. Instead, after they were presented with the opportunity to take a trip, the goal of celebrating or consoling becomes active because of the recent context of completing a semester and taking a difficult exam. When the outcome of the exam is not known, no goal is strongly activated, and there is no strong preference to take (or not take) the trip. Thus, the goal in this case is activated by the presence of an option.

More generally, there are three ways that goals may be activated in the choice setting. First, the individual may already have an active goal. For example, many college students do have an active goal of taking a trip when they complete their final year of school. Given this active goal, they seek out potential trips. Second, as in the example just discussed, the presence of an option may activate a goal. Third, particular aspects of an option may activate specific goals. The second and third situations differ in the connection between the option and the goal. In the second case, the goal is connected to the option as a gestalt (e.g., celebration is connected with taking a trip in general). In the third case, the goal is connected with a particular property (or properties) of the choice option. This third situation requires more discussion.

The specific properties of options may be connected to goals. In the previous section, we described how different attributes of a choice option can be combined when they are related to a common abstract goal. For example, the type of seating in a car, the presence of air conditioning, and the smoothness of ride may all be connected to the goal of having a

---

[2]Shafir, Simonson, and Tversky (1993) considered this phenomenon an instance of *reason-based choice*. That is, they suggested that many choices are made because the decision maker wants to have a reason for making the choice that is easy to explain. We prefer a goal-based explanation for this example, as we think it is the goal that determines what the reason is in this case. However, other types of choices seem better explained as reason based. For example, in the *compromise effect* (Simonson, 1989), people are prone to select a moderately priced, medium-quality item rather than a cheap, low-quality item or an expensive, high-quality item. As suggested by Simonson (1989), people probably use this middle item as an explicit compromise that is easy to justify.

comfortable car. These attributes may be combined to evaluate the degree to which a car may satisfy the goal of being comfortable.

The goals associated with particular properties can often be seen by asking people to evaluate the attributes of objects. In one pilot study, participants were shown an advertisement for a digital camera. They were told about a number of properties of the camera and were asked whether they considered those properties to be good or bad. Then, they were asked why those properties were good or bad. Many of the responses referred to goals. For example, the property that the camera did not have a variable aperture setting was often described by participants as a bad feature, because it did not provide control over the exposure of the image. The property that the camera had to be hooked to a computer was also often considered to be a bad feature, in this case because it required the purchase of additional accessories. Each of these properties was evaluated with respect to a different goal.

One thing of interest is that the goals in this example differ in two ways. First, they differ in content. One goal is focused on the ability to have control over how the pictures are taken. The second is focused on the need for additional equipment. Second, they differ in their orientation. The first goal (having artistic control) is a state of the world that is desirable. That is, it is an approach goal. The feature is evaluated as being a bad one because it fails to achieve an approach goal. The second goal (purchasing additional equipment) is a state of the world that is undesirable. That is, it is an avoidance goal. The feature is evaluated as being bad because it brings about the reference state of an avoidance goal. Thus, features of objects may differ by being connected to goals with different content, and they may also differ by being connected to goals with a different focus.

When one or more goals have been activated, they can then be used to determine the goodness of a choice option. Busemeyer and Townshend (1993; Townshend & Busemeyer, 1995) suggested that the features connected to approach and avoidance goals are weighted and that these weighted properties are combined to determine the goodness of a particular choice option. Their model focused primarily on the speed and ease with which decisions can be made.

Other work has examined the way that goals influence the value of an option. In one study done in collaboration with Patricia Lindemann, we found that people prefer options that completely satisfy an active goal to options that only partially satisfy a goal. Participants were shown the following story (with one of the values in parentheses)

> Imagine that there are a couple of things you need to buy—a ($20/$30) book from BJ's bookstore and a ($20/$30) shirt from Cal's clothing store.

To earn some money, you decide to walk through the Psychology Department to look for an experiment to participate in. There are two experiments currently running. Both pay their subjects with gift certificates. Experiment A is offering a $20 gift certificate to BJ's bookstore. Experiment B is offering a $10 gift certificate to BJ's bookstore along with a $10 gift certificate to Cal's clothing store. Which experiment do you choose?

In the version of the study in which each item cost $20, 64 of 94 participants (68%) preferred Experiment A, which fully satisfied the goal of purchasing the book. In the version of the study in which each item cost $30, participants were essentially indifferent to the options, as 51 of 95 participants (54%) preferred Experiment A. The proportion of people selecting Experiment A in each version is significantly different, $\chi^2(1) = 4.13$, $p < .05$. This result suggests that people have a preference to select options that completely satisfy a single active goal rather than options that partially satisfy a number of active goals.

Another determinant of value is the representativeness of an object to an active goal. As a simple demonstration of this point, Brendl, Markman, and Higgins (1998) gave 187 participants the following scenario.

Three college students are visiting a gambling casino. Each has won $25 in the same gamble. *Student A* received $25 in cash. *Student B* received a gambling chip worth $25 that he can cash at the casino's cashier booth at any time. *Student C* received a cash voucher worth $25 that he can cash at the casino's cashier booth at any time.

Now, all three students are considering another gamble. Each student would put a stake worth $25 on the gambling table. Student A would put cash on the table, Student B a gambling chip, and Student C a cash voucher. There is a 50% chance of losing and a 50% chance of winning. If a student loses, his $25 stake goes to the casino. If he wins, he gets $25 in cash and gets back his $25 (cash, gambling chip, or cash voucher).

It was assumed that people who are gambling have the goal to maximize the cash that they have. The stake types were created so that cash was maximally similar to cash, a gambling chip was least similar to cash, and a cash voucher was intermediate in similarity to cash between cash and a gambling chip. Participants rated the likelihood that each student would accept the new gamble on a 100-point scale. The student risking cash (Student A) was rated as least likely to gamble ($M = 43$), the student risking a cash voucher ($M = 60$) was next, and the student risking the chip was rated as most likely to gamble ($M = 71$). All differences were significant. Given that the objective value of all these stakes was the same, participants were apparently reacting to the relation between the options and the active goal.

The importance of the active goal in determining value can be seen in the results of a second study by Brendl, Markman, and Higgins (1998). In this study, college students were asked how much they would be willing to pay for a ticket to a lottery. Some students were told about a lottery that would give them a chance to win a $1,000 cash prize, and others were told about a lottery that would give them a chance to win a $1,000 waiver of their university bills.[3] Students were approached either while they were standing on line waiting to pay their university bills at the bursar's office (where the goal of paying university bills was likely to be strongly active) or while they were sitting at one of the university cafeterias. Students approached at the bursar's office were willing to pay more when they were asked about a lottery with a bill waiver prize (M = $1.52) than when asked about a lottery with a cash prize ticket (M = $0.93). In contrast, at the cafeterias, students indicated that they would pay more for a cash prize ticket (M = $1.73) than for a bill waiver ticket (M = $1.20). The interaction between the prize type and survey location was reliable in a two by two analysis of variance. This finding makes clear that options are evaluated with respect to active goals. In this case, the goal is activated by the current context. This finding is important, because the same two options were evaluated in each setting. Thus, the cash prize and bursar bill waiver did not have an inherent value, but rather had value in relation to the decision maker's goals in the choice setting.

In sum, the goodness of a choice option is evaluated with respect to active goals. That is, particular properties of options do not have some inherent degree of value. Instead, the value of attributes of options is defined only when there are active goals (Brendl, Markman, & Higgins, 1998; Mellers & Cooke, 1996). When there are no clearly activated goals (as in the study by Tversky and Shafir) then the options cannot be evaluated. When there are clear goals, then options that satisfy goals are preferred to options that only partially satisfy goals. Furthermore, the value of an option increases with its representativeness to active goals. More research must be done to determine other ways that active goals influence the value of options.

CONSTRUCTION AND REPRESENTATION

In this chapter, we have given a brief overview of ways that decision making is dynamic. In sharp contrast to standard economic models, the attributes of choice options have neither an inherent degree of importance

---

[3]All students were screened after the study to ensure that they had at least $1,000 in university bills to pay that semester.

nor an inherent level of utility. Instead, both the importance and utility of choice options are determined during choice processing. The fact that choice is dynamic does not mean that standard representational assumptions cannot be applied to the study of choice. Indeed, we take the opposite view. The only way that the dynamics of choice can be understood is to make assumptions about the way that options and goals are represented. These assumptions are critical for explaining the construction of value.

We described two aspects of the choice setting that influence the importance of attributes of options. First, the structure of knowledge about the options influences importance. In particular, we assumed that choice options are represented with structured representations that permit the determination of the commonalities and alignable differences of a set of options. Consistent with research on structural alignment in similarity and analogy, we assumed that alignable differences are particularly important in choice. Without the assumption that there are structured representations and that these representations can be compared by using a process of structural alignment, the focus on alignable differences cannot be explained.

In addition to structural alignment, goals were shown to influence both the importance of attributes and also their value. An obvious function of goals is to focus people on particular aspects of choice options. In process-tracing studies, people seem to ignore information that is not relevant to active goals (Huffman, 1996; Shen, Markman, & Krantz, 1999). This information is ignored, because the value of an attribute can be determined only with respect to active goals. If an attribute is not relevant to any active goals, then it has no value.

When an attribute is relevant to one or more active goals, it is valuable to the extent that it promotes the satisfaction of an approach goal or impedes the reference state of an avoidance goal. Options that completely satisfy an approach goal (or impede an avoidance goal) are more valuable than those that only partially satisfy (impede) a goal. Finally, the more representative the option is of the goal being satisfied, the more valuable it is.

In this chapter, we have presented examples of preference construction (although our treatment is by no means exhaustive). Evidence for dynamics in cognitive processing has often been used as evidence that there are no representations (Port & van Gelder, 1995; Thelen & Smith, 1994) or that representations are fluid and without structure (Hofstadter, 1995) . In our view, although there is no doubt that cognitive processing is dynamic, a demonstration of this point does not suggest that there are no representations. Instead, it suggests that the processes that operate on cognitive representations allow flexibility. In the case of decision making, the ability to compare options and to evaluate options with respect to active goals permits the construction of preferences. Structured representations are not a hindrance to the dynamics of choice; rather, they work in service of the dynamics. Thus, the dynamics of choice demand representations to be explained.

ACKNOWLEDGMENTS

The research described in this chapter was supported by a National Science Foundation CAREER award SBR-95-10924 and a TRANSCOOP award from the German American Academic Council given to the first author. The authors would like to thank Maya Bar-Hillel, Miguel Brendl, Eric Dietrich, Dedre Gentner, Tory Higgins, Julia Kalmanson, David Krantz, Don Lehman, Patricia Lindemann, Tomislav Pavlicic, Bernd Schmitt, Yung-Cheng Shen, and Takashi Yamauchi for valuable comments and suggestions about this work.

REFERENCES

Bargh, J. A. (1997). The automaticity of everyday life. In R. S. Wyer (Ed.), *Advances in social cognition* (Vol. 10, pp. 1–62). Mahwah, NJ: Lawrence Erlbaum Associates.

Bettman, J. R., Johnson, E. J., & Payne, J. W. (1990). A componential analysis of cognitive effort in choice. *Organizational Behavior and Human Decision Processes, 45,* 111–139.

Brendl, C. M., Markman, A. B., & Higgins, E. T. (1998). Mentale Buchhaltung als Selbst-Regulation: Representativität für ziel-geleitete Kategorien [Mental accounting as self-regulation: Representativeness to goal-derived categories]. *Zeitschrift für Sozialpsychologie, 29,* 89–104.

Busemeyer, J. R., & Townsend, J. T. (1993). Decision field theory: A dynamic-cognitive approach to decision making in an uncertain environment. *Psychological Review, 100*(3), 432–459.

Conover, J. N. (1982). Familiarity and the structure of product knowledge. *Advances in Consumer Research, 9,* 494–498.

Coombs, C. H., & Avrunin, G. S. (1988). *The structure of conflict.* Hillsdale, NJ: Lawrence Erlbaum Associates.

Crowe, E., & Higgins, E. T. (1997). Regulatory focus and strategic inclinations: Promotion and prevention in decision-making. *Organizational Behavior and Human Decision Processes, 69*(2), 117–132.

Gentner, D., & Markman, A. B. (1994). Structural alignment in comparison: No difference without similarity. *Psychological Science, 5*(3), 152–158.

Gentner, D., & Markman, A. B. (1995). Similarity is like analogy. In C. Cacciari (Ed.), *Similarity* (pp. 111–148). Brussels, Belgium: BREPOLS.

Gentner, D., & Markman, A. B. (1997). Structural alignment in analogy and similarity. *American Psychologist, 52*(1), 45–56.

Goldstein, W. M., & Weber, E. U. (1995). Content and discontent: Indications and implications of domain specificity in preferential decision making. In J. Busemeyer, R. Hastie, & D. L.

Medin (Eds.), *Decision making from a cognitive perspective* (pp. 83–136). San Diego, CA: Academic Press.

Goldstone, R. L. (1994). Similarity, interactive-activation and mapping. *Journal of Experimental Psychology: Learning, Memory, and Cognition, 20*(1), 3–28.

Guadagni, P. M., & Little, J. D. C. (1983). A logit model of brand choice calibrated on scanner data. *Marketing Science, 2* (Summer), 203–238.

Hauser, R. R., & Wernerfelt, B. (1989). The competitive implications of relevant-set/response analysis. *Journal of Marketing Research, 26*(4), 391–405.

Hofstadter, D. R. (1995). *Fluid concepts and creative analogies.* New York: Basic Books.

Holyoak, K. J., & Thagard, P. (1989). Analogical mapping by constraint satisfaction. *Cognitive Science, 13*(3), 295–355.

Hsee, C. K. (1996). The evaluability hypothesis: An explanation for preference reversals between joint and separate evaluations of alternatives. *Organizational Behavior and Human Decision Processes, 67*(3), 247–257.

Huber, J., Payne, J. W., & Puto, C. (1982). Adding asymmetrically dominated alternatives: Violations of regularity and the similarity hypothesis. *Journal of Consumer Research, 9,* 90–98.

Huber, J., & Puto, C. (1983). Market boundaries and product choice: Illustrating attraction and substitution effects. *Journal of Consumer Research, 10,* 31–44.

Huffman, C. (1996). Goal change, information acquisition and transfer. *Journal of Consumer Psychology, 5*(1), 1–25.

Huffman, C., & Houston, M. J. (1993). Goal-oriented experiences and the development of knowledge. *Journal of Consumer Research, 20,* 190–207.

Hummel, J. E., & Holyoak, K. J. (1997). Distributed representations of structure: A theory of analogical access and mapping. *Psychological Review, 104*(3), 427–466.

Johnson, M. (1984). Consumer choice strategies for comparing noncomparable alternatives. *Journal of Consumer Research, 11,* 741–753.

Johnson, M. D. (1988). Comparability and hierarchical processing in multialternative choice. *Journal of Consumer Research, 15,* 303–314.

Kahneman, D., & Tversky, A. (1979). Prospect theory: An analysis of decision under risk. *Econometrica, 47,* 263–291.

Kahneman, D., & Tversky, A. (1984). Choices, values, and frames. *American Psychologist, 39*(4), 341–350.

Kardes, F. R., & Kalyanaram, G. (1992). Order-of-entry effects on consumer memory and judgment: An information integration perspective. *Journal of Marketing Research, 29,* 343–357.

Keane, M. P. (1997). Modeling heterogeneity and state dependence in consumer choice behavior. *Journal of Business and Economics Statistics, 15*(3), 310–327.

Lewin, K. (1935). *A dynamic theory of personality.* New York: McGraw-Hill.

Lilien, G., Kotler, P., & Moorthy, S. K. (1992). *Marketing models.* Englewood Cliffs, NJ: Prentice-Hall.

Lindemann, P. G., & Markman, A. B. (1996). Alignability and attribute importance in choice. In G. Cottrell (Ed.), *Proceedings of the 18th annual meeting of the Cognitive Science Society* (pp. 358–363). Hillsdale, NJ: Lawrence Erlbaum Associates.

Maheswaren, D., & Sternthal, B. (1990). The effects of knowledge, motivation, and type of message on ad processing and product judgments. *Journal of Consumer Research, 17,* 66–73.

Maheswaren, D., Sternthal, B., & Gürhan, Z. (1996). Acquisition and impact of consumer expertise. *Journal of Consumer Psychology, 5*(2), 115–133.

Markman, A. B., & Gentner, D. (1993). Splitting the differences: A structural alignment view of similarity. *Journal of Memory and Language, 32*(4), 517–535.

Markman, A. B., & Gentner, D. (1996). Commonalities and differences in similarity comparisons. *Memory and Cognition, 24*(2), 235–249.

Markman, A. B., & Gentner, D. (1997). The effects of alignability on memory. *Psychological Science, 8*(5), 363–367.

Markman, A. B., & Medin, D. L. (1995). Similarity and alignment in choice. *Organizational Behavior and Human Decision Processes, 63*(2), 117–130.

Markman, A. B., & Wisniewski, E. J. (1997). Similar and different: The differentiation of basic level categories. *Journal of Experimental Psychology: Learning, Memory, and Cognition, 23*(1), 54–70.

Medin, D. L., Goldstone, R. L., & Gentner, D. (1993). Respects for similarity. *Psychological Review, 100*(2), 254–278.

Mellers, B. A., & Cooke, A. D. J. (1996). The role of task and context in preference measurement. *Psychological Science, 7*(2), 76–83.

Nedungadi, P. (1990). Recall and consumer consideration sets: Influencing choice without altering brand evaluations. *Journal of Consumer Research, 17*(3), 263–276.

Pavlicic, T., & Markman, A. B. (1997). The structure of the verb lexicon: Evidence from a structural alignment approach to similarity. In M. G. Shafto & P. Langley (Eds.), *Proceedings of the 19th annual conference of the Cognitive Science Society* (pp. 590–595). Mahwah, NJ: Lawrence Erlbaum Associates.

Payne, J. W., Bettman, J. R., & Johnson, E. J. (1988). Adaptive strategy selection in decision making. *Journal of Experimental Psychology: Learning, Memory, and Cognition, 14*(3), 534–552.

Payne, J. W., Bettman, J. R., & Johnson, E. J. (1993). *The adaptive decision maker.* New York: Cambridge University Press.

Port, R. F., & van Gelder, T. (Eds.). (1995). *Mind as motion.* Cambridge, MA: MIT Press.

Roberts, J. H., & Lattin, J. M. (1997). Consideration: Review of research and prospects for future insights. *Journal of Marketing Research, 34*(3), 406–410.

Shafir, E., Simonson, I., & Tversky, A. (1993). Reason-based choice. *Cognition, 49*, 11–36.

Shen, Y. C., Markman, A. B., & Krantz, D. H. (1999). *Goals and attribute integration in choice.* Manuscript in preparation.

Simonson, I. (1989). Choice based on reasons: The case of attraction and compromise effects. *Journal of Consumer Research, 16*, 158–174.

Slovic, P. (1995). The construction of preference. *American Psychologist, 50*(5), 364–371.

Slovic, P., & MacPhillamy, D. (1974). Dimensional commensurability and cue utilization in comparative judgment. *Organizational Behavior and Human Performance, 11*, 172–194.

Thelen, E. (1995). Time-scale dynamics and the development of an embodied cognition. In R. F. Port & T. van Gelder (Eds.), *Mind as motion* (pp. 69–100). Cambridge, MA: MIT Press.

Thelen, E., & Smith, L. B. (1994). *A dynamic systems approach to the development of cognition and action.* Cambridge, MA: MIT Press.

Townshend, J. T., & Busemeyer, J. (1995). Dynamic representation of decision-making. In R. F. Port & T. van Gelder (Eds.), *Mind as motion* (pp. 101–120). Cambridge, MA: MIT Press.

Tversky, A., & Kahneman, D. (1986). Rational choice and the framing of decisions. *Journal of Business, 59*(4), S251–S278.

Tversky, A., & Shafir, E. (1992). The disjunction effect in choice under uncertainty. *Psychological Science, 3*(5), 305–309.

Zhang, S., & Markman, A. B. (1998). Overcoming early entrant advantage: The role of alignable versus nonalignable differences. *Journal of Marketing Research, 35*, 413–426.

Zhang, S., & Markman, A. B. (1999). *The influence of prior knowledge on categories acquired during preference formation.* Manuscript in preparation.

Author Index

Subject Index

ACT-R, 240
Algorithms, 8
Alignable differences, 350–355
Analogy
    and mapping, 234, 267–271
    and structure mapping, 269,
        297–298
    as perspective shift, 265, 284
    paradox of, 283
Antirepresentationalism, 9
Artificial intelligence,
    scientific, 12
Attention, 194
Attraction effect, 348
Auditory cortex, 193

Bezier curves, 206
Binding,
    by synchrony, 245–250
    see also Representation

C (programming language), 17
Categorization, 216
Choices,
    memory-based, 348
    stimulus-based, 348
Classical computer models of mind, 1
Cognition,
    and computationalism, 10–18
    and time, 68–70
    as a continuous system, 68–70
    higher-level, 141–146, 187

Turing machine model of, see
    Computationalism
Watt governor model of, 53–56
Cognitive dynamics, 1, 274–278
    defined, 5–8
Cognitive science,
    and computationalism, 7–8, 31
    and dynamic systems, 6, 51–52
    and the problem of representation,
        31
    better than behaviorism, 79, 93
Competitive learning algorithm, 212
Compositionality, 232–233
Computation, 1
    and continuity of the reals, 12
    and continuous processes, 69
    and explanation, 10–16
    and NP-completeness, 12–14
    over continuous sets, 13
    problems with, 8–10
    see also Virtual machines
Computational hypothesis of mind, 10
Computational model of meaning, 117
Computationalism, 10–18, 292
Concepts,
    and spreading activation, 285
    in analogy, 287
    interacting, 275
    mutability of, 265, 274
    structure of, 287–292
Connectionism, 53, 64–65
    100–step rule, 68
    and analogical inference, 250–257
    and problems with representation,
        83–88
    and semantics, 119
    and synchrony, 245–249
    as inscrutable, 147